Principles and Parameters
in Comparative Grammar

Principles and Parameters
in Comparative Grammar

edited by Robert Freidin

The MIT Press
Cambridge, Massachusetts
London, England

Second Printing, 1992
© 1991 Massachusetts Institute of Technology

This book was set in Times Roman by Asco Trade Typesetting, Ltd., Hong Kong, printed and bound in the United States of America.

Library of Congress Cataloging-in-Publication Data

Principles and parameters in comparative grammar / edited by Robert
Freidin.
    p.   cm.—(Current studies in linguistics series; 20)
Papers from the First Princeton Workshop on Comparative Grammar held in
Mar. 1986.
Includes bibliographical references and index.
ISBN 0-262-06140-6
1. Grammar, Comparative and general—Congresses. I. Freidin, Robert.
II. Princeton Workshop on Comparative Grammar (1st: 1986) III. Series.
P201.P718   1991
415—dc20   90-22164
                                                                 CIP

In memory of Osvaldo Jaeggli
(1954–1990)

Contents

Contents

Acknowledgments

This volume owes its existence to the first Princeton Workshop on Comparative Grammar held March 27–29, 1986 at Princeton University. In addition to the participants, I would like to thank the following sources and individuals whose generosity made the workshop possible: the Andrew D. Mellon Foundation, the Provost's Office at Princeton University, the Princeton University Cognitive Studies Committee, IBM Corporation, Thomas J. Watson, Jr., Dr. Lewis Thomas, Charles Scribner, Jr., Dr. Joseph J. Johnson, Jr., and especially Paul and Julie Campbell for their enthusiastic support of the project from its inception. I am indebted to my former secretary Joan Bassett for indispensable help in organizing the workshop and to our former students Ruth Lanouette, Paul Portner, Christopher Tancredi, and Alice Turk for their help at the workshop. I am also indebted to Alison Hankinson for essential help with preparing the manuscript. And finally I would like to thank Anne Mark whose thoughtful copy editing has enhanced the quality of this volume.

Contributors

Joseph Aoun   East Asian Languages and Cultures, University of Southern California

Adriana Belletti   Faculté des Lettres, University of Geneva

Noam Chomsky   Department of Linguistics and Philosophy, Massachusetts Institute of Technology

Robert Freidin   Program in Linguistics, Princeton University

Wayne Harbert   Department of Modern Languages and Linguistics, Cornell University

Norbert Hornstein   Linguistics Program, University of Maryland at College Park

C. -T. James Huang   Department of Modern Languages and Linguistics, Cornell University

Anthony S. Kroch   Department of Linguistics, University of Pennsylvania

Howard Lasnik   Department of Linguistics, University of Connecticut

Yen-hui Audrey Li   East Asian Languages and Cultures, University of Southern California

David Lightfoot   Linguistics Program, University of Maryland at College Park

Luigi Rizzi   Faculté des Lettres, University of Geneva

Ken Safir   Program in Linguistics, Rutgers University

Beatrice Santorini   Department of Linguistics, University of Pennsylvania

Rex A. Sprouse   Department of Germanic Languages and Literatures, Harvard University

Tim Stowell Department of Linguistics, University of California at Los Angeles

Knut Tarald Taraldsen School of Languages and Literature, University of Tromsø

Lisa deMena Travis Department of Linguistics, McGill University

Edwin Williams Program in Linguistics, Princeton University

Introduction   Robert Freidin

> One of the most important recent innovations in syntactic theory concerns the shift from language-particular, construction-specific rules to analyses to terms of general principles from interacting modules of grammar.
>
> Jaeggli 1986

Contemporary work in comparative grammar, like the comparative work carried out by nineteenth-century grammarians, is concerned with establishing in explanatory basis for the relationships between languages. The work of the nineteenth century focused on relationships between languages and groups of languages primarily in terms of a common ancestry.[1] It assumed a view of linguistic change as by and large systematic and lawful (rule governed) and, on the basis of this assumption, attempted to explain the relationship between languages in terms of a common ancestor (often a hypothetical one for which there was no actual evidence in the historical record). Contemporary comparative grammar, in contrast, is significantly broader in scope. It is concerned with a theory of grammar that is postulated to be an innate component of the human mind/brain, a faculty of language that provides an explanatory basis for how a human being can acquire a first language (in fact, any human language he or she is exposed to). In this way, the theory of grammar is a theory of human language and hence establishes the relationship among all languages—not just those that happen to be related by historical accident (for instance, via common ancestry).

The current paradigm in comparative grammar was made possible by several developments in the theory of generative syntax, beginning in the

I am indebted to Carlos Otero for helpful comments on this introduction.

early 1970s. One of the first important breakthroughs came in the work of Richard Kayne (1975) and Carlos Quicoli (1976a,b), which demonstrated that certain abstract conditions on the application of rules that had been posited by Noam Chomsky for the analysis of English also applied to some very different constructions in Romance. The cross-linguistic application of general conditions on transformations marks the beginnings of comparative studies in generative grammar. A second, equally important step was achieved with the demonstration (Chomsky 1976) that under trace theory the behavior of transformations could be accounted for by general conditions on rules and therefore that transformations themselves could be stated in an extremely general form—essentially the elementary transformational operation (for instance, substitution and adjunction). This view led to the assumption that there was probably only a small number of transformations (for instance, only one movement rule, Move α) whose behavior in various languages could be explained by constraints of the general theory rather than by language-particular stipulations (in terms of structural descriptions and structural changes associated with one or more elementary transformational operations). Thus, transformational rules in this optimally general form could be viewed as rules of Universal Grammar (UG) rather than as language-specific rules of a particular grammar. As a result, there was a significant shift of focus from systems of rules in particular languages to systems of principles in UG. From this new perspective, the important goal in studying languages was to establish how they reflected aspects of UG—which contrasts sharply with the earlier goal of defining a rule system that gives a complete account of the form of the language. A third, related developement was the establishment of a system of principles based on fundamental notions of linguistic structure (such as Case, binding, and bounding) that had clear cross-linguistic applications. This approach gained tremendous impetus when in 1979 Chomsky, developing some fundamental ideas of Jean-Roger Vergnaud on the centrality of concepts of Case and government for UG, proposed the notion of government—a relation derived in large part from the theory of phrase structure that concerned a phrasal head and the constituents of its maximal phrasal projection—as the common thread between the principles of UG. This proposal, published as Chomsky 1981, created a strong link between the theory of phrase structure and the theory of transformations, which until that time had developed essentially independently.

The theory of UG that was developing during the early 1970s emphasized the syntactic similarity of languages—at a certain level of abstraction, of course. Since languages do vary one from another in syntactic structure, it was necessary to provide an account of linguistic variation under the theory or return to a view where variation results from differences between language-particular rules. This problem was first addressed within the theory by Luigi Rizzi (1982; written in 1977), who demonstrated that certain apparent counterevidence to a proposed principle of grammar could be explained as variation in the setting of certain values for a principle of UG. The different values that could be set for a given principle would constitute a parameter of the principle and hence linguistic variation would in part reduce to parametric variation for principles of UG.[2] The discussion of parametric variation has been extended to include differences in construction types—thus, we talk about the "null subject parameter" (or pro drop parameter), which has only two values (positive and negative). A language that is positively specified with respect to this parameter allows finite declarative sentences without overt subjects. Under the theory of grammar it appears that the parameter is related to other syntactic pro-perties—for instance, the occurrence of postposed subjects in null subject languages as opposed to their impossibility in overt subject languages—though how this parameter relates to principles and mechanisms of UG remains to be determined. Thus, in current work the term *parameter* is used in two different ways: to refer to (1) a range of values for settings on principles of UG and (2) data points concerning the output of grammars that seem to divide languages along salient dimensions with respect to the theory. And although we have been investigating cross-linguistic variation from this viewpoint for over a decade, we have barely skimmed the surface of this extremely rich source of data that has already provided us with a certain insight into the nature and structure of the language faculty.

The theory of UG that constitutes the current framework for research in comparative grammar consists of a number of general principles that incorporate basic syntactic notions like c-command, Case, government, binding, and so on. The full set of principles operate in modular fashion to account for the syntactic properties manifested in natural languages. Thus, the theory of UG is viewed as a set of independent subtheories, each with its autonomous principle(s). In addition to the X-bar theory of phrase structure, there are theories of Case, binding, bounding, government, and predicate-argument structure (so-called θ-theory).

Theory	Principle(s)	Mediates
Bounding	Subjacency	distance between a phrase and the position in which it receives an interpretation
Case	Case Filter	distribution of phonetically realized NPs
Government	Empty Category Principle (ECP)	distribution of empty categories
Predicate-argument structure	θ-Criterion	distribution of arguments with respect to predicates
Binding	Principles of binding	distribution of bound elements (anaphors, pronouns, and referential expressions)

This outline is merely a sketch of the more standard subtheories and their respective principles. The precise formulation of these principles continues to be a major topic in current research, as is the investigation of other principles that may supplement or replace these standard examples.

The interactions between this theory of UG and cross-linguistic studies has been both diverse and productive, as illustrated in the papers in this volume, which grew out of work presented at the first Princeton Workshop on Comparative Grammar held in March of 1986. These papers are on the whole quite rich and complex in the issues addressed and the analyses investigated, and the following summary merely sketches some of the broad outlines of the collection.

The first four papers are primarily concerned with binding theory, perhaps the most widely explored area in the theory of UG over the past several decades. Lasnik's paper provides a paradigm case for how cross-linguistic studies within the principles-and-parameters framework contribute to our understanding of UG. Lasnik shows how cross-linguistic variation in binding follows naturally from a parameterized theory of binding principles, thereby providing a powerful argument for the axiomatic (as opposed to derived) nature of such principles. Harbert employs cross-linguistic evidence to argue for the proper formulation of binding domains within the binding theory. Huang discusses the extension of the binding theory to analysis of null objects in Chinese and shows how this analysis generalizes to overt bound pronouns and to emphatic and generic reflexives. Williams investigates an analysis of the binding theory that applies to θ-roles rather than empty categories. This leads to an elimination of pro and an alternative analysis of pro drop phenomena.

The next two papers deal with the syntax—lexical semantics interface as it interacts with the theory of UG. From an investigation of the analysis of implicit arguments, Safir concludes that there are at least two kinds of implicit arguments that do not correspond to empty categories. Belletti and Rizzi demonstrate how the syntactic behavior of psychological predicates (or "psych-verbs") might follow from a theory of UG and hence should not be viewed as idiosyncratic across languages.

Most work on comparative grammar is based on the assumption that the principles of UG do not vary from language to language—with the exception of changes in parameter settings. Under this assumption, strategies other than parameter setting for principles have evolved for accounting for cross-linguistic variation. Aoun and Li assume that certain general principles of scope hold equally for English and Chinese and demonstrate that variation in quantifier interpretation between the languages can be explained by differences in underlying syntactic structure. Stowell proposes an analysis of small clause constructions where differences in the properties of these constructions across languages is accounted for by the application of a restructuring process at different levels of syntactic representations. Thus, if the principles and mechanisms of UG are constant across languages, variation could result from differences in underlying syntactic structure or the syntactic levels at which processes apply.

Cross-linguistic variation in word order phenomena has also been an important topic in recent work, as the next three papers illustrate. Taraldsen offers a parametric account of word order in Scandinavian based on notions of predication and the direction of linking. Kroch and Santorini employ a cross-linguistic study of verb raising constructions in West Germanic to determine the correct analysis of their derived constituent structure. Travis provides an analysis of word order variation in Germanic languages in terms of the ECP and three distinct parameters.

As noted above, the study of how various principles of UG apply across languages provides important insights into the proper formulation of the principles themselves. Hornstein and Lightfoot propose a reformulation of the ECP in which lexical government (as opposed to antecedent government) plays a more extensive role than in standard formulations. Freidin and Sprouse present a detailed analysis of lexical Case phenomena in Russian, German, and Icelandic that shows that the assignment of Case and the licensing of Case are distinct phenomena. This distinction leads to a fundamental modification of Case theory.

In the final paper of this collection, Chomsky explores the consequences for the principles-and-parameters theory of imposing more general guidelines on the nature of derivations and representations—that is, principles of economy that prohibit superfluous symbols in representations and superfluous steps in derivations. These guidelines further restrict the theory of grammar and constitute a promising new approach to the study of comparative grammar.

Notes

1. Wilhelm von Humboldt and those who developed his ideas are, however, a notable exception. See Chomsky 1966 for discussion of the connection between von Humboldt and modern linguistics. Note too that comparative work of the previous century was essentially limited to phonology and morphology, whereas the center of activity in modern work is syntax.

2. See Williams 1987 for discussion of some earlier notions about parameterized theories of grammar.

References

Chomsky, N. (1966). *Cartesian Linguistics*. Harper and Row, New York.

Chomsky, N. (1976). "Conditions on Rules of Grammar." *Linguistic Analysis* 2:303–351.

Chomsky, N. (1981). *Lectures on Government and Binding*. Foris, Dordrecht.

Jaeggli, O. (1986). "Passive." *Linguistic Inquiry* 17:587–622.

Kayne, R. (1975). *French Syntax*. MIT Press, Cambridge, Mass.

Quicoli, A. C. (1976a). "Conditions on Clitic-Movement in Portuguese." *Linguistic Analysis* 2:199–223.

Quicoli, A. C. (1976b). "Conditions on Quantifier Movement in French." *Linguistic Inquiry* 7:583–607.

Rizzi, L. (1982). "Violations of the *Wh* Island Constraint and the Subjacency Condition." In *Issues in Italian Syntax*. Foris, Dordrecht.

Williams, E. (1987). "Introduction." In T. Roeper and E. Williams, eds., *Parameter Setting*. Reidel, Dordrecht.

Chapter 1

On the Necessity of Binding Conditions

Howard Lasnik

I will be concerned in this paper with the binding conditions—the structural requirements governing certain anaphoric relations. I will give particular attention to "Condition C" effects and will argue that, contrary to a currently popular view, something like Condition C does indeed exist. That is, I will display a wide variety of facts motivating Condition C that cannot be handled by, for example, independently motivated pragmatic constraints (see Reinhart 1983 for extensive discussion of such constraints) or by core properties of the theory of "linking" (Higginbotham 1983). A number of the arguments will be seen to carry over to Condition B as well. (It is on these grounds, of course, rather than on logical or biological grounds, that I will attempt to motivate the "necessity" of binding conditions, for one can surely conceive of an organism, even an evolutionarily successful one, whose linguistic system allows, say, the binding of a pronoun within its governing category.) In the course of the discussion, it will become evident that a partial reformulation of Condition C is in order, but its basic nature as a structural constraint on binding will remain intact.

It cannot be denied that there are some discourse-based or pragmatic restrictions relevant to coreference relations. For example, there seems to be a mild prohibition, reasonably regarded as extragrammatical in nature, against repetition of R-expressions. The effect of this can be seen in the slight oddness of a sentence like (1) or a sequence of sentences like (2). (Throughout, I will be concerned only with readings involving coreference (or overlap in reference). I will therefore suppress indices. Inevitably, this will result in certain issues being suppressed as well. See the Appendix, as well as Lasnik 1981, Higginbotham 1983, Sportiche 1985, and Lasnik and Uriagereka 1988, for relevant discussion.)

For very helpful discussion and/or data, I am indebted to Andy Barss, Lan Anh Dang, Bob Freidin, Jim Higginbotham, Mamoru Saito, and Katyanee Svastikula. This paper appeared in slightly different form in Lasnik 1989.

(1) ?After John walked in, John sat down.

(2) ?John walked in. Then John sat down.

This repetition constraint would presumably also be relevant in (3) and (4) but, unaided, is too weak to account for the sharp contrast between these examples, on the one hand, and (1)–(2), on the other.

(3) *John regrets that John wasn't chosen.

(4) *John thinks that I admire John.

This patterning of facts constituted a central part of the argument of Lasnik 1976 for a noncoreference rule. A coreference rule merely *permitting* (or even *requiring*) coreference does not, of itself, preclude coreference, even when such a rule fails to apply. An additional constraint disallowing coreference is needed. Note that this additional constraint seems grammatical in nature, in at least two respects. First, it is crucially dependent on hierarchical structure: the less acceptable examples such as (3)–(4) invariably involve c-command. Second, its effects run directly counter to a plausible discourse principle favoring clarity. The acceptable sentences expressing the contents of the unacceptable (3)–(4) (namely, (5)–(6)), are more, rather than less, vague than their counterparts.

(5) John regrets that he wasn't chosen.

(6) John thinks that I admire him.

Here I disagree with Reinhart (1986). Reinhart presents a pragmatic Gricean analysis of noncoreference effects. In the following quotation the term *bound anaphora* is intended to include not just the usual case of lexical anaphors but also pronouns used as bound variables (that is, all bound pronouns for Reinhart).

In a rational discourse we would expect that if a speaker has the means to express a certain idea clearly and directly he would not choose, arbitrarily, a less clear way to express it. When syntactically permitted, bound anaphora is the most explicit way available in the language to express coreference, as it involves direct dependency of the pronoun upon its antecedent for interpretation. So, if this option is avoided we may conclude that the speaker did not intend coreference. (p. 143)

The difficulty with this, paradoxically enough, is that the notion "explicit" is unclear. As suggested earlier, there is no clear respect in which (5)–(6) are more explicit than (3)–(4), respectively, in their presentation of coreference relations. Just the opposite is true. Thus, the above paradigm is unexplained in these terms.

It is also significant that we find Condition C effects even in unacceptable examples that lack acceptable meaning-preserving bound pronoun counterparts. Anaphoric epithets represent one such striking case.

(7) *John thinks that I admire the idiot.

Though (6) is perhaps a reasonable paraphrase of (4), it does not seem to be a reasonable paraphrase of (7), since it clearly lacks information represented in the latter example. Further, even the mild prohibition against repetition is without effect in such cases. Analogues to (1)–(2) with epithets are not even slightly unacceptable.

(8) After John walked in, the idiot sat down.

(9) John walked in. Then the idiot sat down.

Finally, Condition C effects are even evident in cases involving, not coreference, but mere overlap in reference.

(10) They told John to leave. [They $\neq$ John.]

(11) They told John to visit Susan. [They $\neq$ John. They $\neq$ Susan.]

In these cases it is particularly clear that there is no well-formed alternative to the ill-formed examples. To account for these cases, apparently we need two things: (1) a prohibition on binding (or a requirement of freedom); and (2) a principle giving semantic import to lack of binding. Here, I am particularly concerned with the former requirement. (See Lasnik 1981 for discussion of the interaction between these two mechanisms.)

Arguments similar to some of those above can be constructed for Condition B, as well. For example, (12) seems unacceptable even though it lacks a grammatical bound anaphora alternative, as indicated by (13).

(12) *We like me.

(13) *We like myself.

(14) is a further case.

(14) *John and Mary like him/himself.

(15) is an example of this general type illustrating both Condition B and Condition C effects.

(15) *John told them that Mary should leave.

Thus, even so comprehensive a pragmatic analysis as Reinhart's seems insufficient to account for the full range of effects.[1]

The mechanism of linking was advanced to deal with some of the limitations of the binding theory, including those of the type pointed out in Lasnik 1981 involving plural NPs. The proposals put forward were partially sucessful (for example, an alternative was provided to the account of split antecedence in terms of the formalism of Chomsky 1980),[2] but a number of issues remained unresolved, in particular, some of those outlined above. Further, despite Higginbotham's claim that with linking "no analogue of Chomsky's (C) . . . is required" (p. 405), the attempted elimination of Condition C was not entirely satisfactory, even for a simple case such as (3). To account for (3) in terms of linking, one must first prohibit either occurrence of *John* from being linked to the other. Further, one must explain why coreference is precluded in the absence of a link. Higginbotham, essentially following Evans (1980), denied the factual basis behind the second mechanism, apparently (and incorrectly, I have argued) reducing (3) to (1) or (2). For the first mechanism, he prohibited "downward" linking quite generally. Finally, he prohibited R-expressions from being linked. A direct prohibition would have been tantamount to postulating Condition C, but Higginbotham argued that no such direct prohibition is required (or desired) and that the impossibility of linking an R-expression is instead a special case of (16).

(16) The interpretation of an expression is given in one and only one way.

The idea behind (16) is that since R-expressions receive interpretation internally, by virtue of their lexical content, they cannot also receive interpretation via an antecedent. As it stands, (16) is arguably too strong. As observed by Paul Gorrell (personal communication), in (17) *himself* plausibly receives some of its interpretation internally—person, gender, number—even though it not only allows, but requires, an antecedent.

(17) Leslie likes himself.

A reasonable response in this case is that there is in fact no internal contribution to the interpretation of *himself*. Rather, the observed person, gender, and number reflect a pure agreement phenomenon and not true lexical content. But now note that the semantic difference between reflexives and reciprocals makes it quite clear that anaphors do make an "internal" contribution to the meaning of a sentence. (18) and (19) are not synonymous. Since the antecedent is evidently the same in both cases, the difference resides in the choice of anaphor.

(18) They like themselves.

(19) They like each other.

Suppose, then, that we consider a weaker version of (16) as in (16′).

(16′) If all of the interpretation of an expression is given one way, then none may be given another way.

Unlike (16), (16′) correctly allows (18) and (19). In these cases some of the interpretation of the anaphor is given via the content of the antecedent and some (the difference between a reflexive and a reciprocal) is given in-ternally. As required, (16') still rules out a linked representation for (3), and, for that matter, an upward linked representation for (3'), since all of the interpretation of a name is given internally.

(3') He regrets that John wasn't chosen.

But now consider again example (7), or the modification of it in (7').

(7) *John thinks that I admire the idiot.

(7') *He thinks that I admire the idiot.

Surely, it would be desirable to analogize these to (3) and (3'). And in fact the analogy is basically correct. I argued on essentially these grounds in Lasnik 1976 that anaphoric epithets are like names with respect to bind-ing. That is, in current terms, anaphoric epithets are R-expressions. How-ever, according to Higginbotham (1983), the only relevant property of R-expressions is that they have lexical content. No condition refers directly to R-expressions, a claimed virtue of the theory, and the only indirect reference is in (16). Since we have been forced to reject (16) in favor of (16'), the question now arises whether (16') can account for (the upward linked representations of) (7) and (7'). The answer would seem to be that it cannot. Unlike names, epithets evidently are able to take antecedents. If (8) is not an instance of antecedence (*John* being the antecedent of *the idiot*), then the notion is rather obscure. But, as noted, (8) is entirely well formed. Thus, (16') cannot account for (7) and (7') without incorrectly ruling out (8).

Apparently, the correct generalization is that epithets, and R-expressions more generally, cannot be *bound*, a generalization that linking theory is in principle unable to state. It is in part for this reason that Higginbotham (1985) reintroduces a version of Condition C (and one of Condition B as well), formulated in terms of "obviation."

Patterns of coreference in a variety of languages provide further evidence for a grammatical approach to disjoint reference effects, in particular, a Condition C type approach. The oddness of an English example like (3) or (4) is a fact that must be explained. But in many other languages this fact does not obtain. Evidently, such a distribution constitutes evidence against a pragmatic approach, unless one is willing to posit that speakers of Vietnamese, for example, are less interested in effective communication than are speakers of English. The variation that we find seems parametric in an interesting sense, in ways explicable in terms of the notions of syntactic description, and perhaps only in these terms. In Thai (20) and Vietnamese (21), for example, an R-expression need not be completely A-free.

(20) Cɔɔn khít   wâa Cɔɔn chàlāat.
John thinks that John is smart

(21) John tin   John sẽ thăŋg.
John thinks John will win

That this does indeed reflect a property of the grammars of these languages rather than the desires of individuals for effective communication is suggested by the fact that a Vietnamese/French bilingual found the French analogue to (21) completely unacceptable. Now note that within a clause, Thai and Vietnamese diverge.

(22) Cɔɔn chɔ̂ɔp Cɔɔn.
John likes   John

(23) *John thương   John.
John likes   John

As a first approximation, we have the following: an R-expression is free (English); an R-expression is free in its governing category (Vietnamese); no requirement (Thai). However, if the first NP in (20–23) is replaced by a pronoun (*no* in Vietnamese or *khăw* in Thai), all four examples become ungrammatical, just as they are in English.

(20′) *Khăw khít   wâa Cɔɔn chàlāat.
he   thinks that John is smart

(21′) *Nó tin   John sẽ thăŋg.
he believes John will win

(22′) *Khăw chɔ̂ɔp Cɔɔn.
he   likes   John

(23′) *Nó thương   John.
he likes   John

Apparently, Condition C is really two conditions, and the one just observed, unlike any of the standard binding conditions, involves reference to the binder as well as the bindee.

(24) An R-exression is pronoun-free.

That is, a pronoun may not bind an R-expression. As far as I know, (24) is universal. (24) was not seen as a property of English in earlier work, since its effects all fall under (the English parameterization of) Condition C. If an R-expression must be entirely free, then, in particular, it must not be bound by a pronoun. (24) is not masked in this way in Thai or Vietnamese.

As predicted, sentences with the structure of (7) are well formed in both Thai and Vietnamese.

(25) Cɔɔn khít   wâa ʔâybâa chàlāat.
John thinks that the nut is smart

(26) John tin   cái   thăŋ chó đe' sẽ   thăŋ.
John believes CLASS son of a bitch will win

In Vietnamese, unsurprisingly given (23), anaphoric epithets must be free in their governing categories.[3]

(27) *John thương cái   thăŋ chó đe'.
John likes   CLASS son of a bitch

What is surprising is that this requirement holds in Thai also, a language in which R-expressions need not be free, as seen in (22).

(28) *Cɔɔn chɔ̂ɔp ʔâybâa.
John likes the nut

I will return in a moment to the problem raised by (28).

In all of the languages under discussion, in fact universally as far as I know, a pronominal must be free in its governing category. For Thai, this is illustrated in (29).

(29) *Cɔɔn chɔ̂ɔp khǎw.
John likes him

I suggest that (28) should be analogized to (29), that is, that (28) actually falls under Condition B rather than under any version of Condition C. In particular, I propose that epithets are not merely R-expressions but instead are pronominal R-expressions. We have already seen substantial evidence in English of name-like behavior for epithets. Obviously, no direct evidence of the type provided by (7) is available in Thai, given the lack of pure Condition C effects. However, it is quite clear that epithets in Thai have lexical content, just as they do in English. It is reasonable to conjecture on this basis that they are R-expressions. Further, as bindees, they behave like R-expressions with respect to condition (24), as shown by (30).

(30) *Khǎw khít   wâa ʔâybâa chàlāat.
he   thinks that the nut is smart

The parallelism between (30) and (20') is especially revealing in this connection.

However, there is equally strong evidence indicating pronominal nature for epithets. For example, again as far as (24) is concerned, *ʔâybâa* as a *binder* behaves like a pronoun, *khǎw*, rather than like a name. (31) too has the status of (20').

(31) *ʔâybâa khít   wâa Cɔɔn chàlāat.
the nut thinks that John is smart

Significantly, (31) contrasts sharply with the well-formed (20). Thus, in (31), as in (28), it is evidently the pronominal character of epithets that is playing a crucial role, in the present case, with respect to condition (24), and in the earlier case, with respect to Condition B.

The same effect obtains in Vietnamese as well. (32) is completely parallel to (31).

(32) *Cái thăǹg chó đe' tin John sẽ thăńg.
    CLASS son of a bitch thinks John will win

Recall from (21) that R-expressions may be bound in a structural config-uration such as this one. What is disallowed is the binding of an R-expression by a pronominal, as in (21') and (23'). Plausibly, it is this constraint that is responsible for (32), once again suggesting a pronominal status for epithets.

As observed earlier, epithets generally share one significant property with pronouns: they can have antecedents, as in (8), repeated here as (33).

(33) After John walked in, the idiot sat down.

There is yet another similarity between epithets and pronouns. Both can participate in left-dislocation constructions:

(34) John, I think he should be fired.

(35) John, I think the idiot should be fired.

An R-expression in place of the pronoun or epithet is far less acceptable.

(36) ?*John, I think John should be fired.

Evidently, it is not Condition C that is implicated in (36), for two reasons: first, there is no A-binding here; and second, Condition C would not be expected to distinguish between (35) and (36). Apparently, something like predication is required in this construction, and this demands an open sentence, or a nearly open sentence. The target must not be a complete description. Notice, by the way, that contrary to the proposal made by Chomsky (1977), left dislocation and the *as for* construction must be kept distinct, for they differ markedly in this regard. For example, (37) is much better than (36).

(37) ?As for John, I think that John should be fired.

This accords with the observation that *as for* constructions involve not predication but merely relevance. No open sentence is required, in sharp contrast to the demands of left dislocation in English. The following contrast is representative.

(38) As for sports, I like baseball best.

(39) *Sports, I like baseball best.

Thus, a variety of properties all follow from the assumption that anaphoric epithets are pronominal R-expressions.

Thus far, we have seen substantial evidence that anaphoric epithets are pronominal R-expressions and that R-expressions may not be bound by pronouns (24). Before examining further, potentially problematic data, I would like to consider how the present proposals might be instantiated within the theory. Note that the standard feature analysis of nominal categories of Chomsky (1981, 1982) will not do. According to that theory, there are two independent binary features, $[\pm a]$ and $[\pm p]$, yielding four types of nominals. The $[+a]$ categories—lexical anaphors, NP-trace, and PRO—all satisfy Condition A. The $[+p]$ categories—pronouns, PRO, and pro—all are subject to Condition B. The one remaining feature complex, $[-a, -p]$, is a sort of default. The categories instantiating this feature complex—fully lexical NPs, wh-trace—satisfy Condition C. There is clearly no place in this system for a pronominal R-expression. Such an expression would, of necessity, be $[+p]$. It would not be pronominal otherwise, and hence would not be constrained by Condition B. However, to be an R-expression, it would have to be $[-a, -p]$. Neither of the feature complexes including $[+p]$ satisfies Condition C. Let us tentatively explore alternatives to the standard categorization in an attempt to overcome this difficulty. It is important to keep in mind that the problem is essentially technical, rather than conceptual. A priori, a pronominal R-expression is no more impossible than, for example, a pronominal anaphor, or an anaphoric R-expression, as in the "generalized binding theory" of Aoun (1985).

If we wish to maintain a limit of four classes of expressions, obviously we must maintain a limit of two binary features. Suppose we begin by making R-expressions a substantive category, rather than a default, by positing a feature $[\pm r]$. Lexical NPs, wh-trace, and anaphoric epithets have the plus value for this feature, by hypothesis. To maintain our limit, one feature must now be abandoned. Evidently, $[\pm p]$ must be kept, since the point of the exercise is to allow for the description of pronominal R-expressions. Thus, we have (40).

(40) $[+p, +r]$ $[+p, -r]$ $[-p, +r]$ $[-p, -r]$

The first of these, $[+p, +r]$, is the complex for epithets. As desired, being $[+p]$, they must conform to Condition B, and being $[+r]$, they must conform to Condition C. The second, $[+p, -r]$, is the complex for pure pronominals, and the third, $[-p, +r]$, is the complex for pure R-expressions. This leaves, essentially as a default, the class of anaphors: $[-p, -r]$. This is not obviously incorrect, but there is a substnatial cost associated with it. Whereas before, we could not accommodate the hybrid category pronominal R-expression, now we cannot accommodate the hybrid pronominal anaphor. This raises the question of how to analyze PRO. Clearly, controlled PRO cannot be $[+r]$, since it does not conform to Condition C. This leaves just two possibilities: $[+p, -r]$ and $[-p, -r]$. The first of these satisfies Condition B, but not Condition A. The second satisfies Condition A, but not Condition B. There is then no description for a category satisfying both Conditions A and B, thus, no possibility of deducing the "PRO theorem." According to a number of proposals, this consequence is not undesirable. For example, Bouchard (1983) argues at some length that PRO is sometimes pronominal and sometimes anaphoric but never both simultaneously. Bouchard's account is thus entirely consistent with the feature analysis being considered. However, the only analysis of PRO that I am aware of that fully gives the distributional fact that PRO must not be governed is that of Chomsky (1981) (or its close variant in Chomsky 1986), in which PRO is crucially a pronominal anaphor. (See Chomsky 1981, Huang 1983, and Lasnik and Uriagereka 1988 for problems with trying to deduce the distribution from other properties, including Case requirements.) For this reason, I will tentatively assume that (40) is incorrect.

If a theory with two binary binding features does not provide enough distinctions, the obvious next move is to consider a theory with three features. (I will not consider nonbinary features here, but they are not to be excluded a priori, I assume.) Suppose, then, that we have the three features $[\pm a]$, $[\pm p]$, and $[\pm r]$, where the content of each feature is as before. This gives eight categories, of course, presumably too many. Nevertheless, let us explore the consequences. We require at least five categories, and these will be as in (41).

(41) a. $[+a, +p, -r]$ PRO
     b. $[+a, -p, -r]$ anaphors
     c. $[-a, +p, -r]$ pronouns
     d. $[-a, -p, +r]$ "pure" R-expressions
     e. $[-a, +p, +r]$ anaphoric epithets

Apparently, there are now three additional predicted but nonexistent categories.

(42) a. $[-a, -p, -r]$
     b. $[+a, +p, +r]$
     c. $[+a, -p, +r]$

But are they really all nonexistent? I would like to suggest, first, that (42a) does satisfy a theoretical need. A category with this feature complex would have no binding requirement—it would not have to be free in its governing category, bound in its governing category, or A-free. Now it has become increasingly evident that there is a substantial amount of redundancy in the constraints on the distribution of NP-trace. Case requirements, chain requirements, bounding requirements, proper government requirements, and binding (Condition A) requirements have all been argued for. (For discussion, see Lasnik 1985, and Chomsky 1986, among many other references.) The binding requirement is, perhaps, entirely redundant. It is extremely difficult to find an ungrammatical instance of NP-movement that violates only Condition A. In part for this reason, Chomsky (1986) proposes that the "Nominative Island Condition" (NIC) case of Condition A should be eliminated in favor of the Empty Category Principle (ECP). If this situation obtains more generally, it would be desirable to remove NP-trace from the domain of Condition A entirely. However, it does not seem possible to effect this removal by wholesale elimination of the remainder of Condition A. Central properties of lexical anaphors evidently still must be accounted for in terms of Specified Subject Condition (SSC) requirements. Suppose, then, that we simply assert that NP-trace does not fall under Condition A. How can this be instantiated? Within the traditional categorization, there seems to be no way. In that system, if NP-trace is $[-a]$, to exempt it from Condition A, then it will be either $[-a, +p]$ or $[-a, -p]$. In the former case NP-trace will have to be free in its governing category. In the latter it will have to be entirely free.[4] Neither of these is an acceptable consequence, since, descriptively, NP-trace is always bound in its governing category, hence bound. But now note that (42a) in the three-feature system has precisely the desired properties.

Consider now the remaining two cases in (42), $[+a, +p, +r]$ and $[+a, -p, +r]$. Both of these nominal types would have to be bound in their governing categories by virtue of being $[+a]$. Further, they would both have to be free, a near contradiction reminiscent of Chomsky's analysis of PRO. The two possibilities thus collapse to one. In this case, as in the case of PRO, the expression could occur only in a position where it had no governing category. It could not then be overt, for it would lack Case, being of necessity ungoverned. Thus, what is predicted is a null category (or two such) that must be ungoverned and A-free. In principle, such a category could exist. Possibly, it does: so-called arbitrary PRO seems a not implausible candidate. Arbitrary PRO, like controlled PRO, must be ungoverned. Further, it is not clear that it can ever be bound. Note in particular that when a potentially arbitrary PRO is bound as in (43), it no longer is arbitrary but rather behaves like a controlled PRO. Its value varies with that of its binder.

(43) John$_1$ thinks [that [[PRO$_1$ playing soccer] is easy]].

This is apparently true even when the binder is itself an arbitrary PRO, as in (44).

(44) It is important [[PRO to think [that [[PRO playing soccer] is easy]]]].

It is at least possible, then, that the "extra" categories shown in (42) actually occur. Thus, it is at least possible that the three-feature system is correct. However, I would now like to examine further data suggesting that a different description is in order. Recall constraint (24), repeated here as (45).

(45) An R-expression is pronoun-free.

This constraint handled a wide range of phenomena, including a variety of ill-formed examples in languages lacking a general Condition C effect. Recall further that epithets cannot be bound in their governing categories, even when they are not required to be entirely free, suggesting pronominal binding status for epithets. Finally, recall that with respect to (45), epithets as binders patttern with pronouns, whereas as bindees they pattern with names. Taken together, these properties suggest a consequence that turns out to be completely false. In particular, an epithet should not be able to bind an epithet, yet Vietnamese sentences such as (46) are acceptable.

(46) Cái   thăng cho đe' tin   cái   thăng cho đe' sẽ   thăng.
     CLASS son of a bitch thinks CLASS son of a bitch will win

Under the assumptions developed thus far, (46) evidently violates (45), since a pronominal R-expression (hence, a pronominal) binds a pronominal R-expression (hence, an R-expression). For the present type of case, it might be thought that *pronoun* in (45) should be understood as 'pure pronoun', thus excluding epithets. However, this would give just the wrong result for cases such as the Vietnamese example (32), repeated here as (47), or the Thai example (31), repeated here as (48).

(47) *Cái   thăng chó đe' tin   John sẽ   thăng.
     CLASS son of a bitch thinks John will win

(48) *ʔâybâa khít   wâa Cɔɔn chàlâat.
     the nut thinks that John is smart

In both of these cases the violation stems from the binding of an R-expression by an epithet. Thus, it does not seem desirable to limit the

Table 1.1
Summary of binding relationships between two nominal expressions not in the same governing category

Binder	Bindee		
	Pronoun	Epithet	Name
Pronoun	OK	*	*
Epithet	OK	OK	*
Name	OK	OK	OK

domain of (45) as suggested. Similarly, *R-expression* in (45) cannot be understood as 'pure R-expression' in order to allow (46), since this would incorrectly allow cases such as the Thai example (30), repeated here as (49).

(49) *Khǎw khít   wâa ʔâybâa chàlàat.
     he   thinks that the nut is smart

A pronoun binding an epithet is no better than a pronoun binding a name.

The entire array of facts including (46) does not seem amenable to analysis simply in terms of features that cross-classify the nominal expressions in the way considered above. Before proceeding, I will summarize all of the binding relationships between two nominal expressions not in the same governing category (see table 1.1). Most of these have been illustrated above. The rest are straightforward. I have arranged the categories in table 1.1 in order of what might be regarded as increasing referentiality, from pronoun to name (and name-like definite descriptions). In a sense, this is reflected in the feature analysis proposed, as in (50). (The feature $[-a]$ is suppressed, since it is shared by all three categories being discussed at this point.)

(50) $[+p, -r] < [+p, +r] < [-p, +r]$

This establishes a kind of referentiality hierarchy among the discrete categories given by the features. In these terms, the generalization emerging from table 1.1 is that a less referential expression may not bind a more referential one. (45), the requirement that a pronoun not bind an R-expression, emerges as a special case, as do the other requirements we have seen: that an epithet may not bind a name and that a pronoun may not bind an epithet. However, an epithet is correctly permitted to bind an epithet. For ease of exposition, I state the generalization as (51).

(51) A less referential expression may not bind a more referential one.

One might expect that $[+a]$ categories would also fall under (51), and there is in fact some evidence that this is the case. For example, quite generally, an anaphor cannot bind an R-expression. Further, in Japanese an anaphor may not bind a pronoun, a phenomenon quite reminiscent of the one we have been examining.[5] The contrast between (52), with a pronoun *kare* binding an anaphor *zibun*, and (53), with the anaphor binding the pronoun, is representative.

(52) John-ga [$_S$ kare-ga [$_S$ zibun-ga tensai da to] omotte iru to]
     John   he   self   genius   thinks
     itta (koto).
     said
     'John said that he thinks that self is a genius.'

(53) *John-ga [$_S$ zibun-ga [$_S$ kare-ga tensai da to] omotte iru to] itta (koto).
     'John said that self thinks that he is a genius.'

This contrast obtains in Korean as well.

(54) ?John-nɨn [$_S$ kɨ-ga [$_S$ caki-ga chənjaelako] sengakhanta ko] malhaetta.
     John   he   self   genius   thinks   said
     'John said that he thinks that self is a genius.'

(55) *John-nɨn [$_S$ caki-ga [$_S$ kɨ-ga chənjaelako sengakhanta ko]
     malhaetta.
     'John said that self thinks that he is a genius.'

This suggests that an approach in terms of something like (51) has applicability beyond the treatment of anaphoric epithets.[6]

To summarize, we have seen phenomena in several languages that receive a natural account in terms of principles based on the structural relation of binding. In particular, I have argued that Conditon C does exist, and in fact that it is parameterized, holding in English, for example, but not holding in Thai. Beyond this parameterized requirement that an R-expression be free, there is the further requirement, possibly universal, that a pronoun not bind an R-expression. This requirement is perhaps best viewed as one instantiation of a general prohibition on the binding of a more "referential" expression by one that is less so. Conditions on binding thus seem to play a central role in determining the distribution of nominal expressions of various types.

Appendix

It is well known that the phenomenon of split antecedence raises difficult problems for the theory of indexing. (See Lasnik 1981, and Higginbotham 1983 for detailed discussion.) Here, following Sportiche (1985), and a discarded proposal of Higginbotham (1983), I will present a version of indexing that circumvents these problems to a significant extent.

Suppose that an index is not a single integer but rather is a nonnull set of integers. Suppose further that indices are freely assigned, in the sense that an NP receives an arbitrary set of integers as its index. Consider now the following relational notions:

(56) A binds B if A c-commands B and the index of A is identical to the index of B.

(57) A is free with respect to B if either B does not c-command A or the intersection of the indices of A and B is null.

The binding conditions will be the standard ones, with Condition C revised as in the text. Notice that with the definitions in (56) and (57), whereas *free* entails *not bound*, *not bound* does not entail *free*. That is, an NP might be neither bound nor free, as in (58).

(58) They$_{\{1,2\}}$ like him$_{\{1\}}$.

In (58) *him* is not bound, since its index is distinct from that of *they*. However, *him* is also not free, since its index overlaps with that of *they*. (58) thus violates Condition B. The representation of split antecedence might now be as shown in (59).

(59) John$_{\{1\}}$ told Bill$_{\{2\}}$ that they$_{\{1,2\}}$ should leave.

In a complete account, the semantic import of such a syntactic representation would also be specified. Sportiche indicates that set indexation will be provided "with the obvious interpretation." Here I will attempt, in a preliminary way, to explicate the notion "obvious interpretation."

As is customary in studies of anaphora, I will ignore the problems inherent in such terms as *coreference* and *disjoint reference*. For a clear presentation of a number of these problems, see Higginbotham 1980, and for a promising approach toward a solution, see Heim 1982. For present purposes, I will adopt the pretense that the terms need no explication.

In Lasnik 1981 I showed in some detail that indexing must be given semantic as well as syntactic import and moreover that assignment of semantic import has nontrivial consequences. Obviously, such an argument carries over from a theory with integer indices to one with set indices. Consider, then, the following interpretive conventions.

(60) If the index of A is identical to the index of B, then A, B are coreferential.

(61) If the intersection of the index of A and the index of B is null, then A, B are disjoint in reference.

(60) makes explicit something that is presumably taken for granted in investigations of anaphora. It is required, for example, to guarantee that a reflexive and its "antecedent" corefer. (61) will be part of the account of the ill-formedness of (62).

(62) *I like me.

If *I* and *me* are coindexed, Condition B is violated. If they are contraindexed, (61) contradicts the lexical requirements of those NPs: In a particular utterance, *I* and *me* must be coreferential, hence cannot be disjoint. Now notice that this account generalizes to (63).

(63) *We like me.

Suppose the indices of *we* and *me* overlap. Then, once again, Condition B will be violated, given the definition of *free* in (57). But if the indices do not overlap, then by (61), the two NPs will have to be disjoint in reference, contradicting lexical properties: In a particular utterance, the reference of *we* must include the reference of *me*.

Returning now to split antecedence, neither (60) nor (61) is relevant to example (59). Thus, *they* is not required to be coreferential with either of the other NPs, nor is it required to be disjoint from them (since, although it is not free, it *is* free in its governing category). Thus, *they* is free to include John and Bill in its reference. This is essentially the analysis of Lasnik 1976 restated in the terms of Chomsky 1981, except with set indices replacing integer indices. One might speculate about whether such a representation as (59) should have a more determinate interpretation. Some evidence that it should comes from (64).

(64) Every violinist$_{\{1\}}$ told some pianist$_{\{2\}}$ that they$_{\{1,2\}}$ should play a duet.

Here, the notion "free in reference" does not suffice. *They* cannot be freely picking up the reference of *every violinist* and *some pianist*. Rather, we seem to have true split antecedence: the reference of *they* is *determined* by that of the variables bound by the two quantified NPs. This suggests that (65) should be added to (60) and (61).

(65) If the index of A is included in the index of B, then the reference of A is included in the reference of B.

Given this syntactic and "interpretive" machinery, the standard cases receive a natural account. Higginbotham (1985, fn. 25), however, argues that such an account in terms of set indices must be rejected in favor of a theory based on linking. I will comment briefly on his arguments. His most detailed discussion concerns the ambiguity of (66).

(66) They told each other that they had better leave.

For (66) to be true, each might have told the other (a) "I had better leave," (b) "We had better leave," or (c) "You had better leave." Under linking, Higginbotham points out, (c) can be distinguished from (a) and (b). In the latter case the second *they* would be linked to the first. In the former case *they* would be linked to *each other*. Indexing can make no such distinction, if we assume, as is standard, that *each other* and the first *they* must have the same index. Then, obviously, if the second *they* is coindexed with one of those NPs, it is also coindexed with the other. This gives just one representation, rather than the two provided by linking. Note that even under linking, (a) and (b) are not syntactically distinguished, as Higginbotham acknowledges. Nor does linking provide any account for the ambiguity of (67), from Higginbotham 1981.

(67) They thought they loved each other.

Intuitively, either *they* can be the antecedent of *each other*, yet *each other* must be linked to the lower *they* and only to the lower *they*. To handle all of these cases by the same mechanism, Heim, Lasnik, and May (1991) propose a syntactic analysis in which *each other* is not in fact coindexed with its "antecedent." Rather, roughly along the lines proposed by Lebeaux (1983), *each* undergoes raising at LF, its landing site determining the interpretation. The apparent locality constraints on *each other* will now be constraints on the relation between the trace of *each* and *each* itself. To the extent that such an analysis proves successful, the force of this argument against indexing is correspondingly lessened.

Higginbotham's second argument is that without linking, "We would ... lose the account of the distinctions ... in Montalbetti (1984)." I assume that what Higginbotham has in mind is Montalbetti's argument that in one variety of Spanish, an overt pronominal subject cannot be linked to a formal variable (that is, to the trace left by operator movement). Montalbetti shows that such a pronoun may in fact be *bound* by a formal variable, but only if there is an intervening (null) binder. The implication is that although this can be stated straightforwardly in terms of linking, such is not the case with binding. However, (68) captures nearly all of the facts under consideration.

(68) An overt pronominal subject may not be locally bound by a formal variable.

The notion "local binding," which has wide application in syntactic theory, is that of Koopman and Sportiche (1982) and Chomsky (1982). Essentially, A locally binds B if A binds B and there is no intervening binder. There is

just one class of facts not amenable to this description, illustrated in (69)
(=(59) in Montalbetti 1984: chap. 3).

(69) Nadie   pensó   que las fotos   que él tomó probarían
     nobody thought that the pictures that he took would prove
     que [pro] estuvo ahí.
     that [pro] was   there

Montalbetti reports that this example is fine on the relevant reading, even
though *el* is locally bound by the LF trace of *nadie*. This follows immediately on Montalbetti's account, since *el* need not be linked to that trace
but instead may be linked to pro, which is in turn linked to the trace. Thus,
linking receives some empirical support.[7] It might be noted, though, that
Montalbetti's approach, for reasons that I cannot go into here, relies
heavily on a transitivity condition on linking that Higginbotham, in his
treatment of (66), explicitly rejects. Thus, it is not clear that the phenomenon in (66) and the phenomenon in (68) can simultaneously be arguments
for linking.

   Finally, Higginbotham raises the question of the interpretation of set
indices:

The interpretation could not be that the number *n* [the cardinality of the set]
gives the intended number of the referent; for it must be possible to wave at a
crowd without knowing how many people one is waving at. (p. 573)

Surely this claim is correct. Hence, one cannot claim an interpretive *advantage* for indexing, even set indexing, vis-à-vis linking. That is, there is no
principled correlation between the cardinality of an index on an NP and
the cardinality of the set designated by that NP. Rather, the interpretation
of indices is precisely as in (60), (61), and (65). An individual set index has
no interpretation in this theory, just as an individual integer index has no
interpretation in standard versions of indexing. Choice of, say, *5* rather
than *17* as the index for a particular NP is of no semantic import. There
is nothing necessarily 5-like about the referent of an NP with index *5*. It is
only the relationship between this index and another—identity or non-
identity—that is of consequence. Similarly for set indices. Their contribution to interpretation is purely relational. In this respect, indexing shares
a central property of linking.

Notes

1. There is one further problem for Reinhart's pragmatic account that might be
noted. Consider an example such as (i) ((8) in Reinhart 1986).

(i) Charlie Brown talks to his dog and my neighbor Max does too.

In line with a tradition going back at least to Ross 1967, Reinhart observes that this example is ambiguous. Reinhart characterizes the readings as (1) Max talks to Charlie's dog ("pragmatic coreference"), (2) Max talks to Max's dog ("bound variable"). In fact, Reinhart argues that the first conjunct of (i), even in isolation, is always ambiguous, even if the ambiguity is not always evident. The now familiar characterization of sloppy identity as involving variable binding is also to be found in Lasnik 1976:20, where I argue that the structural requirements governing sloppy identity are precisely those on pronouns used as variables bound by overt quantifiers. The following claim made by Reinhart (1983:63) is thus not entirely accurate: "What has gone unnoticed in the studies of sloppy identity is that, in fact, it obeys precisely the same conditions as quantified NP anaphora . . . ."

Consider now the particulars of Reinhart's (1986) pragmatic analysis.

Speaker's strategy: When a syntactic structure you are using allows bound anaphora interpretation, then use it if you intend your expressions to corefer, unless you have some reasons to avoid bound anaphora.

Hearer's strategy: If the speaker avoids bound anaphora options provided by the structure he is using, then, unless he has reasons to avoid bound anaphora, he didn't intend his expressions to corefer.

These strategies are inconsistent with the claim that the first conjunct of (i) is ambiguous, in the relevant respect, in isolation. This is so because if the speaker intends coreference, bound anaphora must be used in this case, since there are no apparent reasons for avoiding it. Similarly, the hearer will assume that bound anaphora (rather than mere coreference) is being employed. Thus far, this conclusion is without obvious problematic consequences, even if it contradicts Reinhart's claim. Note, in particular, that the initial phenomenon, the ambiguity of (i), is not excluded. Obviously, the bound anaphora reading is made available. Further, pragmatic coreference is possible just in case the speaker has a reason for avoiding the use of a bound variable. And in this case there is a reason: if the speaker intends to report that Max talks to Charlie's dog yet still wants to use an elliptical construction, then he will choose pragmatic coreference. Now, however, consider the following discourse.

(ii) Speaker 1: Charlie Brown talks to his dog.
      Speaker 2: My neighbor Max does too.

As far as I can tell, exactly as in (i), the elided constituent has both a sloppy and a nonsloppy reading. However, the latter reading should not be possible in this case. By hypothesis, Speaker 1 intends coreference. Further, there is evidently no reason whatsoever for that speaker to avoid bound anaphora. Finally, there is no reason for Speaker 2 to assume that Speaker 1 had a reason for avoiding bound anaphora. The conclusion is thus that Speaker 2 cannot intend by his utterance that Max talks to Charlie's dog, since the elided material must include a bound variable. But this is clearly contrary to the facts of the matter.

2. See the Appendix for discussion of an indexing approach to this phenomenon in the spirit of Chomsky 1981.

3. For some speakers, (23) is acceptable. But even for them, (27) is out. Vietnamese and Thai are thus identical in relevant respects for such speakers.

4. This assumes, as is standard, that all nominal expressions are specified for features. For a possible alternative, see Barss 1986.

5. I have not yet been able to examine Vietnamese or Thai in this connection, but in relevant respects Japanese seems very similar, as seen in the following examples.

(i)   *John-ga ano baka-o hometa (koto).
      John   the idiot   praised
      'John praised the idiot.'

(ii) ?John-ga [Mary-ga ano baka-o sonkeisite iru to] omotte iru (koto).
      John   Mary   the idiot   respects   thinks
      'John thinks Mary respects the idiot.'

(iii) *Ano baka-ga [Mary-ga John-o sonkeisite iru to] omotte iru (koto).
      'The idiot thinks Mary respects John.'

(iv) ?Ano baka-ga [Mary-ga ano baka-o sonkeisite iru to] omotte iru (koto).
      'The idiot thinks Mary respects the idiot.'

6. Contary to what we have seen in Japanese and Korean, an anaphor apparently may bind a pronoun in English, as in (i) or (ii).

(i)   John told himself that he should leave.

(ii) John believes himself to have said that he would accept the job.

That is, with respect to constraint (51), overt pronouns and anaphors are equally "referential" in English. Why this should be the case is not clear, but Mamoru Saito (personal communication) points out a correlation. In English both pronouns and anaphors can function as variables bound by operators. (iii) illustrates the former case.

(iii) Who said that he is smart?

This possibility does not exist in Japanese or Korean. Compare the Japanese (iv) and the Korean (v) with (iii).

(iv) *Dare-ga kare-ga atama-ga ii to itta no?
      who   he   smart   said

(v)   *Nu-ka ki-ka ttokttokhata-ko malhaess-ci?
      who   he   smart   said

See Montalbetti 1984 and Hong 1985 for extensive discussion.

7. There is some question about how general the pheomenon in (69) is. There are Spanish speakers who share Montalbetti's judgments, for the most part, but for whom a non-c-commanding pro cannot "save" an overt pronoun. These speakers reject the crucial examples, those with the structure of (69).

References

Aoun, J. (1985). *A Grammar of Anaphora*. MIT Press, Cambridge, Mass.

Barss, A. (1986). "Chains and Anaphoric Dependence." Doctoral dissertation, MIT.

Bouchard, D. (1983). *On the Content of Empty Categories.* Foris, Dordrecht.

Chomsky, N. (1977). "On *Wh*-Movement." In P. Culicover, T. Wasow, and A. Akmajian, eds., *Formal Syntax.* Academic Press, New York.

Chomsky, N. (1980). "On Binding." *Linguistic Inquiry* 11: 1–46.

Chomsky, N. (1981). *Lectures on Government and Binding.* Foris, Dordrecht.

Chomsky, N. (1982). *Some Concepts and Consequences of the Theory of Government and Binding.* MIT Press, Cambridge, Mass.

Chomsky, N. (1986). *Knowledge of Language: Its Nature, Origin, and Use.* Praeger, New York.

Evans, G. (1980). "Pronouns." *Linguistic Inquiry* 11: 337–362.

Heim, I. (1982). "The Semantics of Definite and Indefinite Noun Phrases." Doctoral dissertation, University of Massachusetts, Amherst.

Heim, I., H. Lasnik, and R. May (1991). "Reciprocity and Plurality." *Linguistic Inquiry* 22: 63–101.

Higginbotham, J. (1980). "Anaphora and GB: Some Preliminary Remarks." In J. Jensen, ed., *Proceedings of the Tenth Annual Meeting of NELS.* Department of Linguistics, University of Ottawa.

Higginbotham, J. (1981). "Reciprocal Interpretation." *Journal of Linguistic Research* 1.3: 97–117.

Higginbotham, J. (1983). "Logical Form, Binding, and Nominals." *Linguistic Inquiry* 14: 395–420.

Higginbotham, J. (1985). "On Semantics." *Linguistic Inquiry* 16: 547–593.

Hong, S. (1985). "A and A' Binding in Korean and English." Doctoral dissertation, University of Connecticut, Storrs.

Huang, C. -T. J. (1983). "A Note on the Binding Theory." *Linguistic Inquiry* 14: 554–561.

Koopman, H., and D. Sportiche (1982). "Variables and the Bijection Principle." *The Linguistic Review* 2: 139–160.

Lasnik, H. (1976). "Remarks on Coreference." *Linguistic Analysis* 2: 1–22.

Lasnik, H. (1981). "On Two Recent Treatments of Disjoint Reference." *Journal of Linguistic Research* 1.4: 48–58.

Lasnik, H. (1985). "A Note on Illicit NP Movement." *Linguistic Inquiry* 16: 481–490.

Lasnik, H. (1989). *Essays on Anaphora.* Kluwer, Dordrecht.

Lasnik, H., and J. Uriagereka (1988). *Lectures on Binding and Empty Categories.* MIT Press, Cambridge, Mass.

Lebeaux, D. (1983). "A Distributional Difference between Reciprocals and Reflexives." *Linguistic Inquiry* 14: 723–730.

Montalbetti, M. (1984). "After Binding." Doctoral dissertation, MIT.

Reinhart, T. (1983). "Coreference and Bound Anaphora." *Linguistics and Philosophy* 6:47–88.

Reinhart, T. (1986). "Center and Periphery in the Grammar of Anaphora. In B. Lust, ed., *Studies in the Acquisition of Anaphora, Vol. I.* Reidel, Dordrecht.

Ross, J. R. (1967). "Constraints on Variables in Syntax." Doctoral dissertation, MIT.

Sportiche, D. (1985). "Remarks on Crossover." *Linguistic Inquiry* 16:460–469.

Chapter 2

Binding, SUBJECT, and Accessibility

Wayne Harbert

Under what has been the dominant conception of binding domains within the Extended Standard Theory, responsibility for restricting the reference of pronouns and anaphors has been divided between two conditions: one that defines finite constructions as binding domains (the Tensed-S Condition (TSC)/Propositional Island Condition (PIC) and their successors) and one that defines the domain of a subject nominal as a binding domain (the Specified Subject Condition (SSC) and its successors). This conception is continued in Chomsky 1981, for instance, where the domain of binding is characterized as the domain of an accessible SUBJECT, as defined in (1).

(1) a. SUBJECT = AGR where present, a subject NP otherwise.
   b. γ is accessible to α if and only if α is in the c-command domain of γ and the assignment to α of the index of γ would not violate (1c).
   c. $*[_{\gamma} \ldots \delta \ldots]$ where γ, δ have the same index.

(This characterization differs from earlier ones in three basic ways. First, it takes AGR, rather than Tense, to be the component of "finiteness" responsible for the PIC effect—a claim for which there seems to be substantial cross-linguistic evidence.[1] Second, it reduces the PIC and the SSC to disjunctive subparts of a single principle by means of the notion of SUBJECT. Third, it includes the accessibility provision (1b), about which I will have more to say below.) Under this version of the binding theory, the domain of accessible AGR is in a sense the basic opaque domain, since AGR, when present, takes precedence as SUBJECT over subject nominals.[2] More recently, however, a number of authors, including Freidin and

I would like to thank John Bowers, Chris Brockett, Gennaro Chierchia, Jim Gair, Jaklin Kornfilt, Johan Seynnaeve, S. N. Sridhar, Veneeta Srivastav, Magui Suñer, Jane Tang, and Edwin Williams for their valuable comments. All errors of fact and interpretation are my own.

Harbert (1983), Kayne (1983), Bouchard (1985), and Chomsky (1986), starting out from a variety of premises, have suggested that the PIC is epiphenomenal and that AGR should in fact not be accorded a special role in the defining of binding domains.

I will argue, contrary to these proposals, that a characterization of binding domains in terms of (1) is basically correct. I will show that AGR does have an independent opacity-inducing effect, and I will introduce a consideration suggesting that that effect is in a certain sense stronger than the SSC effect (that is, the opacity-inducing effect of subject nominals), as the hierarchical definition of SUBJECT in (1a) would lead us to expect. The evidence supporting this claim takes the form of an asymmetry in the distribution of the two effects across languages.

Consider first the initial characterization of binding domains in Chomsky 1986, given in (2).

(2)   The local domain for an anaphor or pronoun α is the minimal governing category for α, where a governing category is a maximal projection containing both a subject and a lexical category governing α (hence, containing α).

INFL with the feature [+AGR] plays no special role in defining those domains, under this account, but contributes only insofar as it is a potential governor, for the embedded subject position in (3), for instance.

(3)   *The children* think that [$_S$ *each other/they* INFL[+AGR] are crazy].

Each other in (3) is required by Principle A to be bound in S because S contains the anaphor, its governor (namely, INFL), and a subject—in the form of the anaphor itself—and S is therefore a binding domain with respect to that anaphor, as defined in (2). The same properties define S in (3) as a binding domain for *they*.

The construction in (4) appears problematic for this account, as I have represented it so far, as well as for the binding theory of Chomsky (1981).

(4)   [*They* sold [$_{NP}$ *their/each other's* pictures]].

The NP in (4) seems to function as a binding domain for *their* but not for the anaphor *each other's*; the anaphor can be bound to an NP-external antecedent here, but the pronoun need not be disjoint in reference from any nominal outside of NP. Moreover, this breakdown in the usual complementarity between proximate pronouns and anaphors turns out not to be simply an idiosyncrasy of English; rather, we find that proximate pronouns and anaphors also alternate in the position of possessor/subject of NP in New Testament Greek, as illustrated in (5a–b), Khmer, as illustrated in (6a–b), Japanese, as illustrated in (8a), colloquial Russian, as illustrated in (9a), Chinese, as illustrated in (10a), Dogrib, as illustrated in (12a), and Basque, as illustrated in (13a), for instance.[3] (I have no data on reflexive possessors in Swahili. However, as (7a) shows, here too a pronoun in possessor position can corefer with the subject of the containing clause. The remaining examples in (5)–(13) will be discussed below.)

(5) *New Testament Greek*

    a. Kaì (*autós*) élegen autoîs   en [$_{NP}$ têi didakhêi *autoû*]. (Mark 4:2)
       and he$_i$ spoke to-them in   the teaching his$_i$

    b. Kaì áphes *toùs nekroùs* thápsai [$_{NP}$ toùs *heautôn*
       and let   the dead$_i$ bury   the selves'$_i$
       nekroùs]. (Matt. 8:22)
       dead

    c. Kaì ērôtésen autòn *hapan to   plēthos* ... [$_S$ PRO apelrheîn
       and asked   him$_j$ all   the population   PRO$_j$ to-go
       ap'   *autōn*/(*heautōn). (Luke 8:37)
       from them$_i$/selves$_i$

(6) *Khmer* (Fisher 1985)

    a. *Miin* kəmpun-tae məəl siəwphiw niw knon [$_{NP}$ bəntur *koət*].
       aunt$_i$ in-process-of read book   LOC in   room her$_i$

    b. *Kmaoc* nuh nin cee   pdahsaa dal [baan-pqoun ñiət-səndaan
       spirit$_i$ that FUT curse put   on   relative   relative
       kluən].
       self's$_i$
       'That ghost will put a curse on its relatives.'

    c. *Puu-Sok*   thaa [$_S$ qom-Rin   khəəñ *koət*/*kluən].
       Uncle Sok$_i$ say   Uncle Rin see   him$_i$/*self$_i$.

    d. *Mit teən-pii neaq*   kit   thaa [$_S$ *kluən* ciə kounsəh].
       friend both   CLASSIFIER$_i$ think COMP   self$_i$ be student
       'The two friends think that they are students.'

(7) *Swahili*

    a. *Asha* alimwona [$_{NP}$ mama wa mwalimu *wake*]. (Keach 1980:119)
       Asha$_i$ saw   mother of teacher his$_i$

    b. *Hamisi* alimwamrisha Asadi [$_S$ PRO kumnyaa { $\emptyset$/*yeye*}].
       Hamisi$_i$ ordered   Asadi$_j$ PRO$_j$ INF-shave   him$_i$
       (Iris Alemán, personal communication)

(8) *Japanese* (Oshima 1979)

    a. *John*-wa [$_{NP}$ *kare*-no/*zibun*-no hon]-o   mot-te ki-ta.
       John$_i$-TOP   he$_i$-POSS/self$_i$-POSS book-ACC carrying came

   b. *John*-wa   Mary-ni   [$_S$ PRO *kare*-ni   denwa-o kake]-sase-ta.
      John$_i$-TOP Mary$_j$-DAT   PRO$_j$ him$_i$-DAT to-telephone caused

(9) *Colloquial Russian* (Yokoyama 1980)
   a. *On* podal [$_{NP}$ *ego/svoj*   stakan].
      he$_i$ gave   his$_i$/self's$_i$ cup
   b. Tanju   [$_S$ PRO nalit'   *ej*   vody] poprosila *mat'*.
      Tanja$_j$-ACC   PRO$_j$ to-pour her$_i$ water asked   mother$_i$-NOM

(10) *Chinese* (Huang 1982)
   a. *Zhangsan* kanjian-le [$_{NP}$ *ta/ziji*   de shu].
      Zhangsan$_i$ saw   he$_i$/self$_i$'s book
   b. *Zhangsan* shuo [$_S$ ni   kanjian-le *ta*].
      Zhangsan$_i$ say   you see-ASP   him$_i$
   c. *Zhangsan* shuo [$_S$ *ziji/ta*   hui lai].
      Zhangsan$_i$ say   self$_i$/he$_i$ will come

(11) *Imbabura Quechua* (Peter Cole, personal communication)
   a. *Pay* jaturka [$_{NP}$ *pay*-paj   alku-ta].
      he$_i$ sold   he$_i$-POSS dog-ACC
   b. *Jose* crin   [$_S$ Maria *pay*-ta   rikushka-ta].
      José$_i$ believes   Maria him$_i$-ACC see-NOMINAL-ACC

(12) *Dogrib* (Saxon 1983)
   a. *John* [$_{NP}$ *we*-tà/*?ede*-tà]   xè   nàzè.
      John$_i$ his$_i$-father/self's$_i$-father with hunts
   b. *John* sìi   [$_S$ *we*-gha   ?elà whihtsį̀] yek'èrèzhǫ.
      John$_i$ FOC   him$_i$-for boat I-made   he-knows
      'John knows that I made a boat for him.'

(13) *Basque* (Echavarri-Dailey 1986)
   a. (*pro*) [*elkarren/beren*   etxik]   saldu zituzten.
      they$_i$ each other's$_i$/their$_i$ houses sell   AUX-PAST
   b. *Jonek* [Mirenek *bera/*bere burua* iltzea] ez du nahi.
      John$_i$ Mary   him$_i$/*self$_i$ to-kill not want

Chomsky (1986) observes that we can accommodate the asymmetry in (4) by adopting a particular convention in the identification of binding domains. Informally, the proposal is that a constituent β can constitute a binding domain with respect to an α it contains only if the relevant binding principle could be satisfied within β on some legitimate indexing. The NP in (4) is accordingly a binding domain for the pronoun it contains because that NP contains a governor for the pronoun and a subject nominal (satisfying (2)) and because the pronoun, lacking a potential c-commanding antecedent within NP, would be free in NP under any indexing, thereby satisfying the relevant principle, Principle B, within that NP. On the other hand, NP in (4) cannot constitute a binding domain for the anaphor it contains because it does not contain any potential c-commanding antecedent for that anaphor, and there is therefore no indexing under which Principle A could potentially be satisfied within NP with respect to it. So the anaphor is free to seek an antecedent outside of NP.[4]

The resultant binding theory now appears to be insufficiently restrictive in the case of (3), however. Since the anaphor in (3) is apparently not c-commanded by any potential binder within the embedded clause that could allow potential satisfaction of Principle A, that clause should not constitute a binding domain for the anaphor, just as the NP in (4) does not. Rather, the matrix clause should be the relevant binding domain, and the version of (3) with the anaphor seems to be predicted, incorrectly, to be good.

Chomsky considers but characterizes as somewhat artificial the possibility that it is AGR in (3) that serves as a potential binder for the anaphor, thereby permitting the potential satisfaction of Principle A within the lower clause, and he proposes instead that the version of (3) with the anaphor might in fact not be ill formed with respect to the binding theory at all. Rather, its ill-formedness can be attributed to the *that*-trace effect of the Empty Category Principle (ECP), if we assume that at LF the anaphor in question is raised and adjoined to the INFL of the higher clause, leaving behind an improperly governed trace. (This proposal should be compared to that of Kayne (1983), who also suggests that the NIC effect for lexical anaphors might reduce to an ECP effect, although in a rather different way.)

Once this step is taken, it appears that AGR becomes wholly unnecessary as a factor in the characterization of binding domains, and the binding theory for anaphors and pronouns reduces to the effect of the presence of a subject nominal alone. (I will continue to refer to this effect as the SSC effect.) This reduction seems feasible because the only apparent opacity-inducing effect of AGR in English not duplicated by the SSC, as modified —namely, the "NIC" effect for anaphors reflected in (3)—is now held to fall not under the binding theory but under a different subtheory, the theory of government.[5]

However, I will argue that even if anaphors (or rather, their traces after LF movement) are subject to the ECP in the manner suggested, the PIC effect can still not be reduced to an artifact of the intersection of the SSC and other principles. The argument, in part a restatement of the argument presented in Harbert 1982, 1983, is based on certain systematic differences between languages like English/New Testament Greek and languages like Gothic. In Gothic, unlike English, pronouns could not be used in complement positions in nonfinite clauses to corefer with the subject of the containing clause. When coreference was intended, a reflexive was required. This is illustrated in (14a) for the case of an infinitive complement with a PRO subject, in (14b) for the case of an exceptional case marking complement, and in (14c) for the case of a participal relative construction. Nor could pronouns be used as subjects of NPs in Gothic when coreference with the higher subject was intended. This is illustrated in (15). Again, reflexives had to be used in this context to express coreference.[6]

(14) a. Jah bedun ina   *allai*   *gaujans* ... [$_S$ PRO galeiþan fairra
       and asked him$_j$ all-of-the inhabitants$_i$ PRO$_j$ to-go   from
       sis/(**im*). (Luke 8:37)
       selves$_i$/*them$_i$
       'And all of the inhabitants asked him to go from them.'
       (Greek model has a pronoun)

   b. *þai*-ei ni wildedun   [$_S$ mik þiudanon ufar
       who$_i$ not they-wanted me to-rule   over
       sis/(**im*)] (Luke 19:27)
       selves$_i$/*them$_i$
       'who didn' t want me to rule over them'
       (Greek model has a pronoun)

   c. (*Is*) qaþ-uh -þan [$_{NP}$ þamma   [$_S$ PRO haitandin
       he$_i$ said-and then   to-the-one$_j$ PRO$_j$ inviting
       sik/(**ina*)]] ... (Luke 14:12)
       self$_i$/*him$_i$
       'And then he said to the one inviting him ...'
       (Greek model has a pronoun)

(15) Jah (*is*) qaþ   im   in [$_{NP}$ laiseinai *seinai*/(**is*)]. (Mark 4:2)
     and he$_i$ spoke to-them in   teaching self's$_i$/his$_i$
     'And he spoke to them in his teaching.'
     (Greek model has a pronoun)

It is possible that both of these differences can be accounted for in a unitary way, by claiming that in Gothic, unlike English, the presence of a subject NP is not sufficient to define a phrase as a binding domain for a pronoun or anaphor contained within it. That is, Gothic does not observe the SSC effect. Accordingly, in Gothic the bracketed phrases in (14) and (15) are transparent for purposes of assignment of disjoint reference to pronouns, for example, unlike what happens in English.

Some possible evidence that the differences between English and Gothic reflected in (14) and (15) may in fact be regulated by a single parameter, involving whether or not subject NPs ([NP, XP]) function as SUBJECT in the sense of (1), is provided by the fact that languages resembling English with respect to one of these constructions seem in general to resemble English with respect to the other as well.[7] Thus, (5)–(13) show that in New Testament Greek, Khmer, Swahili, Japanese, colloquial Russian, Chinese, Imbabura Quechua, Dogrib, and Basque, pronoun interpretation works as in English in both constructions, for example. In each of these languages a pronoun occurring in either the position of subject of NP or the position of object of a (nonfinite) complement clause can be understood as coreferring with the subject of the containing clause—unlike Gothic, but like English. Conversely, as (16) and (17) show, pronoun interpretation works in Latin and Icelandic as it does in Gothic with respect to both constructions. In these languages, as in Gothic, a pronoun occurring either as the subject of an NP, as in (16a) and (17a), or as the object of a nonfinite complement, as in (16b) and (17b), must be interpreted as disjoint in reference from the subject of the containing clause.[8]

(16) *Latin*

    a. *(Is)* dixit [$_{NP}$ discipulis   *suis*/(**eius*)] ... (Vulgate Matt. 26:36)
       he$_i$ said   to-the-disciples self's$_i$/*his$_i$

    b. *qui*   noluerunt   [$_S$ me regnare super *se*/(**eos*)] (Luke 19:27)
       who$_i$ not-wanted   me to-rule   over   selves$_i$/*them$_i$

(17) *Icelandic*

    a. *Jón* rétti   Haraldi [$_{NP}$ *sín*/*hans*   föt].[9] (Thráinsson 1976)
       Jon$_i$ handed Harald   self's$_i$/*his$_i$ clothes

    b. *Hann* telur   [$_S$ mig hafa   séð   *sig*/*hann*]. (Andrews 1976)
       he$_i$ believes   me to-have seen self$_i$/*him$_i$

In any case, the SSC effect fails to hold in Gothic, as well as in certain other languages. This failure in turn removes an obscuring factor and provides us with an opportunity to determine whether finiteness plays an independent role in defining binding domains, or whether the PIC effect is an artifact of the intersection of the SSC and other conditions, as has been suggested. Consider (18), in which, given a binding theory incorporating (1), AGR would have constituted the accessible SUBJECT for the italicized position in the embedded clause.

(18) *The children* expected that [Mary INFL[+AGR] would help **each other/them*].

Under the revision proposed by Chomsky (1986) the status of the bracketed clause in (18) as a binding domain for the italicized elements is due solely to the SSC effect, since AGR no longer plays a role in defining binding domains. The pronoun, for example, is required to be free only within the bracketed clause because that clause contains the pronoun, a governor for the pronoun, and a subject nominal, *Mary*. Now if this were correct, then, since the SSC effect does not hold in Gothic, as we have established, we would expect that in Gothic a pronoun occurring in an analogous position in a finite complement would have to be disjoint in reference from the subject of the higher clause, just as it is in infinitive complements. However, comparison of (14a) with (19), for example, demonstrates that this is not the case.

(19) *(Eis)* bedun ina ei   [$_S$ (is) uslaubidedi *im/(*sis)* ...   galeiþan].
      they$_i$ asked him that   he allow[FIN] them$_i$/*selves$_i$ to go
      (Luke 8:32)
      'They asked that he allow them to go.'

Sentences like (19) show that, unlike infinitive clauses, finite clauses do constitute binding domains in Gothic for complement positions contained in them—that is, that the PIC effect holds (and not just in its local "NIC" case), independent of the SSC. This argument can be duplicated in other languages as well, including Icelandic. Also consistent with this conclusion is the fact that languages like Chinese, Khmer, and Korean, which lack morphological realization of subject-verb agreement, in general seem not to observe the PIC effect for lexical anaphors, again suggesting that it is AGR that causes this effect. For instance, the Khmer example (6d) shows that in that language, unlike English, an anaphor can occur in nominative subject position in a finite clause and be bound to the subject of the higher clause. That is, the PIC effect does not hold for anaphors here, although the SSC effect does hold, as illustrated by (6c). But, again unlike English, Khmer is also wholly lacking in subject-verb agreement morphology (hence presumably AGR), so the absence of the PIC effect is unsurprising given a binding theory incorporating (1). See especially Yang 1984 and Fisher 1988 for detailed discussion of such facts. (Malayalam seems to be an exception to the generalization that languages lacking overt subject-verb agreement will lack PIC/NIC effects; even though Malayalam lacks agreement, Mohanan (1983) reports that the strict anaphor *swa-* does not occur in nominative subject position. However, the absence of agreement in

Malayalam seems to be a fairly recent development, and we may therefore simply be dealing here with a case of morphological change lagging behind syntax.)[10]

A characterization of binding domains in terms of (1) thus seems to be correct at least insofar as it captures these classes of facts. The particular formulation of the parameter distinguishing between Gothic and English that I have proposed in other work (for instance, Harbert 1983)—following a suggestion by Alec Marantz (personal communication)—exploits the hierarchical definition of SUBJECT in (1), proposing that languages vary with respect to where on that hierarchy they draw the threshold for SUBJECT hood. In Gothic, unlike English, only the cardinal element on the hierarchy, AGR, constitutes a potential SUBJECT. Thus, Gothic has PIC effects but not SSC effects. Excluded in principle, under this account, is the possibility that binding in some language might observe the SSC but fail to observe the PIC—setting aside, of course, such languages as Khmer, Chinese, and Korean where this is trivially the case because they lack the AGR necessary to cause the PIC effect. To the extent that this implicational prediction is borne out, it provides evidence that the SUBJECT notion is a legitimate generalization, rather than representing simply a conflation of two essentially independent domains. Yang (1984) introduces examples from Kannada claimed to show that that language instantiates the supposedly impossible case, exhibiting the SSC effect but not the PIC effect for lexical anaphors. In fact, however, his examples do not seem to demonstrate this.[11]

The result suggested by the Gothic evidence appears to be contradicted by the conclusion reached in Freidin and Harbert 1983. In that paper we started out by observing that pleonastic subjects ("non-θ-subjects," in our terms) have at most only a weak opacity effect for lexical anaphors in English, as illustrated by the relatively well formed sentence (20a). (As the remaining examples show, pleonastic subjects still define opaque domains for pronouns and NP-traces. See note 20 for further discussion.)

(20) a. (?)*They* expected [it to be reported to *each other* that John is crazy].

   b.   *They* expect [it to be reported to *them* that John is crazy].

   c.   *They$_i$ were expected for [it to be hurt t_i].

We observed next that substituting an agreeing verb for the infinitive verb in the intermediate clause in such constructions as (20a) does not result in significantly diminished grammaticality. This is illustrated in (21), which we do not find appreciably worse than (20a).

(21) (?)*They* expect [it AGR will be reported to *each other* that John is crazy].

We concluded, accordingly, that AGR does not make a strong independent contribution to opacity in such cases and that the strong effect of AGR is limited to the local "NIC" case reflected in (3). This result can in turn be construed as evidence supporting the analysis of Chomsky (1986) (who suggests, as we have seen, that the strong effect in (3) might reflect a fact about the theory of government rather than about the binding theory). Note that the form of the test here is essentially the same as the one based on Gothic that we have just discussed; in a case in which the SSC effect fails to hold for some reason, finiteness is varied to determine whether it has an independent effect on opacity. The outcome in the case of (20a) and (21), though, seems quite different from the outcome in Gothic.

However, there are two grounds for thinking that the evidence of (20a) and (21) does not necessarily argue against a binding theory incorporating the PIC in some form. First, it turns out that the phenomenon reflected in (21) may be a special fact about English, not to be covered by the core binding theory at all. It is at least not universal. (22) shows, for example, that finite (indicative) complements without θ-subjects in Icelandic are not similarly transparent to anaphor binding.

(22) *Jón* veit   að   [það hefur verið beðið eftir *honum/*sér*].
     Jon$_i$ knows that 'it' has   been waited on   him$_i$/*self$_i$
     'Jon knows that he has been waited on.'

This is true even though in Icelandic infinitive complements even referential subject nominals fail to block reflexive binding, as we have seen. Second, even supposing that we do assume (21) to reflect the core case to be accommodated by the binding theory, the two apparently contradictory results—the one arrived at on the basis of (21) and the one arrived at on the basis of the Gothic evidence—might be reconciled by replacing SUBJECT in (1) with a second notion, θ-SUBJECT, defined in an analogous way: AGR, if present, would serve as θ-SUBJECT "by inheritance" just in case it is coindexed with a θ-subject nominal (that is, a nonpleonastic subject NP). This would amount to saying that AGR defines an opaque domain only when linked to a canonical binder—an idea that has at least some conceptual plausibility. (We will return to this idea below.) In (21) the coindexed nominal is pleonastic—that is, a non-θ-subject—so AGR would not count as a θ-SUBJECT and the anaphor would be able to seek a clause-external binder. In (3), on the other hand, the coindexed nominal is not pleonastic, and AGR would therefore constitute a θ-SUBJECT, defining the bracketed clause as a binding domain for the anaphor. In any case, the facts of (21) do not seem necessarily to argue against the claim that AGR contributes to the definition of opaque domains.

If AGR does, after all, define a binding domain for elements that it c-commands, we are led again to the conclusion that (3) falls under the binding theory and, correspondingly, that (23) must reflect a special exemption in Principle A of the sort resulting from the accessibility qualification (1b–c) (an assumption that can be dispensed with so long as the domain of AGR is not taken to be a binding domain).

(3) *They* think that [*each other* AGR are crazy].

(23) *They* think that [[pictures of *each other*] AGR will be on sale].

However, the status of this exemption remains to be determined. Mohanan (1985) has proposed that the sort of apparent "long-distance" binding in (23) should in fact not be covered by the binding theory of Universal Grammar, since it is, he claims, an idiosyncratic phenomenon occurring only in English and a few other languages, and within these languages only in "picture noun phrases."[12] This contention is disputed in Harbert and Srivastav 1986, however, where it is shown that "long-distance" binding of (some) strict anaphors in contexts comparable to (23) is in fact possible in a wide range of languages, including Hindi, as in (24), Dutch, as in (25), Basque, as in (26), Gothic, as in (27), and Malayalam, as in (28).[13] See Harbert and Srivastav 1986 for more complete discussion of these facts.

(24) *Hindu aur Mussalman* laRkõõ ne   deekhaa ki   [[*eek duusre* kee
        Hindu and Muslim   boys   ERG saw   that each other GEN
        ghar]   jal rahee thee].[14]
        houses burning were

(25) *Ze*   zeiden dat [[foto's   van {*hen/elkaar/?zichzelf*}]   te
        they$_i$ said   that pictures of   them$_i$/each-other$_i$/?selves$_i$ for
        koop waren].
        sale were

(26) *Haiek* [[*elkarren*   etxik] salgai zeudela] bazekiten].
        they$_i$ each-other's$_i$ houses on-sale were   know-PAST
        (Echavarri-Dailey 1986)
        'They know that each other's houses were on sale.'

(27) Akei (*is*) *was* kunnands [$_S$ þatei swaleikamma waldufnja
        but   he$_i$ *was* knowing   that by-such   authority
        [$_{NP}$ mahtais *seinaizos* nauþs] ustaiknida wesi]. (Skeireins 1b:12)
        of-power self's$_i$ force   shown   would-be

'But he know that by such authority the force of self's power would
be shown.'

(28) $[_s[_s[_s[$ Swaṇtam suhrəttə] aanaye   nuḷḷi   ennə
           self's   friend-NOM elephant-ACC pinched COMPL
    amma   acchanooṭə parañ̃ñu ennə   r̄aajaawinə tooṇṇi ennə]
    mother to-father said   COMPL. king-DAT felt   COMPL
    maṇṭriye raaṇi wiswasippicu]. (-Mohanan's (44a))
    minister queen believe-caused
    'The queen$_j$ convinced the minister that the king$_i$ felt that the
    mother$_k$ told the father that her$_{j,k}$/his$_i$ own friend pinched the
    elephant.'

It should be noted, since it will become important later, that (24) becomes
ill formed in the indicated indexing for all of the speakers consulted when
the reciprocal is replaced by the reflexive *apnaa*. (However, see Gurtu
1985:77 for a different judgment.) In this regard Hindi resembles Dutch,
in which such long-distance binding, although possible for reciprocals, is
at least questionable for reflexives, as illustrated in (25).[15] A similar asymmetry has been observed in Basque by Echavarri-Dailey (1986); replacement of the reciprocal with the reflexive in (26) also yields bad results.
Lasnik and Freidin (1981) report a generally comparable result for English
as well. In an informal survey they found that reciprocals are also accepted
by a larger number of speakers of English in constructions such as (3) than
are reflexives. I believe this recurrent difference in admissibility between
reciprocals and reflexives in this context in all of these languages is amenable to a common functional explanation, which falls outside the binding
theory. Briefly, in all of these languages pronouns are also possible in the
context in question with intended coreference with the matrix subject. (We
can account for this by assuming, with Huang (1983), that Principle B,
unlike Principle A, does not specify *accessible* SUBJECTs.) These proximate pronouns are of course interpreted in the same way as the corresponding reflexive would be. Accordingly, we may imagine that reflexives in such
contexts are disfavored by something like an "Avoid Reflexive Principle,"
grammaticized to varying degrees in different languages, because other
means, in the form of the proximate pronoun, are available for expressing
reflexive meaning there. On the other hand, no convenient alternative exists
for expressing reciprocal meaning.[16] I have suggested elsewhere that this
"Avoid Reflexive Principle" may also be responsible, either directly or as
a catalyst in linguistic change, for the similar distributional asymmetries
between reflexives and reciprocals illustrated in (29a) and (29b). (See
Harbert 1985 for details.)[17]

(29) a. *They* put the children near *them/each other/?themselves*.
     b. *They* sold [*their/each other's/*theirselves'* pictures].

Since it is improbable that all of these languages allow this type of long-distance binding because of accidental convergence of language-specific properties, we are led to conclude that such binding does result from one of the settings of the parameters of the binding theory (perhaps a marked one) in Universal Grammar. Some additional problems remain for the *i*-within-*i* provision. Yang (1984), for instance, observes that Russian does not admit sentences analogous to (23) with reciprocals (though on the basis of examples to be introduced below I reject his claim that Russian does not exhibit any *i*-within-*i* effects), so clearly some cross-linguistic variation with respect to these effects remains to be explained. On the other hand, the phenomenon of "long-distance" binding of anaphors properly contained in subject nominals, as licensed by the *i*-within-*i* exemption, does not seem to be so restricted in distribution as Mohanan believes.

Moreover, it appears that the effect of the *i*-within-*i* provision for lexical anaphors is not limited to an extension of the domain of binding for anaphors properly contained in subject phrases. As Veneeta Srivastav has observed, and as we have discussed in Harbert and Srivastav 1986, the reflexive form *apnaa* in Hindi is in fact permissible in this context too, as in (30), where, however, it may not be bound but must be interpreted as having arbitrary reference.

(30) a. [*Apnii* zindagii] kiimti hooti hai.
        'self's' life   valuable   is
        'One's life is valuable.'
     b. Ram sooctaa hai ki [*apnii* zindagii] kiimti hooti hai.
        Ram thinks   that 'self's' life   valuable   is
        'Ram thinks that one's life is valuable.'

The arbitrary interpretation is available to *apnaa* in (30), where it is properly contained in the subject of its clause, but not in (31), where it is in an object phrase. This apparent complementarity between reflexive *apnaa* and arbitrary *apnaa* makes it seem quite likely that the arbitrary interpretation of *apnaa* in (30) is a consequence of the accessibility provision of Principle A (rather than, say, reflecting the existence of two different *apnaa*'s, one reflexive and one arbitrary, that happen to be homophonous), especially in view of the fact that an analogous distribution of arbitrary and bound interpretations for reflexives seems to occur in other languages, including Russian, as observed by Rappaport (1986). This is illustrated in (32). Similarly, Giorgi (1984) observes that the usually bound *proprio* in Italian also receives an arbitrary interpretation in the same context.

(31) a. *Ram* [*apnii*   zindagii-se] nafrat kartaa hai.
     Ram$_i$ self's$_i$/*'self's'$_{arb}$ life-ACC   hates
     'Ram hates his own/*one's life.'
  b. *Ram* [*apnaa*   iraada] samajhta   hai.
     Ram self's$_i$/*'self's'$_{arb}$ motives understand is
     'Ram understands self's/*one's motives.'

(32) a. [*Svoja* žizn'] dorože   vsego.
     'self's' life   important all
     'One's own life is the most important.'
  b. Ivan dumaet, čto [[*svoja* žizn' dorože   vsego].
     Ivan thinks   that 'self's' life   important all
     'Ivan thinks that one's/*his life is the most important.'
  c. *Ivan* nenavidit [*svoju*   žizn'].
     Ivan$_i$ hates   self's$_i$/*'self's'$_{arb}$ life
     'Ivan hates his own/*one's life.'
  d. *Ivan* ponimaet   [*svoi*   motivy].
     Ivan$_i$ understands self's$_i$/*'self's'$_{arb}$ motives
     'Ivan understands his own/*one's motives.'

The account proposed in Harbert and Srivastav 1986 for these facts has
the following form: *apnaa* in (30a–b) lacks both a governing category and
a domain-governing category in the sense of Manzini (1983), and we
propose, in the spirit of her analysis, that an anaphor lacking both a
governing category and a domain-governing category need not be bound,
but, lacking intrinsic reference, it must be arbitrary if it does not pick up
reference from an antecedent.[18] The same account will extend to the
parallel examples in Russian.

Two questions arise in connection with this possibility. First, why is an
arbitrary reading not similarly available for other anaphors in the context
in question—for example, the Dutch *zich* in (25) or the Hindi *eek duusre*
in (24)? One might speculate that it is because *zich* is distinctly third person
and *eek duusre* is distinctly plural, and these lexical features must be
licensed by the presence of an appropriate antecedent, independent of the
requirements of the binding theory. *Apnaa* and *svoj*, on the other hand, are
neutral with respect to person, gender, and number and therefore have no
lexical features of these types that require licensing by an antecedent; hence,
they may be arbitrary when the binding theory does not require them to
be bound. It appears, though, that this at least cannot account for all of
the relevant cases, since Mohanan (1985:640n.) suggests that Malayalam
swa-, even though invariant for person and number, does not allow arbi-

trary readings in similar contexts. Conversely, Italian *proprio*, which does not admit first or second person antecedents and therefore appears to be distinctly third person, nonetheless does allow an arbitrary reading in the context under discussion. The question of why some anaphors admit an arbitrary interpretation if not in the domain of an accessible SUBJECT whereas others do not must therefore be left open for the time being. We also do not have an entirely satisfactory answer for the complementary question—why *apnaa* and *svoj*, unlike *eek duusre, cannot* pick up reference from the subject of the higher clause—but again we think that it involves at least in part something like the "Avoid Reflexive Principle" mentioned earlier.

We conclude that *i*-within-*i* effects take two forms in Hindi. A reciprocal properly contained within a subject phrase in a finite clause can be bound to an antecedent in the higher clause, and reflexives in the same position have arbitrary reference. One prediction derivable from this account of arbitrary *apnaa*, however—that the arbitrary reading should be possible for anaphors properly contained in subjects but not in complements—though supported by the nonavailability of that interpretation in (31), for example, turns out to be counterexemplified by other sentences, such as (33).

(33) [Apnee bacõõ]-mẽẽ koii kharabi nahĩĩ hootii.
     'self's' children-in any fault   not is
     'There is no fault in one's children.'

Here, as in (31), the anaphor is free in the domain of an accessible SUBJECT, yet (33), unlike (31), is well formed. The account for this difference advanced in Harbert and Srivastav 1986 exploits the fact that the lower clause subject *Ram* in (31) is a possible binder for the anaphor, whereas *koii kharabi* in (33) is ruled out as a possible binder on semantic grounds. It is proposed that, rather than being defined in terms of accessible SUBJECTs, binding domains for anaphors are in fact defined in terms of potential Binders. (For another suggestion along these lines, see Bouchard 1985.) Among the possible merits of such a reformulation is the fact that it makes feasible the elimination of a redundancy between the definition of binding and the definition of accessibility. As Huang (1983) notes, the two parts of the definition of accessibility—c-command and nonviolation of the *i*-within-*i* condition—also play a role in determining what may constitute Binders for anaphors. Under the proposed account, this would be an expected result.

Further evidence in favor of such a reinterpretation may be provided by the fact that in English, too, there seems to be some connection between the potential of a nominal to serve as an antecedent for an anaphor and its ability to define a barrier for the binding of that anaphor to another nominal. Postal (1974:66) notes that subjects of asymmetric predicates, which are for semantic reasons not possible antecedents of same-clause reflexive objects, also do not strongly block binding of these reflexives by outside antecedents. Consider (34).

(34) Joe$_i$ considers [Mary to be superior to himself$_i$].

Similarly, as pointed out above, Freidin and Harbert (1983) observe that pleonastic subject nominals, which are also not possible antecedents for lexical anaphors because they are not referential, induce at most a very weak SSC effect for lexical anaphors.[19] In each of these cases, therefore, a subject that is not a potential binder for an anaphor for semantic reasons also does not define a strongly opaque domain for binding.

Among the apparent problems facing the proposed replacement of *accessible SUBJECT* in Principle A with *potential Binder* is the fact that, as illustrated in (35), object NPs in English, even though they may antecede anaphors (and are therefore potential Binders), do not prevent them from being bound by more distant antecedents.

(35) They$_i$ gave the children$_j$ pictures of each other$_{i,j}$.

However, the unmarked case across languages seems to be that only subjects count as potential A-Binders; we conclude that it is not surprising that it is only these canonical Binders that define binding domains.

A second apparent problem with such a proposal is that it fails to accommodate the opacity-inducing effect of AGR argued for extensively above, since AGR, as a nonargument and therefore not a sufficient binder for a lexical anaphor, should not define binding domains for lexical anaphors under this account. However, a solution to this problem can possibly be developed along the lines of the discussion surrounding (21). It was concluded there that, although AGR does have the ability to create opacity, that ability might not be wholly independent; rather, it might depend in part on the nature of the nominal coindexed with AGR. In particular, we can amend the proposal developed there in such a way that Principle A is stated in terms of capital BINDER, defined in a way analogous to SUBJECT, with AGR counting as a BINDER just in case the nominal with which it is coindexed is a potential Binder for the anaphor in question.[20] In (21) AGR is coindexed with a nominal that is not a potential Binder for the anaphor because it is nonreferential, and AGR therefore does not count as a BINDER, so defined. The complement in (21) is accordingly transparent to binding. On the other hand, AGR in (3) and

(18) is coindexed with an argument nominal, from which it can inherit the ability to serve as a BINDER, and the anaphor is therefore required to be bound in the domain of that AGR. Finally, the availability of an arbitrary interpretation for the anaphor in (33) might be amenable to a similar account; since the NP *koii kharabi* is not a potential Binder with respect to the anaphor for semantic reasons, neither it nor the coindexed AGR would define a binding domain for that anaphor.

In the absence of AGR, subject nominals themselves would count as BINDER in languages like English just in case they are potential Binders for the anaphor in question (for instance, argument nominals in the case of lexical anaphors). This yields the contrast between (20a) and (36).

(36) *They expected Mary to report to each other that John is crazy.

The availability of this possibility has to be parameterized as suggested earlier, of course, since in languages like Gothic subject nominals never define opaque domains by themselves, as we have seen.

The primary apparent merits of the revision just proposed are that it provides a way of accounting for a variety of apparent exceptions to the PIC effect and the SSC effect of Principle A. However, it also raises numerous questions that space considerations prevent me from addressing here.

Appendix: Accessibility and Predicate Nominals

It also appears that the phenomenon represented by examples (37)–(39) from English, Malayalam, and Icelandic might also be attributed to the *i*-within-*i* provision of Principle A.

(37) *English*
   a. *[*John's* pride] hurt *himself*.
   b. *[Pictures of *John*] are never good likenesses of *himself*.
   c. [$_{NP_i}$ *Their* compositions] AGR$_i$ were [$_{XP_i}$ (stories) about *each other*].

(38) *Malayalam* (Mohanan 1983)
   a. *[*Moohante* makan] *taan* dhiiṟanaaṇə ennə paraññu.
      Mohan's$_i$ son   'self'$_i$ brave-is   that said
      ('Mohan's son said that he was brave.')
   b. *[*Moohante* wiśwaasam] *tanne* ṟakṣiccu.
      Mohan's$_i$ belief   'self'$_i$ saved
      ('Mohan's belief saved him.')
   c. [$_{NP_i}$ *Moohante* wiśwaasam] [$_{S'}$ *taan* dhiiṟanaaṇə ennə] aaṇə.
      [$_{NP_i}$ Mohan's belief]   [$_{S_i}$ 'self' brave-is   that] is
      'Mohan's belief is that he is brave.'

(39) *Icelandic* (Maling 1984)

    a. [Skoðun *Siggu*] fær   mig til að PRO halda   að   *hana/*sig*
       opinion Siggu's leads me to   PRO believe that she-ACC/*self
       vanti hæfileika.
       lacks talent

    b. [$_{NP}$ Skoðun *Siggu*] er [$_{S'}$ að   *sig* vanti hæfileika].
       [$_{NP_i}$ opinion Siggu's is [$_{S_i}$ that self lacks talent]

(37a–b) are ill formed because the anaphor lacks a c-commanding antecedent. (37c) is well formed, however, even though here, too, the anaphor contained in XP appears to have no c-commanding antecedent. Langendoen and Battistella (1982), among others, have attempted to account for these cases by positing a reconstruction process at LF, which substitutes the postcopular phrase in such constructions for some arbitrarily chosen trace in the subject phrase. This account has one rather unsatisfying feature, however: the rule envisioned is not the standard kind of reconstruction rule that inserts moved phrases back into the positions where they belong in logical representations. Thus, for example, in (37c) the predicate nominal phrase would presumably have to be reconstructed into the position of the trace of *their*. (Note that this account also requires that all genitive NPs in the specifier (SPEC) position of NP, even subjective genitives, as in (37c), get to that position by movement, in order to leave a trace as a possible site for reconstruction.)

The alternative I propose exploits the fact that in (37c), unlike the ill-formed (37a), the anaphor is properly contained within a predicate nominal phrase, which, following standard assumptions, we may take to be coindexed by predication with the subject NP. Given this predication coindexing, the anaphor is properly contained in a phrase coindexed with the subject NP, and the latter therefore does not count as a potential BINDER for the former. Evidence that the *i*-within-*i* provision does apply in the suggested manner in predicate nominal constructions is provided by the ill-formedness of (40a), which, as the well-formedness of (40b) shows, cannot be due to a Principle B effect.

(40) a. *He$_i$ is [$_{NP_i}$ his$_i$ cook].

    b. He$_i$ fired [his$_i$ cook].

Thus, I conclude that the *i*-within-*i* provision prevents subjects of clauses with predicate nominals from counting as potential BINDERs for anaphors contained in those predicate nominals. Note, however, that the anaphor in such cases as (37c) is neither excluded nor interpreted as arbitrary in reference, but is rather coindexed with the SPEC of the subject phrase. Why does this occur? In other work (Harbert 1989) I have proposed an account along the following lines: Assume that specifiers, as well as heads, project their indices to the phrases containing them, so that a specified phrase is in effect doubly indexed, having both a head index and a SPEC index. The projection of SPEC indices to the superordinate phrase may be taken to be mediated by SPEC-head agreement. Hence, there is no similar projection of indices from complements to the maximal phrase containing them. Assume further a principle of the following sort (a more precise formulation of which is given in Harbert 1989).

(41) *The Default Binder Principle*
      If $XP_{k,(j)}$ occupies the position of a potential binder of α, where α is a bound element of type A, and if XP_k is a possible Binder of elements of type A, then α may be bound by k (the head index of XP). If XP_k is *not* a potential binder for elements of type A, the binding process may consult the SPEC index (j) of XP.

Since the subject NP in (37c) is not a possible binder (with respect to its head index) for any anaphor in the italicized position, given the i-within-i provision, (41) allows that anaphor to be bound by the SPEC index of that NP, resulting in an apparent relaxation of the c-command condition on binding. (37a) is ruled out on the indicated indexing because the subject NP is (with respect to its head index) a potential binder for a lexical anaphor in the italicized position, and binding by the SPEC index is therefore not licensed by (41). (37b) is ruled out because complements, unlike specifiers, do not project their indices to the superordinate phrase. This analysis can apparently also be extended to the similar facts represented in (38c) from Malayalam and (39b) from Icelandic, where the c-command requirement is also apparently suspended for forms generally requiring c-commanding antecedents, just in case they are contained within predicative phrases. Yang (1984) observes that a phenomenon of the same type occurs in Korean as well. Reinhart (1987) makes a proposal similar in spirit to this, to account for variable binding by operators in SPEC positions that do not c-command those variables. An example of this phenomenon is given in (42).

(42) [Everyone's$_i$ mother] loves him$_i$.

Under the present analysis, such binding would again be licensed by (41). The variable can be bound by the SPEC index of the bracketed phrase because the head index is not associated with an operator feature and therefore does not count as a possible binder for bound elements of this type.

Further extensions of (41) are proposed in Harbert 1989. For example, I argue there that it can also account for certain instances of anaphor binding in Chinese that involve apparent violation of the usual c-command requirement on binding. Tang (1989) has observed that in Chinese, in addition to a subject antecedent condition for anaphors, there is an animacy requirement for reflexive antecedents. However, when the subject of a clause containing a reflexive is not animate, binding can "look down into" the subject to find a non-c-commanding animate antecedent for that reflexive, as in (43a), subject to a kind of path condition that Tang formulates as in (43b) under the name *subcommand*.

(43) a. [*Zhangsan* de jiaoao] hai le   *ziji*.
       Zhangsan$_i$'s pride   hurt ASP self$_i$
       'Zhangsan's pride hurt him.'
   b. β subcommands α if and only if
      a. β c-commands α, or
      b. β is a subject contained in a subject phrase that c-commands α or subcommands α.

The basic idea here is that it must be possible to trace a path of subject phrases from the non-c-commanding antecedent to a subject that does c-command the anaphor. Tang proposes that subcommand is relevant for binding in Chinese as a matter of parametric choice, but not in English, for example. In view of the apparent parallelism between (37c) and (43a), however, I wish to propose that in both instances the apparent binding without c-command is licensed in the same way, namely, through (41). The difference between the two languages with respect to the admissibility of sentences like (43a) is due simply to the fact that Chinese, but not English, observes a systematic animacy requirement on reflexive binding. Thus, the bracketed NP in (43a) is (with respect to its head index) not a possible antecedent for any lexical anaphor in the italicized position, and (41) accordingly allows the anaphor to be bound by the SPEC index of that NP. In the English translation of (43a), however, since there is no general animacy requirement on the binders of lexical anaphors in English, the subject NP would (with respect to its head index) count as a potential binder for the anaphor, and so binding of the anaphor by the SPEC index of that subject would not be allowed under (41).

Notes

1. Turkish (George and Kornfilt 1981) and Portuguese (Zaring 1985, among others) provide evidence that AGR(eement) has an opacity-inducing effect even in the

absence of Tense marking. Further, as observed below, the Nominative Island Condition (NIC) effect for anaphors is systematically lacking in languages such as Chinese, Korean, and Khmer, which do not have subject-verb agreement, again suggesting that it is AGR that is responsible for this effect.

2. Chomsky (1981:209) states that "AGR in [(i)] is a SUBJECT, but NP in [(i)] is not if INFL contains AGR."

(i) NP INFL VP

3. I assume that the italicized possessive genitive phrases in these examples have the role of subject of NP, as their translational equivalents in English are argued to. For some of them, at least, I am aware of evidence involving binding that supports this assumption; in Japanese, Russian, and Chinese, where the ability to antecede a reflexive is characteristically restricted to subjects, possessor phrases may antecede reflexives occurring with them in the same NP. The assumption that possessors in New Testament Greek, as in (5a–b), can be identified, along with English possessors, as subject of NP, may appear somewhat problematic since their distribution is not identical to that of English possessor phrases. The former, unlike the latter, cooccur with the determiner. If we assume, following standard views of NP structure, that the determiner occupies the SPEC of NP position, and if we take the "subject" position in NP to be the SPEC of NP position, then it would seem to follow that the italicized elements in (5a–b) cannot be subjects. I am grateful to an anonymous referee for pointing this out. The objection loses its force, however, under the DP analysis of "noun phrases" developed by Abney (1987), Fukui (1986), and others, under which the position of Subject of NP and the position of determiner are not identified. In particular, *heautôn* can be taken to be the specifier (hence, Subject) of NP and still cooccur with the determiner (the head of DP). A full development of such an analysis would be out of place in the present work. Suffice it to point out that in comparable Chinese constructions the possessor behaves as a subject with respect to anaphor binding even when it occurs to the right of the determiner (Jane Tang, personal communication):

(i) na-ben   *Zhangsan*-de youguan *ziji* de shu
    that-CLASS. Zhangsan's   about   self's book

4. This proposal is conceptually similar to the analysis of Huang (1983), who proposes that Principle A, but not Principle B, specifies the presence of an accessible SUBJECT. The bracketed NP in (4) contains a SUBJECT, in the form of the head N, according to Huang's definition of SUBJECT, but that SUBJECT is not accessible to the pronoun or anaphor, as accessibility is defined in (1). NP is therefore a binding domain only for the pronoun.

5. Note, however, that (3) with the reciprocal does not seem to be as strongly ill formed as ECP violations typically are. Another apparent problem confronting such an analysis involves the existence of languages in which the NIC effect for lexical anaphors and the *that*-trace effect for *wh*-traces fail to converge in the predicted way. For example, the NIC effect holds for lexical anaphors in Dutch, as in (ia), even for those speakers for whom *wh*-traces are not subject to the *that*-trace effect, as in (ib).

(i) a. *Zij   zeiden dat elkaar/zich   gewonnen heeft/hebben.
       they$_i$ said   that each-other$_i$/selves$_i$ won   has/have
    b. Wie denk je   dat [$_{NP}$ e] gewonnen heeft?
       who$_i$ think you that [$_{NP_i}$ e] won   has
       'Who do you think won?'

There are, however, possible accounts of this asymmetry exploiting the fact that
movement in (ib), but not (ia), proceeds through the lower SPEC of C.

6. Since Gothic is an extinct language, the judgments represented in these examples
do not reflect directly elicited responses of native speakers. The distribution of
asterisks presented here may nonetheless be reconstructed with considerable cer-
tainty, since the Gothic text deviates systematically from the otherwise faithfully
imitated Greek model for translation in using reflexives rather than pronouns in
such sentences as (14) when coreference with the matrix subject was intended. This
not only shows that reflexives were possible in such constructions but also suggests
strongly that pronouns were not, since in the absence of such an assumption it
would be hard to account for the consistent deviation from the model for translation that is observed in such cases.

7. However, there also turn out to be languages in which the correlation breaks
down. The behavior of pronouns in the two environments seems to diverge in
Norwegian, for instance (see Yang 1984 and Bresnan, Halvorssen, and Maling
1983). As in Gothic, pronouns occurring in specifier position in NP may not refer
to the subject of the containing clause. Further, as in Gothic, the reflexive seg
occurring in complement positions in a nonfinite clause can corefer with the subject
of the higher clause. Unlike what happens in Gothic, though, pronouns in object
positions in nonfinite clausal complements are not necessarily disjoint in reference
with the subject of the higher clause. That is, unlike Gothic, Norwegian exhibits
an isolated "SSC" effect. According to Steven Franks (personal communication),
the same situation obtains in Polish. Gurtu (1985) reports a similar difference in
Hindi between NPs and nonfinite clauses with respect to the availability of the
proximate interpretation for pronouns, though this language presents some puz-
zling complications.

8. (16b) and (17b) show as well that the SSC effect also fails to hold for reflexives
in these languages, as in Gothic. (ia) and (ib) demonstrate, however, that the
binding of reciprocals and NP-traces is still apparently subject to that effect in
Icelandic.

(i) a. *þeir skipuðu mér að [$_S$ PRO raka   hvor annan.] (Thráinsson 1979)
       they$_i$ ordered me to   PRO shave each other$_i$
    b. *Jón var ákveðið að [$_S$ það   yrði heimsótt [$_{NP}$ t]]. (Everaert, n.d.)
       Jon$_i$ was decided that 'there' was visited   t$_i$
       ('It was decided that Jon was visited.')

9. However, judgments on sentences like the following, in which the pronoun
appears in a nonspecifier position, appear to be less clear, and conflicting results
are reported in the literature.

(i) Jón heyrði lýsingar   (Maríu) á honum.
    Jon heard descriptions (Maria's) of him

One native speaker consulted found coindexation with the clausal subject possible whether or not *Mariu* is present in the noun phrase. I have no account for this apparent contrast between pronouns in specifier position and pronouns in complement position in NPs.

10. I am indebted to Jim Gair for bringing these Malayalam facts to my attention. As reported by Koopman (1983:77), Vata also does not allow its reflexive to occur in nominative subject position, even though it, too, lacks agreement morphology.

11. The example Yang uses to show absence of the PIC effect, repeated here as (i), is not well chosen. The predicate in the complement is a predicate nominal, which agrees with the subject of the complement with respect to plurality; the example is thus analogous to English constructions like *They consider each other fools*. Accordinging to S. N. Sridhar (personal communication), comparable examples such as (ii) in which the complement clause contains a finite *verb* are ill formed.

(i)   Ā   ibbaru hudugaru [obbarannobbaru buddhivantar- endu]
       the two   boys$_i$ each-other$_i$ clever-PL   that
       tiḷididdāre.
       think-PRES. PERF. -3PL

(ii)   *Ā   ibbaru hudugaru [obbarannobbaru hōdar   -endu] tiḷidaru.
       the two   boys$_i$ each-other$_i$ went-PL that   think-PAST PL

12. Thus, Mohanan claims that, for example, sentences like (i) are ill formed.

(i) The boys thought that each other's girlfriends were pretty. (= Mohanan's (13a))

However, neither I nor other native speakers I have consulted concur with this judgment.

13. The Malayalam facts are from Mohanan 1983. The reflexive form *swa-* is generally a strict anaphor, which, when it occurs in a complement NP, can refer only to the subject of its own clause, and which never occurs in nominative subject position. However, when properly contained within a subject NP, as in (28), it need not be bound within its own clause, but may be bound to the subject of a higher clause. English and Malayalam differ in that in Malayalam *any* higher subject may antecede such an anaphor, whereas in English only the subject of the immediately higher clause is a possible antecedent. Accordingly, we must envision some extra, limiting condition for English—perhaps along the lines suggested by Giorgi (1984). However, this does not negate the fact that anaphors admit long-distance binding in both languages as predicted under the accessibility provision.

14. Mohanan claims that long-distance binding of the type in question is not possible in Hindi. However, all of our informants found (24) and similar sentences to be well formed. Note again, incidentally, that the noun in question here is not a picture noun.

15. Yang (1984), considering only the case of the reciprocal in prenominal specifier position, concludes that long-distance binding is marginal in Dutch. The version of this sentence with *elkaar* in postnominal position seems to be wholly well formed, however.

16. Chomsky (1981:230n.) advances a similar idea in a different context. Lebeaux (1983:724n.) also considers an account of this type for the contrast in (29b) and

similar constructions, but rejects it in favor of a grammatical account, under which reflexives but not reciprocals, in addition to being subject to Principle A, are required to be properly governed—a requirement derived from the ECP under the assumption that reflexives are raised at LF, leaving traces. Reflexives are thus excluded from genitive subject position in NPs, for instance, not by the binding theory but by government theory. This position is of course similar to the one adopted in Chomsky 1986. In spite of Lebeaux's interesting arguments, however, there seem to be reasons for preferring the functional account sketched above.

First, as we have seen, Gothic and Icelandic, which differ from English in not allowing pronouns as subjects of NPs to refer to the subject of the containing clause, also differ from English in allowing reflexives to occur as subjects of NPs. This state of affairs follows directly from the functional account, but not from Lebeaux's structural account. (However, Kornfilt (1986) reports a similar asymmetry between reciprocals and reflexives in certain Turkish gerundive constructions for which the functional account advocated here does not work. Reciprocals may appear in subject position in these constructions but reflexives cannot, even though a pronoun in that position cannot refer to the subject of the containing clause.)

Second, the "Avoid Reflexive" account also covers cases like (29a), where again the pronoun can be used to express reflexive meaning, and where the reflexive is found by most speakers to be odd whereas the reciprocal is perfectly unobjectionable. The oddness of the reflexive here cannot be attributed to the effect of the ECP since the position in question must be properly governed, as evidenced by the fact that it may be occupied by a trace, as in (i).

(i) Who did they put the children near [$_{NP}$ e]?

17. Some account of the difference in severity of ill-formedness between (29a) and (29b) is probably in order. With a reflexive, (29a) is somewhat odd, whereas (29b) is wholly impossible. As I have suggested elsewhere, this is because (29b) exhibits a *historical* effect of the Avoid Reflexive Principle; that principle has operated diachronically to cause the loss of the genitive reflexive in English (which occurred nowhere other than in the position of subject of NP). (29b) is consequently ruled out not only because it violates the Avoid Reflexive Principle but also because it contains a non-English form. (See Harbert 1985 for details.)

18. *Domain-governing category* is defined as follows:

(i) γ is a domain-governing category for α if and only if
    a. γ is a governing category for the minimal maximal category dominating α, and
    b. γ contains a subject accessible to α.

19. Considerations of this sort also no doubt play a role in the relative well-formedness, pointed out by Chomsky (1973), of such sentences as (i):

(i) Why are John and Mary letting honey drip on each other's feet?

20. Alternatively, under the assumption that AGR and a coindexed nominal form a chain, we could say that an element α is in the domain of a BINDER if it is c-commanded by the head of a chain one of whose members is a (canonical) potential Binder, and is not properly contained in a component of that chain.

It should be noted, incidentally, that the observation made earlier about (20c)—namely, that pleonastic subjects in English have a weak effect for lexical anaphors but a strong effect for traces—finds a possible explanation given a characterization of binding domains in terms of BINDER. Pleonastic subjects are not possible Binders for lexical anaphors, since lexical anaphors require referential antecedents. They therefore also fail to define binding domains for lexical anaphors. However, pleonastic subjects are possible Binders for traces, as in (i).

(i) There$_i$ seem t$_i$ to be unicorns in the garden.

They therefore would define binding domains for traces, under the proposed account.

References

Abney, S. (1987). "The English Noun Phrase in Its Sentential Aspect." Doctoral dissertation, MIT.

Andrews, A. (1976). "The VP Complement Analysis in Modern Icelandic." *Proceedings of the Sixth Annual Meeting NELS*. GLSA, University of Massachusetts, Amherst.

Bouchard, D. (1985). "The Binding Theory and the Notion of Accessible SUBJECT." *Linguistic Inquiry* 16:117–133.

Bresnan, J., P.-K. Halvorssen, and J. Maling (1983). "Invariants of Anaphoric Binding Systems." Paper presented at Cornell University.

Chomsky, N. (1973). "Conditions on Transformations." In S. Anderson and P. Kiparsky, eds., *A Festschrift for Morris Halle*. Holt, Rinehart and Winston, New York.

Chomsky, N. (1981). *Lectures on Government and Binding*. Foris, Dordrecht.

Chomsky, N. (1986). *Knowledge of Language: Its Nature, Origin and Use*. Praeger, New York.

Echavarri-Dailey, A. (1986). "Basque and Binding Theory." Ms., Cornell University.

Everaert, M. (n.d.). "Icelandic Long Reflexivization and Tense-Connectedness." In *Working Papers in Scandinavian Syntax* 12. Linguistics Department, University of Trondheim.

Fisher, K. (1985). "The Syntax and Semantics of Anaphora in Khmer." Master's thesis, Cornell University.

Fisher, K. (1988.) "Agreement and the Distribution of Anaphors." In M. L. Hammond, E. Moravscik, and J. Wirth, eds., *Studies in Syntactic Typology*. Benjamins, Amsterdam.

Freidin, R., and W. Harbert (1983). "On the Fine Structure of the Binding Theory: Principle A and Reciprocals." In *Proceedings of the Thirteenth Annual Meeting*, *NELS*. GLSA, University of Massachusetts, Amherst.

Fukui, N. (1986). "A Theory of Category Projection and Its Applications." Doctoral dissertation, MIT.

George, L., and J. Kornfilt (1981). "Finiteness and Boundedness in Turkish." In F. Heny, ed., *Binding and Filtering*. MIT Press, Cambridge, MA.

Giorgi, A. (1984). "Toward a Theory of Long Distance Anaphors: A GB Approach." *The Linguistic Review* 3:307–361.

Gurtu, M. (1985). "Anaphoric Relations in Hindi and English." Doctoral dissertation, Central Institute of English and Foreign Languages, Hyderabad.

Harbert, W. (1982). "In Defense of Tense." *Linguistic Analysis* 9:1–18.

Harbert, W. (1983). "Germanic Reflexives and the Implementation of Binding Conditions." In I. Rauch and G. Carr, eds., *Language Change*. Indiana University Press, Bloomington.

Harbert, W. (1985). "Markedness and the Bindability of Subject of NP." In *Proceedings of the Twelfth University of Wisconsin-Milwaukee Linguistics Symposium*. Plenum, New York.

Harbert, W. (1989). "Subjects of Prepositions." Paper presented at the Conference on Views of Phrase Structure. University of Florida.

Harbert, W., and V. Srivastav (1986). "Principle A and Accessibility." Ms., Cornell University.

Huang, C.-T. J. (1982). "Logical Relations in Chinese and the Theory of Grammar." Doctoral dissertation, MIT.

Huang, C.-T. J. (1983). "A Note on the Binding Theory." *Linguistic Inquiry* 14:554–561.

Kayne, R. (1983). "Connectedness." *Linguistic Inquiry* 14:223–249.

Keach, C. (1980). "The Syntax and Interpretation of the Relative Clause Construction in Swahili." Doctoral dissertation, University of Massachusetts, Amherst.

Koopman, H. (1983). *The Syntax of Verbs*. Foris, Dordrecht.

Kornfilt, J. (1986). "Binding and Agreement in Turkish." Paper presented at Princeton University.

Langendoen, D. T., and E. Battistella (1982). "The Interpretation of Predicate Reflexive and Reciprocal Expressions in English." In *Proceedings of the Twelfth Annual Meeting, NELS*. GLSA, University of Massachusetts, Amherst.

Lasnik, H., and R. Freidin (1981). "Core Grammar, Case Theory and Markedness." In A. Belletti, L. Brandi, and L. Rizzi, eds., *Theory of Markedness in Generative Grammar*. Scuola Normale Superiore, Pisa.

Lebeaux, D. (1983). "A Distributional Difference between Reciprocals and Reflexives." *Linguistic Inquiry* 14:723–730.

Maling, J. (1984). "Non-Clause-Bounded Reflexives in Icelandic." *Linguistics and Philosophy* 7:211–241.

Manzini, M. R. (1983). "On Control and Control Theory." *Linguistic Inquiry* 14:421–446.

Mohanan, K. P. (1983). "Grammatical Relations and Anaphors in Malayalam." In *MIT Working Papers in Linguistics* 5.4. Department of Linguistics and Philosophy, MIT.

Mohanan, K. P. (1985). "Remarks on Control and Control Theory." *Linguistic Inquiry* 16:637–648.

Oshima, S. (1979). "Conditions on Rules: Anaphora in Japanese." In G. Bedell, E. Kobayashi, and M. Muraki, eds., *Explorations in Linguistics: Papers in Honor of Kazukuo Inoue*. Kenkyusha, Tokyo.

Postal, P. (1974). *On Raising*. MIT Press, Cambridge, Mass.

Rappaport, G. (1986). "On Anaphor Binding in Russian." *Natural Language and Linguistic Theory* 4:97–120.

Reinhart, T. (1987). "Specifier and Operator Binding." In E. Reuland and A. ter Meulen, eds., *The Representation of (In)definiteness*. MIT Press, Cambridge, Mass.

Saxon, L. (1983). "Disjoint Reference between Anaphor and Antecedent." Paper presented at the LSA Annual Meeting, Minneapolis.

Tang, J. (1989). "Chinese Reflexives." *Natural Language and Linguistic Theory* 7:93–121.

Thráinsson, H. (1976). "Reflexives and Subjunctives in Icelandic." In *Proceedings of the Sixth Annual Meeting, NELS*. GLSA, University of Massachusetts, Amherst.

Thráinsson, H. (1979). *On Complementation in Icelandic*. Garland Publishing, New York.

Yang, D. W. (1984). "The Extended Binding Theory of Anaphors." *Theoretical Linguistic Research* 1:195–218.

Yokoyama, O. (1980). "Studies in Russian Functional Syntax." In S. Kuno, ed., *Harvard Studies in Syntax and Semantics* 3, Department of Linguistics, Harvard University.

Zaring, L. (1985). "The Syntactic Role of Verbal Inflection in French and Brazilian Portuguese." Doctoral dissertation, Cornell University.

Chapter 3

Remarks on the Status of the Null Object	C.-T. James Huang

1 Introduction

Null objects present interesting problems for the theory of empty categories. According to the classical Government-Binding Theory presented in Chomsky 1981, 1982, empty NPs are categorized on a par with overt elements on the basis of the features [α anaphor], [β pronominal], either as their intrinsic features or functionally according to the status of the elements that locally bind them. Regardless of how it is defined, each empty category (EC) is subject to general conditions of well-formedness that apply to both overt and empty elements (such as the conditions of the binding theory), and to conditions of licensing and identification that are more specifically defined over ECs (such as principles of control and pro drop as well as the Empty Category Principle (ECP)). Since null objects were not considered in the formulation of this framework, questions arose about whether and how they might fall under the same general principles and parameters of Universal Grammar.

In Huang 1982, 1984 the existence of null objects in various languages was first presented as a problem for the theory of ECs. Given appropriate environments, null objects are allowed in many languages. In each of the Chinese examples below, a null object is used with the referential interpretation of an overt deictic pronoun:

The materials incuded in this paper were presented, in part, at the Princeton Workshop on Comparative Grammar in 1986 and at the Workshop on Japanese Syntax at Connecticut College in 1987. I am indebted to the organizers of these conferences, Robert Freidin, J. J. Nakayama, and Wako Tawa, for the opportunities to present these materials, and to Robert Freidin and an anonymous reviewer for very useful comments on an earlier draft.

(1) Zhangsan renshi [e].
    Zhansan   know
    'Zhangsan knows him/her/them/you...'

(2) Zhangsan shuo Lisi bu renshi [e].
    Zhangsan say   Lisi not know
    'Zhangsan said that Lisi does not know him/her/them/you...'

It is obvious that null objects of this type do not immediately fall under the system proposed in Chomsky 1981, 1982. A null object cannot be a PRO, since it occurs in a governed (and Case-marked) position. Also, it has neither the appearance of an NP-trace, since it is not A-bound to a non-θ-position, nor that of a *wh*-trace or variable, since it is apparently also not Ā-bound. By these considerations a null object looks most like a pro, the pure pronominal EC; but this possibility is also ruled out, since it does not meet the requirements of licensing and identification (that is, by a rich enough agreement system).

One easy way to accommodate the null objects is to simply admit them into the inventory of ECs as a new, distinct type of EC. A more interesting strategy is to regard the null objects as pros and to revise the theory of licensing and identification so that although some pros (for example, subject pros) must be licensed and identified by a rich anaphoric agreement system, others (null objects) need not be licensed or identified in the same way. In Huang 1982, 1984 I argued, however, that the null objects exemplified in (1)–(2) should each be analyzed, not as a pro, but as a variable bound by a null topic, or more generally, by a null operator. The proper representation for (2) is therefore (3):

(3) e_i, [Zhangsan shuo [Lisi bu renshi t_i]]
    Zhangsan say   Lisi not know

The difference between Chinese and, say, English with respect to the existence of null objects therefore lies, not in whether or not the languages allow an object pro, but in whether or not they permit null topics.

A major reason for this postulation is the fact that the null object can only be interpreted deictically. Thus, in (2) the EC cannot be interpreted as being A-bound by the matrix subject *Zhangsan* (or the embedded subject *Lisi*). It must be interpreted as referring to a person whose reference has been established in discourse (that is, a discourse topic). In contrast, an overt pronoun in the position of the null object is capable of being used deictically or anaphorically, referring to the discourse topic or to the matrix subject, respectively:

(4) Zhangsan shuo Lisi bu renshi ta.
     Zhangsan say   Lisi not know him
     'Zhangsan said that Lisi does not know him.'

The deictic interpretation of the null objects is aptly captured if (2) is represented as in (3), on a par with ordinary topic structures in which an overt topic binds an object variable. The fact that the null object cannot be interpreted as being A-bound by the matrix subject follows as a case of strong crossover, from the requirement of Condition C of the binding theory that variables (and R-expressions in general) must be A-free. If the null object were simply analyzed as a pro, its referential possibilities would be expected to be the same as those of the overt pronoun, and the interpretive contrast between (2) and (4) would be unexplained.

As for why the pro is excluded from the object position, it was made to follow from the interaction of the binding theory and a proposed generalized version of control theory. The latter theory requires that both PRO and pro are subject to the requirement that they be controlled in their control domain. A somewhat simplified statement of this requirement was given in Huang 1984 (see Huang 1989 for a more detailed formulation):

(5) *Generalized Control Rule* (GCR)
     Coindex an empty pronominal with the closest nominal element.

If a pro occurred in object position, then according to the GCR it must be coindexed with its own subject, the closest nominal element. But this coindexing would violate Condition B. Therefore, a pro is excluded from the object position. On the other hand, a null object is not excluded from this position because it is a variable, which is subject to Condition C, but not to the GCR.

This EC-as-variable hypothesis has been supported by data from other languages, including Portuguese (see Raposo 1986), Spanish (Campos 1986), German (Huang 1984), KiNande (Authier 1988), Japanese (Hasegawa 1984/85), and American Sign Language (Lillo-Martin 1986). At the same time, the hypothesis has aroused controversy: some have argued the non-universality of the claim (see, for example, Chung 1984; Cole 1987; Rizzi 1986), whereas others have directly challenged aspects of the proposed analysis (see Xu 1986; Hoji 1985).

In this paper I will make four points concerning the status of the null object. Note that, although the EC-as-variable hypothesis provides an attractive account of certain central facts, what is crucial in this analysis is that the null object is analyzed as a R-expression.[1] In section 2 I will show that the null object shares important properties with the anaphoric epithet and may be considered the null counterpart of an epithet. This idea looks particularly appealing in light of a new typology of overt categories along the lines suggested by Lasnik in chapter 1 of this volume. The hypothesis eliminates the need for a null operator as an abstract $\bar{\text{A}}$-binder, solving certain problems associated with the earlier hypothesis, though also raising new problems. In section 3 I will show that certain null objects exhibit properties of null VPs typically associated with VP-ellipsis constructions and that such ECs may be better analyzed, not as genuine null objects, but as null VPs in disguise. In section 4 I will discuss bound pronouns in Chinese and show that their distribution receives a natural explanation under Montalbetti's (1984) Overt Pronoun Constraint (OPC), if the null object is not analyzed as a pro. Finally, in section 5 I will show that this same hypothesis about the object EC explains the distribution of the emphatic reflexive in Chinese. Thus, except for those apparent instances of the null object that are more properly analyzed as instances of elliptical VPs in disguise, the facts discussed in this paper give additional support for the general treatment of the null object as a referential expression, and not as a pure pronominal.

2   Null Epithets

The central idea that underlies the EC-as-variable hypothesis is that the object EC must be prevented from being identified as PRO, pro, or an anaphor, since it cannot be A-bound inside or outside its governing category. This means that the EC is an R-expression in the sense of the binding theory. Within the typology of NPs proposed in Chomsky 1982, the only candidate for the object EC is the variable, since it is the only empty R-expression recognized. This system also recognizes exactly one overt R-expression, which includes names, definite descriptions, and anaphoric epithets. As Lasnik points out in chapter 1, however, there is reason to distinguish two kinds of overt R-expressions: anaphoric epithets on the one hand, and names on the other. Lasnik's point is that anaphoric epithets behave like names in one way and like pronominals in another with respect to the binding theory, which requires pronominals to be free in their governing categories (Condition B), and R-expressions to be free throughout (Condition C). In English the difference between epithets and names is not evident, because Condition C effects override Condition B effects. In some languages, however, the effects of Condition C are very weak or invisible, whereas those of Condition B are not, and the difference between names and epithets can be seen very clearly. Thus, in English both names and epithets obey Condition C, since they cannot be bound inside or ouside their governing categories:[2]

(6) *John likes John.

(7) *John likes the bastard.

(8) *John thinks that John is smart.

(9) *John thinks that the bastard is smart.

However, in Thai Condition C does not seem to apply, and as indicated in (10)–(11), both names and epithets in this language may be A-bound outside their governing categories:

(10) Cɔɔn khít wâa Cɔɔn chàlāat.
     John think that John smart
     'John thinks that John is smart.'

(11) Cɔɔn khít wâa ?âybâa chàlāat.
     John think that nut   smart
     'John thinks that the nut is smart.'

In their governing categories, however, though names may also be bound as expected, epithets may not:

(12) Cɔɔn chɔ̂ɔp Cɔɔn.
     John like   John
     'John likes John.'

(13) *Cɔɔn chɔ̂ɔp ?âybâa.
     John likes   nut
     '*John likes the nut.'

This range of facts may be explained if epithets are taken to have the properties of both R-expressions and pronominals, whereas names are pure R-expressions. Assuming that epithets are R-expressions, the ill-formedness of (9) follows from Condition C, on a par with the ill-formedness of (6)–(8). The well-formedness of (10)–(12) is also explained if we assume that Condition C does not apply in Thai. On the other hand, if epithets are also assumed to be pronominals, (13) will be correctly excluded by Condition B.[3] That Condition B applies in Thai is independently shown in (14):

(14) *Cɔɔn chɔ̂ɔp khăw.
     John like   him
     '*John likes him.'

The pronominal nature of epithets is further evidenced by the fact that, although names may bind names (as shown in (10) and (12)), epithets and pronouns cannot (as shown in (15) and (16)). In this respect, epithets and pronouns behave alike, in contrast to names.[4]

(15) *Khǎw khít wâa Cɔɔn chàlāāt.
      he   think that John smart
      '*He thinks that John is smart.'

(16) *ʔâybâa khít wâa Cɔɔn chàlāāt.
      nut   think that John smart
      '*The nut thinks that John is smart.'

Lasnik's idea that epithets should be characterized as both R-expressions and pronominals leads to a reformulation of the typology of lexical categories in terms of the two features [α pronominal] and [β referential]:[5]

(17) [−pronominal], [−referential]   lexical anaphors
      [+pronominal], [−referential]   pronouns
      [−pronominal], [+referential]   names
      [+pronominal], [+referential]   epithets

We may now ask how ECs fit into this system. NP-traces and variables seem very naturally to fall under the same categories as lexical anaphors and names, respectively, whereas PRO and pro both fall under the category of pronouns.[6] This leaves us with a gap corresponding to the category of epithets:

(18) [−pronominal], [−referential]   NP-trace
      [+pronominal], [−referential]   PRO/pro
      [−pronominal], [+referential]   variable
      [+pronominal], [+referential]   ?

A possible candidate for the last category in (18) is the null object in Chinese. Besides filling an otherwise peculiar gap in the universal inventory of empty categories, the assumption that the object EC is a null epithet receives additional support from the following facts. Note that an epithet in English or Chinese has the following three properties: (a) it may not be A-bound, (b) it may be Ā-bound, and (c) it need not be Ā-bound:

(19) a. *Zhangsan yiwei [zhege bendan hen youqian].
          Zhangsan think this   idiot   very rich
          '*Zhangsan thinks that the idiot is very rich.'

     b. Zhangsan, wo bu xihuan zhege wangbadan.
          Zhangsan I   not like   this   bastard
          'Zhangsan, I don't like this bastard.'

    c.   Wo bu xihuan zhege wangbadan.
        I   not like   this   bastard
        'I don't like the bastard.'

(20) a. *John thinks that the bastard is rich.
      b.   John, I saw the bastard.
      c.   Did you see the bastard?

Not all these properties of an epithet are shared by names or variables. For example, names do not share the second property because they resist $\bar{\text{A}}$-binding (compare (20b) with ??*John, I like John*). Variables do not share the third property since they must be $\bar{\text{A}}$-bound. On the other hand, the null object in Chinese apparently has all three properties of an epithet: it cannot be A-bound, it can be $\bar{\text{A}}$-bound, and it need not have an overt $\bar{\text{A}}$-binder. Earlier we saw that the null object cannot be A-bound. The grammaticality of sentences like (1)–(2) also shows that null objects do not need an overt $\bar{\text{A}}$-binder. The following sentence shows that null objects can be $\bar{\text{A}}$-bound if an $\bar{\text{A}}$-binder is available:

(21) Neige ren$_i$, Zhangsan shuo Lisi bu   renshi e$_i$.
      that   man Zhangsan say   Lisi not know
      'That man, Zhangsan said Lisi does not know.'

Furthermore, epithets and null objects share a fourth property in that they may be coindexed with an argument as long as the argument does not c-command them. That this is true of epithets is shown in (22)–(23):

(22) a. When I saw the sissy, John was cheating.
      b. When I saw John, the sissy was cheating.
      c. The woman who met John fell in love with the sissy.
      d. The woman who met the sissy fell in love with John.

(23) Ruguo ni   xiang jian Zhangsan, wo jiu   pai   ren qu zhao zhe
      if   you want see   Zhangsan I   then send man go look this
      xiaozi.
      sissy
      'If you want to see Zhangsan, I will send someone to look for the sissy.'

That it is true of null objects in Chinese is shown in (24)–(25):[7]

(24) Ruguo ni   bu xihuan zheben shu, jiu   qing   bie   mai [e].
      if   you not like   this   book then please don't buy
      'If you don't like this book, then please don't buy [it].'

(25) Ni yi   kanwan zheben shu, jiu   qing   huan [e] gei wo.
     you once read-up this   book then please return   to me
     'Once you finish reading this book, please return [it] to me.'

Even more interestingly, although anaphoric epithets fit well in examples
like (22) and (23), such an epithet cannot occur in an object position taking
the possessor of its subject as its antecedent:

(26) *John$_i$'s mother saw the idiot$_i$.

(27) *Zhangsan$_i$ de mama   kanjian-le neige bendan$_i$.
     Zhangsan 's mother see-PERF   that   fool
     'Zhangsan's mother saw the fool.'

Correspondingly, a null object in the place of the epithet also cannot be
coindexed with the possessor, as Whitman (1986) has correctly observed:[8]

(28) *Zhangsan$_i$ de mama   kanjian-le e$_i$.
     Zhangsan 's mother see-PERF
     'Zhangsan$_i$'s mother saw e$_{*i/j}$.'

An overt pronoun in the object position of (28) can readily take the
possessor as its antecedent (as is also the case in English):

(29) Zhangsan$_i$ de mama   kanjian-le ta$_i$.
     Zhangsan 's mother see-PERF   him
     'Zhangsan's mother saw him.'

Null objects thus share quite a number of properties with epithets. This
property sharing is explained if we assume that the null object is the null
counterpart of an epithet, but not if it is analyzed as pro.

In sum, Lasnik's new typology of NPs opens up the possibility of treating the null object as an empty category that is both pronominal and
referential. This possibility is quite similar in spirit to the EC-as-variable
analysis, and the two may be regarded as two variants of the same analysis, in crucial contrast to the treatment of the null object as a pure
pronominal.[9,10]

3 VP-Ellipsis

One interesting property of the null object in Chinese is that it often occurs
in situations where, in languages like English, one would find a VP gap.
Consider the following examples:

(30) Zhangsan xihuan zheben shu, Lisi bu xihuan.
     Zhangsan like   this   book Lisi not like
     'Zhangsan likes this books, but Lisi doesn't.'

(31) John kanjian-le tade mama, Mary ye   kanjian-le.
     John see-PERF   his mother Mary also see-PERF
     'John saw his mother, and Mary did, too.'

In the second clause of these sentences, the object is missing. But as one can see from the English translations, sentences like these are on a par with VP-ellipsis sentences in English. In the following English example, the second clause has a missing VP:

(32) John saw his mother, and Mary did [$_{VP}$ e], too.

But in the Chinese examples (30)–(31), the second clause repeats the verb of the preceding clause but does not contain an auxiliary corresponding to *do*. The repetition of the verb in the second clause in (30)–(31) appears to serve no more purpose than that of "*do*-support" in English. As Kuno (1978) points out, the apparent lack of VP-deletion in Japanese correlates with its lack of a process of "*do*-support" to license VP-deletion. (Both VP-deletion and VP-movement require the presence of an auxiliary in English. This may be due to the requirements of the ECP.) The same generalizaton can apply to Chinese. To capture this generalization, however, we can postulate that the second occurrence of the verb is, in fact, an instance of "*do*-support" and that there is actually a process of VP-deletion in the language. In particular, we may assume that the verb has been moved into an abstract INFL node in the second clause. This will lexicalize the INFL, enabling the latter to L-mark (and properly govern) the VP, thus allowing the latter to appear as an empty category. According to this hypothesis, what follows the repeated verb in the second clause is an empty VP, not merely a null object. Alternatively, one might assume that the second occurrence of the verb is a sort of "resumptive" pro-VP, which covers up an improperly governed [$_{VP}$ e] that would otherwise be excluded by the ECP. In either case what appears on the surface as a null object in fact does not exist as a null object. In such cases the question of whether the apparent null object is a pronominal or a nonpronominal does not arise.

It is of course possible to simply assume that the ECs in (30)–(31) are indeed null objects and that the phenomenon of VP-deletion simply does not happen in Chinese, since a VP is not properly governed in this language. There is reason to suppose that such sentences do involve VP-ellipsis, however. This has to do with the fact that such constructions may exhibit strict/sloppy ambiguity of the sort typical of VP-ellipsis. Thus, just as (32) in English is ambiguous between a strict (referential) reading and a sloppy (bound variable) reading of the deleted pronoun *his*, the Chinese sentence

(31) is ambiguous in a similar way. In both (31) and (32), either John and Mary saw the same woman (the strict reading), or they each saw their own respective mothers (the bound variable reading). There is no third reading: if John and Mary saw different women, then they must have seen their own mothers. This range of facts in English receives a natural explanation from the theory developed by Sag (1976) and Williams (1977). According to Sag's account, for example, (32) is characterized as well formed just in case the empty VP corresponds in LF to a lambda expression that is an "alphabetic variant" of the lambda expression associated with the antecedent VP. If the antecedent VP in (32) is translated into λx (x *saw his mother*), the pronoun *his* is taken to be referential. The empty VP will be translated into the same expression, and we have the strict reading. On the other hand, if the antecedent is translated into λx (x *saw x's mother*), then the pronoun is taken to be a variable bound to whoever the lambda predicate is a predicate of, and we have the sloppy reading. This account correctly predicts a locality requirement on the sloppy reading, namely, that the antecedent of the sloppy pronoun is restricted to the binder of the lambda expression (the subject of the empty VP). Thus, although (33) has a sloppy reading according to which Bill saw Bill's mother, it does not have another sloppy reading according to which Bill saw Mary's mother:

(33) John saw his mother, and Mary knew that Bill did, too.

Now, crucially, all this is achieved under the assumption that the availability of a sloppy reading depends on the existence of a category corresponding to a lambda expression. Turning now to the Chinese example (31), if it is hypothesized that the second clause contains a null VP whose verb has been raised to INFL, the strict/sloppy ambiguity of the sentence follows immediately, and so does the lack of a second sloppy reading (meaning Bill saw Mary's mother) in (34):

(34) John kanjian-le tade mama, Mary zhidao Bill ye   kanjian-le.
    John see-PERF his mother Mary know Bill also see-PERF
    'John saw his mother, and Mary knew that Bill did, too.'

If, on the other hand, the second clause of (31) is assumed to have merely a null object, such an empty category would not be translated into a lambda predicate, since NPs denote individuals but not properties. In order to allow for one (but not more than one) sloppy reading in (31) and (34), it would be necessary to state ad hoc conditions on the null object that duplicate precisely Sag's and Williams's account, and this would miss a generalization otherwise captured by that account.

The discussion in this section is not meant to suggest that all null objects are null VPs in disguise. There are clearly null objects that cannot be so analyzed, but there is good reason to believe that such null objects are better analyzed not as pure pronominals but as null R-expressions, either as variables or as null epithets. In the rest of this paper I will cite two more pieces of evidence for the theory that excludes empty pronominals from the object position in Chinese.

4 Bound Pronouns

In recent years several scholars have called attention to a distinction between overt and empty pronouns with respect to their ability to be construed as bound variables. Saito and Hoji (1983) observe that in Japanese overt pronouns cannot be related to quantificational NPs as bound variables, though they can be anteced by referential NPs. Montalbetti (1984) further observes that the same constraint applies to certain overt pronouns in Italian and Spanish, specifically when such pronouns occur in subject position. At the same time, it is clear that this constraint does not hold in English. Thus, although (35) is good in English with the pronoun being related to the matrix subject, the Spanish and Japanese sentences are bad under the same bound variable interpretation of the pronoun:

(35) Nobody$_i$ believes that he$_i$ is intelligent.

(36) *Nadie$_i$ cree   que él$_i$ es inteligente.
      nobody believe that he is intelligent

(37) *Daremo$_i$-ga [kare$_i$-ga Mary-o sukida] to   omotte iru.
      everybody he   Mary like   that think
      'Everybody believes that he will like Mary.'

Montalbetti makes the important observation that this contrast between English on the one hand and Spanish-Japanese (and Italian, etc.) on the other is mirrored by the well-known fact that although English does not allow pro drop, Spanish, Japanese, and Italian do. Note that the Spanish and Japanese sentences (36)–(37) are well formed under the same interpretation once the overt pronoun is replaced by pro:

(38) Nadie$_i$ cree que pro$_i$ es inteligente.

(39) Daremo$_i$-ga [pro$_i$ Mary-o sukida] to omotte iru.

The relevant generalization is that the constraint against the use of an overt pronoun as a bound variable applies only where there is an empty pronoun for the same purpose. The constraint does not apply to English precisely because English does not allow the option of an empty pronoun in the context of (35). Montalbetti directly expresses this generalization with his Overt Pronoun Constraint:

(40) *Overt Pronoun Constraint* (OPC)
  Overt pronouns cannot link to formal variables if and only if the alternation overt/empty obtains.

The generalization that the OPC expresses is entirely reasonable and has an obvious functional explanation. In fact, the OPC may be collapsed with Chomsky's Avoid Pronoun Principle. The principle was originally intended to capture facts like those in (41):

(41) a. ??John$_i$ enjoyed [his$_i$ reading the poems].
  b. John$_i$ enjoyed [PRO$_i$ reading the poems].

Note that although the proximate reading of *his* can be forced in (41a), with a quantificational antecedent the sentence is totally unacceptable:

(42) a. *Who$_i$ enjoyed [his$_i$ reading the poems]?
  b. *Everybody$_i$ enjoyed [his$_i$ reading the poems].
  c. *Nobody$_i$ enjoyed [his$_i$ reading the poems].

The sentences in (42) can evidently be explained by the OPC. A comparison of (42) with (41) shows that OPC effects are stronger than "Avoid Pronoun" effects. But this difference between the two principles may be explained by the fact that in (41a), although *his* cannot be bound to *John*, it can still refer to *John* as a result of accidental coreference. On the other hand, in (42) with quantificational antecedents, the possibility of coindexing by accidental coreference is ruled out, since quantificational NPs have no reference. Abstracting away from this difference, then, we might say that the OPC and the Avoid Pronoun Principle are two sides of the same coin.

Whatever the source of the OPC, an important prediction it makes is that in Italian and Spanish it excludes overt bound pronouns only from the subject position, but not from the object or other nonsubject positions, since pro drop occurs only in subject position in these languages. The following Spanish sentences are all well formed:

(43) Muchos estudiantes quieren que María se case con ellos.
  'Many students want Mary to marry them.'

(44) Nadie quiere que María hable de él.
  'Nobody wants Mary to talk about him.'

(45) Muchas mujeres dijeron que el libro fue escrito por ellas.
'Many women said that the book was written by them.'

That the OPC expresses a valid generalization (regardless of its ultimate explanation) thus seems to be beyond doubt. Now, let us turn to relevant facts in Chinese. Aoun and Li (1989) have observed (see also Montalbetti 1984; Xu 1986) that, for many speakers, the overt pronoun cannot be interpreted as a bound variable in sentences like (46) and (47):

(46) *Shei$_i$ xiwang [ta$_i$ neng kanjian Lisi]?
     who hope   he can   see   Lisi
     'Who hopes that he can see Lisi?'

(47) *Meiyou ren$_i$ shuo [ta$_i$ hen xihuan Lisi].
     no   man say   he very like   Lisi
     'Nobody says that he likes Lisi.'

This is entirely expected from the OPC, given the possibility of subject pro drop in this language:

(48) Shei$_i$ xiwang [pro$_i$ neng kanjian Lisi]?
     'Who hopes that [he] can see Lisi?'

(49) Meiyou ren$_i$ shuo [pro$_i$ hen xihuan Lisi].
     'Nobody says that [he] likes Lisi.'

Aoun and Li (1989) observe, in addition, that the constraint against using an overt pronoun does not apply when the pronoun occurs in object position.[11]

(50) Shei$_i$ xiwang [Lisi hui kanjian ta$_i$]?
     who hope   Lisi will see   him
     'Who hopes that Lisi will see him?'

(51) Meiyou ren$_i$ shuo [Lisi hen xihuan ta$_i$].
     no   man say   Lisi very like   him
     'Nobody says that Lisi likes him.'

Given the OPC, this means that a pro cannot occur in object position in Chinese. This situation is entirely expected under the hypothesis that the null object is a referential expression, but inconsistent with the hypothesis that it is a pro. The OPC and the contrast between (46)–(47) and (50)–(51) thus provide a new piece of evidence for the proposed analysis.[12]

5 Emphatic *Ziji*

As is well known, the English reflexive *himself* can be used either as an anaphor or as a marker for emphasis. As Bickerton (1987) shows, the emphatic *himself* appears in either an adverbial position as in (52) or an adnominal position as in (53)–(54):

(52) John talked to Mary about the decision himself.

(53) John himself talked to Mary about the decision.

(54) John talked to Mary herself about the decision.

Expressions like *John himself, Mary herself* seem to occur freely in any position where an NP can occur. Bickerton further observes that if the head of the NP is a pronoun, as in *he himself* and the like, then such adnominal constructions are less natural in object positions:[13]

(55) He himself saw me.

(56) ?I saw him himself.

Tang (1989) has independently observed the following facts concerning the emphatic use of *ziji* 'self' in Chinese. Like the English reflexive, it can appear in adverbial position as in (57), or in adnominal position as in (58)–(59).

(57) Zhangsan hui ziji qu.
     Zhangsan will self go
     'Zhangsan will go himself.'

(58) Zhangsan ziji hui gen Lisi shuo.
     Zhangsan self will with Lisi say
     'Zhangsan himself will talk to Lisi.'

(59) Wo hui gen Lisi ziji shuo.[14]
     I   will with Lisi self say
     'I will talk to Lisi himself.'

The adnominal construction *pronoun + ziji* is also acceptable, though sometimes less natural in object position:[15]

(60) Ta ziji kanjian-le Lisi.
     he self see-PERF Lisi
     'He himself saw Lisi.'

(61) Wo xiang gen ta   ziji tan.
     I   want with him self talk
     'I want to talk to him himself.'

(62) ?Wo zhi piping ta   ziji.
     I   only criticize him self
     '?I only criticize him himself.'

The availability of emphatic expressions in the form *overt pronoun + ziji* leads one to expect that, in a pro drop language like Chinese, it is possible to have emphatic adnominal constructions in the form *pro* + *ziji*. That is, a bare *ziji* in Chinese should be analyzable either as an adnominal construction of the form *pro* + *ziji* or as a simple anaphor of the form *ziji*. According to the former analysis, *ziji* is used to emphasize a null pronoun argument; and according to the latter analysis, *ziji* is used itself as an argument. As pointed out by Battistella and Xu (1987), however, this expectation is fulfilled only partially. In particular, although the bare *ziji* can be used immediately after a missing subject to intensify the null subject, it cannot be used immediately after a null object to intensify the null object. The contrast between (63) and (64) is a manifestation of this subject-object asymmetry:

(63) Zhangsan shuo [ziji hui hui   jia].
     Zhangsan say   self can return home
     'Zhangsan said that he himself can go home.'
     (No need for a ride, etc.)

(64) Zhangsan shuo [wo zhi   piping   ziji].
     Zhangsan say   I   only criticize self
     'Zhangsan said that I only criticized myself.'
     (Not: 'Zhangsan said that I only criticized him himslef, and no one else.')

As indicated in the translation, the reflexive *ziji* can be used emphatically in (63) but not in (64). Assuming that the emphatic *ziji* is an adnominal following *pro*, this means that the form *pro* + *ziji* is possible in subject position (as in (63)), but not in object position (as in (64)).

   Battistella and Xu (1987) further obseve that distribution of the so-called generic *ziji* exhibits a similar asymmetry.

(65) Lisi shuo ziji zuo shi,   ziji dang.
     Lisi say   self do thing self be-responsible
     'Lisi said that if one does a thing, then one (should) take
     responsibility for it oneself.'

(66) Lisi xihuan piping   ziji.
     Lisi like   criticize self
     'Lisi likes to criticize himself.'

In (65) neither occurrence of *ziji* needs to refer to *Lisi*; both can be understood as having generic reference. But in (66) the postverbal *ziji* must be understood as bound by *Lisi*, thus lacking generic reference. Tang (1987) has argued that the so-called generic *ziji* is really simply an instance of emphatic *ziji* modifying a generic pro. On this analysis, the contrast between (65) and (66) can be reduced to the contrast between (63) and (64), namely, a subject-object asymmetry regarding the distribution of emphatic *ziji*.

These states of affairs again point to the generalization that the null object cannot be a pro and, as pointed out by Tang (1987), further support the theory that excludes pro from the object position. In particular, according to the Generalized Control Rule mentioned in section 1, a pro has to be coindexed with the closest nominal element. If a pro were to occur in object position, it would need to be bound by its own subject. But this would lead to a violation of Condition B, which requires it to be free from the subject. Hence, pro cannot occur in object position. If pro is excluded from object position in principle, then emphatic and generic *pro + ziji* are also excluded from that position.

6 Summary

In this paper I have shown that there are a number of ways to analyze the null object. In certain cases null object constructions are better analyzed on a par with VP-ellipsis constructions. In other cases true null objects exhibit properties similar to those of referential expressions. These properties are captured if the null object is analyzed as the null counterpart of an epithet or as a variable bound by a null operator, but not as a pure pronominal. The same hypothesis also provides a straightforward account of the distribution of overt bound pronouns and of the emphatic and generic reflexives in Chinese.

Notes

1. In Huang 1984 I adopted the functional definition of empty categories proposed in Chomsky 1982, according to which an EC is a variable if and only if locally Ā-bound. The analysis assumed that an EC may start out as a pro and turn into a variable if it comes to be coindexed with a local Ā-binder. In recent years the functional definition has been called into question (notably by Brody (1984) and Chomsky (1986)), and it may be that ECs are never allowed to change status in the course of a derivation. Note, however, that the analysis in Huang 1984 can be made quite independent of the functional definition. The crucial assumption is that the null object is Ā-bound. If a null object is base-generated as a pro, then it must be an Ā-bound pro. Moreover, both true variables and Ā-bound pros must be defined as R-expressions in the sense of the binding theory, to be distinguished from A-bound pros, which are pure pronominals.

2. The sentences are starred on the coreferential reading only. This applies to other relevant examples that follow.

3. (7) can also be excluded by Condition B if epithets are assumed to be pronominals. But this assumption is not enough to rule out (9). To exclude (9), it is necessary to assume that epithets are also R-expressions.

4. Given the well-formedness of (10)–(12), sentences (15)–(16) clearly cannot be ruled out by Condition C. This means that Condition C, as formulated by Chomsky (1981) incorporating the results of Lasnik (1976) and Reinhart (1976), should be split into two conditions: one that prohibits R-expressions from being A-bound and one that prohibits R-expressions from being A-bound by pronominal expressions. The latter condition would recapture the spirits of earlier works like those of Langacker (1969) and Ross (1969), who were more specifically concenred with pronoun-antecedent pairs than Lasnik and Reinhart, who were concerned simply with A-bound R-expressions. Lasnik argues, correctly I think, that the latter condition (call it *Condition D*) should be formulated in more general terms as something like the following ((51) in chapter 1):

Condition D
A less referential expression may not bind a more referential one.

The notion of relative anaphoricity or referentiality can be defined in such a way as to rank names, epithets, pronouns, and anaphors in that order, where names are most referential and least anaphoric, and anaphors are least referential and most anaphoric. This condition, besides accounting for the facts given in the text, also correctly predicts that epithets can bind epithets in Thai, though pure pronouns cannot, assuming that although Condition C does not obtain in Thai, Condition D does (perhaps universally):

(i)   ʔâybâa khít wâa ʔaybâa chàlāat.
       'The nut thinks that the nut is smart.'
(ii)   *khǎw khít wâa ʔâybâa chàlāat.
       '*He thinks that the nut is smart.'

Incidentally, for many speakers of English the effects of Condition C also seem much weaker than those of Condition D, thus providing further support for the split of Condition C and the separation of epithets from names:

(iii) a. ??John thinks John is smart.
       b. ??The nut thinks that the nut is smart.
       c. *The nut thinks that John is smart.
       d. *He thinks that John is smart.
       e. *He thinks that the nut is smart.

5. This is essentially the proposal made in Lasnik 1982, though in chapter 1 of this volume Lasnik gives a more elaborate system.

6. There is good reason to believe that the PRO/pro distinction is unnecessary and that there is only one pure pronominal EC, Pro. Given the generalized control theory developed in Huang 1984, 1989, the distribution and reference of both PRO and pro can be accounted for without reference to any difference between them.

7. The well-formedness of sentences like (24)–(25) has also been pointed out for Japanese by Kuroda (1965) and for Portuguese by Chao (1983), suggesting the generality of the phenomenon.

8. A similar restriction in Japanese has been pointed out by Kuno (1985).

9. This discussion is not intended to suggest that the null object cannot be analyzed as a variable as well. Indeed, the facts discussed here can also be accommodated by the EC-as-variable analysis, once a null operator is assumed. Furthermore, there are cases in which the EC-as-variable analysis is clearly superior to the null epithet hypothesis. For example, the facts from German discussed in Huang 1984 argue strongly for treating the null object in that language as a variable bound by a null topic. There is also some evidence that the distribution of the null object is constrained by Subjacency and the Condition on Extraction Domains, as Raposo (1986) indicates for European Portuguese and Authier (1988) for KiNande. In such cases the null object is better analyzed as a variable created by the movement of a null operator.

10. The null object may also be likened to a "*donkey* pronoun" and analyzed as the null counterpart of the latter.

(i) Everone who owns a donkey beats it.

(ii) John saw a soldier. Then he shot him.

This is especially appealing in view of Evans's (1980) argument that *donkey* pronouns are definite descriptions (or epithets, which are special instances of definite descriptions). (See also Parsons 1978 and Cooper 1979.) Thus, *it* in (i) may be translated as 'the donkey he owns' and *him* in (ii) as 'the solder he saw'. Heim (1982) analyzes such pronouns as variables in a framework of "unselective binding." Again, the crucial assumption is that such pronouns are also referential expressions. This assumption predicts that there is an anti-c-command relationship between the *donkey* pronoun and its antecedent. This prediction is correct, since (iii) and (iv) cannot have the interpretation of *donkey* sentences:

(iii) Every donkey believes that I will beat it.

(vi) A soldier told John to shoot him.

(iii) cannot be paraphrased as 'Every donkey believes that I will beat the donkey', nor can (iv) be paraphrased as 'A soldier told John to shoot the soldier'. The pronouns in these sentences must be interpreted as bound pronouns, which are true anaphoric pronouns but not referential expressions. The anti-c-command requirement of the *donkey* pronoun is a property shared by the null object.

11. Not every speaker finds (46)–(47) ungrammatical under the bound variable reading. But the relevant point is that *all* speakers find (50)–(51) entirely grammatical.

12. Given that similar facts have been observed concerning the null object in Japanese, one wonders whether similar evidence is available from bound pronouns in Japanese for the analysis of the null object as a referential expression. It turns out that the facts in Japanese are not parallel to those of Chinese in this regard. As shown below, the overt pronoun *kare* cannot be construed as a bound variable in either the subject or the object position (see Saito and Hoji 1983 and Montalbetti 1984):

(i) *Daremo$_i$-ga [kare$_i$-ga Mary-o sukida] to   omotte iru.
everybody   he   Mary   like   that think
'Everybody thinks that he likes Mary.'

(ii) *Daremo$_i$-ga [Mary-ga kare$_i$-o sukida] to   omotte iru.
everybody   Mary   he   like   that think
'Everybody thinks that Mary likes him.'

This fact might favor the view that the null object in Japanese may be a pro, as Hoji (1985) has argued. On the other hand, if the asymmetries pointed out by Hasegawa (1984/85) represent a real generalization, one might still want to exclude pro from the object position and explain the impossibility of binding the overt pronoun in (ii) in some other way. It is worth noting that (ii) becomes entirely well formed if the reflexive *zibun* is used:

(iii) Daremo$_i$-ga [Mary-ga zibun$_i$-o sukida] to omotte iru.

Quite possibly, then, it is the availability of the option of using a reflexive that makes (ii) ill formed. This suggests that the Avoid Pronoun Principle or the OPC should be generalized so as to exclude an overt pronoun from a position where a pro or a reflexive is in general available as an option. (Since the use of a long-distance reflexive in Chinese is subject to fairly strict restrictions, but not *in general* available as an alternative to an overt bound pronoun, the latter is not excluded from the object position.)

13. (56) is natural if used as an answer to *Did you see anyone besides John?*

14. The use of adnominal *ziji* is not acceptable to all speakers, but many speakers do accept it. Speakers who do not accept adnominal expressions like *Zhangson ziji* tend to replace them which expressions like *Zhangsan ben ren* 'Zhangsan himself, not anyone else'.

15. This adnominal construction should be distinguished from the compound reflexive *taziji* 'himself/herself', *niziji* 'yourself', and so on. The compound reflexive can itself be used emphatically in an adnominal construction, as in *Wo zhi xihuan Zhangsan taziji* 'I only like Zhangsan himself'.

References

Aoun, J., and Y.-H. A. Li (1989). "Minimal Disjointness." In *Proceedings of the Seventh West Coast Conference on Formal Linguistics*. Stanford Linguistics Association, Stanford University.

Authier, J.-M. P. (1988). "Null Object Constructions in KiNande." *Natural Language and Linguistic Theory* 6: 19–38.

Battistella, E., and Y. Xu (1987). "Reflexivization in Chinese." Ms., University of Alabama, Birmingham.

Bickerton, D. (1987). "*He Himself*: Anaphor, Pronoun, Or . . . ?" *Linguistic Inquiry* 18: 345–348

Brody, M. (1984). "On Contextual Definitions and the Role of Chains." *Linguistic Inquiry* 15: 355–380.

Campos, H. (1986). "Indefinite Object Drop." *Lingusitic Inquiry* 17:354–359.

Chao, W. (1983). "Discourse-Based Null Elements and the Typology of Empty Categories." Ms., University of Ottawa.

Chomsky, N. (1981). *Lectures on Government and Binding*. Foris, Dordrecht.

Chomsky, N. (1982). *Some Concepts and Consequences of the Theory of Government and Binding*. MIT Press, Cambridge, Mass.

Chomsky, N. (1986). *Barriers*. MIT Press, Cambridge, Mass.

Chung, S. (1984). "Identifiability and Null Objects in Chamorro." In C. Brugman and M. Macaulay, eds., *Proceedings of the Tenth Annual Meeting, BLS*. Berkeley Linguistics Society, University of California, Berkeley.

Cole, P. (1987). "Null Objects in Universal Grammar." *Linguistic Inquiry* 18:597–612.

Cooper, R. (1979). "The Interpretation of Pronouns." In F. Heny and H. Schnelle, eds., *Syntax and Semantics 10: Selections from the Third Groningen Round Table*. Academic Press, New York.

Evans, G. (1980). "Pronouns." *Linguistic Inquiry* 11:337–362.

Hasegawa, N. (1984/85). "On the So-called 'Zero Pronouns' in Japanese." *The Linguistic Review* 4:289–342.

Heim, I. (1982). "The Semantics of Definite and Indefinite Noun Phrases." Doctoral dissertation, University of Massachusetts, Amherst.

Hoji, H. (1985). "Logical Form Constraints and Configurational Structures in Japanese." Doctoral dissertation, University of Washington.

Huang, C.-T. J. (1982). "Logical Relations in Chinese and the Theory of Grammar." Doctoral dissertation, MIT.

Huang, C.-T. J. (1984). "On the Distribution and Reference of Empty Pronouns." *Linguistic Inquiry* 15:531–574.

Huang, C.-T. J. (1989). "Pro Drop in Chinese: A Generalized Control Theory." In O. Jaeggli and K. Safir, eds., *The Null Subject Parameter*. Kluwer, Dordrecht.

Kuno, S. (1978). "Japanese: A Characteristic OV Language." In W. P. Lehmann, ed., *Syntactic Typology*. University of Texas Press, Austin.

Kuno, S. (1985). "Anaphora in Japanese." In S.-Y. Kuroda, ed., *Papers from the First SDF Workshop on Japanese Syntax*. University of California at San Diego.

Kuroda, S.-Y. (1965). "Generative Grammatical Studies in the Japanese Language." Doctoral dissertation, MIT. (Published by Garland, New York 1979.)

Langacker, R. (1969). "Pronominalization and the Chain of Command." In D. Reibel and S. Schane, eds., *Modern Studies in English*. Prentice-Hall, Englewood Cliffs, N.J.

Lasnik, H. (1976). "Remarks on Coreference." *Linguistic Analysis* 2:1–22.

Lasnik, H. (1982). "Is Condition C Necessary?" Talk given at the Cornell Conference on Government and Binding Theory, Cornell University.

Lillo-Martin, D. (1986). "Two Kinds of Null Arguments in American Sign Language." *Natural Language and Linguistic Theory* 4:415–444.

Montalbetti, M. (1984). "After Binding." Doctoral dissertation, MIT.

Parsons, T. (1978). "Pronouns as Paraphrases." Ms., University of Massachusetts, Amherst.

Raposo, E. (1986). "On the Null Object in European Portuguese." In O. Jaeggli and C. Silva-Corvalan, eds., *Studies in Romance Linguistics*. Foris, Dordrecht.

Reinhart, T. (1976). "The Syntactic Domain of Anaphora." Doctoral dissertation, MIT.

Rizzi, L. (1986). "Null Objects in Italian and the Theory of *pro*." *Linguistic Inquiry* 17:501–557.

Ross, J. R. (1969). "On the Cyclic Nature of English Pronominalization." In D. Reibel and S. Schane, eds., *Modern Studies in English*. Prentice-Hall, Englewood Cliffs, N.J.

Sag, I. (1976). "Deletion and Logical Form." Doctoral dissertation, MIT.

Saito, M., and H. Hoji (1983). "Weak Crossover and Move Alpha in Japanese." *Natural Language and Linguistic Theory* 1:245–259.

Tang, J. (1987). "Chinese Reflexives: Two Uses or Three Uses." Ms., Cornell University.

Tang, J. (1989). "Chinese Reflexives." *Natural Language and Linguistic Theory* 7:93–122.

Whitman, J. (1986). "Discourse Ellipsis and the Identity of Zero Pronouns." In *Selected Papers from SICOL 1986*. Linguistic Society of Korea, Seoul.

Williams, E. (1977). "Discourse and Logical Form." *Linguistic Inquiry* 8:101–139.

Xu, L. (1986). "Free Empty Category." *Linguistic Inquiry* 17:75–93.

Chapter 4

| The Argument-Bound | Edwin Williams |
| Empty Categories | |

If implicit arguments are unassigned θ-roles, and if implicit arguments are "visible" to the rules of syntax, to the binding theory in particular, then the status of the empty categories (ECs) is thrown into question. What might be thought to demonstrate the syntactic presence of an EC might in fact be taken to demonstrate the syntactic visibility of the θ-role that is assigned to the posited EC. In Williams 1985, 1987a, b I have developed the thesis that the binding theory holds, not of the NPs to which θ-roles are assigned, but of the θ-roles themselves. Such a thesis suggests a program of research involving a systematic reanalysis of the constructions in which ECs are though to play a role, a reanalysis that eliminates the ECs in favor of an elaboration of the θ calculus. In this paper I will first review the formulation of the binding theory as it applies directly to θ-roles. I will then outline how this theory might facilitate the elimination of small pro, as I have done for the other ECs (PRO, NP-trace) in the papers just mentioned.

I would add that I am myself very uncertain whether this alternative is superior, and I sometimes wonder whether it is empirically different from the standard view. Still, I consider it important to work out this alternative, if for no other reason than to force a sharpening of the ideas that constitute the standard view. If θ-roles are visible at all in syntax, and they certainly are, at least for θ-role assignment, and arguably as antecedents of control relations, then why not for everything?

1 Implicit Arguments and the Binding Theory

One ordinarily speaks of NPs as referring. However, since the θ-roles in a sentence are in one-to-one correspondence with NPs, thanks to the θ-criterion, one might just as easily speak of θ-roles as referring; the NP would then be a condition on the reference of the θ-role:

(1) John$_i$ left.

      (A$_i$)

Here, we might say that A refers and that that reference must be consistent with the restriction *John* (x).

If the θ-Criterion requires a one-to-one correspondence, then it might be impossible to determine what refers, NPs or θ-roles, and one would seek a theory that sidesteps the question. However, it appears that there are θ-roles that are not assigned (implicit arguments), and these θ-roles do have reference.

Implicit arguments in the sense under discussion are incompatible with the θ-Criterion of (for example) Chomsky (1981), which requires that every θ-role be assigned; instead, what we need is something like Freidin's (1978) Argument Uniqueness Principle. Suppose we break the θ-Criterion down into parts, as follows:

(2) *θ-Criterion.*
    a. Every NP is assigned a θ-role.
    b. No two NPs are assigned the same θ-role.
    c. Every θ-role is assigned.
      i. *Every internal θ-role is assigned.
      ii. Every external θ-role is assigned.
    d. No two θ-roles are assigned to the same NP.

To account for implicit arguments, we will want to give up only (2ci)—this will permit unassigned internal arguments. The reason we don't give up all of (2c) is that there appear to be no implicit external arguments, though of course this is conceivable. In some sense, the obligatoriness of the external argument might derive from its being the "head" of the argument structure—it is the argument whose index is passed up to a maximal projection—and heads are generally obligatory.

What is interesting about (2) with (ci) subtracted is that the remaining parts can be gathered into a single statement, under a certain assumption about what constitutes θ-role assignment. Since nouns have external arguments as well as verbs, we can view θ-role assignment as the linking of the external argument of an NP with a verbal θ-role:

(3) Man bites   dog.

    (R̲$_i$) (A̲$_i$B$_j$) (R̲$_j$)

Since the N has an R external θ-role, the θ-Criterion requires that it be assigned; but to what is it assigned? It is assigned to the verbal θ-role it is coindexed with. Therefore, the fact that an NP must receive a θ-role follows from the fact that external θ-roles must be assigned. We may therefore summarize all the parts of the θ-Criterion that we want to retain as follows:

(4) External θ-roles must always be uniquely assigned.

This says nothing about internal θ-roles; sometimes they must be assigned (like the object of *put*), but sometimes they may not be (like the experiencer role of *interesting*).

In Williams 1985, 1987a, b I make the case that unassigned θ-roles are directly visible as the "antecedents" for various control relations (see also Roeper, to appear) and for various applications of the binding theory. For example, it is plausible that the control and disjointness facts noted in (5) are connected to binding theory relations involving an unexpressed argument of the head noun:

(5) Control: the attempt to leave (attempter = leaver)

Condition A: Respect for oneself is important (respecter = respectee)

Condition C: the realization that John was unpopular (realizer = John

Condition B: admiration of him (admirer = admiree)

Of course, it is always possible that there is an EC to which the θ-role in question is assigned, and that it is this EC with respect to which the binding theory operates; a likely site for such an EC is the SPEC position. But (6)–(9), in which the SPEC position is occupied, show this suggestion to be untenable:

(6) a. yesterday's attempt to leave (attempter = leaver)
     b. yesterday's realization that John was sick (realizer = John)

(7) John performed Mary's operation.

(8) John$_i$ performed [Mary's$_j$ operation].
     $(\underline{A}_i\ th_k)$ $(\underline{R}_k\ A\ th_j)$
     A controls A
     of argument th

(9) John performed his first operation.
    (not "first on him"; rather, "first by him")
    *John$_i$ performed his$_i$ first operation.
     $(\underline{A}\ ...)$ $(\underline{R}\ A\ th_i)$

(9) is especially revealing on this point. It is ungrammatical only on the reading where the theme of *operation* is assigned to *his* and *his* is corefer-

ential with *John*—Condition B says that A and th cannot be coreferential. But where *his* is linked to the A of *operation* (already controlled by the A of *perform*), Condition B is irrelevant, since only one argument of *operation* is indexed with *i*. Clearly, positing ECs will not help to distinguish these two readings. In sum, then, the binding theory can see unassigned θ-roles.

If the binding theory can see θ-roles, we might wonder whether that is all that it can see. In other words, even when the binding theory seems to hold between two overt NPs, maybe it is really holding between the θ-roles that are assigned to those two overt NPs. In other words, the overt expression of a θ-role would be incidental to its behavior with respect to the binding theory.

But this cannot be correct, for binding theory behavior depends on, for example, whether a θ-role is realized as reflexive or not. Therefore, this aspect of the expression of θ-roles must still play a role. Suppose we let the typology of overt elements (anaphors, pronouns, names) induce a typology of θ-roles, as follows:

(10) *The θ-binding theory elements*
A *t-anaphor* is a θ-role assigned to an anaphor.
A *t-pronoun* is a θ-role assigned to a pronoun.
A *t-R-expression* is a θ-role assigned to an R-expression.

We will then say that the θ-binding theory holds of these elements, not of the overt expressions that these are connected to under θ-role assignment. We might model the θ-binding theory directly after the binding theory as closely as possible:

(11) *The θ-binding theory*
A. A t-anaphor must be bound in ...
B. A t-pronoun must be free in ...
C. A t-R-expression must be free.

We then will want to redenfine *bound* and *free* to refer to θ-roles, not to overt NP positions:

(12) *t-bound*
X is t-bound if there is a θ-role conindexed with and c-commanding X.
t-free
X is t-free if not t-bound.

In addition, we must define *c-command* in such a way that it can hold between θ-roles. A mechanical mimic of the binding theory notion of c-command might be the following:

(13) *θ-command*
    θ-role 1 θ-commands θ-role 2 if the predicate of which θ-role 1 is
    an argument c-commands the predicate of which θ-role 2 is an
    argument.

However, I feel a more appropriate definition will involve a recursive
definition in terms of θ-role assignment:

(14) a. X θ-commands Y either if X is a coargument of Y or if X
        θ-commands B and B is assigned to an NP whose head has Y in
        its argument structure.

    or

    b. X θ-commands Y either if X is a coargument of Y or if X
        θ-commands B_i and Z_i (external) θ-commands Y.

(14b), equivalent in its coverage to (14a), takes advantage of the fact that
θ-role assignment always results in the coindexation of the external θ-role
of the assignee with a θ-role of the assigner.

So the θ-command relations of tree (15) are as indicated:

(15)

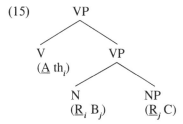

A θ-commands th R_i B R_j C
th θ-commands A R_i B R_j C
R_i θ-commands B R_j C
B θ-commands R_i R_j C
R_j θ-commands C

These definitions have the rough effect that if NP_1 c-commands NP_2,
then T_1 (assigned to NP_1) will θ-command T_2. However, there are discrepancies between the two relations.

To begin with, the notion "coargument" does not distinguished subject
from object, whereas "c-command" does. Thus, under the θ-binding theory we do not expect the following:

(16) a. John likes himself.
    b.* Himself likes John.

Under Condition A of the θ-binding theory, both of these should be grammatical, since in both cases the t-anaphor is θ-commanded by the other argument. It appears that it will be necessary to import the subject-object structural asymmetry into the flattened argument structure. Actually, though, θ-theory already has this distinction. Since the subject, or external θ-role (being the head of the argument structure), is the one whose index is percolated to the top of the VP, the VP of (15b) will have the following form:

(17)

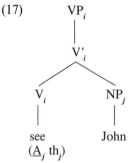

The i-index dominates the j index in a clear sense: there is a constituent with the i index that dominates a constituent with the j index. If $i = j$, then we have a violation of the version of Condition C in Williams 1982, or an i-within-i violation. In terms of the theory under discussion, we will want to say that X θ-commands Y if X dominates Y. A further problem posed by (16) is that (16a) violates Condition C, in that the t-R-expression A is θ-commanded by the t-anaphor th; this again displays the problem with the flat argument structure. One solution to this problem would be to articulate the argument structure further, so that the external argument was not θ-commanded by the internal arguments:

(18) (A (th G))

We will not adopt this proposal; instead, for Condition C we will substitute the following principle borrowed and adapted from Higginbotham 1983:

(19) A pronoun may not asymmetrically θ-command its antecedent.

We will then take (16b), but not (16a), to violate (19).

    One reason for rejection (18), in which the needed asymmetry is introduced into the argument structure itself, is that it will be necessary for internal arguments to c-command external arguments in other circumstances:

(20)

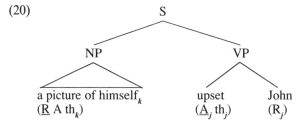

Here, t-John (the θ-role assigned to *John*) θ-commands t-himself, so anaphora is possible; but it does so only because it θ-commands the θ-role assigned to the subject. The asymmetry of (18) would block this.

It is well known that "backward" reflexivization is limited by predicate type, as the following contrast illustrates:

(21) a.   Pictures of each other impressed John and Mary.
     b.   *Pictures of each other hit John and Mary.

Johnson (1985), Pesetsky (1987), and Belletti and Rizzi (1986) seek to normalize these cases to the "forward" cases, by putting the subject of the experiencer verbs (like *impress*) in the VP in D-Structure (in different ways in the papers just cited):

(22) e impress John and Mary pictures of each other

If anaphora is done on this representation, then it may be said that all anaphoric binding is done under strict structural c-command.

This result is incompatible with the view of binding taken here, where the realization of arguments should not matter for binding, and where in particular structural c-command should not govern binding. The one exception to this has already been discussed in connection with (16b), where the anaphor is the external argument.

If (21a) and (21b) cannot be differentiated structurally, then they must be differentiated directly in terms of the θ-roles themselve. Suppose that experiencers can bind into coarguments, but patients cannot. Rozwadowska (1985, personal communication) has made just such a proposal. She ranks the θ-roles in the following way:

(23) Patient < Causer < Experiencer < Agent

Binding by X into Y may take place only if X > Y. Thus, experiencers can bind into their causer subjects, but patients cannot bind into their agent subjects.

It turns out that this law can be shown to hold of cases not implicated in the backward binding problem:

(24) *The books impressed each other's authors.

    (Bozena Rozwadowska, personal communication)

Here the causer subject binds into the experiencer; but this is athwart the hierarchy. What is most important about (24) is that binding by the subject should be permitted at S-Structure, regardless of θ-role; but it is not. Substituting a nonexperiencer verb greatly improves the example:

(25) The books refer to each other's authors.

If this account is correct, then what needs to be added to θ-command is some theory like Rozwadowska's (which itself is like Jackendoff's (1972)); what is not needed is structural predicates like c-command.

2 θ-Command and Adjuncts

Stating the binding theory in terms of θ-command implies that it will treat adjuncts and complements differently. This is evident in the following example:

(26) a.   John$_i$ bought a coatrack for him$_i$ to hang his coats on.

     b. *John$_i$ arranged for him$_i$ to leave.

Because there is no θ-connection between *John* and the adjunct purpose clause in (26a), *John* does not θ-command *him* in this sentence, and Condition B does not apply. In (26b), by contrast, *John* does θ-command *him*.

The role of θ-command in the binding theory can also be seen in the following examples, noted by Chomsky (1982):

(27) a.   *The books were sold without noting the prices.

     b. The books can be sold without noting the prices.

In both cases *sell* has an implicit agent argument. Why can it control the adjunct only in the second case? The difference lies in the θ-structure of the two sentences. Suppose that the modal *can* takes two arguments, the "one who is able" (enabled) and the "thing he or she is able to do" (ability) (*John* and *swim*, respectively, in *John can swim*). Suppose further that adjuncts are a part of the complement structure of modals. In particular, the *without*-phrase is a complement (C in the argument structure below). Then the θ-structure of a simple sentence with *can* will be as follows:

(28) John   can swim without drowning.

    (enabled ability   C)

Finally, suppose that controllers must θ-command. In the structure of (28), *John* θ-commands the *without*-phrase, because the *without*-phrase is a coargument of t-John. In the passive, the enabled argument is unassigned:

(29) The book can be read without turning the pages.
        enabled = implicit
        ability = the book can be read
        C = without turning the pages

Here, the implicit enabled argument controls, because it θ-commands the *without*-phrase. Where there is no modal, the implicit argument of the verb does not θ-command the *without*-phrase, because the *without*-phrase is not a complement of the verb and control by the implicit argument is therefore not possible.

Condition B can be seen to interact with the modal argument structure in the following contrast:

(30) a.   John can be robbed without him knowing it.
        b.   *John can enter the house without him making a noise.

In (30b) *John* is the enabled argument and thus θ-commands the adjunct; in (30a), on the other hand, *can* has the following θ-structure:

(31) enabled-implicit
        ability = John be robbed
        C = without him knowing it

Here, *John* does not θ-command *him*, so Condition B does not apply.

The same contrast exists in (32), where the modal *must* has an obligated argument, an obligation, and a C realized as an *in order to* clause:

(32) a.   *John must run fast in order for him to win.
                obligated = John
                obligation = run fast
                C = in order for him to win
        b.   The fish must be drained in order for it to stay fresh.
                obligated = implicit
                obligation = the fish be drained
                C = in order for it to stay fresh

In (32b) *the fish* does not θ-command the pronoun, so Condition B does not apply; but in (32a) the obligated role, *John*, does θ-command the pronoun, so Condition B does apply.

The major point to be derived from these examples is that the phrase structure by itself does not make the discriminations; instead, the θ-structure makes the discriminations without the phrase structure. This bolsters the argument that the binding theory regulates θ-relations, not relations between structural positions. Whether or not the surface subject is an argument of the modal determines whether or not it will be the antecedent for an application of Condition B. There is no coherent way to translate this into structural terms. For example, one might suppose that in (32a) the *in order to* clause was generated inside S, whereas in (32b) it was generated outside S, so that the subject would c-command in the former but not the latter. In this case the binding theory in terms of c-command could be maintained. But there is no logical connection between whether or not the surface subject is interpreted as an argument of the modal and whether the clause is generated inside or outside S, so the (a) cases are still predicted to be grammatical, just with the clause outside S.

That subtle adjustments in phrase structure are not the way to solve these problems is made very clear by (33), where there is no doubt that *John* does not c-command the pronoun but where Condition B applies with full force:

(33) *For him to win would upset John.

Since *John* does θ-command *him*, however, the application of Condition B is expected under the θ-binding theory.

There is much more to be learned about how modals are assigned their arguments. For example, when the enabled (for *can*) or obligated (for *must*) θ-roles are unassigned, then the ability or obligation θ-role is the discontinuous phrase consisting of the subject and the VP. It is my guess that in such cases the modal first functionally composes with the VP to derive a predicate that is then applied to the subject. On the other hand, when the enabled or obligated θ-role is assigned to the surface subject, then it controls the external argument of the VP, which by itself then constitutes the ability or obligation argument.

3 Small Pro

I will now explore a reanalysis of the constructions that are said to involve small pro, the Case-marked EC. I will consider separately the role of small pro in subject position, where it has been implicated in the pro drop phenomena, and in object position, where it is implicated in general argument drop. I will seek to eliminate its role in the account of these constructions in favor of an account that relies directly on θ-roles and relations between them.

3.1 Small Pro in Subject Position

Recall that the θ-Criterion requires that external arguments be assigned. Small pro satisfies the external argument of the VP when no overt subject is present:

(34) pro VP

But since the VP's external argument is itself referential, one must ask, what is the small pro for?

If we are to maintain the θ-Criterion as a universal, then we might posit small pro here to satisfy the VP's external θ-role. But if we are to eliminate small pro, then we must attribute the satisfaction of the θ-Criterion in subjectless sentences to something else in the sentence.

In the standard view, some (parameterized) property of INFL is responsible for "licensing" small pro in subject position. Suppose instead that INFL itself were capable of satisfying the VP's external θ-role; then small pro would be unnecessary, at least as far as the θ-Criterion is concerned. We may make INFL capable of satisfying the external θ-role of the VP by giving it a θ-role of its own, an R θ-role:

(35) INFL mangia (Italian)
      $(\underline{R}_i)$ $(\underline{A}_i)$
             'eats'

The coindexation of INFL's θ-role with the external θ-role of the verb satisfies it.

Italian INFL will have [R], but English INFL will not, since English is not a pro drop language. Actually, Italian INFL will have [R] only optionally: the overt expression of the subject is of course possible, and the overt expression would be incompatible with a [R] INFL, since this would violate the uniqueness part of the θ-Criterion.

Assigning [R] to INFL tells us nothing about the difference between English and Italian with respect to expletive subjects, since expletive subjects do not satisfy θ-roles. For this we assume another INFL property, [CASE]. English INFL has [CASE] (which entails an overt subject), but Italian INFL lacks [CASE], or, in fact, is optionally Case-assigning, which we might represent as [(CASE)].

If INFL can have either or both of these properties, the [R] θ-role and the [CASE]-assigning property, and if it can have either optionally, independent of the other, then we have nine different kinds of INFL:

CASE R	CASE	R
CASE (R)	(CASE) (R)	(CASE) R
(CASE)	(R)	——

Are all of these attested? One certainly is not, and that is INFL [R, CASE]. Such an INFL would allow an overt expletive to be the subject of a verb with an external θ-role: *It arrived* in English, meaning 'They arrived'. I take it that this is impossible in general. This is perhaps because the two features [R] and [CASE] conflict with each other—having the θ-role [R] is a nominal property, but having the [CASE]-assigning property is a verbal property. If this is so, then not only is INFL [R, CASE] not available, but some of the other INFLs have reduced instantiations. If *[R, CASE], then six INFLs remain:

CASE	R	not (CASE & R)
English	Breton	Italian
(CASE)	(R)	——
Dutch	(Breton?)	only null expletive subjects

INFL [CASE] is English; an overt subject is always required, since Case assignment is obligatory.

INFL [R] is the person-marking INFL of Breton, where overt expression of a subject is impossible (see Anderson 1982; (36a–b) are Anderson's (3c) and (3a), respectively):

(36) a. *Bemdez e lennont ar vugale eul levr.
         every day 3PL-read the kids a book
     b. Bemdez e lenn   ar vugale eul levr.
         every day 3SG-reads the kids a book
         'The kids read a book every day.'

Only the "default" 3rd singular is compatible with an overt subject; it will be [CASE], but the rest of the Breton paradigm will be [R]. Actually, 3rd singular will be [(R)], in order to permit 3rd singular subjects to be omitted or expressed.

Italian INFL is [(CASE)(R)], though of course the two features cannot be realized simultaneously. This is the INFL of full pro drop of referential subjects (which have [R]) and expletive subjects (which lack [CASE]), and of course the full expression of subjects is allowed. In fact, expletives are allowed in Italian—the [CASE] variant of INFL, with a VP with no external argument. It is an accident, then, that Italian actually displays no overt expletive. Perhaps this could be explained on functional grounds. If not, then this must count against the view outlined here. In fact, it may be that Italian has an overt expletive, *ci*, which appears in existential sentences:

(37) Ci   e uno studente al telefono.
     there is a student   on the telephone
     (Belletti 1986)

As in the case of Breton, we find that Italian has several INFLs, with different properties. It seems in general that pro drop is parameterized not at the level of the language, as we might prefer on general grouds, but at the level of INFLs. For example, Italian participles ending in -*ndo* are [(CASE)], meaning that expletives can be dropped, but not referentials:

(38) a. *... avendo lei/*∅ combinato questo, pasticcio ...
       'him having made this mess'
     b. ∅ essendo molto improbabile che ... ,
       '(it) being very improbable that
       (Rizzi 1982:128)

It is important to note here that Rizzi's most general thesis about pro drop, that it correlates with the availability of postposed subjects, cannot be maintained in the framework under discussion. In Rizzi's account, both these constructions involve the licensing of pro in preverbal subject position; hence, they occur together. Here, however, the ability to drop the subject follows from INFL's having the R θ-role; but this is incompatible with the expression of the subject in pre- or post-VP position. Postposing must be effected by another mechanism, one having to do with the manner of Case assignment or θ-role assignment. A number of researchers have questioned Rizzi's generalization, for in a number of languages the correlation does not hold up; see, for example, Chao's (1980) discussion of Portuguese and Safir's (1985) discussion of Trentino and related languages.

Another generalization that cannot be maintained is Perlmutter's (1971) generalization that pro drop accompanies the ability to violate the *That-Trace Filter*. Again, pro drop is available with an INFL that has [R], but a *wh*-trace in subject position (either pre- or post-VP) is compatible only with an INFL that lacks [R].

To continue our tour of the world's INFLs, the INFL [(CASE)] is the INFL of a language that drops only expletives, never referentials; this is apparently the INFL of Dutch. In fact, it is predicted, as in the case of Italian, that the expletive will be optionally present, and in Dutch this appears to be so:

(39) Deny heeft me verteld dat (er) beweerd wordt dat ...
     Deny has me told   that it was claimed that
     (Travis 1984:232)

The expletive is not optional in matrix clauses:

(40) *Wordt beweerd dat ...
     (Travis 1984:232)

This could be because a matrix clause beginning with a verb is interpreted as a question, and only the overt expletive can prevent this. See the work cited for a related though different analysis; Travis regulates null subjects with an INFL feature [+c], which INFL passes to pro, permitting pro to be unrealized. Her system does not permit optional expletives, so the examples cited above are given a treatment not compatible with the present framework.

Hebrew is another language that shows INFL-by-INFL parameterization. The present tense is [(CASE)], permitting expletives to be dropped, but not referentials:

(41) a. *(ʔani) ʔoxelet ʔet ha-banana.
        (I)   eat   the banana
     b. Nirʔe   se-ʔitamar suv meʔaxer.
        (It) seems that Itamar again is late
        (Borer 1983:128, 130)

In the past tense, though, the INFLs of first and second person are [(R)(CASE)], permitting the dropping (or expression) of referentials and expletives:

(42) (ʔani) ʔaxalti ʔet ha-banana.
     (I)   ate   the banana
     (Borer 1983:128)

And as in Dutch, there is an *it*-type "substandard" expletive, *ze*, which can always be dropped:

(43) ze nirʔe se-ʔitamar suv meʔaxar.
     'It seems that Itamar is late again.'

Finally, we arrive at the INFLs [R] and [——]. These already exist as subcases of some of the other INFLs, but the question now is, Can they exist on their own. The [R] INFL would not allow the overt expression of referentials but would allow an overt expletive. It is unlikely that a language would settle for this as its only INFL. Still less likely is [——]. A language with this as its only INFL would not only not allow the overt expression of referential subjects (lacking [CASE]); it would not allow covert referential subjects either (for which it would need [R]). The only sentences it could have would be sentences with covert expletive subjects. Hence, we might find these as part of a family of INFLs in a language (Breton, for example) but not by themselves.

Some of the content of the theory outlined here resides in the use of parentheses to collapse INFLs; for example, Italian is [(CASE)(R)]. The empirical content of this proposal lies in the fact that only certain combinations of properties can be combined in this way. For example, there can be no INFL that optionally deletes referentials but obligatorily expresses expletives. This, unfortunately, is what is found in Bangla (Gautam Sengupta, personal communication):

(44) a. eTa Thik je   nOgon lokkhi   chele.
         it   true that Nayan well-behaved boy
         'It is true that Nayan is a well-behaved boy.'
     b. *Thik je nOgon lokkhi chele.
     c. (ami) baRi jacchi.
         (I)   home am-going
         'I am going home.'

To get this set of properties, we must assign INFL either [CASE] or [R], but not both (this is universally ruled out) and, importantly, not neither. If we attempted this will [(CASE)(R)], we would get [——] as a subinstantiation, predicting optional expletives.

Of course, we might predict that there are two homophonous INFLs in Bangla, one [CASE] and one [R]; after all, we have posited INFLs with different properties in a number of languages. However, in all the other cases the INFLs were different in form as well as marking, the implicit claim being that for each different form, the induction of INFL markings could proceed autonomously.

3.2 Small Pro in Object Position

Rizzi (1986) presents several arguments that small pro can occupy object position in Italian. He shows that the null object in various constructions seems to be available as a syntactic controller. ((45a–d) are Rizzi's (11a), (9a), (14a), (16a).)

(45) a. *Anaphors*
         La buona musica riconcilia con se stessi.
         *'Good music reconciles with oneself.'
     b. *Complement control*
         Il bel tempo invoglia a PRO restare.
         *'The nice weather induces to stay.'
     c. *Small clause adjunct control*
         Un dottore serio visita nudi.
         *'A serious doctor visits one nude.'
     d. *Small clause complement control*
         Questa musica rende allegri.
         *'This music renders happy.'

To begin the discussion, it will be useful to divide the above cases into two sorts: (45a–b), which involve anaphors and control of PRO, and (45c–d), which do not. It is plausible that in the latter two cases, which we may call the *small clause* cases, the θ-Criterion is implicated, whereas in the former two, which we may call the *pure control* cases, the θ-Criterion is irrelevant, since PRO and the reflexive are assigned their own θ-role independent of their antecedent.

In the context of the theory developed here, the facts of Italian for the pure control cases are not surprising—given that control is by θ-roles, and not by overt NPs, we expect all control relations to remain unaltered by the deletion of the controller. What is surprising is the facts of English, where reflexive and PRO object controllers must be present (Bach's generalization; Bach 1980):

(46) a. *Good music reconciles with oneself.

     b. *Such things persuade PRO to stay.

This part of Bach's generalization, the part that is clearly independent of the θ-Criterion, is called into question by two kinds of facts. First, English nominals show that reflexive and PRO controllers need not be overt, as pointed out in Williams 1985:

(47) a. Disappointment in oneself is inevitable.

     b. Any attempt PRO to leave will be thwarted.

Second, lack of "implicit" controllers in verbal complement structure appears to be indepent of control, since the verbs involved do not allow null objects even when control is not a factor:

$$(48) \quad *\text{Such things} \left\{ \begin{array}{l} \text{persuade} \\ \text{convince} \\ \text{tell} \\ \text{remind} \\ \text{inform} \end{array} \right\} \left\{ \begin{array}{l} \text{to leave} \\ \text{that one should leave} \end{array} \right\}.$$

If these are representative, then we may safely subtract them from the cases to which Bach's generalization must answer.

This leaves (45c–d), cases where a bare predicate is missing its subject, which plausibly reduce to the θ-Criterion. Still, for these cases, there is a clear difference between Italian and English, Italian apparently violating the θ-Criterion in two different ways. It would still be legitimate to posit small pro in Italian (but not English) to account for the apparent violation of the θ-Criterion in these two cases.

However, a comparison of the facts of English, French, and Italian suggests that this is not the correct approach:

	English	French	Italian
(49) a. Such things disappoint.	yes	yes	yes
b. That makes sad.	no	yes	yes
(complement small clause)			
c. He photgraphs seated.	no	no	yes
(adjunct small clause)			

Here we see that Italian differs from English in the way already discussed; however, French is like English in disallowing implicit subjects of adjunct small clauses (*Il photographe assis*), but like Italian in permitting implicit subjects of complement small clauses (*Ça rend triste*). Clearly, the availability of small pro in object position cannot account for the three-way distinction this chart illustrates.

We might suppose that there are two parameters, but the [±pro] parameter cannot be either of these, since [+pro] will permit both complement and adjunct control, and [−pro] will permit neither, thus drawing a two-way distinction where we need three.

Let us consider first the parameter on which French and Italian coincide, namely, (49b). Both these languages, but not English, permit subjects of small clause complements to be omitted. Why does this omission not violate the θ-Criterion? We know independently that the causative constructions of French and Italian are subject to a kind of reanalysis (Rouveret and Vergnaud 1980; Williams 1979), by virtue of which the verb and the small clause complement are construed as a single complex predicate:

(50) a. Ça fait [vomir]$_{VP}$ ⇒
    b. Ça [fait-vomir]$_V$
      'That makes vomit.'

(50a) does violate the θ-Criterion, since the predicative XP *vomir* has no external argument; but in (50b) the predicative XP has been incorporated into a lexical item, *fait-vomir*, and hence is immune to the θ-Criterion, which is a sentence-level requirement on XPs. Thus, omitting the object after reanalysis is just like deleting any direct object, the direct object of *fait-vomir*.

If we suppose that such reanalysis is limited to complement small clause constructions and applies in French and Italian, but not English, then we account for (49b). The reason that reanalysis affects only complement small clauses is that the reanalysis is essentially a lexical process, and a lexical process can operate only on the argument structure of lexical items. Thus, one of the parameters distinguishing these three languages will be the presence versus absence of reanalysis of small clause constructions.

Fortunately, this parametric analysis of these languages is documented quite independently of the question of omitted objects, so no parametric variation must be posited here that is not needed anyway.

The other parameter has to do with the possibility of omitting subjects of adjunct small clauses, as in (49c). Here the parameter must distinguish English and French on the one hand from Italian on the other. Again, it is tempting to relate this to another parameter on which these languages differ, namely, pro drop: English and French are not pro drop languages, but Italian is.

Recall that pro drop in the theory under discussion is accomplished by assigning the external argument of predicates to something other than a structural subject (INFL in the cases discussed in section 2). In the case of Italian, but not French or English, suppose that the external argument of the small clause predicate is satisfied by coindexation with the verbal θ-role that it modifies:

(51) a.   Un dottore serio visita   nudi$_j$.
               $(\underline{A}, th_j)$
      b.   *A serious doctor visits   nude$_i$.
               $(\underline{A}, th_i)$
      c.   A serious doctor visits   patients nude$_i$.
               $(\underline{A}, th_i) (\underline{R}_i)$

In order to accomplish this, we must stipulate that in English and French, external arguments can be satisfied only by the R θ-role that occurs with true Ns. Hence, (51b) is ungrammatical, because the external θ-role of *nude* is linked with the verbal θ-role th(eme), a linking that yields θ-role satisfaction only in Italian; in (51c) it is linked to an R, so this sentence is grammatical. Therefore, a second parameter distinguishing the languages is $\pm$ R-nec (Is an R θ-role necessary for θ-role satisfaction?), with French and English + R-nec, and Italian − R-nec.

This parameter may plausibly be related to the subject pro drop parameter in the following way. Recall that the subject pro drop parameter of section 2 has to do with assigning INFL a θ-role that satisfies the external θ-role of the VP. But since INFL is not an N, suppose that INFL cannot bear the R θ-role and that it must bear some other θ-role. Then, in order for any pro drop effects to be detected, the language would have to be − R-nec. But then adjuncts controlled by implicit objects should be possible. A clear prediction thus emerges: subject pro drop implies implicit object control of adjuncts.

In fact, the prediction is somewhat finer than this: only a language allowing implicit referential subjects will allow implicit object control of adjuncts, since it is only the dropping of referential subjects that would require the language learner to endow INFL with a θ-role and set R-nec to the negative value.

If this prediction is borne out (and I do not presently know whether it is), then we can have some confidence that we have identified something like the correct dimensions of variation, and we will have then succeeded in relating both of the parameters needed to distinguish the languages in (49) to parameters already present in the system: the presence versus absence of reanalysis for (49b), and the R-nec parameter connected to subject pro drop for (49c).

We have almost succeeded in entirely eliminating small pro from the analysis of the difference between English and Italian. For the case in (49a), which all three languages exhibit, we simply have an unassigned internal argument. The (49b) case in French and Italian reduces to the (49a) case, thanks to reanalysis. And the (49c) case reduces to subject pro drop, for which we eliminated small pro in section 2.

The case of small pro that remains is the case of expletive small clause subjects, which exist in French and Italian, but not in English. ((52) is Rizzi's (1986) example (52).)

(52) Gianni ritiene —— probabile che Mario venga.
     Gianni believes   likely   that Mario comes

Since Italian and French both lack accusative expletives, if such small clause structures are to exist in those languages, they must take the form V-predicate-S, as in (52). The question is, Why is that form possible in French and Italian, but not in English:

(53) *John believes probable that George is here.

We have connected the obligatory presence of an expletive subject to the obligatory presence of a Case that must be assigned. We might say then that in English, verbs that take small clause complements have accusative Case to assign, obligatorily ([ACC]), whereas in French and Italian, this Case is optionally assigned ([ACC]).

Recall that the optionality of Case assignment does not predict that referential NPs can be dropped. For that, the external θ-role of the complement XP would have to be linked to some implicit θ-role (of the verb, presumably). However, since the verb does not take the small clause complement subject as an argument, there is no such θ-role; hence, referential small clause subjects cannot be dropped, as Rizzi points out. ((54) is his (57).)

(54) *Considero pro intelligenti.
     I consider   intelligent

I am uncomfortable about two aspects of this account. First, I am forced to ascribe the systematic exclusion of null expletive small clause subjects to a lexical generalization: the fact that no verb taking small clause complements lacks the [ACC] feature. Why aren't there a few, or even one? Second, this appears to be a second parameter distinguishing English and French from Italian, a parameter in addition to the pro drop parameter. Actually, though, the pro drop parameter itself is a kind of lexical generalization, albeit a generalization across the INFLs of a language. In the theory we have set up, it is permitted that each INFL have a different set of pro drop possibilities, and in fact we have found languages that differ from INFL to INFL. Hence, a "uniform" pro drop language (like Italian) can result only from a generalization across all the INFLs of the language; similarly for a uniformly non–pro drop language (like English). Therefore, the uniformity of small-clause-taking verbs in a language with respect to the oblgatoriness of [ACC] is perhaps less surprising, though nonetheless troubling.

One of the interesting, or perhaps worrisome, properties of small pro is that it has no fixed interpretation, even within a given language. In Rizzi's (1986) work on Italian, for example, it is definite and referential in subject position, generic in object positions, and expletive in small clause subject constructions. The differences are ascribed to the "content" small pro gets from its context. In the theory developed here, the differences are directly differences in the context, rather than differences in small pro induced by the context. For example, the definiteness of subject pro drop is attributed to a property of INFL itself: the θ-role borne by INFL is interpreted as having definite reference. On the other hand, the generic nature of omitted objects is connected to the referential value associated with unassigned internal θ-roles. And the fact that the expletive can be omitted in Italian and French is connected to the fact that the verb does not obligatorily assign accusative Case.

Not only does small pro have different interpretations in different positions in the same language; its interpretation in object position is found in other languages that according to Rizzi do not have small pro in object position, such as English. English does not have small pro because it does not have null small clause subjects, and so on, but English missing objects have the same generic interpretation that small pro gets in Italian object position. In light of this, Rizzi in fact associates the generic interpretation directly with the object θ-role, even in Italian, and not with small pro, even though small pro is the overt expression of that θ-role.

This suggests that the pivot of the missing object construction in Italian and English is a θ-role, not an empty position. This is confirmed by further observations made by Rizzi, to the effect that only certain types of θ-roles can be null ("affected patients"). The simple generalization is that unexpressed affected patients are interpreted generically. The role of small pro in this system has nothing to do with this generalization. It is posited simply to account for (the failures of) Bach's generalization; but we have seen accounts of this that are more adequate both empirically and theoretically.

References

Anderson, S. (1982). "Where's Morphology." *Linguistic Inquriy* 13:571–612.

Bach, E. (1980). "In Defense of Passive." *Linguistics and Philosophy* 3:297–341.

Belletti, A. (1986). "Unaccusatives as Case Assigners." In *Lexicon Project Working Papers* 6. Center for Cognitive Science, MIT.

Belletti, A., and L. Rizzi (1986). "Psych-Verbs and Th-Theory." In *Lexicon Project Working Papers* 13. Center for Cognitive Science, MIT.

Borer, H. (1983). *Parametric Syntax: Case Studies in Semitic and Romance Languages.* Foris, Dordrecht.

Chao, W. (1980). "Pro Drop Languages and Non-obligatory Control." Ms., University of Massachusetts, Amherst.

Chomsky, N. (1981). *Lectures on Government and Binding.* Foris, Dordrecht.

Chomsky, N. (1982). *Some Concepts and Consequences of the Theory of Government and Binding.* MIT Press, Cambridge, Mass.

Freidin, R. (1978). "Cyclicity and the Theory of Grammar." *Linguistic Inquiry* 9:519–549.

Higginbotham, J. (1983). "Logical Form, Binding, and Nominals." *Linguistic Inquiry* 14:395–420.

Jackendoff, R. (1972). *Semantic Interpretation in Generative Grammar.* MIT Press, Cambridge, Mass.

Johnson, K. (1985). "Subjects and θ-Theory." Ms., MIT.

Perlmutter D. (1971). "Deep and Surface Constraints in Syntax." Doctoral dissertation, MIT.

Pesetsky, D. (1987). "Binding Problems with Experiencer Verbs." *Linguistic Inquiry* 18:126–140.

Rizzi, L. (1982). *Issues in Italian Syntax.* Foris, Dordrecht.

Rizzi, L. (1986). "Null Objects In Italian and the Theory of *pro.*" *Linguistic Inquiry* 17:501–557.

Roeper, T. (1987). "Implicit Arguments and the Head-Complement Relation." *Linguistic Inquiry* 18:267–310.

Rouveret, A., and J.-R. Vergnaud (1980). "Specifying Reference to the Subject: French Causatives and Conditions on Representation." *Linguistic Inquiry* 11:97–202.

Rozwadowska, B. (1985). "Shortcomings of the Existing Theta Theories." Ms., University of Massachusetts.

Safir, K. (1985). *Syntactic Chains.* Cambridge: Cambridge University Press.

Travis, L. (1984). "Parameters and Effects of Word Order Variation." Doctoral dissertation, MIT.

Williams, E. (1979). "The French Causative Construction." Ms.

Williams, E. (1982). "The NP Cycle." *Linguistic Inquiry* 13:277–295.

Williams, E. (1985). "PRO and Subject of NP." *Natural Language and Linguistic Theory* 3:297–315.

Williams, E. (1987a). "NP Trace in Theta Thoey." *Linguistics and Philosophy* 10:433–447.

Williams, E. (1987b). "Implicit Arguments, the Binding Theory and Control." *Natural Language and Linguistic Theory* 5:151–180.

Chapter 5

Evaluative Predicates and the Representation of Implicit Arguments

Ken Safir

253218

This paper concerns the nature and distribution of understood but unpronounced thematic arguments. The key issue I will address can be stated in broad terms as follows: How much of our ability to appropriately construe unpronounced arguments is due to purely (innately shaped) syntactic knowledge, and how much is due to simply knowing what words mean and what likely situations are (that is, to lexical semantic and pragmatic information)? Guided by this concern, I will argue that there exist at least two kinds of unpronounced arguments that do not correspond to any of the currently proposed empty category types. I will suggest further, in contrast to Williams (1987), that one of these "implicit argument" types is probably not syntactically represented at all.

In order to investigate these issues, I will devote a good deal of attention to the complementation of a little-known class of predicates that I call *evaluatives*. Evaluative predicates are especially interesting for three reasons: (A) their gerundive and derived nominal complements typically lack overt objects and yet are understood as transitive, (B) the understood object of the complement is construed as identical to the matrix subject of the evaluative predicate, and (C) the properties described in (A) and (B) can come about in any one of three very distinct ways, depending on the choice of predicate and of complement type. By means of these variations across a narrow class of predicates, a number of apparently similar constructions may be neatly distinguished in theoretically interesting ways.

I would like to thank Mona Anderson, Howard Lasnik, James Pustejovsky, Richard Sproat, Yoshio Endo, and an anonymous reviewer for comments on earlier drafts of this paper that improved it in a variety of ways. Thanks also to Bob Freidin for his editorial acumen. I am indebted to the Rutgers Research Council and the NEH Summer Stipend program for grants that supported this research.

Indeed, I will trace these distinctions in some detail in order to stress the empirical consequences of each analysis.

I will begin by showing that gerundive evaluative predicate complements come to have properties (A) and (B) either through *wh*-movement of a null operator binding a *wh*-trace in object position, or through NP-movement of PRO to pregerundive position where the PRO is controlled by the matrix subject. In section 3 I will turn to derived nominal complements, which, by contrast, come to have properties (A) and (B) without recourse to movement or control, but rather by a process I will describe as coconstrual of an implicit argument with a particular thematic role. After the coconstrual mechanism is carefully distinguished from movement in sections 3 and 4, I will conclude by examining the implications of the coconstrual analysis for the distribution of implicit arguments.

At the outset I will take it as well established that many understood arguments are syntactically represented (by one device or another) even though they are phonetically null. I will further assume, following without argument the standard references in Government-Binding Theory (see Chomsky 1981, 1982), that such phonetically null arguments are represented by "empty categories" and that at least four varieties of these empty categories exist, namely, *wh*-trace, NP-trace, PRO, and pro.

1 Gerundive Complements of Evaluative Predicates

The goal of this section is largely to provide an analysis of movement mechanisms and their empirical consequences that will render the properties of the nonmovement mechanism, introduced in sections 3 and 4, more distinct. Many of the observations and some of the analysis of this section are based on earlier work by Hantson (1984), Clark (1985), and Safir (1984), and I will draw liberally from these sources in what follows.[1]

1.1 Worth
Let us begin by considering the gerundive complement of *worth*.

(1) a. It is worth considering this issue further.
    b. This issue is worth considering further.
    c. *This issue is worth considering it further.

The paradigm in (1) is familiar in that it is just like that of other complex adjectival predicates, such as those of the *tough* variety.

(2) a.   It is tough to trust John.
    b.   John is tough to trust.
    c.   *John is tough to trust him.

In both cases the subject of the matrix clause can be filled by the impersonal pronoun *it*, and in both cases when the subject is thematic, there must be a gap in the clause following the adjective.

These parallels with Chomsky's (1977, 1981) *tough*-predicate analysis seem to indicate that (1b) is derived by *wh*-movement to an empty operator position within the S′ following *worth* (see Hantson 1984:102), as in (3).

(3) This issue is worth [*wh*-o$_i$[PRO considering e$_j$]].

The null operator is then controlled by the subject of *worth*.

On the other hand, one might argue that the construal of the understood gerundive object with the matrix subject in examples like (1b) may involve control of a PRO subject that is in turn derived by NP-movement from underlying object position, as in (4).

(4) [This issue]$_i$ is worth [PRO$_i$ considering e$_i$]$_{S'}$.

The operation of NP-movement in these cases would then be structurally identical to NP-movement in the passive construction.[2]

Although I will argue later that some evaluative predicate complements should be analyzed along the lines of (4), there is abundant evidence that gerundive complements to *worth* are derived by *wh*-movement as in (3) and not by NP-movement.

One argument against the NP-movement analysis of *worth*-complements is based on dethematization. If the PRO subject in (4) were moving to the pregerundive subject position by NP-movement, then the gerund must have been dethematized—in other words, the agent of *considering* must have been suppressed as in passive constructions. Thus, we would expect that a *by*-phrase could be inserted to express the agent thematic role of *considering*, and this is not possible, as indicated in (5) (also noted by Hantson (1984:102)).[3]

(5) *This issue is worth considering by experts.

Another argument against the NP-movement analysis shows that the subject of the gerund is not controlled by the subject of *worth*. In (6a) it is impossible to account for binding of the reciprocal over a long distance unless the gerund PRO subject is controlled by *the men*, and not by *John*. The failure of reciprocal binding in the embedded passive construction in (6b) can then be attributed to the lack of a PRO subject binder for the reciprocal.

(6) a.   The men$_i$ thought that John would be worth PRO$_i$ introducing
   to [each other]$_i$.

   b.   *The men$_i$ thought that (it was good that) John was introduced
   to each other$_i$.

Finally, a number of typical *wh*-movement diagnostics argue in favor of
the *wh*-movement analysis (as also pointed out by Hantson (1984)). First,
prepositions that can be stranded by *wh*-movement but not by passive can
be stranded in the *worth*-construction.

(7) a.   *Gary was given a chance to.

   b.   Who did Geoff give a chance to?

   c.   The men though Gary was worth giving a chance to.

Second, the construal relation can cover a relatively long distance, as
illustrated in (8a), and can support a parasitic gap, as in (8b). (On parasitic
gaps, see Engdahl 1981, Chomsky 1982, and references cited there.)

(8) a.   John's support is worth trying to get Mary to lobby for.

   b.   This report is worth reading t before filing e.

Thus, an analysis along the lines suggested for *tough*-constructions using
wh-movement of a null operator seems to be in order for the *worth* gerundive complement construction.

1.2   Evaluative Verbs

It would seem, however, that *worth* is a fairly exceptional adjective, because
very few other adjectives take a gerundive complement that serves as a
domain for *wh*-movement.[4] On the other hand, a semantically related class
of verbs seems to have similar properties. The verbs in (9), which I will call
evaluative verbs, strand prepositions but do not license a *by*-phrase.

(9) a.   These proposals do not merit working on (*by the doctors).

   b.   ?This essay repays talking about (*by writers).

   c.   That idea doesn't deserve looking into (*by scholars).

   d.   This player bears keeping track of (*by scouts).

   e.   ?These possibilities warrant looking at (*by the experts).

Like *worth*, these predicates license gerundive complements that permit
parasitic gaps.

(10) a.   These proposals merit reading before filing.

   b.   ?This essay repays talking about after reading.

   c.   ?This idea deserves looking into before rejection.

   d.   ??This player bears watching before deciding about.

   e.   ??These possibilities warrant considering before acting upon.

All of the verbs in (9–10) show the same freedom (more or less) to strand prepositions in a manner that contrasts with passive (as in (7a) and (12)).

(11) a.   This student does not merit giving a chance to.
   b.   ??This recidivist will not repay giving a chance to.
   c.   ?Guys like that don't deserve crying your eyes out for.
   d.   This player bears keeping an eye on.
   e.   These students warrant going to some trouble for.

(12) a.   *Guys like that shouldn't be cried your/one's eyes out for.
   b.   *This player was kept an eye on.
   c.   *These students were went/gone to some trouble for.

These evaluative verbs differ slightly from *worth*, however, in that they generally do not permit an impersonal subject (as pointed out by Clark (1985)).

(13) a.   *It merits reading this sort of proposal carefully.
   b.   ?*It repays talking about such proposals.
   c.   *It deserves thinking about this idea.
   d.   ??It bears keeping this guy in mind.
   e.   *It warrants considering such things carefully.

This difference in no way prejudices the *wh*-movement analysis any more than it does for the paradigm in (14) (see Chomsky 1982:56–57).

(14) a.   *It is pretty to look at Mary.
   b.   Mary is pretty to look at.
   c.   *Mary is pretty to look at her.

Thus, it seems that the evaluative verbs are more similar to complex adjectivals of the *pretty to look at* variety and that predicates like *worth* are more similar to *tough*-predicates, but both sorts of predicates involve *wh*-movement in their gerundive complements.

1.3   Gerundive Complements with Determiners

There is an important distinction yet to be made about the *worth*-construction that sheds further light on the evaluative verbs in (9)–(10). Clark (1985:86–89) points out that the parasitic gap evidence for the *wh*-movement analysis disappears when any noun specifier precedes the gerund, even though preposition stranding (a property that may also be attributed to NP-movement) still appears to be possible.[5]

(15) a.   Picasso's later paintings are worth a lot of looking at.
   b.   Picasso's later paintings are worth (*a lot of) looking at before criticizing.

Similarly, the argument that PRO provides the antecedent for *each other* in sentences like (6) also fails under these conditions. Compare (16a), which presumably allows *wh*-movement, with (16b), which has a specifier and does not permit *wh*-movement.

(16) a.   The men didn't think this fool would be worth talking to about each other.
  b.   ?The men didn't think this fool would be worth a thorough talking to about Bill/*each other.

These sorts of *worth*-complements, where the gerund has a specifier, appear to genuinely parallel passive constructions. The evaluative verbs show the same sensitivity; moreover, *by*-phrases often become viable.

(17) a.   These proposals merit some working on by experts.
  b.   ?This essay would repay some careful analyzing by lawyers.
  c.   That idea doesn't deserve any talking about by serious scholars.
  d.   ?This player doesn't bear any keeping track of by scouts.
  e.   ?This evidence warrants a good looking at by the experts.

The presence of the *by*-phrase in these examples suggests that the missing agent role of the gerunds is in fact like the agent role of passive constructions when it does not appear in a *by*-phrase (for instance, *John was killed*) and that the pregerundive position is occupied by PRO controlled by the matrix subject of the evaluative verb. This immediately explains why there is no binder of *each other* in (16b), as the pregerundive position is not PRO controlled by *the men*. Moreover, when the gerund has a specifier, preposition stranding not permitted by passive is not permitted by the gerundive complement either.

(18) a.   *This student does not merit some giving a chance to.
  b.   *This recidivist will not repay any giving a chance to.
  c.   *Such politicians don't deserve any giving the time of day to.
  d.   *This player bears a lot of keeping an eye on.
  e.   *These students warrant a great deal of going to some trouble for.

These contrasts strengthen the argument that the evaluative verbs involve *wh*-movement in their complement clauses when no specifier is present while at the same time confirming the essentially "passive" analysis proposed by Clark for those cases where the specifier is present.[6]

1.4   Verbs of Requirement

With these distinctions in mind, however, it is perhaps worthwhile to distinguish the evaluative verbs in (9)–(10) from some verbs discussed by

Clark and by Hantson that do not support *wh*-movement at all. Besides not permitting parasitic gaps or preposition stranding not parallel with passive, the verbs in (19) and (20) permit a *by*-phrase more easily than those in (9) even when there is no noun specifier.[7]

(19) a.   This student needs (some careful) looking after.
     b.   *This student needs talking to without insulting.
     c.   *This student needs going to some trouble for.
     d.   This student needs looking after by a caring parent.

(20) a.   That overcoat wants (a thorough) cleaning.
     b.   *That overcoat wants cleaning without getting wet.
     c.   *That overcoat wants going to some trouble for.
     d.   That overcoat wants cleaning by an expert.

(21) a.   This idea could use (some careful) working through.
     b.   *This idea could use working through before accepting.
     c.   *?This player could use keeping an eye on.
     d.   ??This player could use looking after by a good coach.

The verbs in (19)–(21), then, are more restricted than the "[+wh]-evaluatives" mentioned earlier in that they do not permit the *wh*-structure, although the "[−wh]-evaluatives" do permit the passive-like structure even when there is no noun specifier.[8]

2 Retroactive Gerunds as Selected Complements

Although this issue is not my main concern, it is reasonable to ask what mechanism of selection permits the existence of gerundive complements with traces in them (which, following Hantson (1984:102, fn. 1), I will call *retroactive gerunds*). In this section I will outline a rather cursory conservative approach to these matters, but one that will serve to contrast retroactive gerunds with the deverbal nominal complements discussed in section 3.

Little need be said about the *wh*-movement complements, which presumably will receive the same sort of treatment as the *pretty to look at* cases mentioned earlier, whatever that treatment turns out to be. Perhaps the evaluative predicate selects certain kinds of features in the complement COMP, but in any event I will assume that the complement selected is an S'.

The NP-movement retroactive gerunds raise more complex issues. Clark (1985) proposes to account for these cases by assuming that the matrix evaluative selects an *-ing* affix that triggers passive-like dethematization in the complement XP headed by the -*ing*. It is the retroactive -*ing* affix that, like the passive -*ed*, can trigger reanalysis. Though I will not accept more of Clark's account than this,[9] I believe he is right to treat these as the key properties that license movement. Clearly, I also adopt Clark's assumption that the retroactive gerundive complement has a PRO subject controlled by the matrix subject, an assumption that I will justify indirectly in section 4 (but see Clark 1985).

Natural questions arise. First, what sort of XP is headed by the -*ing* affix: an NP, an S, or an S'? Second, where is the PRO "subject" of the gerund positioned, especially when the retroactive gerund permits noun specifiers to precede the head. Finally, what sort of assumption can permit reanalysis to "skip" the noun specifiers and the derived subject PRO when the gerund and a following preposition are reanalyzed? My answers to these questions are very incomplete and somewhat stipulative, but they are designed mostly to facilitate the presentation of the issues raised in the next section.

To begin, let us suppose that the predicates of requirement, for example, select a clausal complement headed by the inflection -*ing* just as a verb like *require* may also select a subjunctive.

(22) a.   I require that you be here.
     b. *I hope that you be here.

It is generally assumed either that INFL is the head of S', or else that INFL is the head of S (IP, in Chomsky 1986a), and COMP is the head of S' (CP, in Chomsky 1986a). Under most theories of government, the first assumption would allow the selecting verb to select the head of its complement, in this case -*ing*. Alternatively, it could be that CP is selected and that the COMP head of CP selects an IP headed by -*ing*. The latter analysis might be appropriate for the *wh*-movement cases, which require a landing site for the null operator in CP; but for the NP-movement cases, no CP-level constituent is otherwise motivated. Let us assume that the lexical head of the complement phrase -*ing* is ambiguous between INFL[+ V, − N] and [+ V, + N] properties, in which case the maximal projection of the gerundive complement is either a verbal sort of IP or a nominal sort of IP, respectively. We may then assume that the retroactive gerunds that allow specifiers are headed by the [+ N] -*ing*. In order to refer neutrally to the categorial status of these complements, let us simply refer to the maximal phrasal category of a retroactive gerundive complement as *ING*^{max}.[10]

We may then assume, as mentioned above, that retroactive -*ing* has the properties of passive -*ed*; that is, it triggers both dethematization and reanalysis (to permit preposition stranding).

In the case of a requirement predicate the structure of a retroactive gerund complement without specifiers may look roughly as in (23), where preposition stranding is licensed by reanalysis (which I will simply notate by cosuperscripting, though I make no commitment to the actual account proposed by Rouveret and Vergnaud (1980)). Thus, the complement of the matrix verb, ING^{max}, is selected and the -ing head triggers reanalysis and dethematization within the retroactive gerund. I will treat the retroactive gerund as a verb and assume, for the sake of argument, that the verb raises to ING at a later level (perhaps PF).

(23)

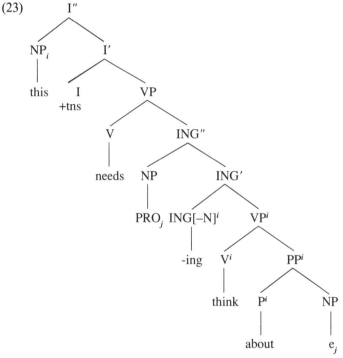

In the case of NPs with specifiers, such as the elements *any*, *some*, and *careful*, these intervening elements can be licensed by a [+N] -*ing*, but since the evaluative predicate is still selecting for the -*ing* head, the prenominal material (including the landing site for NP-movement of PRO) will be irrelevant for determining the nature of the nominal as retroactive.[11] In every other respect, retroactive gerund complements with specifiers behave like those without specifiers; that is, the head -*ing* triggers reanalysis within the gerund, as well as dethematization.

(24)

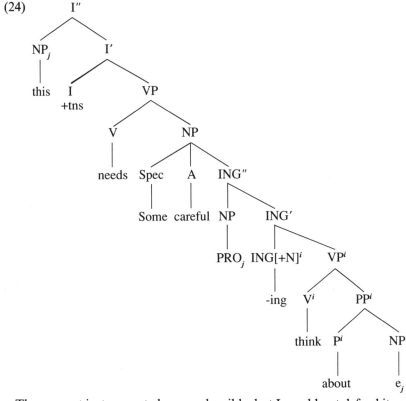

The account just presented seems plausible, but I would not defend it as more than a convenient point of departure for the next section, which is concerned with how retroactive gerundive complements compare with deverbal nominal ones. Is the same sort of analysis, including dethematization and reanalysis, appropriate for deverbal nominal complements?

3 Derived Nominal Complements: The Movement Analysis

The foregoing analysis of evaluative verbs has established that some gerundive complements involve *wh*-movement and some involve NP-movement of PRO to pregerundive position, an operation similar to passive, as in the examples of gerunds with determiners and the gerundive complements of requirement verbs. As a point of departure, I will now highlight the problems that arise if the same sort of account is extended to deverbal nominal complements of evaluative verbs.

Deverbal nominal complements of evaluative verbs appear to have the same salient property observed in the case of the retroactive gerundive complements: as illustrated in (25), the nominalization is understood as an action that the subject of the evaluative verb will undergo.

(25) a. This idea merits further consideration.
   b. These bylaws repay close investigation.
   c. This proposal deserves careful analysis.
   d. This document bears careful perusal.
   e. This approach warrants careful treatment.

Two questions now arise: Is the understood object of the action expressed by the deverbal nominal represented structurally by an empty category in syntax? and if so, is it a trace left by the *wh*-movement or NP-movement?

If the construction in question is based on *wh*-movement and not NP-movement, then we would expect a parasitic gap to be licensed, and in examples parallel to those in (10) this appears to be true.

(26) a. This application merits rejection without consideration
   b. This proposal deserves reorganization before resubmission.
   c. ?This evidence bears reconsideration before exclusion.
   d. This result warrants retabulation before complete acceptance.

On the other hand, if the construction is based on NP-movement and not *wh*-movement, then we would expect the derived nominal to support a *by*-phrase, a possibility the *wh*-evaluatives do not allow.

(27) a. This application merits rejection by the parole board.
   b. This result deserves final acceptance by the planning committee.
   c. ?This evidence bears reconsideration by defense counsel.
   d. This initiative warrants reevaluation by our policy-makers.

The evidence considered so far appears to raise a paradox in that mutually exclusive structural analyses of the derived nominal complements of evaluatives both receive some support. The paradox, however, is only apparent.

3.1 The *Wh*-Movement Analysis

There is some strong evidence to show that a *wh*-movement analsysis of deverbal nominal complements must be rejected in spite of the apparent import of (26).

Argument 1 The parallel between the parasitic gap construction and the examples in (26) is spurious. As illustrated in (28a), requirement predicates allow the same construals as those in (26), yet we know that such predicates do not license parasitic gaps with retroactive gerundive complements.

Thus, (28b) is ungrammatical (where *revising* is construed transitively, of course), but (28c) is once again grammatical (where *these laws* controls the subject of the adjunct gerund *being revised*). Finally, (28d) shows that the derived nominal does not employ the *wh*-movement strategy even though the evaluative predicates *merit* and *deserve* would otherwise permit it with a gerund.

(28) a. These laws need/could use reinterpretation after revision.
     b. *These laws need/could use reinterpreting/reinterpretation after revising.
     c. These laws need/could use reinterpreting/reinterpretation after being revised.
     d. ?These laws merit/deserve reinterpreting/*reinterpretation after revising.

The ungrammaticality of the parasitic gap following *revising* in (28d) is thus linked to the absence of a *wh*-movement strategy when the evaluative predicate complement is a derived nominal. In section 4 I will return to some of these examples in order to explain how it is possible to construe both *reinterpretation* and *revision* transitively in (28a).[12]

Argument 2   This argument shows that derivation by movement depends crucially on the presence of gerundive structure. If this were not so, we would expect the deverbal nominal examples to strand an *of* (in a case where there is no corresponding passive). This is possible only when a gerund intervenes as in (29a), contrasted with (29b).

(29) a. This issue is worth having a discussion of.
     b. *This issue is worth discussion of.

These two arguments show conclusively that the patient argument of the evaluative deverbal nominal complement is not construed via the *wh*-movement strategy.

3.2   The NP-Movement Analysis
Deverbal nominal complements contrast with retroactive gerund complements in a way that also seems to exclude an NP-movement analysis.

Argument 1   As Clark (1985) has observed, construal of the matrix subject with the object of the retroactive gerund requires that the subject of the retroactive gerund be empty, and this restriction does not extend to the deverbal nominal case.

(30) a. *These reports could use our careful examining.
     b. These reports could use our careful examination.

Since the prenominal genitive NP position is filled, there could be no movement into it, and yet construal of the deverbal nominal object with the matrix subject is not hampered. This makes sense if the direct object is not structurally present but is understood by some lexical semantic process of construal, not involving an empty category or a projected argument.[13]

Argument 2   As discussed earlier, the NP-movement analysis is licensed by some sort of dethematization of the complement gerund. This process is very local in that it affects the first gerund of the complement and cannot skip a gerund, as in (31c).

(31) a. This plan needs fixing up.
     b. This plan needs thinking about.
     c. *This plan needs thinking about fixing up.

Now notice that both the gerund and the deverbal nominal can be understood transitively in (32), but the gerund doesn't allow this (or any) interpretation in (33)—once again, because the selection/dethematization relation is very local.

(32) a. This plan deserves resubmission/reconsideration.
     b. This plan deserves resubmitting/?(some) reconsidering.
     c. The old law needs (careful) revision/preparation.
     d. The old law needs (careful) revising/preparing.

(33) a. This proposal deserves reconsideration for/?of resubmission.
     b. *This proposal deserves reconsideration for/of resubmitting.
     c. The old law needs further preparation for/?of revision.
     d. *The old law needs further preparation for/of revising.

The grammaticality of (33a) shows that the object reading for the deverbal nominal is not dependent on local selection/dethematization in the way that the object reading for retroactive gerund complements is; the construal of the implied deverbal nominal object with the matrix subject must therefore arise without NP-movement. This conclusion supports the suggestion that the interpretation in (33a) arises by pragmatic construal unrelated to structurally represented arguments.

Argument 3   This argument is much like argument 2 of section 3.1, in that deverbal nominal complements of evaluative predicates generally disallow passive-like reanalysis of prepositions, just as they disallow preposition stranding in the fashion of *wh*-movement. To show this, it is necessary to pick deverbal nominals of verbs that normally select prepositions that can be stranded by passive.[14]

(34) a. ?These documents don't deserve relying on/*reliance on.
  b. ?These permits don't bear depending on/*dependence on.
  c. These writs don't need replying to/*a reply to.
  d. This grant requires reapplying for/*reapplication for.
  e. ?This problem could use some concentrating on/*concentration on.

To summarize so far, it would appear that neither the NP-movement analysis nor the *wh*-movement analysis is appropriate for deverbal nominal complements of evaluative predicates. Instead, although (35a–b) seem parallel, they must apparently be analyzed differently.

(35) a. These laws could use/need revising.
  b. These laws could use/need revision.

One obvious difference is that since deverbal nominal complements have no selected *-ing*, no dethematization and subsequent reanalysis (where are deverbal nominal selects a preposition) is necessarily expected.

3.3 Against an Unselected NP-Movement Analysis

So far I have argued that the deverbal nominal complements to evaluative predicates do not have movement derivations. However, it might be objected that if NP-movement is generally possible in nominals, then it would be exceptional if this possibility were excluded only for evaluative deverbal nominal complements. Put another way, it might be supposed that some sort of movement analysis is still generally possible for deverbal nominals whether they are complements or not, as in (36a).

(36) a. [the city's]$_i$ destruction [e]$_i$
  b. [This proposal]$_i$ needs [$_{NP}$[PRO]$_i$ revision [e]$_i$].

It might then be argued that examples like (35b) are derived the same way, the only difference being that the NP moved to prenominal position is PRO, which must be controlled by the higher predicate, as in (36b) (of course, it must be assumed that PRO is somehow not governed in prenominal genitive position).

In Safir 1987 I have argued against the general availability of such a movement derivation for derived nominals. But even if deverbal nominals like (36a)/(37a), where *the city* is understood to be the patient of *destruction*, were derived by movement, notice that (37b) is simply unacceptable.

(37) a.   The city's destruction took a long time.

　　 b.   ?*The proposal's revision took a long time.

The deverbal nominal in (37b) is excluded because it violates Anderson's (1979) Affectedness Constraint, which captures the generalization that the patient of a deverbal nominal cannot appear in prenominal genitive position if the patient is not somehow changed or transformed by the action described by the deverbal nominal. Though *revision* does describe a change, the proposal is still a proposal at the end of the revision; but a city is not still a city if it is destroyed. Although the distinction is not so clear for a deverbal nominal like *revision*, some (semantically) clearer cases are presented below where deverbal nominals that do not permit a prenominal genitive patient argument can nonetheless appear with an evaluative predicate where the patient of the deverbal nominal is construed with the matrix subject.

(38) a.   This report needs criticizing/criticism.

　　 b.   *This report's criticism took a long time.

(39) a.   This suggestion is worth discussing/(careful) discussion.

　　 b.   *This suggestion's (careful) discussion took a long time.

(40) a.   Some implications warrant ?investigating/(lengthy) investigation.

　　 b.   *Some implication's investigation will take a long time.

The Affectedness Constraint thus provides a way of showing that the construal of the implicit deverbal nominal object with the matrix subject is not mediated by NP-movement of PRO within the deverbal nominal complement.[15]

It can now be demonstrated that no syntactic empty category could be playing a role in the relevant construal in (35b). Consider (41a–b), in which transitive interpretations of *revision* and *rejection* are both available and preferred.

(41) a.   These laws need/could use reinterpretation after revision.

　　　　 (= (28a))

　　 b.   John's ideas will merit investigation before rejection.

I have already shown that there is no parasitic gap following this nominal; thus, if there were an empty category in postnominal position, it could not be a variable. Nor could it be PRO, since it is generally assumed that PRO is ungoverned. It is not likely to be the pure pronominal pro, either, since pro must be identified by a governing lexical category that provides it with agreement features (see Chomsky 1982) and no such governor is available here. Thus, if there is an empty category following *revision* in (41a), it must be an NP-trace, which would have to be locally bound. However, we know that the Affectedness Constraint would rule out such a movement, even if we were willing to admit (and I am not) that such movements are allowed generally. In fact, (28b) provides evidence that selection by a higher predicate is not circumventing the Affectedness Constraint by dethematization, since *revision* is not even a complement of *need/could use*. Thus, there can be no empty categories mediating the transitive interpretation available for the noun *revision*. Q.E.D.

4 The No-Movement Analysis—First Pass

If there is no movement and control of a prenominal PRO in (35b), as there is in (35a), then how is the relationship between the matrix subject and the understood patient of *revision* effected?

Such considerations bring to mind the discussions of "implicit arguments" in nominals and the properties they have been held to display by Roeper (1986, 1987), Williams (1985, 1987), Chomsky (1986b), and Safir (1987), among others. Whereas Roeper treats the implicit arguments in nominals as prenominal PRO, Williams claims that no structural position should be assigned to such arguments, even when they interact with the binding theory. Rather, Williams proposes that implicit arguments are those that are represented by indices on a predicate that may interact with syntactic processes.

For example, as originally noted by Ross (1967), *Oscar* cannot corefer with *him* in examples like (42b), although it can in (42a).

(42) a. That Oscar$_i$ was unpopular upset him$_i$.
     b. The realization that Oscar$_i$ was unpopular upset him$_i$.

If the disjoint reference effect here is attributable to Principle C ("A name must be free"), then some element coindexed with *him* must c-command *Oscar*. Moreover, a realization implies the existence of one who realizes, in this case *Oscar*, and so the implicit realizer and the c-commanding index can both be represented by either a prenominal PRO, as Roeper suggests (43a), or by an index on the deverbal nominal that represents the unsaturated argument, as in Williams's approach (43b).

(43) a. [The PRO$_i$ realization [that Oscar$_i$ was unpopular]] upset him$_i$.
     b. [The realization$_i$ [that Oscar$_i$ was unpopular]] upset him$_i$.

Of course, Roeper's approach requires that the PRO be permitted in a position where it is governed. Although it has been suggested that the prenominal genitive position in deverbal nominals might be treated as an ungoverned one (as it is in gerunds), perhaps because it can be treated as a specifier position, it would be very difficult to argue that the postnominal complement position in a nominal is ungoverned. After all, government was designed to permit a predicate to be a governor for its (in English, right-) adjacent complements. But notice that it is the internal arguments of deverbal nominals such as *revision* and *rejection* that are construed with the matrix subject in (44a) and many other examples discussed above. Thus, it would appear that we must either accept the untenable proposition that PRO may be in the internal argument position of a nominal at S-Structure as in (44b) (a position that Roeper does not hold), or else adopt an approach similar to that of Williams and assume that an index representing the internal arugment of these predicates is instantiated on the derived nominal itself. The coindexing then expresses coconstrual of the internal argument and the matrix subject.

(44) a. John's claims merit/deserve investigation/rejection/revision.
     b. [John's claims]$_i$ merit [$_{NP}$ investigation PRO$_i$].
     c. [John's claims]$_i$ merit [$_{NP}$ investigation$_i$].

An additional argument that deverbal nominal complements do not involve an empty postnominal category may be based on a generalization examined in Safir 1987. There I argued (contra Williams (1982)) that derived nominals do have external arguments if and only if the internal argument of the derived nominal is realized by a lexical NP or an empty category. As evidence for this contention, I provided contrasts like those in (45) and (46).

(45) a. John's discussion of the issue drunk did not clarify matters.
     b. Discussion of the issue drunk did not clarify matters.
     c. *Discussion drunk did not clarify matters.
     d. *John's discussion drunk did not clarify matters.
     e. John's discussing the issue drunk did not clarify matters.

(46) a. John's treatment of Mary naked would cause a scandal.
     b. Treatment of Mary naked would cause a scandal.
     c. *Treatment naked would cause a scandal.
     d. *John's treatment naked would cause a scandal.
     e. (John's) treating Mary naked caused a scandal.

In both (45) and (46) the adjectival adjunct is supported by the agent of *treatment* and *discussion* only where there is an overt *of*-object, and the same pattern of adjunct support is observed even when the prenominal genitive NP is missing. Thus, (45a–b) and (46a–b) act like the gerunds in (45e) and (46e), respectively, with regard to adjunct support. In this respect, the available construal of an agent external argument was shown to be dependent on the full projection of syntactic lexical structure (as in (35)). (An agentive reading for *John* in *John's treatment* is derived by direct appeal to the lexical conceptual structure of *treatment*, bypassing syntactically relevant lexical structure. See Safir 1987 for details.)

Now notice that conconstrual of an implicit internal argument with a matrix subject, a process that is not limited to evaluatives, as will be discussed in section 4.1, does not enable an adjectival adjunct to be supported by the deverbal nominal agent. ((47a) has an irrelevant interpretation where Undine, rather than John, it drunk.)

(47) a. Undine underwent (John's) investigation/surgery drunk.
     b. *Suzy's suggestion suffered (John's) rejection/reinterpretation/ vicious attack drunk.
     c. *This report will be susceptable to (John's) revision/ misinterpretation/vicious attack drunk.

Some evaluative predicates show a minimal contrast between gerunds and deverbal nominal complements in this regard (where adjectival adjuncts are possible at all). The relevant judgment involves narrow scope for the adjunct, where it is understood that the receiving agent deserves/requires/is worth a certain kind of activity, namely, discussion in a drunken state or investigation in a sober state.[16]

(48) a. Crazy stories are worth discussing/?*discussion drunk.
     b. These frivolus charges don't deserve/require investigating/ ?*investigation sober.

These considerations thus show that internal implicit arguments do not license adjunct interpretations for external ones. They do not do so because internal implicit arguments of deverbal nominals are not represented by empty categories, and therefore control of object PRO is not involved.

If we were to stop here, we could conclude that Williams's treatment of implicit arguments as unsaturated thematic indices is more successful than one where patient arguments of deverbal nominals are treated as PRO, and so there must exist implicit arguments represented as indices of nominal predicates that remain unsaturated by a full syntactic empty category or lexical argument. However, an important question, one that leads to a third approach, remains unanswered.

4.1 Forced Conconstrual

Why is it that the object of a deverbal nominal complement usually *must* be construed with the subject of the matrix evaluative verb? If we were to assume, contrary to what has just been argued, that the deverbal nominal contains a PRO in object position, we might at least account for the coconstrual on the grounds of some sort of obligatory control of the (partially) anaphoric PRO, which prefers an antecedent.[17] But if this sort of account is not available, then how is coconstrual forced?

Let us examine the coconstrual in question more closely. Typically, a deverbal nominal complement that is understood as an activity must be understood transitively, where the matrix subject is patient, as in (49a); but this is not *always* the case, as illustrated by the ambiguities in (49b).

(49) a. John's proposal deserves study/investigation/careful evaluation.

b. John's proposal requires study/investigation/careful evaluation.

In addition to the interpretation of (49b) whereby John's proposal is studied investigated/evaluated, it could be the case that John's proposal requires that some unnamed matters be studied/investigated/evaluated. Let us refer to this second reading as the *free deverbal nominal* reading. Now notice that the coconstrual reading can be favored by simply changing the nature of the subject: in (50) it is very hard to understand that *these matters* require the study, investigation, or evaluation of anything other than themselves.

(50) These matters require study/investigation/careful evaluation.

Perhaps the reason the *proposal* permits a free deverbal nominal reading is that a proposal, unlike *matters*, may imply agency in the same way that a plan does: it may have intent. Thus, (51a) is odd in a way that (51b) is not.

(51) a. These matters are intended to irritate me.

b. This proposal is intended to irritate me.

Moreover, the subject of *deserve* is not an agent, whereas the subject of *require* can be. It seems that the ambiguity of (49b) is thus triggered by the two possible thematic roles that the ambiguous verb *require* can assign to its subject.

But the relationship between what we may call a *receiving patient* argument and the complement of the verb that selects it is more general than this. Consider how the deverbal nominal complements in (52) are construed with the subjects of the predicates (none of them evaluatives) that select them.

(52) a. Rex received benediction/remuneration/(a) suspension.

b. Undine underwent investigation/surgery.

c. Suzy's suggestion suffered rejection/reinterpretation/vicious attack.

d. This report will be susceptible to (John's) revision/
misinterpretation/vicious attack.

All of the nominal complements in (52) must be understood as involving
an activity that the receiving patient subject is submitted to. This is especially interesting since many of these nominal complements are not derived
nominals at all, such as *surgery* and *benediction*, although the relevant
readings are that Undine was operated on and that Rex was blessed (or
remunerated, or suspended). Morevoer, deverbal nominals like *attack*
normally select a specific preposition (*the attack on/*of the city*) when
construed transitively. A noun like *surgery* does not even appear to take
overt arguments in the sense that typical derived nominals do (compare
??Mary's surgery on/*of John with *Mary's investigation of John*).[18]

The basic generalization may be stated as follows:

(53) *Receiving Patient Coconstrual* (provisional)
      Whenever a receiving patient is selected by some predicate P, then
      a deverbal nominal complement that describes the activity that the
      receiving patient is related to must be understood as an activity that
      the receiving patient is a nonvolitional participant in.

We must ask, however, whether (53) is a reflex of any syntactic process of
control, or is simply the result of the pragmatic employment of lexical
semantic properties. I believe, following arguments in Roeper 1986 and
Safir 1987, that the latter is the case insofar as it supplies a sufficient
explanation for coconstrual in deverbal nominal complements, once (53)
and the semantics of specific predicates is taken into account. Moreover,
the lexical semantic approach will not oblige us to express a syntactically
active thematic structure for a noun like *surgery* that otherwise does not
seem to require it.[19]

If (53) is a correct generalization about lexical semantics, then it immediately accounts for the unacceptability of the examples in (54) and the
partial acceptability of the examples in (55).

(54) a. *Rex received suspension of Bill's privileges.
      b. *Undine underwent investigation of Inez's taxes/surgery on
          Serge.
      c. *Suzy's suggestion suffered rejection of a new law/
          reinterpretation of Bill's motives/vicious attack on Mary.

(55) a. Rex received suspension of his privileges.
      b. Undine underwent investigation of her taxes/surgery on her
          spleen.

c. Suzy's suggestion suffered rejection of its central tenets/vicious attack on its motivations.

Though they vary in acceptability, the examples in (55) are much improved over those in (54) because the receiving patient is implicated as undergoing the activity at least in part (inalienable possession works best). Examples like those in (54) can sometimes be acceptable too, though more tenuously, if there is a way to construe Undine, for example, as somehow suffering the auditing experience through her friend Inez. Moreover, (53) seems a more accurate account of examples like (56).

(56) Mary suffered/is susceptible to indigestion.

Though it refers to an ongoing malady affecting an inalienable body part (that is, a process with a thematic argument), *indigestion* could not have *Mary* as one of its arguments; but it is an activity in which Mary is a nonvolitional participant (see also note 20). If this is on the right track, then we likewise predict that predicates that can select a different thematic role for their subject will allow their nominal complement to choose a patient argument freely or not at all. Thus, whereas *undergo*, *suffer*, and *receive* all force coconstrual where the nominal complement can possibly allow it, *invite* does not necessarily select a receiving patient subject, although it allows for one (as in (57a)). Thus, (57b) could be said in a situation where Sylvan, who has known Mary for years, is normally very forthcoming about Mary's motives, except on that particular day he had laryngitis. (57c) could mean that the guys in question bring disaster on themselves or cause disaster generally.

(57) a. Sylvan's silence invited overinterpretation.
   b. Sylvan's silence invites overinterpretation of Mary's motives.
   c. Guys like that invite disaster.

Even though Sylvan's silence may itself be nonvolitional (laryngitis), the silence is still not necessarily the recipient of the action described by the complement of *invite*.[20,21]

It is important to note that coconstrual for deverbal nominal complements via the generalization in (53) is not grammaticalized in the way that it is for retroactive gerunds, where we have assumed control of "passivized" PRO is involved (following arguments in Clark 1985). If (53) applied to both in the same way, then we would expect that retroactive gerund complements could be salvaged in the manner of (55), and this is not possible, as illustrated in (58).

(58) a. *These proposals merit reading their titles.
   b. *This essay repays talking about its contents.

   c. *This idea deserves talking about its origin.
   d. *This player bears watching his progress.
   e. *These shirts need/could use washing their sleeves.

This shows that syntactic dethematization plays a crucial role in retroactive gerunds that it does not play in the coconstrual of deverbal nominal complements with a matrix subject.

If (53) is a generalization about lexical semantics not resulting from any structural requirement that PRO must be controlled or that a deverbal nominal complement must be dethematized, then it is reasonable to ask what the status of notions like "receiving patient" and "activity undergone" might be. I would like to propose that what they refer to need not be any hypothesized thematic role independently represented by an index; rather, the relationship between the receiving patient and the activity undergone may be stated directly on the descriptions of meaning assigned to each lexical predicate.

This approach can be expressed by employing what Hale and Keyser (1986) have called the *lexical conceptual structure* (LCS) of a lexical entry. The LCS is stated independently of thematic argument assignment to syntactic entities in their theory; hence, a deverbal nominal like *revision* will have a lexical entry like (59).

(59) revision$_N$:

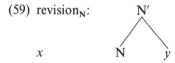

   LCS: *x* engages in the activity of changing, reordering, or modifying *y*

A more revealing account of the meaning described by the LCS might be attempted by one more interested in lexical semantics per se. The important property of this representation is merely that the variables expressing the valency of the nominal are separately stated in the syntactic lexical structure (the tree and unconnected external argument) and in the semantic LCS. My claim, then, is that the generalization in (53) refers directly to the LCS and not necessarily to the lexical structure.

5 Two Kinds of Implicit Arguments

In Safir 1987 I suggested that there are essentially two kinds of implicit arguments. One kind is the external argument implied when lexical structure is mapped onto syntax, and it is this external argument of the nominal, implicit or overt, that is capable of supporting an adjectival adjunct. The other kind is the one just described, an internal argument that is not represented in lexical structure at all. Although he does not appeal directly to Hale and Keyser's lexical structure/LCS distinction, this also appears to be Roeper's (1987) position, except that he explicitly treats the external implicit arguments as PRO.

By contrast, Williams (1987) assumes that there is no difference between implicit arguments in derived nominals that are external arguments of corresponding verbs. This is a necessary conclusion within his framework of assumptions because he has argued (in Williams 1982) that there are no external arguments in nominals. But (assuming, contra Williams, that there is such a distinction) do internal implicit arguments indeed act differently from external ones? I believe there is some evidence that they do.

As noted earlier, external arguments of nominals (prenominal genitives, when overt) can support adjectival adjuncts if the internal argument is represented, but they cannot do so when it is not. *Of*-objects, however, can generally support adjectival adjuncts in nominals, albeit awkwardly, but implicit objects of nominals do not. That is to say, *Dina* in (60a) can be the one drunk, but no such interpretation is available in (60b).

(60) a. Jack's observation of Dina drunk led to her dismissal.
     b. *Jack's observation drunk led to her dismissal.

This is not so surprising in that one could claim that the implicit argument is at best optional in (60b) and perhaps must be forced to exist by a requirement like (53). An example like (61a), however, where the coconstrual requires an understood patient, is not revealing because *undergo* is always contemporaneous with the activity described by its complement; hence, it may be that *drunk* simply modifies the matrix subject directly. When this is controlled for by placing the adjectival adjunct in a temporal adjunct phrase, the implict object clearly does not support the adjectival adjunct.

(61) a. Oona underwent the examination drunk.
     b. *Oona underwent the operation after Andy's examination drunk.
     c. *Dina underwent a thorough tongue-lashing after Jack's
         observation drunk.

This difference between internal and external implicit arguments suggests not only that internal implicit arguments and external ones differ but also that internal implicit arguments do not play a role in syntax, in that they do not provide a sufficient antecedent for structurally dependent adjectival adjuncts.[22]

On the other hand, Williams presents some evidence that would appear to disconfirm the proposal that internal implicit arguments, unlike external ones, are strictly semantic entities drawn from the LCSs of relevant predicates. Recall that Williams contends that implicit arguments are argument indices (construed as pronominals) on predicates. He claims that representing all implicit arguments in this way is necessary to account for patterns of coreference within nominals.

To see why this is so, note that none of the nominals in (62) can be interpreted reflexively, no matter what the agent of these nominals is assumed to be.

(62) a. Discussion of him implicated John's brother.
     b. Investigation of him will cause trouble.
     c. Treatment of him will be harsh.

If the implicit external argument contributes (at the least) an argument index as part of its syntactic role, then it follows that the pronouns will be disjoint from the index on the c-commanding predicate. This is still consistent with the view that external implicit arguments differ from internal ones in that only the former are syntactically active.

But the same sort of evidence appears to favor the view that the internal implicit arguments are also represented by indices. None of the nominals in (63) can be interpreted reflexively, although some permit interpretations along the lines of (55).

(63) a. Rex received his examination.
     b. Undine underwent her investigation/surgery.
     c. Suzy suffered her rejection/overinterpretation/vicious attack.
     d. These men will be susceptible to their liberation/
        misinterpretation/vicious attack.

The reflexive interpretations are excluded here if the patient of *examination*, for example, bears an argument index identical to that of the overt (agentive) pronoun, hence violating Principle B, which requires a pronoun (in this case, the implicit argument) to be free in its domain.

If the reflexive readings in (63) were indeed excluded via the binding theory, then we would have to agree with Williams that internal and external arguments get symmetric syntactic treatment, at least in this regard. However, all of the missing interpretations in (63) are immediately attributable to something else, namely, the coconstrual generalization in (53). Notice that reflexive construals in (63) would in every case render the matrix receiving patient a *volitional* participant in the activity to which that patient is related. Thus, examples like (63) require no appeal to the binding theory, and there is thus no evidence that internal implicit arguments must be represented in syntax at all.[23,24]

Before concluding, it is perhaps worthwhile asking why a subset of the predicates that permit receiving patient coconstrual are also those that select *wh*-movement and/or NP-movement derived retroactive gerund complements. After all, the retroactive gerunds, like deverbal nominal complements, describe an activity in which the receiving patient is a non-volitional participant. The difference between the movement derived complements and the derverbal nominal complements is that only in the former complements are empty categories generated that need antecedents, and only in the NP-movement cases is dethematization required by the selection of an -*ing* complement. Exactly how the null operator of the *wh*-evaluatives gets its antecedent, or how the controller antecedent of PRO is determined for NP-movement evaluatives may now be attributed to (53) if it is generalized as in (64), so that it can motivate the instances of control under discussion.[25]

(64) *Receiving Patient Coconstrual* (final version)
Whenever a receiving patient is selected by some predicate P, then a complement of P that describes the activity that the receiving patient is related to must be understood as an activity that the receiving patient is a nonvolitional participant in.

The line between syntactic and semantic analysis is delicate in the treatment I have outlined so far, and so it is perhaps worth pointing out that it is neither entirely novel, nor entirely in accord with some similar approaches to the syntax/semantics line(s) of demarcation that have recently been put forth. One trend, the guiding thought of which is well expressed by Dowty (1985:296–297), runs as follows.

... there is no reason why the intuition of the "missing subject" of *win* in *Mary tried to win* should not be accounted for as a lexical entailment of *try* in the same way as ... other lexical entailments. ... Rather the plausible solution [to the parallel entailments of *John attempted the problem* and *John attempted to VERB the problem*, KS] is that our intuition of both abstract verb and its "controlled" subject in these cases are to be explained solely as lexical (and pragmatic) entailments of the verbs *attempt*, *want*, etc. But if lexical semantics must be able to perform such tasks as these, how strong an objection can there be to attributing control to lexical meaning where is a "real" infinitive complement?

Dowty goes to propose a treatment of control that does not employ the structural presence of a PRO subject for infinitives.

One of the results of this study is that the coconstrual entailments that are similar across the three types of evaluative complementation simply do not bear on the issue of whether or not the entailments have direct syntactic representations. In other words, even if Dowty is right about generalizations that can be achieved for a given predicate across lexical entailments for both its nominal and its infinitive complements, the question of whether or not coconstrual is effected by control, coconstrual with a syntactically represented implicit argument, or coconstrual with an inferred (not syntactically represented) thematic role remains an issue that can only be resolved by syntactic analysis.

6 Conclusion

The analysis of the complementation of evaluative predicates has provided us with a laboratory in which to examine the variety of unpronounced but understood thematic arguments. Three distinct analyses turn out to be involved in what appear to be similar structures. The analysis of derived nominal complements emerges as the most theoretically interesting, in that it provides a means of isolating a forced coconstrual mechanism that is distinct from both movement and control. Moreover, based on the analysis of the internal implicit arguments of derived nominal complements of evaluatives, some insight into the contrast between internal and external implicit arguments has been achieved. If correct, latter distinction suggests a new approach to one of the more intriguing borders between syntactic representation and lexical semantics.

Notes

1. Safir 1984, which is cited and discussed in Clark 1985, is entirely incorporated into this paper as part of section 1.

2. One might also imagine an object-raising analysis of (1b) that would presumably look something like (i).

(i) [this issue]$_i$ is—worth—PRO—considering e$_i$

The dashes indicate that some sort of reanalysis would have to be assumed to apply in these cases to permit NP-movement across both a clause boundary and a specified subject, given that evidence to be presented in (6a) shows that the subject must be PRO not controlled by the surface subject of *worth*. Though some restructuring rules have been proposed for Romance languages that permit a form of complex predicate formation across PRO (see, for example, Rizzi 1982), the process is otherwise unattested in English.

3. Of course, middles are often analyzed as NP-movement constructions and yet they do not permit *by*-phrases. I will show later, however, that the optionality of

by-phrases is typical of gerundive complements that may be otherwise diagnosed as permitting NP-movement.

4. A reviewer points out that the following adjectives, whose gerundive complements are embedded in prepositional phrases, also appear to permit a *wh*-movement analysis (although I find (ii) very marginal).

(i)   This book is finally ready for cataloguing without reading.

(ii) Sometimes, a politician is ripe for voting against without challenging openly.

(iii) This pianist is worthy of keeping an eye on.

Worth is exceptional in another respect in that it appears to assign Case directly to an NP complement (see Maling 1983 for extensive discussion). In this it contrasts with *pretty* and *tough*.

(i)   Mary is worth the trouble.

(ii) *Mary is pretty a girl.

(iii) *Mary is tough a person.

5. Clark is responding on the pages cited to Safir 1984.

6. A reviewer points out that the examples in (18) are not arguments against a *wh*-movement analysis because the gerundive complements are ungrammatical even with a full lexical NP in prepositional object position.

(i) a. *Some giving a chance to this student will be disappointing.
   b. *Any giving the time of day to such politicians is irritating.
   c. *A lot of keeping an eye on Bill would prove his innocence.
   d. *A great deal of going to some trouble for these students would be a waste of time.

Notice, however, that the passive complements of (17) would, for the most part, be excluded in the same contexts.

(ii) a. *Some working on these proposals (by experts) will reveal a pattern.
   b. *Some careful analyzing this essay will be disappointing.
   c. ??Any talking about that idea (*by serious scholars) would result in an indictment.
   d. *Any keeping track of that player by scouts will reveal his talent.
   e. ??A good looking at this evidence (*by the experts) will support our view.

Thus, the success of the gerundive complements in (17) must be due to the licensing of NP-movement by the higher predicate, whereas the failure of the complementation in (18) must be due the failure of licensed movement.

Notice also that all of the retroactive gerund complements with specifiers are chosen so as to avoid cases of lexicalized expressions that occur freely, such as *A good talking to might straighten the boy out* or, more marginally, *A careful looking into might reveal deep flaws*.

7. Clark applies the term *predicates of requirement* more broadly than I do here. I limit this term to the class of verbs in (19)–(21). This distinction might be further justified by the implicit oblique readings of predicates like *worth* and *repay*, which imply datives ("worth something to someone"), and those like *warrant*, *deserve*,

and *merit*, which imply animate, if somewhat indirect, sources ("something from someone"). The predicates of requirement—*require, need, could use, could stand,* and *wants*—do not necessarily imply human agency. Compare (i) and (ii).

(i)   These clapboards need/require/could use weathering.

(ii) *These clapboards warrant/deserve/merit weathering.

8. As pointed out by a reviewer, gerundive complements can be pseudoclefted more easily in sentences where it is clear that *wh*-movement is not the strategy being employed.

(i)   *Keeping an eye on is exactly what this player bears.

(ii)   *Crying your eyes out for is not what guys like that deserve.

(iii) *?Working on is exactly what these proposals merit.

(iv)   ??Looking into is exactly what that idea deserves.

(v)   Some careful looking after is what this student needs.

(vi)   Some careful working through is what this idea could use.

Although the reviewer (who provided (iii)–(vi)) stars (iii)–(iv), I believe that with appropriate emphasis they can be improved. This may be because the predicates in question allow both *wh*-movement and NP-movement strategies. In (i)–(ii), where the preposition could only be stranded by *wh*-movement, there is no means of improving the examples by special emphasis. The reviewer suggests that contexts where the empty object is not c-commanded by its ultimate antecedent may thus be seen to distinguish the NP-movement from the *wh*-movement strategy. Compare control clauses in pseudoclefts (*Talking to John is what I regret most*) with null operator constructions (**To play with is why Mary bought it*).

9. Clark's analysis is embedded in a number of assumptions that I will not attempt to evaluate here. Essential in his analysis is the assumption that deverbal nominals do not normally assign θ-roles in the same sense that verbs do. As argued at length in Safir 1987, and discussed further in section 4, I believe, on the contrary, that a derived nominal assigns θ-roles in contexts where it takes an overt *of*-object. The latter claim has a number of consequences.

10. Of course, there is strong evidence for a gerundive sentential structure for the [+wh] evaluatives, insofar as *wh*-movement is involved, and this implies the presence of COMP. These sentences contain a thematic subject represented by PRO (see (6a)), and the gerund must assign accusative Case, like a verb rather than a nominal, insofar as *wh*-trace must be Case-marked.

   Nonetheless, the issue of whether NP-movement gerundive complements have sentential or nominal internal structure can be very theory-dependent. For example, it is a peculiar fact about reanalysis that none of the gerundive complements can be treated as nouns taking thematic *of*-objects (i), unless the corresponding verb also takes the *of*-object (ii).

(i) a. This document needs signing (*of).
     b. This book repays careful reading (*of).
     c. This book merits a tough reviewing (*of).

(ii) a. ?This book doesn't even deserve any talking of.
    b. ?That guy doesn't merit any speaking of.

This might be simply taken to indicate that when an -*ing* gerund takes an *of*-object (as in *the signing of the document*), it is a noun; otherwise, it is a verb in a sentential structure (this is the view I assume, although little depends on it). On the other hand, in the sentential analysis it is necessary to assume that accusative Case is suppressed to generate the passive-like derivation, whereas this follows from the analysis that treats gerunds in both constructions as nouns, which do not assign Case (so *of* must be inserted).

11. Something special will have to be said about certain degree expressions that have the form of partitive N heads, such as *a whole lot of*. Such cases are not true partitives, but frozen expressions like *a great deal*. Less idiomatic partitive amounts are very marginal in this construction (for example, *?*This problem deserves exactly three years/a week of thinking about*). Nonetheless, such structures are problematic for the proposal in the text if *lot* or *deal* must be taken as an intervening head selected by the matrix predicate. I leave this problem unsolved.

12. The control relations in (i)–(ii) also reveal a contrast with the typical *wh*-movement derivations.

(i) This proposal merits reconsideration after resubmission.
(ii) This proposal merits reconsidering after resubmitting.

Notice that although the understood subjects of *resubmission* and *reconsideration* need not be the same, the understood subjects of the *wh*-retroactive gerunds must be identical. Thus, (ii) requires that the agent of the resubmitting act be the one who subsequently reconsiders, whereas (i) allows an additional interpretation whereby the one who reconsiders is not the one who resubmits.

13. Clark (1985:61) points out a number of unacceptable cases of deverbal nominal complements with agent prenominal genitives and assumes that such deverbal nominal complements are not permitted. I more or less agree with Clark's judgments for (ii)–(iii), though a star seems rather extreme for (i) and I believe it is not hard to find acceptable examples, such as (iv)–(vi).

(i) *This scoundrel deserves the jury's prompt conviction.

(ii) *John fully merits the government's ostracization.

(iii) *This body needs the mortuary's rapid cremation.

(iv) This statute deserves the government's ongoing support/approval.

(v) This issue doesn't merit our examination.

(vi) These institutions need the press's ongoing criticism/?investigation.

I am not sure why (i)–(iii) should have a different status, but it may be related to the fact that the deverbal nominal complements in these sentences satisfy Anderson's (1979) Affectedness Constraint whereas those in (iv)–(vi) do not. Richard Sproat (personal communication) suggests further that the more natural, if silly, interpretation of the nominals in (i)–(iii) in isolation would be to construe the prenominal genitive as a patient (for instance, *John's conviction/ostracization/cremation saddened his family*). Thus, he suggests, there is no free internal argument to be construed with the matrix subject. These facts are consistent with the discussion in section 3.3 and the rule of coconstrual presented in section 4.1.

14. A reviewer points out that the inability of the deverbal nominal complement to strand prepositions may be independent of its NP-movement possibilities, a suggestion that cannot be excluded in principle. This brings to mind the discussion in note 9, where I reject Clark's (1985:60, 73–74) assumption that θ-assignment in nominals is defective unless the nominal is specially selected by some verb. It is also fair to say that for the same reason I cannot derive the main benefit of Clark's assumption, which was to explain why retroactive gerunds allow preposition stranding and derived nominal complements do not. I must stipulate this as a property of the -*ing* affix, whereas Clark is slightly less dependent on this device. See his discussion for details.

15. James Pustejovsky (personal communication) suggests that aspectual distinctions rather the Affectedness Constraint may be the factor excluding the (b) examples in (37)–(40). He suggests that the failure of process/event type readings for the nominals in question is what excludes them, and claims further that such examples can be improved if the process reading, rather than the result reading, is favored. He points out that the Affectedness Constraint world not predict the (for him) perfect acceptability of *The criminal's investigation lasted for two hours.* I find such examples slightly marginal, but better than the Affectedness Constraint would lead us to expect. If Pustejovsky is correct in attributing the failure of the relevant examples to aspectual problems, then the argument in the text could be undermined only if it could be shown that aspectual limitations normally imposed on such nominals were exceptionally alleviated by the matrix evaluatives that select them. Then it would have to be argued that NP-movement is possible once this aspectual limitation is removed. I argue in Safir 1987 that the latter claim is not viable, but I leave the former one as an unexplored possibility, although I know of no evidence for it.

16. Some gerunds do not allow the adjunct freely, for reasons I do not understand.

(i)   ?*This issue needs/could use discussing/discussion drunk.

(ii) ?*This proposal warrants discussing/discussion drunk.

There seems even to be a slight preference for the derived nominal in (i) and perhaps for the gerund in (ii), possibly for aspectual reasons. However, neither the gerund nor the derived nominal is as acceptable as those in (45a, b, e) or (46a, b, e), nor are they as acceptable as the gerunds in (47). On the other hand, a reviewer finds the derived nominal in (iii) more acceptable than those in (48), which would be contrary to expectation.

(iii) ?This article is not so bad that it only merits discussion drunk.

I do not agree with this judgment, although I do find this example marginally acceptable where the assessment of the article as meriting discussion is made when those making the assessment are drunk. I will leave further speculation about these murky data aside.

17. Yoshio Endo (personal communication) suggests that the object of deverbal nominal complements might be introduced by a null preposition that somehow

does not govern or assign Case to its null object, permitting PRO postnominally. It is not clear what sort of independent evidence could justify such a move, or what additional predictions such an analysis would be committed to, but it would seem to make the wrong predictions for cases like (48). I will not pursue this possibility further.

18. At this point my discussion closely parallels that of Roeper 1986, 1987. Roeper 1987 is the earlier of the two articles. See notes 19, 20, 22, and 24.

19. This is essentially the same conclusion that Roeper (1987:282–283) reaches for slightly different reasons. He is at pains to show that a plural deverbal nominal cannot have a syntactically active internal argument, and so he must explain why *The lawn has undergone several mowings* cannot have an internal argument represented in its θ-grid. He concludes that "an object (like *the lawn*) can be connected by *inference* to an action nominalization in the plural." The arguments in the text support this view. Similarly, Roeper (1987:300) distinguishes "implied" and "inferred" θ-roles, where the latter are not syntactically represented (see also Safir 1987). But on Roeper's view, see note 24.

20. It may be of some interest that the receiving patient and the nonvolitional participant do not necessarily overlap. In an example like (57b), *Sylvan's silence* could be a nonvolitional participant even though it is not a receiving patient. For this reason, the proposal in the text, though very much guided by the same intuition, is more specific than Roeper's (1986:17–18) remark that "the higher verb selects a thematic *role* in a complement nominalization without providing an *argument* for the nominalization" (emphasis Roeper's).

21. As pointed out by a reviewer, the coconstrual generalization extends beyond cases where the receiving patient is a subject. The following examples (provided by the reviewer) show that object and indirect object receiving patients can evoke the same effects.

(i)   John gave Bill a punch.

(ii)   Let's give this article the once-over.

(iii) Mary dished up stern criticism to Bill.

22. Although the considerations surrounding (30) might suggest otherwise (but note that there is no represented internal argument in (30)), these results remain consistent with Roeper's (1986, 1987) view that external implicit arguments, at least as these are identified in Safir 1987, are actually represented syntactically by PRO. This would require a revision of government with respect to PRO, as pointed out in the latter work.

23. A reviewer finds (i) acceptable. I do not agree with the judgment (except marginally where *in each other's homes* modifies the whole predicate *not deserve Bills' rude cross-examination* instead of just *Bills' rude cross-examination*).

(i)   John and Mary didn't deserve Bill's rude cross-examination in each other's homes.

The reviewer's judgment may be related to our disagreement over (iii) in note 16. I have no account of the reviewer's judgment of (i).

24. Roeper (1986) ultimately diverges from his earlier (1987) view that internal implicit arguments are not represented in syntax. He cites examples like (i)–(iii) to argue that "the theme-linking process continues to work … it loses the capacity to assign thematic roles to argument positions but the thematic roles remain" (p. 19).

(i)   You will have to undergo our interrogation program.

(ii)   You cannot avoid undergoing the examination system.

(iii) The manuscript must undergo our review system.

The coconstrual generalization in (53), which is a generalization about lexical semantics and not syntax, captures the fact that such examples are both pragmatically possible and, as Roeper puts it, "obscure." Thus, I am diametrically opposed to the conclusion drawn in the last two sentences of the following quotation from Roeper 1986:

The upshot of this discussion is that the use of a verb like *undergo* can assume an inferential connection to its complement. However if an unconnected thematic grid is present then the thematic grid must be invoked. In this fashion, which is admittedly indirect, we can argue that it is not via pragmatics that the semblance of the thematic linking arises. Thematic linking occurs as a genuine formal process. (p. 33)

25. A reviewer suggests that Receiving Patient Coconstrual might be strengthened as in (i) to account for cases like *John promised to be killed*, where *John* must be understood as volitional.

(i) *Receiving Patient Coconstrual*
     Given a predicate P that selects an argument denoting an activity A, if P
     selects another argument B that is related to A, then B is to be construed as a
     nonvolitional participant in the activity denoted by A if and only if B is a
     receiving patient.

The biconditional makes the stronger claim that agents cannot ever be nonvolitional participants in complements to which they are related. I am not certain such a strengthening is empirically viable, given examples such as *John rejected Mary's criticism*, where John is not a receiving patient yet *Mary's criticism* could certainly be understood as criticism of John. Such issues extend beyond the immediate goals of this study, however, and so I leave them for future research.

References

Anderson, M. (1979). "Noun Phrase Structure." Doctoral dissertation, University of Connecticut, Storrs.

Chomsky, N. (1977). "On *Wh*-Movement." In P. Culicover, T. Wasow, and A. Akmajian, eds., *Formal Syntax*. Academic Press, New York.

Chomsky, N. (1981). *Lectures on Government and Binding*. Foris, Dordrecht.

Chomsky, N. (1982). *Some Concepts and Consequences of the Theory of Government and Binding*. MIT Press, Cambridge, Mass.

Chomsky, N. (1986a). *Barriers*. MIT Press, Cambridge, Mass.

Chomsky, N. (1986b). *Knowledge of Language: Its Nature, Origin, and Use.* Praeger, New York.

Clark, R. (1985). "Boundaries and the Treatment of Control." Doctoral dissertation, UCLA.

Dowty, D. (1985). "On Recent Analyses of the Semantics of Control." *Linguistics and Philosophy* 8:291–331.

Engdahl, E. (1981). "Parasitic Gaps." *Linguistics and Philosophy* 6:5–35.

Hale, K., and S. J. Keyser (1986). "Some Transitivity Alternations in English." In *Lexicon Project Working Papers* 7. Center for Cognitive Science, MIT.

Hantson, A. (1984). "Towards an Analysis of Retroactive Gerunds." In W. de Geest and Y. Putseys, eds., *Sentential Complementation*. Foris, Dordrecht.

Maling, J. (1983). "Transitive Adjectives: A Case of Categorial Reanalysis. "In F. Heny and B. Richards, eds., *Linguistic Categories: Auxiliaries and Related Puzzles*. Reidel, Dordrecht.

Rizzi, L. (1982). *Issues in Italian Syntax*. Foris, Dordrecht.

Roeper, T. (1986). "Implict Arguments, Implicit Roles, and Subject/Object Asymmetry in Morphological Rules." Ms., University of Massachusetts, Amherst.

Roeper, T. (1987). "Implicit Arguments and the Head-Complement Relation." *Linguistic Inquiry* 18:267–310.

Ross, J. R. (1967). "Constraints on Variables in Syntax. " Doctoral dissertation, MIT.

Rouveret, A., and J.-R. Vergnaud (1980). "Specifying Reference to the Subject: French Causatives and Conditions on Representations." *Linguistic Inquiry* 11:97–202.

Safir, K. (1984). "Worth." Ms., Rutgers University, New Brunswick.

Safir, K. (1987) "The Syntactic Projection of Lexical Thematic Structure", to appear in *Natural Language and Linguistic Theory* 5:561–601.

Williams, E. (1982). "The NP Cycle." *Linguistic Inquiry* 13:277–295.

Williams, E. (1985). "PRO and Subject of NP." *Natural Language and Linguistic Theory* 3:297–315.

Williams, E. (1987). "Implicit Arguments, the Binding Theory, and Control." *Natural Language and Linguistic Theory* 5:151–180.

Chapter 6

Notes on Psych-Verbs, θ-Theory, and Binding

Adriana Belletti
Luigi Rizzi

Psychological verbs (psych-verbs) raise serious problems for any principled attempted to constrain the mapping of thematic representations (θ-grids) into initial syntactic configurations (D-Structure representations). The same θ-grid (experiencer, theme) is projected to a variety of syntactic configurations in an apparently arbitrary way, depending on the lexical choice. Putting aside processes of derivational morphology, which obviously multiply the possibilities, we find three primitive lexical classes in Italian:

(1) Gianni teme l'inflazione.
Gianni fears inflation

(2) L'inflazione preoccupa Gianni.
inflation   worries   Gianni

(3) La musica piace   a tutti.
music   pleases to everyone
'Music pleases everyone.'

(1) and (2) seem to be simple transitive sentences with an apparent inversion in the assignment of θ-roles. (3) is a variant of (2) with a different Case structure: the VP-internal experiencer is dative, not accusative. Such a variety is not peculiar to Italian, nor does it appear statistically marked: similar inversions are frequently found across languages. This state of affairs has sometimes been interpreted as showing that any principled approach is doomed to failure in this domain and that the mapping problem is simply a matter of lexical idiosyncrasy.

*This paper is an adapted version of sections 1 and 2 of Belletti and Rizzi 1986, published in a revised form as Belletti and Rizzi 1988 and reprinted here with permission from Kulwer. Academic Publishers. Belletti is responsible for section 1; Rizzi is responsible for section 2. We wish to thank Luigi Burzio, Noam Chomsky, Guglielmo Cinque, Richard Kayne, Mary Laughren, and Beth Levin for comments and suggestions.

We would like to argue against this pessimistic conclusion, basically agreeing on this point with earlier ideas of Generative Semantics (see Postal 1970). The bulk of this paper is devoted to showing that the D-Structure representations of (1), (2), and (3) differ, but not as drastically as prima facie evidence would suggest. Our claim is that the D-Structure representation of (1) is the uncontroversial (4), whereas the D-Structure representation of (2) and (3) is (5), a kind of double object construction with nonthematic subject position:

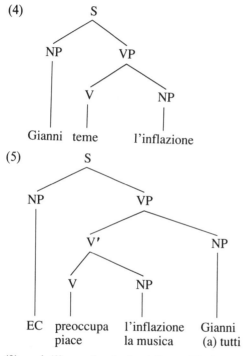

(4)

       S
      / \
    NP   VP
    | / \
    | V   NP
    | | |
 Gianni teme l'inflazione

(5)

       S
      / \
    NP   VP
    | / \
    | V'   NP
    | / \ |
    | V NP |
    | | | |
   EC preoccupa l'inflazione Gianni
      piace   la musica   (a) tutti

(2) and (3) can be derived from (5) through movement of the theme to subject position.

If this hypothesis is correct, then the argument can be reversed: there *must* be principles constraining the mapping of θ-grids to D-Structure representations; otherwise, why should the language learner depart from the null hypothesis for (2) and (3), and postulate initial syntactic representations that do not surface as such?

In spite of the obvious differences in linear order and category labels, (4) and (5) have an important property in common: in both cases the verb directly θ-marks the theme, and the constituent verb + theme compositionally θ-marks the experiencer; hence, θ-marking relations are held constant. This amounts to saying that even in the problematic domain of psych-verbs the theory constraining the syntactic projection of θ-grids has an important regularity to capture.[1]

Specific proposals about how this regularity is to be represented and on the mapping problem in general are beyond the aims of this paper. Our main goal here is to discuss in detail one type of empirical evidence supporting the hypothesis that (5) is the D-Structure representation of (2). In a nutshell, the evidence is that the subject of (2) has a cluster of properties typical of derived subjects. Four variants of this argument are given in section 1. Section 2 shows that adopting this hypothesis allows us to explain certain well-known puzzles raised by the behavior of psych-verbs with respect to the binding theory. The analysis of the binding facts will lead us to explore, among other things, a new approach to the so-called reconstruction problem. For a more complete presentation of the empirical justification of (5), see Belletti and Rizzi 1988, which also provides an analysis of (3) and a discussion of the mapping problem in general.

1 The Subject of Preoccupare Is Not a Deep Subject

1.1 Anaphoric Cliticization

A very reliable test discriminating deep and derived subjects in Romance is the ability to bind an anaphoric clitic. Consider the following contrast:

(6) Gianni si   è fotografato.
     Gianni himself photographed

(7) *Gianni si   è stato affidato.
     Gianni to + himself was entrusted

(8) *Gianni si   sembra simpatico.
     Gianni to + himself seems   nice

The deep subject of (6) can bind the reflexive clitic, whereas the derived subjects of the passive and raising constructions (7) and (8) cannot. In Rizzi (1986a) it is argued that the ill-formedness of these examples can be derived from the following assumptions: (1) arguments in non-θ-positions must be connected to traces in θ-position through a chain formation algorithm in order to ensure satisfaction of the θ-Criterion at S-Structure; (2) the chain formation algorithm only connects positions in configurations of local binding (that is, (a, b) is a possible link of a chain only if a is the closest binder of b). (7), (8), and any other similar example involving a derived subject are ill formed because the argument filling the non-θ subject position cannot be connected to its trace due to the intervention of the coindexed clitic:

(9) *NP$_i$...si$_i$...e$_i$

Now, the *temere* and the *preoccupare* classes contrast very systematically with respect to this diagnostic:

(10) a. Gianni si   teme.
         Gianni himself fears
         'Gianni fears himself.'
    b. *Gianni si   preoccupa.
         Gianni himself worries

(11) a. Io mi   conosco.
         I myself know
         'I know myself.'
    b. *Io mi   interesso.
         I myself interest

(12) a. Maria si   accetta.
         Maria herself accepts
         'Maria accepts herself.'
    b. *Maria si   attrae/attira.
         Maria herself attracts

(13) a. Gianni si   ammira.
         Gianni himself admires
         'Gianni admires himself.'
    b. *Gianni si   commuove.
         Gianni himself moves

The hypothesis that the *preoccupare* class involves a derived subject is thus supported.[2]

The contrasts of (10)–(13) are somewhat weaker with nonclitic anaphors, and they tend to disappear if the anaphor receives focal stress:

(14) a.   Gianni conosce se stesso.
          Gianni knows   himself
    b. *?Gianni preoccupa se stesso.
          Gianni worries   himself
    c. (?)Ultimamente, Gianni preoccupa perfino se stesso.
          lately   Gianni worries   even   himself

In English, examples correspondig to (14b) are judged deviant to some extent, varying from "?" (Jackendoff 1972) to "*" (Postal 1970). Stress seems to affect the acceptability of other deviant structures for which a chain formation analysis has been proposed, for example, the impossibility of anaphors in the *by*-phrase of the passive construction (Roberts

1985):[3]

(15) a. *John was fired by himself.
      b.   John was fired by HIMSELF.

It thus appears that the intervention effect illustrated in (9) can be weakened by stress. A possible analysis is that elements receiving focal stress are assigned a special focal index at S-Structure (call it F), which is later identified, at LF, with a normal referential index. We would then have the following representations:

(16) SS: Gianni$_i$ preoccupa e$_i$ [$_{NP_F}$ perfino se stesso]
      LF: same with $F = i$

At the level of application of the chain formation algorithm, S-Structure, there would be no intervention effect. This option, of course, is unavailable in principle with anaphoric clitics, which by definition cannot bear stress—whence the higher degree of ill-formedness of examples like (10b) with respect to (14b) and the corresponding English examples, in which the option of stressing the anaphor is always available.

There is a second factor that can improve the (b) examples of (10)–(13) to full acceptability. With some verbs of this class a human subject can be interpreted as voluntarily inducing the psychological process or state of the experiencer. Under this interpretation (pragmatically more natural when a reciprocal is involved, and prompted by such adverbs as *voluntarily* and *intentionally*), sentences corresponding to the (b) examples can reach full acceptability:

(17) Quei due si   spaventano intenzionalmente ogni volta
      these two each-other frighten   intentionally   every time
      che ne   hanno   l'occasione.
      that of-it (they) have the opportunity
      'These two guys frighten each other intentionally every time that
      they have the opportunity.'

This is not surprising: here the subject is an agent; hence, there is no reason to assume anything else than a simple transitive structure with a deep agentive subject. The compatibility with an anaphoric clitic is therefore expected.[4]

There is a class of cases in which the agentive-nonagentive distinction correlates with an important modification in meaning. Consider the following pair:

(18) a. Gianni mi ha colpito con un bastone.
          Gianni me struck   with a   stick
          'Gianni struck me with a stick.'

b. Gianni mi ha colpito per la sua prontezza.
   Gianni me struck   by his   quickness
   'Gianni struck me by his quickness.'

(18a) illustrates the primary meaning of *colpire*, a verb of physical activity involving an agent and a patient. Such verbs admit a derivative psychological interpretation illustrated in (18b) (see Ruwet 1972: chap. 5 for important discussion): the subject is a theme, the nonintentional trigger and content of the psychological process, and the object is the experiencer. As expected, the first case, which involves a simple transitive configuration, is compatible with an anaphoric clitic, whereas the second is not:

(19) a. Gianni si   è colpito con un bastone.
         Gianni himself struck   with a   stick
         'Gianni struck himself with a stick.'
     b. *Gianni si   è colpito per la sua prontezza.
         Gianni himself struck   by his   quickness

In conclusion, nonagentive themes of psychological processes pattern syntactically with derived subjects with respect to this test.

1.2 Arbitrary Pro

In Italian a pro subject grammatically specificed as third person plural (a specification visible from the verbal agreement), in addition to the usual definite pronominal interpretation ('they'), allows a kind of arbitrary interpretation in which the plural specification does not imply semantic plurality: there is simply no commitment about the real number of the argument in question. For instance, a sentence like (20)

(20) pro ti   stanno chiamando.
     pro you are calling

can mean 'They are calling you' (where *they* refers to a group of people already identified in discourse, or somewhat salient) or 'Somebody is calling you.' In the latter interpretation, the structure could have the following continuation in a coherent discourse,

(21) ... deve   essere Gianni.
     (it) must be   Gianni

in which the referent of the grammatically plural argument is identified as a single individual. The relevant property of this phenomenon is that the arb interpretation is not possible with all verb classes and structures:[5]

(22) a. pro hanno telefonato a casa mia.
         pro telephoned   to my place
         'Somebody telephoned to my place.'

    b. pro mi   hanno mandato un telegramma.
       pro to-me sent   a telegram
       'Somebody sent me a telegram.'

    c. pro hanno arrestato Gianni.
       pro arrested   Gianni
       'Somebody arrested Gianni.'

    d. pro hanno visto Gianni in giardino.
       pro saw   Gianni in the garden
       'Somebody saw Gianni in the garden.'

(23) a. *pro sono arrivati a casa mia.
       pro arrived   at my place
       ('Somebody arrived at my place.')

    b. *pro mi   sono sembrati matti.
       pro to-me seemed   crazy
       ('Somebody seemed crazy to me.')

    c. *pro sono stati arrestati dalla polizia.
       pro has been arrested by-the police
       ('Somebody has been arrested by the police.')

    d. *pro sono stati visti in giardino.
       pro has been seen in the garden
       ('Somebody has been seen in the garden.')

The discriminating property seems to be that arb interpretation can be assigned to deep subject pros only: it is incompatible with ergative structures (23a), raising (23b), and passive (23c–d).[6] It thus appears that arb interpretation is licensed through θ-marking. For concreteness, let us make the following assumption on the θ-marking of deep subjects: the external θ-role of the VP is first assigned to INFL under sisterhood and is then transmitted by INFL to the subject NP under government. It would then follow that pro in subject position can have arb interpretation when the licensing INFL θ-marks it.[7]

    The two classes of psych-verbs again pattern differently:

(24) a.   Evidentemente, in questo paese per anni pro hanno temuto
           evidently   in this country for years pro feared
           il terremoto.
           the earth quake
           'Evidently, in this country people feared the earthquake for
           years.'

    b.   *Evidentemente, in questo paese per anni pro
           evidently   in this country for years pro

hanno preoccupato il governo.
worried   the government
('Evidently, in this country people worried the government for years.')

(25) a.   Qui pro hanno sempre $\begin{Bmatrix} \text{ammirato} \\ \text{apprezzato} \end{Bmatrix}$ gli americani.

'Here, people always $\begin{Bmatrix} \text{admired} \\ \text{liked} \end{Bmatrix}$ the American people.'

b. ??Qui *pro* hanno sempre $\begin{Bmatrix} \text{entusiasmato} \\ \text{commosso} \end{Bmatrix}$ gli americani.

('Here, people always $\begin{Bmatrix} \text{moved} \\ \text{excited} \end{Bmatrix}$ the American people.')

Similary, agentive *colpire* 'strike' admits the arb interpretation, whereas psychological *colpire* does not:

(26) a.   pro hanno colpito il giornalista con un bastone.
          'Somebody struck the journalist with a stick.'
     b.   *pro hanno colpito il giornalista per la gentilezza.
          ('Somebody struck the journalist by his kindness.')

We thus have additional evidence for the derived nature of the subject with the *preoccupare* class.

1.3   The Causative Construction

Burzio (1986) has shown that structures containing a derived subject cannot be embedded under the causative construction in Italian:

(27) a.   Gianni ha fatto telefonare (a) Mario.
          Gianni made call   (to) Mario
          'Gianni made Mario call.'
     b.   *Gianni ha fatto essere licenziato (a) Mario.
          Gianni made   to-be fired   (to) Mario
          ('Gianni caused Mario to be fired./Gianni got Mario fired.')

This fact follows, under Burzio's analysis, from the derived structure of causative sentences: the causative rule applies to abstract representations like (28a–b) and extracts the VP from the embedded clause:

(28) a.   Gianni ha fatto [Mario telefonare]
     b.   Gianni ha fatto [Mario$_i$ essere licenziato e$_i$]

(29) a.   Gianni ha fatto [$_{VP}$ telefonare] [Mario VP].
     b.   *Gianni ha fatto [$_{VP}$ essere licenziato e$_i$] [Mario$_i$ VP].

(29b) is excluded because the trace is not bound by its antecedent at S-Structure; moveover, proper binding cannot be restored through reconstruction of the moved VP for reasons discussed by Burzio (1986).

Our two classes of psych-verbs differ sharply with respect to the possibility of embedding under a causative verb. Given the potential sources in (30), only (30a) has acceptable counterparts produced by the causative rule:

(30)

a. Questo ha fatto sì che Mario lo { apprezzasse / temesse / ammirasse } ancora di più.

    this   caused   that   Mario him { liked / feared / admired } even more

    'This made Mario like/fear/admire him even more.'

b. Questo ha fatto sì che Mario lo { preoccupasse / commuovesse / attraesse } ancora di più.

    this   caused   that   Mario him { worried / moved / attracted } even more

    'This made Mario worry/move/attract him even more.'

(31)

a. Questo lo   ha fatto { apprezzare / temere / ammirare } ancora di più a Mario.

    this   him caused { like / fear / admire } even more   to Mario

    'This made Mario like/fear/admire him even more.'

b. *Questo lo   ha fatto { preoccupare / commuovere / attrarre } ancora di più a Mario.

    this   him caused { worry / move / attract } even more   to Mario

    ('This made Mario worry/move/attract him even more.')

Moreover, whereas the potential source (32a) admits both the physical and the psychological sense of *colpire* 'strike', the corresponding causative structure (32b) admits only the physical interpretation:

(32) a.　Questo ha fatto sì che io lo　colpissi.
　　　　this　　caused that　I　him struck
　　　　'This made me strike him.'

　　b. (*)Questo me lo　ha fatto colpire.
　　　　This　me him caused strike
　　　　'This made me strike him.'

Burzio's test thus further discriminates between the two classes of psych-verbs. The contrast is accounted for, given our hypothesis that the embedded subject of (31b) is a derived subject. The relevant representation is given in (33):

(33) questo lo$_i$ ha fatto [$_{VP}$ preoccupare e$_j$ e$_i$] [a Mario$_j$ VP]

Here, e_j is not properly bound by its antecedent, and the structure is excluded on a par with (27b)/(29b).[8,9]

1.4 Passive

It is well known that structures with nonthematic subjects cannot undergo passivization: in general, natural languages do not allow (further) passivization of passive, raising, or ergative verbs. For example, French allows impersonal passive with intransitives but not with ergatives:

(34) a.　Il a été discuté　sur la question.
　　　　it was discussed on the matter

　　b. *Il a été venu chez moi.
　　　　it was come to my house

Different theoretical accounts of this incompatibility have been proposed (Perlmutter and Postal 1977; Burzio 1986; Marantz 1984; Baker, Johnson, and Roberts 1989). Whatever the correct analysis, we seem to have here another clear diagnostic environment for derived subjects. At first sight, our hypothesis is contradicted: at least some of the verbs of the *preoccupare* class seem to allow perfectly natural passive sentences:

(35) a.　Gianni è disgustato dalla corruzione　di questo paese.
　　　　Gianni is disgusted by the corruption of this country

　　b. Gianni è affascinato da questa prospettiva.
　　　　Gianni is fascinated by this perspective

We claim that syntactic passivization is indeed excluded with psych-verbs of the *preoccupare* class and that apparent passive structures like (35) are instances of adjectival passivization. That these structures *can* involve adjectival passives is straightforwardly shown by the possible occurrence of typical adjectival morphology like the superlative suffix *-issimo*: *Gianni è affascinatissimo, preoccupatissimo,* ... 'Gianni is very fascinated, very worried ...'. If it can be shown that this is the only possibility and that structures like (35) cannot be verbal passives, the prima facie counter-evidence would in fact provide additional support for our hypothesis.

A very clear test discriminating verbal and adjectival passives in Italian is given by the fact that only verbal passives can bear a clitic pronoun in reduced relatives (a subcase of the general fact that only verbs can bear clitics). Consider the following paradigm discussed by Chomsky (1981):

(36) a. la notizia che gli   è stata comunicata
         the news that to-him was communicated
     b. la notizia che gli   è ignota
         the news that to-him is unknown

(37) a. la notizia comunicata   a Gianni
         the news communicated to Gianni
     b. la notizia ignota   a Gianni
         the news unknown to Gianni

(38) a. la notizia comunicatagli
         the news communicated to-him
     b. *la notizia ignotagli
         the news unknown to-him

Now, the *da*-phrase in (35a–b) can be pronominalized with *ne*, and the whole structure can occur in a reduced relative, but the participial form cannot bear the clitic:

(39) a. la sola persona che ne   è affascinata
         the only person that of-/by-it is fascinated
     b. la sola persona affasicnata da questa prospettiva
         the only person fascinated by this perspective
     c. *la sola persona affascinatane
         the only person fascinated of-/by-it

If sentences like (35) were structurally ambiguous between verbal and adjectival passivization, we would expect (39c) to be possible as a verbal passive, contrary to fact.

Further evidence supporting the same conclusion is provided by the selection of the passive auxiliary. Whereas *essere* be is compatible in Italian with both verbal and adjectival passive, *venire* 'come' used as a passive auxiliary allows only verbal passive. For instance, (40a) is ambiguous between the adjectival interpretation (the door is in the state of being closed at five) and the verbal interpretation (somewhat marked with present tense, but still possible: somebody closes the door at five); (40b) is not ambiguous, only the verbal interpretation being allowed:

(40) a. La porta è chiusa alle cinque.
        the door is closed at five
     b. La porta viene chiusa   alle cinque.
        the door "comes" closed at five

Now, verbs of the *temere* and *preoccupare* classes systematically contrast in the expected way:

(41) a. Gianni viene temuto   da tutti.
        Gianni "comes" feared by everyone
     b. Gianni viene apprezzato dai suoi concittadini.
        Gianni "comes" liked   by his fellow-citizens
     c. Questa scelta viene rispettata   dalla maggioranza
        this choice   "comes" respected by-the majority
        degli elettori.
        of-the voters

(42) a. *Gianni viene preoccupato da tutti.
        Gianni "comes" worried   by everyone
     b. *Gianni viene affascinato   da questa prospettiva.
        Gianni "comes" fascinated by this perspective
     c. *Gianni viene appassionato dalla politica.
        Gianni "comes" excited   by politics

A third piece of evidence is that some verbs of the *preoccupare* class do not naturally allow the regular participial form:

(43) le sue idee mi stufano/stancano/entusiasmano.
      his ideas   me tire/excite
      'His ideas tire/excite me.'

(44) *Sono   stufato/stancato/entusiasmato dalle sue idee.
      (I) am tired/excited   by his ideas

These verbs correspond to irregular adjectival forms:

(45) Sono stufo/stanco/entusiasta delle sue idee.
     (I) am tired/excited   of his ideas

The contrast between (44) and (45) recalls Kiparsky's (1973) Blocking Principle: the existence of an irregular adjectival form blocks the regular formation of the adjectival participle. But notice that this natural analysis also implies that these structures do hot allow verbal passive participles: if they did, the Blocking Principle would still exclude the formation of the regular adjectival form in the lexicon, but could have no effect on the formation of the regular verbal participle in the syntax; hence, (44) should be possible, contrary to fact.[10]

In conclusion, the subject of the *preoccupare* class cannot bind an anaphoric clitic and does not allow arb interpretation; moreover, the structure cannot be embedded under the causative construction, nor does it allow syntactic passivization. These four properties consistently point to the conclusion that the subject position is nonthematic and that the surface subject is moved there from a VP-internal position.

2   Pysch-Verbs and the Binding Theory

2.1   Local Anaphors and D-Structure Binding

Perhaps the most notorious puzzle raised by psych-verbs of the *preoccupare* class is their anomalous behavior with respect to the binding theory. The experiencer in object position can bind an anaphor contained within the subject, in apparent violation of the usual c-command requirement on the antecedent-anaphor relation. Compare (46) with the expected behavior of a non-psych-verb (47):

(46)   Questi pettegolezzi   su di *sé*   preoccupano *Gianni*
       these pieces of gossip about himself worry   Gianni
       più di ogni altra cosa.
       more than anything else

(47)   *Questi pettegolezzi   su di *sé*   descrivono *Gianni*
       these pieces of gossip about himself describe   Gianni
       meglio di ogni biografia ufficiale.
       better than any official biography

A fairly standard approach to this problem, initiated by Jackendoff (1972), is to exploit the thematic difference between these structures. The basic idea is that the notion of "prominence" relevant for assigning an antecedent to an anaphor is not (purely) configurational, but involves some kind of thematic hierarchy: an experiencer is intrinsically more prominent than a theme belonging to the same thematic complex.

In fact, given the standard view that (46) is a simple transitive structure, contrasts such as the one between (46) and (47) do raise a major difficulty for any configurational approach to anaphora. But we now have strong independent evidence that the structure of (46) is more complex. This offers a fresh perspective on the binding problem. Given our assumptions, the D-Structure representation of (46) has the following form (irrelevant details omitted):

(48)

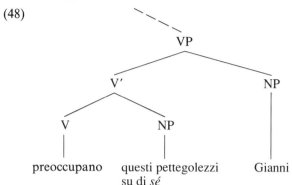

Then, there is an important structural difference between (46) and (47), a bona fide simple transitive sentence: the c-command requirement on the antecedent-anaphor relation is met in the D-Structure representation of (46), whereas it is not met at any level of representation of (47). The most straightforward theoretical interpretation of this state of affairs seems to be that Principle A of the binding theory, which requires anaphors to be bound in their governing category, can be satisfied at D-Structure; this means that if a correct binding configuration holding at D-Structure is destroyed later on, the structure remains well formed.

Is it reasonable to assume that Principle A can be satisfied at D-Structure? Standard evidence against its application at D-Structure and for its application at S-Structure (or LF) is provided by sentences like (49),

(49) They$_i$ seem to each other$_i$'s parents [e$_i$ to be intelligent].

in which, given the usual raising analysis, the correct binding configuration arises only at S-Structure. But, of course, (49) simply shows that Principle A can be satisfied at S-Structure, not that it cannot be satisfied at D-Structure. In fact, (49) is in a sense the mirror image of (46) under our interpretation. There is a general consensus that Principle A differs from the Projection Principle in that it does not have to be satisfied at all levels of representation. What (46) and (49) jointly suggest is that it suffices for Principle A to be met somewhere, either at D-Structure or at S-Structure or, perhaps, at LF. Our claim, then, is that Principle A is a kind of anywhere principle, an assumption that does not seem conceptually less desirable that the standard assumption that it applies at some arbitrarily chosen level.

Considerable empirical evidence supports this veiw. Consider the well-known "reconstruction" problem—that is, the fact that a structure remains well formed even if *wh*-movement destroys the configuration required by Principle A:

(50) Which picture of himself$_i$ do you think [that Bill$_i$ likes e best]?

Standard interpretations of this fact are either that Principle A can be satisfied at a level preceding *wh*-movement (say, Van Riemsdijk and William's (1981) NP-Structure), or that Principle A applies after a reconstruction procedure has put back (part of) the *wh*-phrase into the position of the variable (Belletti and Rizzi 1981; Cinque 1984; Barss 1985). Our hypothesis that Principle A is an anywhere principle in a sense trivializes the reconstruction problem: if the D-Structure configuration already satisfies the binding requirements for anaphors, subsequent applications of *wh*-movement cannot affect the acceptability of the structure.

The literature offers detailed discussions of cases of reconstruction arising from applications of *wh*-movement, but there is virtually no discussion of cases determined by NP-movement. This asymmetry is easily understandable. The relevant abstract configuration is one where an application of Move α destroys a well-formed binding configuration by extracting (the container of an anaphor from the c-domain of its antecedent:

(51)

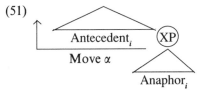

Concrete instances of this configuration are much easier to find for α = *wh* than for α = NP, because *wh*-movement is much freer than NP-movement (a difference that in turn follows from various factors: the anaphoric status of NP-traces versus the nonanaphoric status of *wh*-traces; the different classes of "landing sites"; and so on). Still, we believe that it is not impossible to find relevant cases involving NP-movement. Under our analysis psych-verbs are one such case.

There are other similar cases involving NP-movement:

(52) *I propri$_i$ genitori gli$_i$ hanno telefonato ieri.
     his own parents   him called   yesterday

(53) I propri$_i$ genitori gli$_i$ sembrano [e i più simpatici].
     his own parents   to-him seem   e the nicest

When the anaphoric possessive *proprio* modifies a deep subject, as in (52), it cannot be bound by a lower antecedent, as the familiar c-command condition predicts. When *proprio* modifies a derived subject, it can be bound by a lower antecedent, provided that the antecedent c-commands it in the D-Structure representation; such a representation for (53) is the following:

(54) e gli$_i$ sembra [i propri$_i$ genitori i più simpatici]
     e to-him seems   his own parents   the nicest

Again, D-Structure satisfaction of the binding requirements seems to suffice for a structure to be well formed.

Now consider the following cases:

(55) a. Gli$_i$ hanno fatto commentare queste spiacevoli voci
         him (they) made comment on these unpleasant pieces of gossip
         su di sé$_i$ nel corso della conferenza stampa.
         about himself during the press conference
     b. Queste spiacevoli voci   su di sé$_i$ gli$_i$
         these unpleasant pieces of gossip about himself to-him
         sono state fatte commentare   nel corso della conferenza stampa.
         have been made comment on during the press conference
     c. Queste spiacevoli voci   su di sé$_i$ sembrano
         these unpleasant pieces of gossip about himself seem
         essergli$_i$ state fatte commentare
         to-him to have been made comment on
         nel corso della conferenza stampa.
         during the press conference

In (55a) the dative subject of the causative construction binds the anaphor embedded within the direct object. In Italian it is possible to passivize the causative construction (*I to + him made wash the car* ⇒ *the car to + him was made wash*), as in (55b); and the derived subject can be further raised, as in (55c). In the latter two cases the anaphor *sé* has been extracted from the domain of its D-Structure antecedent *gli*, with no significant loss of acceptability ((55b) and (55c) appear slightly more awkward than (55a), as structures in which the anaphor precedes the antecedent generally are; but the contrast is much weaker than in examples involving violations of the binding theory, such as (47)).

A comparable example can be found in English. The following contrast was pointed out to us by K. Johnson (also see Johnson 1985):

(56) a.   Replicas of themselves$_i$ seemed to the boys$_i$ [e to the ugly].
     b. *Replicas of themselves$_i$ promised the boys$_i$ [PRO to become ugly].

At D-Structure *themselves* is bound by *the boys* in the raising structure (56a), but not in the control structure (56b).

Consider also the following contrast between raising and control, pointed out by Langendoen and Battistella (1982):

(57)   Friends of each other$_i$ seemed [e to amuse (e) the men$_i$].
(58)   *Friends of each other$_i$ wanted [PRO to amuse (e) the men$_i$].

According to our analysis, in the D-Structure representation of (57) *each other* is bound by *the men*, whereas at no level of representation is *each other* bound by its only potential antecedent in the control structure. Hence, the binding theory is violated in (58) but not in (57).

Moreover, Burzio (1981: chap. 4, fns. 5, 10) points out that the marginal acceptability of structures in which an anaphor contained in the object is bound by a dative is not affected by passivization:

(59)   a.   ?John gave a picture of each other to the kids.

       b.   ?Pictures of each other were given to the kids.

In sum, there seems to be clear evidence that as far as Prinicple A is concerned, the reconstruction issue arises in exactly the same form for both *wh*-movement and NP-movement structures, which strongly supports the view that Principle A can be satisfied by both input and output structures of Move α.[11]

2.2   An Asymmetry between Principle A and the Other Binding Principles

There is an important empirical problem that our approach must deal with. The object of a psych-verb can bind an anaphor properly contained within the subject but cannot bind an anaphor that *is* the subject:

(60)   a.   Pictures of himself$_i$ worry John$_i$/him$_i$.

       b.   *Himself$_i$ worries John$_i$/him$_i$.

Given our assumptions, (60b) cannot no longer be excluded as a violation of Principle A. At D-Structure *himself* is bound by *John/him* in both cases:

(61)

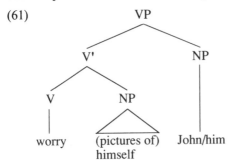

Hence, (60b) must be excluded in an independent way.

A natural device to differentiate the two examples can still be found within the binding theory. In general, although anaphors must be bound, pronominals and referential expressions must be (locally) free, a fact stated by Principles B and C. The obvious difference between (60a) and (60b) is that only in the latter is the antecedent c-commanded by the anaphor at S-Structure. Hence, (60b) is ruled out by either Principle B or Principle C at S-Structure.[12]

This analysis implies a fundamental asymmetry in the application of Principle A and Principles B and C. The latter cannot be regarded as anywhere principles in the same sense as Principle A: in D-Structure representations like (61) the whole binding theory is satisfied with a bound anaphor and a free antecedent. Therefore, if we assumed full symmetry between Principle A and Principles B and C, (60b) could not be ruled out as proposed. In fact, there is clear independent evidence that satisfaction of Principles B and C at D-Structure is not sufficient and that the two principles must be met at S-Structure:

(62) a. It seems to him$_i$ [that it is likely [that he$_i$ will win]].
     b. *He$_i$ seems to him$_i$ [e to be likely [e to win]].

(63) a. It seems to Bill$_i$'s sister [that he$_i$ is the best].
     b. *He$_i$ seems to Bill$_i$'s sister [e to be the best].

Sentences like (62a) and (63a) are well formed, and in particular Principles B and C are not violated. Since the D-Structure representations of the (b) examples are identical to those of the (a) examples in the relevant respects, if it was sufficient for Principles B and C to be satisfied at D-Structure, all the examples of the paradigm should be well formed, contrary to fact. The (b) examples are correctly excluded if we assume that Principles B and C must be satisfied at S-Structure. Once this assumption is independently granted, the impossibility of (60b) can be accounted for in the proposed manner.[13]

One might wonder what excludes an example like (64) in which the experiencer is also anaphoric:

(64) *Each other$_i$ worried themselves$_i$.

At D-Structure each other would be bound by *themselves* and at S-Structure *themselves* would be bound by *each other*; hence, the example would technically satisfy the requirements of Principle A. Of course, what is wrong with this example is the circularity in assigning a referent to the anaphors: in general, if *a* is the antecedent of *b*, then *b* cannot be taken as the antecedent of *a*. (See Higginbotham 1983.) In fact, if the circularity is broken and one of the two elements can have a different antecedent, structures comparable to (64) are more or less acceptable:

(65) ?They$_i$ believe themselves$_i$ to worry each other$_i$.

(Of course, they still produce a weak violation of the chain condition; recall (14).)[14]

2.3 Long-Distance Anaphors

Let us now try to determine more precisely what kind of D-Structure configuration the evidence discussed so far implies. The arguments given in section 1 show that the subject is nonthematic (hence, moved from some VP-internal position); but they do not give us any clue about the internal structure of the VP. In principle, there are four possibilities (order irrelevant in (66a) and (66b)):

(66)

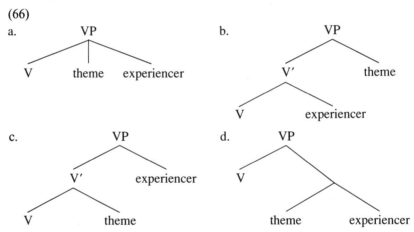

So, either we have a flat tripartite structure (66a), or the theme is more prominent than the experiencer (66b), or vica versa (66c), or theme and experiencer form a small clause (66d). We will now have to choose among these options on empirical and theoretical grounds. The binding facts already reduce the indeterminacy in part: (66b) cannot be the right structure because neither at D-Structure nor at S-Structure would the experiencer c-command the content of the theme (assuming that Reinhart's (1976) original definition holds, as seems to be correct for the binding theory). Theoretical considerations narrow the options further. If Kayne's (1984) unambiguous path approach to phrase structure is correct, then (66a) should be discarded as a case of nonbinary branching. If we adopt a strong enough version of the Projection Principle, (66d) should be discarded as well, there being no plausible θ-role for the small clause constituent. We would then single out (66c) as the only structure compatible with the empirical evidence and with plausible theoretical assumptions.

The study of long-distance anaphors provides interesting evidence in favor of this conclusion. Here we will rely on Giorgi's (1984) analysis of the long-distance anaphor *proprio* in Italian. We have already seen that *proprio* can function as a local anaphor; it also allows long-distance binding (naturally for some speakers, marginally for others). As a local anaphor, it behaves as expected; we find symmetric binding options with the *preoccupare* class, and asymmetric options with the *temere* class:

(67) a. I propri sostenitori preoccupano Gianni.
         his own supporters worry   Gianni
     b. Gianni preoccupa i propri sostenitori.
         Gianni worries   his own supporters

(68) a. *I propri sostenitori temono Gianni.
         his own supporters fear   Gianni
     b. Gianni teme i propri sostenitori.
         Gianni fears his own supporters

In our terms, (67a–b) are both possible because the anaphor is bound by *Gianni* at D-Structure and S-Structure, respectively. (68a) is excluded because at no level of representation is the binding requirement satisfied.

Things get more complicated with long-distance *proprio*. Giorgi points out that, whereas the *temere* paradigm remains unchanged (70), the *preoccupare* paradigm becomes asymmetric (69): the experiencer can bind a long-distance *proprio* embedded within the theme, but the theme cannot bind a long-distance *proprio* embedded within the experiencer, even though at S-Structure the c-command configuration would hold:

(69) a. Chiunque dubiti della propria$_i$ buona fede preoccupa Gianni$_i$.
         whoever doubts of his own good faith   worries   Gianni
     b. *Gianni$_i$ preoccupa chiunqe dubiti della propria$_i$ bouna fede.
         Gianni worries   whoever doubts of his own good faith

(70) a. *Coloro che vogliono sostenere la propria$_i$ candidatura temono
         those who want to support   his own candidacy   fear
         Gianni$_i$.
         Gianni
     b. Gianni$_i$ teme coloro che voglione sostenere
         Gianni fears those who want to support
         la propria$_i$ candidatura.
         his own candidacy

These judgments are quite subtle, and the usual "OK" versus "*" notation is perhaps not appropriate to characterize similar contrasts; still, there seems to be a detectable systematic difference in the indicated direction. The problematic and interesting case is the relative ill-formedness of (69b). Giorgi interprets it through a special binding principle for long-distance anaphors that makes direct reference to a thematic hierarchy, an option that we have dispensed with in our analysis of local anaphors with psych-verbs. It would seem desirable to give a purely structural analysis of long-distance anaphors as well.[15]

A natural way to account for the contrast between (69b) and (70b) within our system would be to take advantage of the hypothesis that the subject position is nonthematic in (69b). The following possibility comes to mind:

(71) A long-distance anaphor must be bound from a θ-position.[16]

The adequacy of (71) can easily be checked on independent grounds: it suffices to look at structures like (49), in which the short-distance anaphor is bound from a non-θ-position. The prediction is that long-distance anaphors could not survive in this environment. The prediction appears to be correct:

(72) a. *Gianni$_i$ sembra [e essere efficiente] a chiunque sostenga
       Gianni seems   e to be efficient   to whoever supports
       la propria$_i$ candidatura.
       his own candidacy
    b. Gianni$_i$ promette [di PRO essere efficiente] a chiunque
       Gianni promised to PRO be efficient   to whoever
       sostenga la propria$_i$ candidatura.
       supports his own candidacy

Again, the contrast is subtle, comparable to the contrast between (69) and (70). If it is systematic and representative, as it seems to us, then a principle like (71) is supported.[17]

This approach has a direct impact on the choice of the a priori possible D-Structure configurations. In fact, it gives the optimal result of picking exactly one of the four possibilities given in (66). Only configuration (66c) allows a correct characterization of the facts: a long-distance anaphor contained within the theme can be bound by the experiencer (at D-Structure the c-command configuration is met). A long-distance anaphor contained within the experiencer cannot be bound by the theme: the peculiar binding requirement of long-distance anaphors is met neither at D-Structure nor at S-Structure; at S-Structure the theme NP has been moved to subject position, but this position, being nonthematic, is not available for long-distance binding, according to principle (71). Whence the ill-formedness of (69b).

(66b), already excluded by short-distance binding, also gives an incorrect result for long-distance binding: this asymmetric c-command configuration would predict reversed grammaticality judgments on (69a–b). (66a) and (66d) also give a wrong results. In these respresentations the two θ-positions symmetrically c-command each other; hence, we would expect symmetric binding possibilities in (69), contrary to fact.[18]

In conclusion, the syntax of long-distance anaphors supports the choice of (66c) as the correct D-Structure representation for the *preoccupare* class.

3 Conclusion

We have provided different kinds of evidence that sentences involving verbs of the *preoccupare* class have nonthematic subjects and that both the theme and the experiencer are VP-internal at D-Structure. The syntax of long-distance anaphors further suggests a specific internal structure of the VP, with the experiencer higher than the theme. In Belletti and Rizzi 1988 we provide further evidence supporting the same conclusion. In addition to the implications for the binding theory, the major theoretical consequence of this result involves the mapping problem. Let us consider the proposed D-Structure representations of the *temere* and *preoccupare* classes:

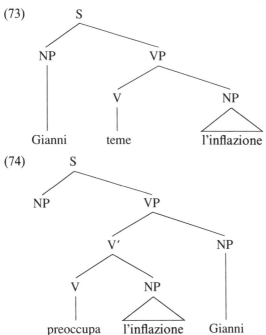

(73)

(74)

The two representations share one important property: in both cases the experiencer is structurally higher than the theme. How can this generalization be acquired by the language learner? Notice that the order of the two arguments in (74) never surfaces as such;[19] moreover, the evidence showing the derived nature of the subject is largely negative and, in any event, too "exotic" to manifest itself with sufficient frequency in the primary data. This strongly suggests that the generalization is driven by a mapping principle that enforces a structural assumption not granted by overt evidence for the case of (74). The natural format for this principle is a thematic hierarchy constraining the formation of D-Structure representations from θ-grids: when an experiencer and a theme are members of the same θ-grid, the experiencer must be projected to a higher structural position.[20] This leaves only two possibilities: the experiencer can be selected as the external argument or not; if not, it will remain within the VP in a higher position than the theme; all other possibilities, in particular selection of the theme as the external argument, are excluded in principle. This restricts the class of the possible D-Structure representations projected from (experiencer, theme) to (73) and (74), which are the empirically motivated cases.

Notes

1. See Guéron 1986, Johnson 1985, Pesetsky 1987, Stowell 1986, and Den Besten 1982 (on German and Dutch) for slightly different approaches having in common the assumption that at some level of representation the structure of (2) and (3) is more complex than superficial evidence might suggest. Also see Georgopoulos 1987 for evidence that (5) is the correct representation (modulo categorial and linear adjustments) for psych-nouns in Palauan.

2. The (b) sentences of (10) and (13) are acceptable on an irrelevant reading. In addition to the construction "theme V experiencer," the verbs in these sentences admit the construction "experiencer *si* V P theme" with an inchoative sense. For instance:

(i) Questo commuove/preoccupa Gianni.
     this   moves/worries   Gianni

(ii) Gianni si commuove/preoccupa di questo.
     Gianni *si* moves/worries   of this

Here *si* is nonthematic, presumably akin to the ergative marker *si* discussed by Burzio (1986). The PP designating the theme can be omitted, so that, for instance, (10b) is acceptable in the interpretation corresponding to (ii), 'Gianni gets worried of something unspecified'. (10b) and (13b) are impossible with thematic *si* corresponding to the experiencer. The irrelevant reading does not arise with the verbs of (12b), which do not occur in the inchoative construction. As for the verb in

(11b), it does occur in the inchoative construction, but it does not allow for the omission of the PP; hence, no irrelevant reading arises in this case either.

3. In Roberts's analysis the intervention responsible for the ill-formedness of (15a) is not directly provided by the anaphor, which presumably does not c-command the object trace, but instead is provided by the *en*-morpheme coindexed with the *by*-phrase (hence, by transitivity, with the object trace).

4. Examples (21b) of Rizzi 1986 is amenable to this analysis.

5. The "*" on the examples of (23) refers to the arb interpretation. All the examples are in fact acceptable with the definite pronominal interpretation of the null subject: 'They arrived at my place', and so on. In this section we freely draw from a talk given by Alfredo Hurtado at MIT (fall, 1984) on the corresponding construction in Spanish.

6. The contrasts are very sharp when the structures refer to specific events as in (22)–(23). In such cases arb is close to existential quantification. There are weaker but still detectable contrasts when the structures are generic (in which case arb is close to universal quantification or to generic NPs like *people*):

(i)   Qui hanno sempre rispettato gli americani.
        here (people) always respected Americans

(ii)   ?Qui sono sempre stati rispettati   dagli americani.
        here (people) were always respected by Americans

(iii)   ??Qui mi   sono sempre sembrati filo-americani.
        here to-me (people) always seemed friendly toward Americans

The contrast is probably weakened because the definite pronominal interpretation and arb interpretation in generic contexts (*they* and *people*) are more difficult to tease apart than in specific contexts (*they* and *somebody*).

7. This formal condition would then parallel the assignment of arb interpretation to pro in V-governed positions, which is also contingent upon θ-marking (see Rizzi 1986b). Still, arbitrary interpretation of pro subjects (call it *arb'*) differs from what is generally referred to as *arb interpretation* (assigned to uncontrolled PRO, impersonal *si*, and pro in object position) in at least two respects: (1) ordinary arb can be intepreted as including the speaker, whereas arb' is always exclusive; (2) arb is grammatically singular in some languages (Spanish) and plural in others (Italian), whereas arb' is always plural. We will leave open the question whether one should factor out a unique procedure responsible for the assignment of arb and arb', or two independent mechanisms should be admitted to exist. See Jaeggli 1986, Suñer 1982, Otero 1985.

8. Notice that if the embedded subject is cliticized to the main verb, the structure does not improve:

(i) questo glie$_j$lo$_i$ ha fatto [$_{VP}$ preoccupare e$_j'$ e$_i$] [e$_j''$ VP]
    this to-him it made   worry

The same is true in cases like (27b). This shows that the clitic cannot count as the antecedent for the NP-trace e$_j'$, a result that can be obtained if the assumption is made that the relation between a clitic and an empty category in the VP is to be assimilated not to the NP-trace relation but to the licensing relation of pro (see Rizzi 1986b).

9. The unacceptability of the *preoccupare* class in the *fare da* construction (Kayne 1975; Burzio 1986; Zubizarreta 1985) is less significant because the *temere* class also seems to give rise to deviant *fare da* structures:

(i) *?Questo lo   ha fatto temere   da tutti.
      this   him made to be feared by everybody

(ii) *Questo lo   ha fatto preoccupare da tutti.
      this   him made to be worried by everybody

The generalization seems to be that only agentive subjects can occur in this construction (Trigo 1985); hence, *da* is a real θ-marker here and does not simply transmit the external θ-role assigned by the VP as in the passive construction. Still, (ii) appears to be more deviant than (i), suggesting that more is involved here than simple thematic incompatibility. The additional deviance of (ii) can be related to the derived status of the subject, given Burzio's (1986) hypothesis that the *fare da* construction is monoclausal and involves selection of a bare VP:

(iii) questo lo$_i$ ha fatto [$_{VP}$ preoccupare e$_i$ e] da tutti

Here, the VP-internal trace corresponding to the experiencer could not be properly bound.

    The acceptable structure (iv)

(iv) Questo lo   ha fatto preoccupare.
      this   him made worry

would derive, not from a source corresponding to (ii) via optional omission of the *da*-phrase, but from a source corresponding to (v)

(v) Questo ha fatto sì che lui si preoccupasse.
     this   caused that he *si* worried

(see note 2 on this inchoative contruction) via deletion of the nonargument *si*, which always takes place in the causative construction. Compare:

(vi) a. Questo ha fatto sì che lui si pentisse.
        this   caused that he *si* repented
     b. Questo lo   ha fatto pentire.
        this   him made   repent

10. An additional fact to notice is that some of these participial structures cannot cooccur with the regular *da*-phrase of passives, and require a different preposition:

(i) a. Gianni è interessato a/*da Maria.
     Gianni is interested to/by Maria
    b. Gianni è appassionato di/*dalla poesia.
     Gianni is fond   of/by poetry

These lexical idiosyncrasies again appear more easily compatible with the view that the only possibility here is adjectival formation in the lexicon. No analogous idiosyncratic selection is found with the *temere* class, nor with other plausible cases of syntactic passivization.

That the regular formation of the verbal past participle is not affected by the existence of the adjectival form is shown by the fact that sentences correspnding to (43) show the regular participal form in compound tenses:

(ii) Le sue idee mi hanno stufato/stancato/entusiasmato.
    his ideas   me have tired/excited
    'His ideas have tired/excited me.'

11. Our evidence is also compatible with a representational approach to reconstruction, phrased in terms of syntactic chains read off of S-Structure (or LF) representations. See Cinque 1984, Barss 1985, and Hornstein 1984 for different formulations of the representational approach. In the discussion in the text we have chosen the derivational approach merely for reasons of perspicuity. It should be clear, however, that our substantive contribution to the reconstruction problem can be phrased in neutral terms with respect to the derivations versus representations controversy; "reconstruction" for Principle A is a property of X-chains (X = A or $\bar{\text{A}}$), and not only of $\bar{\text{A}}$-chains, as is generally assumed.

Notice that a potential case of satisfaction of Principle A only at LF is example (14c), if analyzed as proposed in the text.

12. There are some cases in which an anaphor seems to be allowed to c-command its antecedent at S-Structure. This happens when the anaphor and the antecedent c-command each other. This is perhaps the case in the following Italian examples in which the direct object can bind an anaphoric indirect object or vice versa, provided that the antecedent precedes the anaphor:

(i) a. Ho affidato Maria a se stessa.
        (I) gave   Maria to herself
    b. Ho affidato a Maria se stessa (e la sua famiglia).
        (I) gave   to Maria herself   (and her family)

Why isn't Principle C violated in these examples? The obvious difference between these examples and (60b) is that in (ia–b) c-command is symmetric. If we assume that binding is intrinsically asymmetric (Higginbotham 1983), in cases of symmetric c-command we have to choose the direction of the binding relation (perhaps linear order gives the favored direction). Then the antecedent would be free in (ia–b) even if it is c-command by the anaphor. This option does not materialize in the case of (60b), where c-command is asymmetric; hence, the only possible binding relation at S-Structure is that the anaphor binds the antecedent, which produces a violation of Principle B or Principle C.

13. Examples like (60b), (62b), and (63b) show that satisfaction of Principles B and C at D-Structure is insufficient to grant well-formedness. Is it also unnecessary? The answer depends on a notoriously murky domain: noncoreference effects under pied piping. Consider the following paradigm adapted from Van Riemsdijk and Williams 1981:

(i) a. *He likes John's picture of Mary.
    b. *He likes this picture of John.
    c. *He likes pictures that John saw.

(ii) a.   *Mary, *John's* picture of whom *he* likes e.
  b.   ??Which picture of *John* did *he* like e?
  c.   Which picture that *John* saw did *he* like e?

(i) illustrates ordinary cases of Principle C violations. (ii) shows that the disjunction effect is preserved under *wh*-movement in some cases, weakened or eliminated in others. If we take (iia) to be the representative case, the conclusion is that satisfaction of Principle C at D-Structure is necessary (even if not sufficient, given (63b); if we take (iic) as representative, the conclusion is that satisfaction of Principle C at D-Structure is neither sufficient nor necessary (that is, this principle does not concern D-Structure representations). A satisfactory answer to this question would require a detailed analysis of this complex empirical domain, a task we cannot undertake here.

14. Given the asymmety we have introduced between Principle A and B, one might wonder whether the PRO theorem can still be derived. What excludes a governed PRO in cases like the following?

(i) Pictures of PRO_i pleased the $boys_i$.

The anaphoric properties of PRO could be satisfied at D-Structure and its pronominal properties at S-Structure, and no contradiction would arise. This unwanted result is excluded if the binding theory of Chomsky (1986) is adopted: neither at D-Structure nor at S-Structure would there be an indexation binding-theory-compatible for PRO (that is, simultaneously satisfying the pronominal and anaphoric properties); hence, PRO would be governed but could not receive a governing category, a situation explicity excluded in Chomsky's system.

15. Giorgi's system includes the following definitions and principles:

(i)   P-domain: "... each lexical head defines a thematic domain (θ), i.e. the set of arguments θ-marked by that head. One of the arguments of this thematic domain can be said to be 'prominent' with respect to the others, and the set of the remaining ones, with all the material they dominate, can be called its P-domain. ... The prominent argument should be identified with the highest one in the following thematic hierarchy: 1) agent; 2) experiencer; 3) theme and others" (p. 64).

(ii) α is P-bound by β if and only if α is coindexed with β and α is in the P-domain of β.

(iii) A long-distance anaphor is P-bound.

(69b) would then be ruled out because the theme would not be thematically prominent with respect to *proprio* embedded within the experiencer; hence, it would not qualify as a binder for a long-distance anaphor.

16. Alternatively, we might assume that binding of a long-distance anaphor is checked at D-Structure, where all potential binders are in θ-positions. The two formulations appear equivalent for all the cases we will consider. Of course, any such statement is only a partial characterization of the properties of long-distance anaphors. Familiar work on Japanese, Korean, and the Scandinavian languages suggests that other conditions are operative. See note 18 for a more structured conjecture.

17. Compare also:

(i) *Gianni$_i$ pare   intelligente a chiunque accetti le proprie$_i$ idee.
    Gianni seems intelligent to whoever accepts his own ideas

(ii) Gianni$_i$ dà aiuto a chiunque accetti le proprie$_i$ idee.
    Gianni helps   whoever accepts his own ideas

18. Recent work on long-distance anaphors in different languages suggests that (71) cannot be a complete characterization of long-distance anaphora: other conditions must be operative as well. One such condition is subject orientation (not always respected, though; see (69a), with the qualification that if the long-distance anaphor is contained within an adverbial clause, the immediate superordinate subject cannot function as a binder. That is, in (i)

(i)

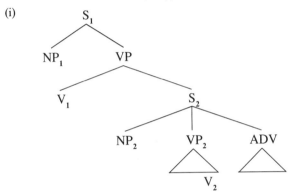

a long-distance anaphor α can be bound by NP$_1$, but not by NP$_2$ (see Kuroda 1965; Hellan 1983). This effect can be captured by a more structured principle referring to θ-positions, namely, (ii),

(ii) A long-distance anaphor α must be bound from the highest θ-position of a
    thematic complex containing α.

where *highest θ-position* is simply defined as the one that c-commands (perhaps asymmetrically; see note 12) all the other positions in the thematic complex. Now, NP$_1$ and NP$_2$ are θ-positions in (i). However, NP$_2$ does not qualify as a binder because it is not contained within its thematic complex (which only contains V$_2$ and its arguments). NP$_1$, on the the other hand, does qualify as a possible binder because it is the highest θ-position of the thematic complex of V$_1$, which contains α (α is contained in S$_2$, an argument of V$_1$). In (69a) the experiencer qualifies as a possible antecedent for the same reasons. Principle (ii) amounts to a minor reformulation of Giorgi's approach (see note 15) within a framework that bans direct reference to thematic hierarchies in formal grammar. *Prominence within a thematic complex* is now defined in purely structrual terms. The principle reflects thematic hierarchies only indirectly, inasmuch as structural prominence is determined by thematic prominence through the principles projecting θ-grids into D-Structure. As for the other important property of long-distsance anaphors, the parametric variation concerning the opacity-creating factor, our assumptions are compatible with an approach of the type proposed by Manzini and Wexler (1987).

19. We have left open the question why the theme but not the experiencer can be moved to subject position. For a Case-theoretic account, see Belletti and Rizzi 1988.

20. This partial thematic hierarchy is perhaps a consequence of intrinsic compositionality relations between θ-roles. A better understanding of the notional content of "experiencer," "theme," and so on, is likely to shed light on this point.

Apparent violations of the proposed hierarchy involve structures containing an experiencer in a VP-internal PP and a subject theme, as in (i):

(i) This is pleasant for Bill.

One possible analysis is that the theme actually starts in D-Structure from an AP-internal position lower than the experiencer PP. Alternatively, the hierarchy could be restricted to apply to coarguments, arguments directly or compositionally θ-marked by the same head; hence, it would not apply in cases like (i), where the experiencer is θ-marked by the preposition.

References

Baker, M., K. Johnson, and I. Roberts (1989). "Passive Arguments Raised." *Linguistic Inquiry* 20:219–251.

Brass, A. (1985). Synatx generals paper, MIT.

Belletti, A., and L. Rizzi (1981). "The Synatx of *ne*: Some Theoretical Implications," *The Linguistic Review* 1:117–154.

Belletti, A., and L. Rizzi (1986). "Psych-Verbs and Th-Theory," In *Lexicon Project Working Papers* 13. Center for Cognitive Science, MIT.

Belletti, A., and L. Rizzi (1988). "Psych-verbs and Theta-Theory," *Natural Language and Linguistic Theory* 6:291–352.

Besten, H. den (1982). "Some Remarks on the Ergative Hypothesis." Ms., University of Amsterdam.

Burzio, L. (1981). "Intransitive Verbs and Italian Auxiliaries." Doctoral dissertation, MIT.

Burzio, L. (1986). *Italian Syntax*. Reidel, Dordrecht.

Chomsky, N. (1981). *Lectures on Government and Binding*. Foris, Dordrecht.

Chomsky, N. (1986). *Knowledge of Language: Its Nature, Origins, and Use*, Praeger, New York.

Cinque, G. (1984). "Island Effects, Subjacency, ECP/Connectedness and Reconstruction." Ms., University of Venice.

Georgopoulos, C. (1987). "Psych Nouns." In *Proceedings of the Seventeenth Annual Meeting, NELS*, GLSA, University of Massachusetts, Amherst.

Giorgi, A. (1984). "Toward a Theory of Long Distance Anaphors. A GB Approach." *The Linguistic Review* 3:307–361.

Guéron, J. (1986). "Le verbe *avoir.*" Ms., Université de Paris VIII.

Hellan, L. (1983). "Anaphora in Norwegian and the Theory of Binding." In *Working Papers in Scandinavian Syntax.* Linguistics Department, University of Trondheim.

Higginbotham, J. (1983). "Logical Form, Binding, and Nominals." *Linguistic Inquiry* 14:395–420.

Hornstein, N. (1984). *Logic as Grammar.* MIT Press, Cambridge, Mass.

Jackendoff, R. (1972). *Semantic Interpretation in Generative Grammar.* MIT Press, Cambridge, Mass.

Jaeggli, O. (1986). "Arbitrary Plural Pronominals." *Natural Language and Linguistic Theory* 4:43–76.

Johnson, K. (1985). "Subjects and θ-theory." Ms., MIT.

Kayne, R. (1975). *French Syntax.* MIT Press, Cambridge, Mass.

Kayne, R. (1984). *Connectedness and Binary Branching.* Foris, Dordrecht.

Kiparsky, P. (1973). "Elsewhere in Phonology." In S. R. Anderson and P. Kiparsky, eds., *A Festschrift for Morris Halle.* Holt, Rinehart and Winston, New York.

Kuroda, S.-Y. (1965). Generative Grammatical Studies in the Japanese Language." Doctoral dissertation, MIT. (Published by Garland, New York, 1979.)

Langendoen, T., and E. Battistella (1982). "The Interpretation of Predicate Reflexive and Reciprocal Expressions in English." In *Proceedings of the Twelfth Annual Meeting, NELS.* GLSA, University of Massachusetts, Amherst.

Manzini, M. R., and K. Wexler (1987). "Parameters, Binding Theory, and Learnability." *Linguistic Inquiry* 18:413–444.

Marantz, A. (1984). *On the Nature of Grammatical Relations.* MIT Press, Cambridge, Mass.

Otero, C. (1985). "Arbitrary Subjects in Finite Clauses." Ms., UCLA.

Perlmutter, D., and P. Postal (1977). "Towards a Universal Characterization of Passivization." In *Proceedings of the Third Annual Meeting of the Berkeley Linguistics Society.* University of California, Berkeley.

Pesetsky, D. (1987). "Binding Problems with Experiencer Verbs." *Linguistic Inquiry* 18:126–140.

Postal, P. (1970). *Cross Over Phenomena.* Holt, Rinehart and Winston, New York.

Reinhart, T. (1976). "The Syntactic Domain of Anaphora." Doctoral dissertation, MIT.

Riemsdijk, H. van, and E. Williams (1981). "NP-Structure." *The Linguistic Review* 1:171–218.

Rizzi, L. (1986a). "On Chain Formation." In H. Borer, ed., *Syntax and Semantics 19: The Syntax of Pronominal Clitics*. Academic Press, New York.

Rizzi, L. (1986b). "Null Objects in Italian and the Theory of *pro*." *Linguistic Inquiry* 17: 501–557.

Roberts, I. (1985). "The Representation of Implicit and Dethematized Subjects." Doctoral dissertation, University of Southern California.

Ruwet, N. (1972). *Théorie syntaxique et syntaxe du français*, Editions du Seuil, Paris.

Stowell, T. (1986). "Psych-Movement in the Mapping between D-structure and LF." Abstract, GLOW newsletter, 1986.

Suñer, M. L. (1982). "Big PRO and Little *pro*." Ms., Cornell University.

Trigo, L. (1985). Syntax generals paper, MIT.

Zubizarreta, M. L. (1985). "The Relations between Morphophonology and Morphosyntax: The Case of Romance Causatives." *Linguistic Inquiry* 16: 247–289.

Chapter 7

The Interaction of Operators   Joseph Aoun and Yen-hui Audrey Li

1 Introduction

In the process of characterizing general grammatical principles, language variation plays a privileged role. Thus, the difference in the distribution of *wh*-elements in English, Italian (Rizzi 1982), and French (Sportiche 1981) revealed that the choice of bounding nodes relevant for the Subjacency Condition should be parameterized (see Rizzi 1982). Language similarity may also be relevant. The existence of similar facts in different languages usually offers insights into the proper characterization of general linguistic principles. For example, even though a putative linguistic principle may account for a set of facts in one language, it ought to be replaced by a more general one if it cannot simultaneously account for the same facts in other languages.

In this paper we illustrate the relevance of language variation and language similarity in the proper formulation of general linguistic principles. Specifically, our purpose will be to provide a principled account for the interaction of various operators.

As a starting point, we will study the interaction of QPs with other QPs, showing how this interaction is subject to language variation (see Aoun and Li 1989). For instance, Chinese active sentences, in contrast to English active sentences, are not ambiguous:

(1) a. Someone loves everyone.   (ambiguous)
   b. Liangge laoshi hui jiao   meige xuesheng.   (unambiguous)
      two   teacher will teach every student
      'Two teachers will teach every student.'

We wish to thank Wesley Hudson for his help.

Meige laoshi hui jiao liangge xuesheng.   (unambiguous)
every teacher will teach two   student
'Every teacher will teach two students.'

Next we will turn to the interaction of QPs with *wh*-operators. Whereas the interaction of QPs with other QPs is subject to language variation, the interaction of QPs with *wh*-operators is similar across languages. Consider, for instance, sentences like (2) and (3), originally discussed by May (1985):

(2) What did everyone buy?
(3) Who bought everything?

Sentence (2) is ambiguous; sentence (3) is not. May attributes the existence of such a contrast to the well-known subject-object asymmetry governing extraction in English. May's approach leads us to expect QPs and *wh*-elements to interact differently in languages that exhibit different types of asymmetries under extraction. This expectation, however, does not appear to be fulfilled. We will show that the contrast illustrated in English in (2) and (3) also exists in widely differing languages like Chinese, which displays no subject-object asymmetry.

Our task will then be to provide a unified account for the cross-linguistic similarities in the interaction of QPs and *wh*-operators and the cross-linguistic differences in the interaction of QPs and other QPs. We will argue that the main features of such a unified account will incorporate the following two principles: the Minimal Binding Requirement (MBR) and the Scope Principle.

(I) *Minimal Binding Requirement*
     A variable must be bound by the most local potential $\bar{\text{A}}$-binder.

(II) *Scope Principle*
      A quantifier A has scope over a quantifier B in case A c-commands a member of the chain containing B.

2 Interaction of QPs with QPs: Language Variation

It has been widely observed that the interaction of QPs with other QPs in Chinese is different from that in English (see S. F. Huang 1980; C.-T. J. Huang 1982; Lee 1986). For example, in contrast to the English sentence (4), which is ambiguous, the corresponding sentence (5) in Chinese is unambiguous:

(4) Someone loves everyone.   (ambiguous)

(5) a. Liangge laoshi[1] hui jiao   meige xuesheng.   (unambiguous)
       two   teacher will teach every student
       'Two teachers will teach every student.'
   b. Meige laoshi hui jiao   liangge xuesheng.   (unambiguous)
       every teacher will teach two   student
       'Every teacher will teach two students.'

This contrast has led to the postulation of an Isomorphic Principle, stated
in (6), and a restructuring process constrained by the phrase structure rules
of particular languages (see C.-T. J. Huang 1982). Simply put, the effect
of the Isomorphic Principle is manifested in Chinese but not in English.[2]

(6) *Isomorphic Principle*
    Suppose A and B are QPs. If A c-commands B at S-Structure, then
    A c-commands B at LF.[3]

    "C-command" is defined as in Reinhart 1976: A c-commands B if A
    and B do not dominate each other and the first branching node
    dominating A also dominates B.

According to the Isomorphic Principle, the c-command relation at S-
Structure is preserved at LF. Therefore, the subject QP that c-commands
the object QP at S-Structure must also c-command the object QP at LF.
By the Isomorphic Principle account, (5) is unambiguous because the
subject QP must have scope over the object QP.

    In contrast, English does not display an Isomorphic Principle effect (see
note 2). The c-command relation at S-Structure need not be preserved at
LF. Therefore, the English sentence (4) is ambiguous.

    This approach leads us to expect that a Chinese sentence containing two
QPs in an asymmetric c-command relation is always unambiguous. On the
other hand, it also leads us to expect that an English sentence can always
be ambiguous. However, such predictions are not borne out. We find
instances in Chinese where a sentence is ambiguous even though it contains
two QPs asymmetrically c-commanding each other. This situation arises
in passive sentences, as in (7):

(7) a. Liangge xiansuo hui bei meigeren zhaodao.   (ambiguous)
       two   clue   will by everyone find
       'Two clues will be found by everyone.'
   b. Meige xiansuo hui bei lianggeren zhaodao.   (ambiguous)
       every clue   will by two men   find
       'Every clue will be found by two men.'

Moreover, we find instances in English where the Isomorphic Principle
seems to have an effect. This is the case of double object structures [V NP$_1$

NP$_2$] given in (8):

(8) John assigned someone every problem.   (unambiguous)

In (8) *someone* asymmetrically c-commands *every problem*, as suggested in Barss and Lasnik 1986 (also see Larson 1988). If we take the Isomorphic Principle to apply in this instance, the unambiguity of (8) is captured.

In brief, contrary to what the Isomorphic Principle approach predicts, there are sentences in English that exhibit an Isomorphic Principle effect and there are sentences in Chinese that do not. We summarize these problems in (9):

(9) a. Active sentences are ambiguous in English but unambiguous in Chinese (see (4)–(5)).
   b. Passive sentences in Chinese, unlike active sentences, are ambiguous (see (6)).
   c. Double object structures [V NP$_1$ NP$_2$] in English are unambiguous (see (8)).

In order to account for the different behavior of QPs in Chinese and English, Aoun and Li (1989) assume that a maximal category can adjoin to any maximal projection that is a nonargument (Chomsky 1986). We further suggest that LF adjunction rules are constrained by the following Minimal Binding Requirement:

(I) *Minimal Binding Requirement*
   A variable must be bound by the most local potential $\bar{\text{A}}$-binder.

The MBR has the effect of ruling out representations (10a–b) and allowing representation (10c). In these representations the variables x_1 and x_2 are traces generated by raising QP$_1$ and QP$_2$, respectively, at LF:

(10) a. [IP QP$_1$[IP QP$_2$[IP x_1[VP ... x_2 ...]]]]
    b. [IP QP$_2$[IP QP$_1$[IP x_1[VP ... x_2 ...]]]]
    c. [IP QP$_1$[IP x_1[VP QP$_2$[VP ... x_2 ...]]]]

In (10a) QP$_2$ is the first available $\bar{\text{A}}$-binder for x_1 and x_2. According to the MBR, x_1 and x_2 must both be bound by QP$_2$. This is not the case, however, since x_1 is coindexed with QP$_1$ by movement. (10a) will therefore be ruled out by the MBR. Notice that (10a) cannot be salvaged by reindexing x_1 with QP$_2$. After this reindexing process, not only would both variables be bound by one QP but QP$_1$ will not bind any variable, thus violating the prohibition against vacuous quantification (May 1977) or, alternatively, the Bijection Principle (Koopman and Sportiche 1982). (10b) is ruled out in the same manner: QP$_1$ is the most local potential antecedent for both x_1 and x_2. In contrast, the traces in (10c) are properly bound. The most local potential antecedent for x_1 is QP$_1$; the most local potential antecedent for x_2 is QP_2. Both traces are bound by the most local potential antecedent, obeying the MBR.

Because of the MBR, the Chinese active sentence (5a) will have only one possible LF representation, shown in (11). Similarly, the English double object structure (8) will have only one possible LF representation, shown in (12):

(11) [$_{\text{IP}}$ liangge laoshi$_i$ [$_{\text{IP}}$ x_i [$_{\text{VP}}$ meige xuesheng$_j$ [$_{\text{VP}}$ hui jiao x_j]]]]
     two   teacher   every student   will teach
     'Two teachers will teach every student.'

(12) John [$_{\text{VP}}$ someone$_i$ [$_{\text{VP}}$ assigned [$_{\text{SC}}$ x_i [$_{\text{PRED}}$ every problem$_j$ [x_j]]]]]

These two sentences are therefore unambiguous.

In contrast, a Chinese passive sentence is ambiguous. An important distinction between an active sentence and a passive sentence lies in the existence or nonexistence of an NP-trace. A passive sentence like (7a), in contrast to an active sentence like (5a), will have the LF representation shown in (13):

(13) [$_{\text{IP}}$ liangge xiansuo$_i$ [$_{\text{IP}}$ x_i [$_{\text{VP}}$ meige   ren$_j$ [$_{\text{VP}}$ hui bei x_j zhaodao t_i]]]]
     two   due   everyone   will by   find
     'Two clues will be found by everyone.'

In order to determine the relative scope relations between QPs, the following Scope Principle is proposed in Aoun and Li 1989.

(II) *Scope Principle*
     A quantifier A has scope over a quantifier B in case
     A c-commands a member of the chain containing B.

The MBR and the Scope Principle provide a straightforward account for the contrast between the nonambiguity of Chinese active sentences like (5a) and the ambiguity of Chinese passive sentences like (7a). (5a) has the LF representation in (11); (7a) has the LF representation in (13). In (11) the subject QP adjoins to IP and the object QP adjoins to VP. The traces thereby meet the MBR. Other adjunction possibilities—adjunction of the object QP to IP, for example—will be ruled out by the MBR. Since the raised subject QP and its trace c-command the raised object QP and its trace, (11) yields only a reading where the subject QP has scope over the object QP, according to the Scope Principle. In (13) the passive subject QP adjoins to IP and the *by*-QP adjoins to VP, so the MBR is satisfied. This representation will yield two readings according to the Scope Principle: the subject QP c-commands and has scope over the *by*-QP; the *by*-QP also has scope over the subject QP because it c-commands t_i, a member of the chain containing the subject QP. Therefore, an active sentence in Chinese is unambiguous but a passive sentence in Chinese is ambiguous.

Turning to the contrast between an active Chinese sentence and its corresponding sentence in English, Aoun and Li assume with Koopman and Sportiche (1985), Kuroda (1988), and Zagona (1988) that an English sentence has the S-Structure representation given in (14). That is, subjects in English are generated in the Specifier (SPEC) position of VP and then raised to the SPEC position of INFL:

(14)

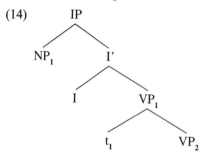

In the framework of Chomsky (1986), subject raising in (14) is made possible by a process of V-raising to INFL. This process allows VP_1 not to count as a barrier for subject raising. Aoun and Li claim that in Chinese the degenerate nature of INFL prevents V-raising from taking place. As a consequence, subject raising is not available in this language; that is, a Chinese sentence does not have an NP-trace like t_1 in (14). The representations for the Chinese sentences in (11) and (13) can be maintained.

Once the basic distinction between the constitutent structures of Chinese and English is recognized, the ambiguity of an English active sentence, in contrast to the nonambiguity of its corresponding Chinese sentence, is accounted for straightforwardly by the MBR and the Scope Principle. The English active sentence (4), repeated here, has the LF representation in (15), according to the MBR:

(4)   Someone loves everyone.

(15) $[_{IP}$ someone$_i$ $[_{IP}$ x_i $[_{VP_1}$ everyone$_j$ $[_{VP_2}$ t_i loves $x_j]]]]$

In (15) the variable in object position also satisfies the MBR. Even though the NP-trace t_i generated by subject raising intervenes between everyone$_j$ and x_j, it does not create a violation with respect to the MBR. An NP-trace is an A-anaphor that requires an A-binder rather than an Ā-binder. The raised everyone will not qualify as a potential antecedent. This representation is thus well formed with respect to the MBR. According to the Scope Principle, it yields two readings because someone is c-commanded by everyone and c-commands t_i, a member of the chain containing everyone.

Therefore, (4) is ambiguous, in contrast to the Chinese active sentence (5a), which is unambiguous.

The discussion in this section shows how the different behavior of QPs in Chinese and English can be uniformly accounted for by an analysis incorporating the MBR and the Scope Principle. We will see in the following sections that this analysis can also be used to account for the interaction of QPs with *wh*-operators.

3 Interaction of QPs with *Wh*: Language Similarity

The discussion of interactions between QPs and *wh* will show how language similarity can shed light on the proper formulation of linguistic analyses.

May (1985) points out that there is a subject-object asymmetry in English sentences like (16a–b):

(16) a. What did everyone buy?   (ambiguous)
     b. Who bought everything?   (unambiguous)

Depending on whether the QP is in subject or object position, the sentences can be ambiguous or unambiguous. When the QP is in subject position, the sentence is ambiguous. *Everyone* in (16a) can have either a distributive or a collective reading. In contrast, when the QP is in object position, the sentence is unambiguous. *Everyone* in (16b) can have only a collective reading. In terms of scope, when the QP is in subject position, it can have scope over the *wh*-word. When the QP is in object position, however, it cannot have scope over the *wh*-word (see May 1985, 1988, and Hoji 1986 for a detailed discussion of scope ambiguity in such cases).

Interestingly, the same contrast is found in Chinese and some other languages.[4]

(17) a. Meige ren dou maile   shenme?   (ambiguous)
        everyone all   bought what
        'What did everyone buy?'
     b. Shei maile   meige dongxi?   (unambiguous)
        who bought every thing
        'Who bought everything?'

May's (1985) treatment of the contrast between (16a) and (16b) in English cannot account for the same contrast in Chinese. Indeed, May's account is directly related to the subject-object asymmetry governing extraction in English, as in (18):

(18) a. *[Who wondered [what$_j$ [who saw x_j]]]?
     b. [Who wondered [who$_i$ [x_i saw what]]]?

Objects, but not subjects, can undergo long-distance extraction in English. Chinese, on the other hand, does not display any asymmetry with respect to extraction, as indicated by Huang (1982). Thus, both subjects and objects can undergo long-distance extraction:

(18) c.Ta xiang-zhidao shei mai sheme?
      he wondered   who buy what
      i. 'Who (x), he wondered what (y) x bought y?'
      ii. 'What (y), he wondered who (x) x bought y?'

May's account for the contrast between (16a) and (16b) would lead us to expect that Chinese does not have the same contrast as the one existing between (16a) and (16b) in English.

On the other hand, the analysis of QP scope discussed in section 2 offers an account for the identical contrast between (16a) and (16b) in English and between (17a) and (17b) in Chinese. Before we turn to this account, however, we must digress somewhat to clarify an important distinction with respect to the binding theory between variables bound by *wh*-words and variables bound by QPs. This discussion will also clarify the notion of "potential $\bar{\text{A}}$-binder" incorporated in the MBR.

4 Variable Types

Even though variables bound by QPs obey the MBR straightforwardly, variables bound by *wh*-words do not seem to obey this principle. The variable bound by *what* in the following example seems to violate the MBR:

(19) ?What$_j$ did you wonder who$_i$ x_i bought x_j?

In (19) the most local antecedent for both x_i and x_j is the *wh*-word in the embedded clause, *who*. However, (19) is generally taken as only somewhat unacceptable, because of a Subjacency violation. In other words, this sentence should not be ruled out by the MBR. How, then, is the MBR satisified in this case?

The answer to this question lies in recognizing an important distinction between variables bound by *wh*-words and variables bound by QPs with respect to the binding theory. Chomsky (1981) assumes that variables coindexed with *wh*-operators are name-like expressions that are subject to Principle C of the binding theory. By contrast, Aoun and Hornstein (1985) argue that variables coindexed with standard QPs (such as *everyone* or *someone*) are *not* subject to Principle C. This contrast suggests that the apparent violation of the MBR in (19) can be resolved by sharpening the notion of "potential $\bar{\text{A}}$-binder" encoded in the MBR. We assume that

(20) A qualifies as a potential $\bar{\text{A}}$-binder for B if and only if A
c-commands B, A is in an $\bar{\text{A}}$-position, and the assignment of the
index of A to B would not violate the Binding Principles.

The characterization of a potential $\bar{\text{A}}$-binder in (20) disqualifies *who* in the embedded COMP position of (19) as a potential $\bar{\text{A}}$-binder for the variable x_j in the object position: assignment of the index *who* to the object variable would entail that this object variable be coindexed with the variable x_i in subject position. Since the subject variable is in an A-position, such coindexing would create a violation of Principle C with respect to the object variable. Therefore, *what* in the matrix COMP position, but not *who* in the embedded COMP position, qualifies as the most local potential antecedent. Since no other potential antecedents intervene between *what* and the object variable, the object variable is bound by the most local potential antecedent, thus satisfying the MBR.

Summarizing, we have seen that variables bound by *wh*-operators and variables bound by QPs obey the MBR. The basic distinction between these two variable types is that variables bound by *wh*-operators are subject to Principle C, but variables bound by QPs are not. This distinction will dictate whether or not an $\bar{\text{A}}$-binder is a potential antecedent as defined in (20).

Having clarified the distinction between QP-variables and *wh*-variables with respect to Principle C and the notion of potentiality in the MBR, we proceed to extend our analysis of QPs to the cases involving QP/*wh* interaction.

5 Syntax of QP/*Wh* Scope

In this section we show that the contrast between the English sentences (16a–b) and the contrast between their counterparts in Chinese can be uniformly accounted for by the analysis outlined in the previous sections. We start with the ambiguous English sentence (16a) and its counterpart in Chinese (section 5.1). Then we turn to the unambiguous English sentence (16b) and its counterpart in Chinese (sections 5.2 and 5.3).

5.1 Interaction of *Wh* and Subject QPs
First consider the ambiguous English sentence (16a), repeated here:

(16) a. What did everyone buy?   (ambiguous)

At S-Structure, *what* is moved to SPEC of COMP and the subject NP is moved from the SPEC of VP position to the SPEC of I' position as a result of subject raising. At LF, quantifier raising (QR) applies, deriving the LF representation in (21):

(21)

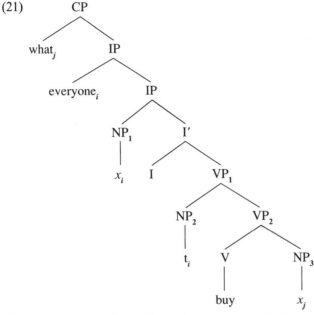

This representation is well formed according to the MBR. The raising QP *everyone* is the most local potential antecedent for x_i, meeting the MBR. The object variable generated by *wh*-raising must also be bound by its most local potential antecedent. The raised subject QP *everyone* does not qualify as a potential Ā-binder for this variable. Indeed, assignment of the index of *everyone* to the object variable would trigger a Principle C violation since this variable would end up being A-bound by t_i or x_i. In short, *everyone* does not qualify as a potential antecedent for this variable. No other potential antecendent intervenes between *what* and the variable in the object position. *What* counts as the most local potential antecedent. Thus, the MBR is satisified.

Note that (21) yields two readings according to the Scope Principle. *What* c-commands *everyone* and its trace, yielding the reading where *what* has scope over *everyone*. In turn, *everyone* and its trace c-command the trace of *what* in NP_3 position, yielding the reading where *everyone* has scope over *what*. Sentence (16a) is thus ambiguous.

The same account directly extends to the Chinese counterpart of (16a), the ambiguous (17a), repeated here:

(17) a. Meige ren dou maile   shenme?   (ambiguous)
        everyone all   bought what
        'What did everyone buy?'

This sentence has the LF representation given in (22). This representation is generated by the LF movement of the *wh*-word *shenme* to the SPEC of COMP and the LF movement of the subject QP to IP:

(22) $[_{CP}$ shenme$_j$ $[_{IP}$ meige ren$_i$ $[_{IP}$ x_i $[_{VP}$ maile $x_j]]]]$

The MBR is satisfied in (22) as in (21). 'Everyone' is the most local potential antecedent for the subject variable x_i. The object variable generated by *wh*-raising is properly bound by its most local potential antecedent 'what'. This well-formed representation yields two readings since 'what' c-commands 'everyone' and 'everyone' c-commands x_j, a member of the chain containing 'what'. Sentence (17a) is therefore ambiguous.

As we have shown, then, the analysis of QP scope outlined in section 2 offers a unified account for the interaction of QP/*wh* operators in the ambiguous English sentence (16a) and its counterpart in Chinese. The MBR constrains the well-formed representations. The Scope Principle, which crucially makes use of the chain containing the operators and their variables, derives the scope relations.

Next we show how the same analysis accounts for the nonambiguity of the English sentence (16b) and its counterpart in Chinese. Since the account for Chinese is more straightforward, we discuss that case first.

5.2   Interaction of *Wh* and Object QPs
The Chinese counterpart of the unambiguous English sentence (16b) is (17b), repeated here:

(17) b. Shei maile   meige dongxi?   (unambiguous)
         who bought every thing
         'Who bought everything?'

Our analysis incorporating the MBR and the Scope Principle, coupled with the claim that variables bound by *wh*-operators but not variables bound by QPs are subject to Principle C, accounts for the nonambiguity of this sentence. At LF 'who' is moved to the SPEC of COMP and the QP 'everything' undergoes QR. VP and IP are both possible adjunction sites for QR, as shown in (23a–b):

(23) a. $[_{CP}$ shei$_i$ $[_{IP}$ x_i $[_{VP_1}$ meige dongxi$_j$ $[_{VP_2}$ maile $x_j]]]]$
     b. $[_{CP}$ shei$_i$ $[_{IP}$ meige dongxi$_j$ $[_{IP}$ x_i $[_{VP}$ maile $x_j]]]]$

Only (23a), however, is well formed with respect to the MBR. In (23a) both x_i and x_j are bound by the most local potential $\bar{A}$-binder, thus obeying the MBR. In contrast, (23b) is ruled out by the MBR: the most local potential antecedent for both x_i and x_j is 'everything'. Thus, (23a) is the only well-formed LF representation for (17b). This representation yields only one interpretation where 'who' has scope over 'everything' because both the *wh*-operator and the variable bound by the *wh*-operator c-command the QP and the variable bound by the QP. Therefore, (17b) is ambiguous.

In brief, the nonambiguity of the Chinese sentence (17b) follows straightforwardly from the MBR and the Scope Principle. We show in next section that the nonambiguity of the English sentence (16b) can be accounted for by the same analysis provided that we clarify the nature of the chain entering into scope relations.

5.3 NP-Traces and Scope Assignment
As mentioned earlier, the English sentence (16b) is unambiguous:

(16) b. Who bought everything?

This sentence has the S-Structure representation in (24) (see section 3):

(24)

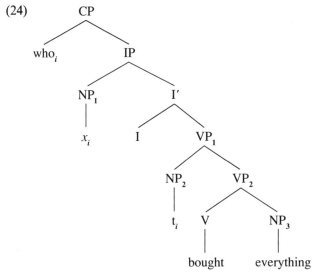

In (24) the object QP *everything* can adjoin to VP_2 or VP_1:

(25) a. $[_{CP}$ who$_i$ $[_{IP}$ x_i $[_{VP_1}$ t$_i$ $[_{VP_2}$ everything$_j$ $[_{VP_2}$ bought $x_j]]]]]$
      b. $[_{CP}$ who$_i$ $[_{IP}$ x_i $[_{VP_1}$ everything$_j$ $[_{VP_1}$ t$_i$ $[_{VP_2}$ bought $x_j]]]]]$

Representation (25a) yields one reading: *who* has scope over *everything* because the chain (*who$_i$, x_i, t$_i$*) c-commands both *everything* and its trace x_j. Representation (25b) should yield two readings: *who* c-commands and has scope over *everything* and *everything* c-commands *t*, a member of the chain containing *who*. According to the Scope Principle, *everything* must also have scope over *who*. However, this is not the case: (24) is unambiguous. It has the reading where *who* has wide scope but not the reading where *everything* has wide scope. Note that this impossible reading is derived because *everything* c-commands *t*, the NP-trace coindexed with *who*. This seems to indicate that the NP-trace *t* in (24) should not play a role in determining scope relations. This conclusion conflicts with the one reached in section 3, where we indicated that NP-traces play a role in determining scope relations between QPs in sentences like (26):

(26)

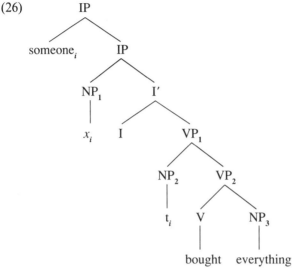

In (26) *everything* crucially can have scope over *someone*. We accounted for this interpretation by adjoining *everything* to VP$_1$. *Everything* would then c-command the NP-trace coindexed with the subject QP *someone*. This means that the NP-trace in NP$_2$ position must interact with the object QP *everything*.

In brief, then, it seems that an NP-trace plays a role in the determination of scope relations between two QPs but not between a QP and a *wh*-word.

(27) In the representation [wh$_i$ ... x$_i$ ... t$_i$]

where x_i is a variable coindexed with *wh$_i$* and t_i is an NP-trace coindexed with x_i,

t_i does not constitute a member of the chain relevant to the determination of scope;

whereas in the representation [QP$_i$ ... x$_i$ ... t$_i$]

where x_i is a variable coindexed with *QP$_i$* and t_i is an NP-trace coindexed with x_i,

t_i constitutes a member of the chain relevant to the determination of scope.

A detailed account for the generalization in (27) is given in Aoun and Li, forthcoming.[5] The generalization in (27) is necessary not only to account for the contrast between (25) and (26) but also to account for a wider range of examples in English. Consider the following raising constructions in English:

(28) a. Someone seems to [t love everyone].   (ambiguous)
     b. Who seems to [t love everyone]?   (unambiguous)

In (28a–b) there is an NP-trace generated by subject-to-subject raising. (28a) is ambiguous but (28b) is unambiguous. This contrast can only be captured by assuming that NP-traces play a role in the determination of relative scope relations for QPs but not for *wh*-elements. Consider first (28a). After the subject QP *someone* is raised by QR as in (29a), *everyone* can have scope over *someone* by adjoining to VP_3 or IP_3 of the embedded clause. In either case, *everyone* c-commands the NP-trace t_i, which is a member of the chain containing *someone* and thus may have scope over *someone*. Notice that the wide scope reading of *everyone* can be obtained only if the NP-trace in NP_3 or NP_4 position enters into scope relations.

(29) a.

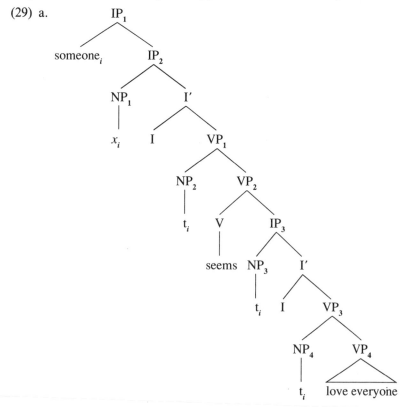

Next consider (28b). This sentence basically has the same structure as (28a):

(29) b.

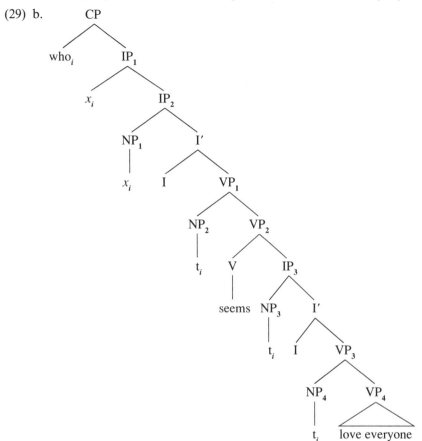

Once again, *everyone* can have scope over *who* by adjoining to VP$_3$ or IP$_3$ of the embedded clause. However, the wide scope reading of *everyone* must be barred. The nonambiguity of this sentence supports the claim that NP-traces do not play a role in the determination of the relative scope of *wh*-elements.

In brief, the contrast between the ambiguity of (28a) and nonambiguity of (28b) can be captured only if an NP-trace coindexed with a QP enters into scope relations but an NP-trace coindexed with a *wh*-operator does not.

The same discrepancy between the role of NP-traces for QPs and their role for *wh*-elements reappears in passive constructions, which contain an NP-trace in object position:

(30) a. Someone is loved by everyone t.   (ambiguous)

b. Who is loved by everyone t?   (unambiguous)

Here too, the NP-trace plays a role in the determination of the scope relations between QPs but not between a QP and a *wh*-operator, since *who* cannot have narrow scope with respect to *everyone* in (30b).

This discrepancy between the role of an NP-trace coindexed with a *wh*-word and the role of an NP-trace coindexed with a QP noted for English also exists in Chinese, as the following passive sentences illustrate:

(31) a. Liangge xiansuo hui bei meige ren zhaodao t.   (ambiguous)

two   clues   will by every man find

'Two clues will be found everyone.'

b. Naxie xiansuo hui bei meige ren zhaodao t?   (unambiguous)

which clue   will by every man find

'Which clues will be found by everyone?'

Again, the contrast between the ambiguity of (31a) and the nonambiguity of (31b) can be captured by the different roles an NP-trace plays in determining scope relations. The generalization in (27) captures this recurrent contrast.

Recapitulating, our analysis based on the MBR and the Scope Principle uniformly accounts for the scope relations between *wh*-operators and QP operators in English and Chinese.

6 Conclusion

Our purpose in this paper has been to account for the interaction of operators in Chinese and English. The discussion has led to interesting results. We have shown that at least operators and variables play a role in the determination of scope relations. The relevance of both operators and variables in determining scope relations may be illustrated by (16a), *What did everyone buy?*, with its LF representation in (32):

(32) $[_{CP}$ what$_j$ $[_{IP}$ did everyone$_i$ $[_{IP}$ x_i buy $x_j]]]$

Sentence (16a) is ambiguous. The reading where *what* has scope over *everyone* can only be accounted for if operators play a role in determining scope relations: *what*, but not its variable, c-commands the QP *everyone* and thus may have scope over this QP. Furthermore, the reading where *everyone* has scope over *what* can only be accounted for if variables play a role in determining scope relations. *Everyone* c-commands the variable bound by *what*, but not the operator *what*, and thus may have scope over *what*.

In order to establish the main features of our analysis, we have contrasted the behavior of operators in English and Chinese. This contrastive study revealed that the interaction between QPs in Chinese differs from their interaction in English. On the other hand, the interaction of QPs with *wh*-elements is identical in Chinese and English. The challenge was to devise an analysis that provides a unified account for these differences and similarities. We hope to have provided the foundations for such an analysis in terms of the MBR and the Scope Principle.

Notes

1. Chinese does not have an expression like *someone*. The expressions that are closest to *someone* are bare NPs or *mogeren* 'a certain person' or *you (yi) ge ren* 'there is a person'. In fact, Chinese generally does not allow an indefinite NP in subject position unless a modal occurs in the sentence, the subject is preceded by *you* 'have, exist', or the indefinite NP occurs in a conditional (see Lee 1986 and Hudson 1986 for accounts of such phenomena):

(i) a. *Sange ren lai   le.
       three men come ASP
       'Three men came.'
    b. Sange ren hui lai.
       three men will come
    c. *You* sange ren lai   le.
       have three men come ASP
       'There existed three men that came.'
    d. Yaoshi sange ren lai   le ...
       if   three men come ASP
       'If three men came, ...'

2. Huang accounts for the difference in the behavior of QPs in Chinese and English by postulating an Isomorphic Principle in Universal Grammar and a restructuring process constrained by the phrase structure rule of individual languages. As shown in Aoun and Li 1989, the restructuring process seems to play a role only in sentences where the Isomorphic Principle is relevant but not in sentences where other grammatical principles (such as the binding principles) are involved. Therefore, for the purpose of this discussion, we will simply state that Chinese displays an Isomorphic Principle effect but English does not.

Even though we will simplify the discussion in this way, we should point out that Huang's analysis of QP interaction and our analysis share the same spirit: in both accounts, the variation in the interpretation of QPs in English and Chinese is traced back to a difference in the constituent structures of the two languages.

3. For concreteness, we assume the definition of *c-command* in Reinhart 1976 (strict c-command). The definition of *c-command* given in Aoun and Sportiche 1983 (m-command) could have been chosen as well.

A similar characterization of the scope interaction is assumed in Williams 1988.

4. This contrast is also found in Spanish, for example. Aoun and Li (forthcoming) discuss in detail how the analysis proposed here accounts for the Spanish facts.

5. Aoun and Li (forthcoming) eliminate the discrepancy between the role NP-traces play in chains headed by quantifiers and the role they play in chains headed by *wh*-operators. They devise a system where only elements in $\bar{\text{A}}$-position—that is, the operator and its intermediate trace(s) that occur in $\bar{\text{A}}$-position—play a role in the determination of relative scope. As evidence for this, they discuss contrasts like the one in (ia–b):

(i) a. $[_{CP_1}$ what$_i$ $[_{IP_1}$ you $[_{VP_1}$ t$_{1_i}$ $[_{VP_1}$ think $[_{CP_2}$ t$_{2_i}$ $[_{IP_2}$ everyone $[_{VP_2}$ t$_{3_i}$ $[_{VP_2}$ bought $x_i]]]]]]]]$

   b.   ?$[_{CP_1}$ what$_i$ $[_{IP_1}$ you $[_{VP_1}$ t$_{1_i}$ $[_{VP_1}$ wonder $[_{CP_2}$ whether $[_{IP_2}$ everyone $[_{VP_2}$ bought $x_i]]]]]]]$

The distribution of the intermediate traces in (ia–b) is determined by the Empty Category Principle (ECP). In (ib) no intermediate trace can be left within the embedded clause. Otherwise, the ECP would be violated: this intermediate trace would not be properly governed (see Chomsky 1986).

Unlike (ia), (ib) is unambiguous. (ia) and (ib) should both be ambiguous if variables are relevant to the determination of relative scope: *everyone* c-commands the variable x_i left by the *wh*-element. Assuming, on the other hand, that only $\bar{\text{A}}$-elements determine relative scope, the contrast between (ia–b) may be accounted for. In (ia) *everyone* c-commands the intermediate trace t_{3_i} left by *what* and *what* c-commands *everyone*. Thus, (ia) is ambiguous. On the other hand, in (ib) *everyone* does not c-command an intermediate trace left by the extraction of the *wh*-element: only the *wh*-element has scope over *everyone*.

References

Aoun, J., and N. Hornstein (1985). "Quantifier Types." *Linguistic Inquiry* 16:623–636.

Aoun, J., and Y.-H. A. Li (1989). "Scope and Constituency." *Linguistic Inquiry* 20:141–172.

Aoun, J., and Y.-H. A. Li (forthcoming). *Syntax of QP Scope*. MIT Press, Cambridge, Mass.

Aoun, J., and D. Sportiche (1983). "On the Formal Theory of Government." *The Linguistic Review* 2:211–236.

Barss, A., and H. Lasnik (1986). "A Note on Anaphora and Double Objects." *Linguistic Inquiry* 17:347–354.

Chomsky, N. (1981). *Lectures on Government and Binding*. Foris, Dordrecht.

Chomsky, N. (1986). *Barriers*. MIT Press, Cambridge, Mass.

Hoji, H. (1986). "Scope Interpretation in Japanese and Its Theoretical Implications." In *Proceedings of the Fifth West Coast Conference on Formal Linguistics*. Stanford Linguistics Association, Stanford University.

Huang, C.-T. J. (1982). "Logical Relations in Chinese and the Theory of Grammar." Doctoral dissertation, MIT.

Huang, S. F. (1980). "On the Scope Phenomena of Chinese Quantifiers." *Journal of Chinese Linguistics* 226–243.

Hudson, W. (1986). "Predication and Licensing of Indefiniteness." Ms., University of Southern California.

Koopman, H., and D. Sportiche (1982). "Variables and the Bijection Principle." *The Linguistic Review* 2:139–160.

Koopman, H., and D. Sportiche (1985). "Theta-theory and Extraction." *GLOW Newsletter.*

Kuroda, S.-Y. (1988). "Whether We Agree or Not: Rough Ideas about the Comparative Syntax of English and Japanese." *Lingvisticae Investigationes* 21:1–46.

Larson, R. (1988). "On the Double Object Construction." *Linguistic Inquiry* 19:335–391.

Lee, T. (1986). "Studies on Quantification in Chinese." Doctoral dissertation, UCLA.

May, R. (1977). "The Grammar of Quantification." Doctoral dissertation, MIT.

May, R. (1985). *Logical Form: Its Structure and Derivation.* MIT Press, Cambridge, Mass.

May, R. (1988). "Ambiguities of Quantification and *Wh*: A Reply to Williams." *Linguistic Inquiry* 19:118–135.

Reinhart, T. (1976). "The Syntactic Domain of Anaphora." Doctoral dissertation, MIT.

Rizzi, L. (1982). *Issues in Italian Syntax.* Foris, Dordrecht.

Sportiche, D. (1981). "Bounding Nodes in French." *The Linguistic Review* 1:219–246.

Williams, E. (1988). "Is LF Distinct from S-Structure? A Reply to May." *Linguistic Inquiry* 19:135–146.

Zagona, K. (1988). *Verb Phrase Syntax.* Kluwer, Dordrecht.

Chapter 8
Small Clause Restructuring   Tim Stowell

1 Adjectival Small Clauses

1.1 A Small Clause Typology
Adjectival small clauses come in at least three grammatical varieties:

(1) a. I consider John foolish.
    b. This will make John angry.

(2) a. John is considered foolish.
    b. John seems foolish.

(3) a. John left the party angry.
    b. Bill ate the meat raw.

(1) is a small clause analogue of exceptional Case marking (ECM): the NP *John* is θ-marked by the adjectival predicate but is assigned Case by the matrix verb. (2) is a small clause version of raising: the matrix subject is θ-marked by the adjectival predicate, and not by the matrix verb. (3) is a small clause counterpart to an infinitival adjunct clause with a PRO subject controlled by the matrix subject or object. In these examples, small clauses mirror the properties of infinitival complements, a situation that syntactic theory must account for.

But there are no small clause analogues to subcategorized control complements; the structures in (4) are ungrammatical.

(4) a. *John tried happy.   "John tried to be happy"
    b. *Fred told Bill quiet.   "Fred told Bill to be quiet"

Evidently small clauses do *not* mirror the syntactic properties of infinitives in at least one respect, and this is a fact that must be explained too. (Some further small clause/infinitive asymmetries are discussed below.)

1.2   Two Structures

There has been much debate in the literature about the structure of small clauses, as in the case of infinitives. In previous work (Stowell 1980, 1983) I have suggested that small clauses like (1a) have the structure in (5):

(5)

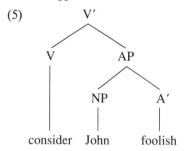

The small clause structure in (5) is a close analogue of the infinitival ECM structure in (6):

(6)

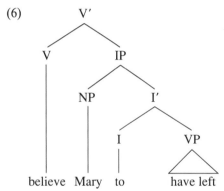

(5) treats the structural relationship between the subject and predicate of a small clause as being identical to that holding between the subject and predicate of the infinitive, which is analyzed as IP in (6), following Chomsky (1986a).[1] In each case, the clause is a maximal projection XP, containing a subject NP in its SPEC position and a predicate phrase X'. This structural parallel can be attributed to the interaction of X-bar theory and θ-theory if domains of predication are defined as in (7):

(7) A domain of predication is an XP, such that the X' category directly dominated by XP is predicated of the SPEC of XP.

If every predicate phrase must be predicated of a subject, as suggested by Rothstein (1983), then (7) forces the structure in (5), where the small clause is an AP containing a subject NP and a predicate phrase A'.[2] I will refer to (7) as the *clausal theory* of predication.

Williams (1983) argues against (5) and in favor of (8), giving a "non-abstract" analysis of constructions like (1a):

(8)

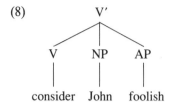

consider   John   foolish

Williams's analysis holds that "small clauses" are not true structural clauses; instead, the subject NP is really a structural object NP, and the adjectival predicate is an independent AP complement of V. In X-bar terms, this means that a predicational "subject" need not appear in a SPEC position; in (8) it occurs as a direct object. Thus, Williams maintains that there is no uniform X-bar structure assigned to the subject-predicate relation. Rather, this relation arises from a rule of predication, whose major structural conditions are those in (9):

(9) a. The subject must be an NP.
    b. The predicate must be a maximal projection XP.
    c. The subject must c-command the predicate.

In (6) the predicate satisfying (9b) is VP; in (8) it is AP.

   The conflicting assumptions of these two theories of predication give rise to another dispute, over the structure of examples like (2b). The clausal theory of predication implies that (2b) involves raising from the subject of a small clause, as in (10a), since A' may not be directly predicated of the matrix subject. On the other hand, Williams's theory of predication (9) does not need to posit raising, since the AP can be directly predicated of the c-commanding matrix subject NP:

(10) a.   b.

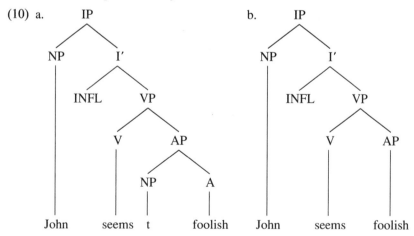

If D-Structure is a pure representation of θ-structure, as in Chomsky 1981

(*LGB*), then small clauses should be true constituents at D-Structure, as in (5) and (10a), since the matrix verb is dyadic, taking an external human argument and an internal clausal complement. This conclusion is unavoidable, unless we change central assumptions about the nature of D-Structure or the semantics of small clause complements.[3]

Williams's theory rejects the assumption that D-Structure is a pure reflection of internal argument structure in the sense defined by the Projection Principle. First, it allows verbs to select complement NPs that they do not θ-mark, as in (8); this leaves no obvious way to block subject-to-object raising in the case of infinitives. Second, it allows a predicate such as AP to assign θ-roles at a distance, to NPs that are not directly combining with it.

1.3   Small Clause Restructuring

Although I have argued elsewhere that the structure in (5) is correct in its essentials, I now believe that when a small clause appears as the complement of a verb, it undergoes restructuring in the derivation of its LF representation. The output of restructuring is the configuration in (11), where the head of the small clause has been adjoined to the governing matrix verb:

(11)

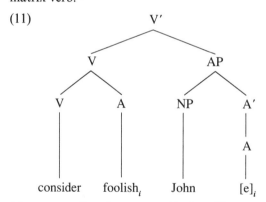

More generally, the proposal is that (5) correctly portrays the (universal) D-Structure representation of small clauses and that (11) correctly portrays their (universal) LF representation.

Although I have referred to the operation mapping from (5) to (11) as *restructuring*, it is possible that it is a subcase of Move α. Specifically, (11) is derivable from (5) by means of head-to-head adjunction, that is, as a process of incorporation in the sense proposed by Baker (1988). The pros and cons of this formal interpretation of the restructuring operation are discussed in sections 3 and 4 below.

The structure in (11) partly resembles the D-Structure representation assigned to small clauses by Chomsky (1975) (*LSLT*). According to *LSLT*, the verb first combines with the adjectival predicate to form a complex predicate taking an NP direct object; the adjectival predicate is then moved to the right of the object by a transformational rule. My current proposal is a kind of mirror image of the *LSLT* account, assuming that the complex predicate is formed at LF rather than at D-Structure.

Rizzi (1986) has proposed that a small clause reanalysis rule applies within the grammar of Italian in the mapping from D-Structure to S-Structure. (See section 3.1 below.) My LF restructuring rule is both an extension and an elaboration of Rizzi's basic idea. Suppose that the D-Structure representation (5) and the LF representation (11) are both universal; then restructuring must always apply somewhere in the mapping from D-Structure to LF. But this does not determine whether it applies between D-Structure and S-Structure or between S-Structure and LF. If grammars may vary on this point, then restructuring "in the syntax" versus restructuring "at LF" would resemble Huang's (1982) parameter involving *wh*-movement in questions.

1.4 Outline

The rest of the paper is structured as follows. In section 2 I provide evidence for the claim that (5) represents the D-Structure form of small clauses, as well as their S-Structure form in languages like English. In section 3 I review Rizzi's evidence for small clause restructuring in Italian and discuss the relative merits of treating restructuring as an instance of Move α. I then provide evidence that small clause restructuring applies at LF in English. In section 4 I address theoretical consequences of the analysis and provide a set of principles to force restructuring.

2 Support for Small Clauses

2.1 How Small Clause Subjects Resemble Objects

Before turning to the evidence supporting the existence of small clauses, I will review some of the traditional reasons for assuming a structure like (8). These mostly involve observations that small clause subjects behave like direct objects in many respects. Like objects, they (i) are assigned accusative Case, (ii) can be reflexive pronouns, (iii) can undergo NP-movement in passive constructions, and (iv) may not be occupied by control PRO.

But within the framework of Government-Binding (GB) Theory, these similarities are not reliable tests for objecthood; they simply show that the subject of a small clause complement is governed by the matrix verb. Thus, *government* rather than *objecthood* is taken to be the only significant similarity between small clause subjects and true direct objects. V assigns accusative Case to an adjacent NP provided that no barrier intervenes between them; thus, the accusative Case on the small clause subject simply shows that the small clause is transparent to government by V (more on this shortly).

The reflexive and passive data are explained in a similar way, since reflexive pronouns and NP-traces are both subject to Condition A of the *LGB* binding theory, which is also sensitive to government. Condition A requires that an anaphor be bound in its governing category (the minimal XP containing the anaphor, its governor, and an accessible subject). Hence, the subject of a small clause may be an anaphor (such as a reflexive pronoun or NP-trace), provided that it is bound within the clause containing its governor (the matrix verb).

Finally, the fact that the subject of a small clause may not be control PRO follows from the fact that PRO may only appear in an *ungoverned* position. (In *LGB* this follows from the assumption that PRO is a pronominal anaphor.) Thus, within the framework of assumptions of GB Theory, these object-like properties of small clause subjects are not reliable diagnostics for true objecthood; instead, they are diagnostics for government. So long as it is agreed that the matrix verb governs the NP in question, the choice between the two theories of small clause constructions must be made on the basis of other criteria.

2.2   Constituency Tests

2.2.1   English   According to the clausal theory of predication, the subject and predicate of a small clause form a structural constituent. But the location of a null category is difficult to establish conclusively—especially when its existence is in dispute, as in (2). Therefore, constituency tests can be applied with definitive results only when the subject of the small clause is overt, as in (1).

One syntactic environment that provides an apparently reliable positive test for constituency is the preverbal subject position, and small clauses with overt subjects usually do not occur there. But this is predictable from current assumptions about Case and government. Since a small clause lacks an internal Case assigner for its subject, that subject may be overt only when it is governed by some external Case-assigning head. Chomsky (1986a) posits that XP is transparent to government only if it is *L-marked*, where L-marking corresponds to θ-*government*. (X θ-governs Y if and only if X governs Y and X θ-marks Y.) An XP occurring in the subject position of IP is not L-marked, since it is not θ-marked by the category that governs it (INFL). Therefore, a subject XP is a barrier to government by any potential external Case-assigning category. So small clauses with overt subjects should never occur in a subject position, as (12) seems to confirm:[4]

(12) *[Workers angry about their pay] proves that the ad campaign has failed.

But Safir (1983) shows that small clauses with overt subjects can occur in the subject position of IP, provided that the matrix verb is *be*:

(13) [Workers angry about their pay] is precisely the situation that the ad campaign was supposed to avoid.

Presumably the subject of the small clause in (13) is Case-marked by some external governor, and the likeliest candiate is the verb *be*. We can explain this by assuming that *be* is used in (13) as a dyadic predicate, asserting an identity relation between its two arguments.[5] This implies that *be* θ-marks its subject (unlike other auxiliary verbs in INFL). If INFL governs the subject of IP, then *be* also L-marks its subject, accounting for the contrast between (13) and (12). Regardless of how (13) is licensed by Case theory, the basic point is that if small clauses are possible constituents here, then some ad hoc principle would be required to block their occurrence as constituents in (1)–(3).

2.2.2 Irish A similar conclusion follows from Chung and McCloskey's (1987) study of small clauses in Irish, where Case assignment in nonfinite clauses seems to work according to a different set of principles than in English. Overt lexical NPs are free to occur as the subjects of infinitives and small clauses in Irish, even in non-ECM contexts, and Chung and McCloskey suggest that this is due to a general rule assigning accusative Case to the subject of a nonfinite clause.

This makes it possible to apply a battery of positive constituency tests to small clauses with overt NP subjects, and they all support the basic architecture of the structure in (5). For instance, small clauses may be pseudoclefted or focused, as is characteristic only of constituents:

(14) a. Séard a   chonaic mé ná tusa ar meisce.
        what COMP see(PAST) I PTC you drunk
        'What I saw was you drunk.'

    b. agus gan ach sinn i dtosach   ár ngreise
       and NEG but us in beginning our attack(GEN)
       'and us only beginning our attack' (lit.)

If small clauses are possible in Irish, then they should be able to occur in other languages, including English, provided that the effects of Case theory are controlled for.

2.3 Interpolation of Main Clause Constituents

Although many constituents of VP (adverbs, PPs, control infinitives, and so on) are freely ordered with respect to each other, an object NP must be string-adjacent to the verb that Case-marks it (see Chomsky 1980, 1981; Stowell 1981). The subject of a small clause behaves just like an object in this respect:

(15) a. *John lost carelessly his book.
      b. *John considers seriously [Bill foolish].

The shared adjacency effect in (15) is not a diagnostic for objecthood, since it follows from the adjacency condition on Case assignment: NP must be adjacent to the governing verb in order to be Case-marked.

    Now whereas manner adverbials may not separate a verb from an NP that it must Case-mark, they are otherwise free to intervene between a verb and its complements. The matrix verb assigns the θ-role *manner* to the adverbial, yielding a main clause construal:

(16) a. John ran carelessly [through the park].
      b. John$_i$ promised repeatedly [PRO$_i$ to leave].

But if a manner adverbial occurs within a subconstituent of VP, it is interpreted as modifying that subconstituent, and not the full VP; if this construal is impossible, the result is ungrammatical:[6]

(17) a. John believed [Mary repeatedly to have left].
        (she left repeatedly)
      b. *John believed [Mary sincerely to have left].

Thus, the main clause construal serves as a diagnostic for main clause constituency. If Williams's structure is correct, a matrix adverb should be able to intervene between a small clause predicate and the preceding "object" NP, yielding a main clause construal; if the small clause theory is correct, this should be impossible. In fact, this option is disallowed:

(18) a. John sincerely considers Bill foolish.
        (John's opinion is sincere)

b. John considers Bill sincerely foolish.
   (Bill's foolishness is sincere)
c. John found Bill repeatedly annoying.
   (Bill is repeatedly annoying)

This supports the small clause structure in (5).

2.4   Binding Evidence

If the subject of a small clause is a true subject, it ought to induce opacity effects for the binding of anaphors and pronouns. This is correct, as noted in Stowell 1980. An anaphor in a small clause predicate must be bound within the small clause, by the subject:[7]

(19) a. Mary considers Bill$_i$ kind to himself$_i$.
     b. Mary made Bill$_i$ angry at himself$_i$.
     c. *Mary$_i$ considers Bill kind to herself$_i$.
     d. *Mary$_i$ made Bill angry at herself$_i$.

The same is true of adjunct emphatic anaphors; if an emphatic reflexive occurs within an ECM infinitive or small clause, it must be A-bound by that subject:[8]

(20) a. John$_i$ told Mary himself$_i$ to leave.
     b. *John$_i$ believes [Mary himself$_i$ to be foolish].
     c. *John$_i$ considers [Mary himself$_i$ foolish].
     d. John$_i$ considers [Mary (to be) foolish] himself$_i$.

A pronoun in a small clause predicate need only be A-free within the small clause; it may be bound by the subject of the matrix clause:

(21) a. Mary$_i$ considers Bill too kind to her$_i$.
     b. *Mary considers Bill$_i$ too kind to him$_i$.

These facts suggest that small clauses count as governing categories for anaphors and pronouns occurring within their predicates. This follows if a small clause is an XP containing a subject, since according to the *LGB* definition, a governing category must be an XP containing a subject. Within the framework of Chomsky's (1986b) binding theory, the inclusion of the subject within the small clause XP makes that XP a complete functional complex (CFC), yielding an equivalent result.

Williams's structure in (8) can accommodate these data only if the binding theory can derive the opacity effect without having to refer to a notion of *subject* defined in terms of a particular S-Structure position. Bresnan (1982) and Williams (chapter 4 of this volume) respond to this by reformulating the binding theory in terms of conditions on abstract hierarchical representations of thematic argument structure.

Actually, Williams's theory could accommodate (19–21) with a less radical departure from a syntactically based binding theory if opacity were defined in terms of *predication domains*. In essence, this would require that the governing category for α be defined as the minimal predication domain containing the element governing α, where a predication domain is defined as the minimal phrase containing a predicate phrase P and an NP that P is predicated of. (This corresponds roughly to Chomsky's (1986b) notion of a (CFC) The question arises whether only maximal projections should be eligible to count as governing categories (and/or predication domains). This depends on whether the subject of a sentence originates inside or outside VP. If it originates outside VP (the traditional view), then governing categories can be restricted to XPs. But if the subject of IP always originates within VP, as is now widely assumed,[9] then V′ would have to be permitted to count as a governing category for the anaphors and pronouns in (19)–(21).

Summarizing, the binding evidence weakly supports (5) over (8), since no special assumptions about the binding theory are needed to sustain (5). It also provides weak indirect support for (5) as the D-Structure representation for small clauses, since no known rule-type could create an S-Structure representation like (5) from a D-Structure representation like (8).

2.5 Subject Condition Effects

Kayne (1984) points out that the subject of a small clause behaves like a normal subject with respect to *Subject Condition* effects in the sense proposed by Chomsky (1973):

(22) a. *Who_i would [[for John to visit t_i] bother you]?
    b. Who_i would it bother you [for John to visit t_i]?
    c. *Who_i would [[John's having visited t_i] bother you]?
    d. Who_i were you annoyed at [John's having visited t_i]?
    e. *Who_i do you believe [[the oldest sister of t_i] to have left]?
    f. Who_i did you tell [the oldest sister of t_i]$_j$ [PRO_j to leave]?

(23) a. ?*Who_i do you consider [[the oldest sister of t_i] foolish]?
    b.   ?*Which $book_i$ did you find [[the author of t_i] very eloquent]?
    c.   ?*Who_i do you judge [[John's having visited t_i] very unwise]?

Although there is some variability in the judgments in (23), it seems safe to assume that the effect is significant. But the import of these data for the small clause controversy depends on the precise formulation of the principle responsible for Subject Condition effects. Kayne attributes them to his Connectedness Condition. Simplifying somewhat, this condition dictates that nothing can be extracted from a constituent that is not *canonically governed*:

(24) A category α canonically governs a category β if and only if
    a. α governs β, and
    b. β is a sister of α (or of a projection of α), and
    c. α precedes β (head-initial languages) or
       α follows β (head-final languages).

English is a head-initial language, so NP is canonically governed only by a category that precedes it. In (23) the Subject Condition effect indicates that the subject of the small clause is not canonically governed. This is true of the small clause structure, where the subject is not a sister of V, but not of Williams's structure, where it is.[10]

But both structures are compatible with the data in (23) if Chomsky's (1986a) theory of barriers and Subjancecy is adopted. This theory attributes Huang's (1982) Condition on Extraction Domains (CED) effects, including both Subject Condition effects and Adjunct (Adverbial Island) Condition effects, to Subjacency. Simplifying somewhat, the theory holds that a category α may be extracted from a phrase YP only if there is some γ such that γ *L-marks* YP. (Recall that γ L-marks YP if and only if γ θ-marks and governs YP.)[11]

Thus, Subject Condition effects are interpreted as diagnostics for L-marking (θ-government) rather than for subjecthood, and (23) shows only that the subject of a small clause is not L-marked. The only category that θ-marks the subject is the adjectival head of the small clause, so the adjective is its only potential L-marking governor. If the adjectival head of a small clause fails to govern the small clause subject, the Subject Condition effects would follow.

To ensure this result, the relation of government would have to be defined so as to confine the domain of government of a head X to the predicate phrase containing X. One way of doing this is to define government and c-command as in (25):

(25) a. α *governs* β if and only if
      i. α c-commands β, and
      ii. for all δ, δ a barrier for β,
         if δ dominates β, then δ dominates α.
    b. α *c-commands* β if and only if
      every category dominating α also dominates β.

Note that (25b) does not distinguish between maximal and nonmaximal categories, so the c-command domain of a head X is confined to the X′

dominating it. Then if all predicative heads are assumed to be dominated by a predicate phrase X', regardless of whether X' is branching, (25) ensures that the head of the small clause predicate neither c-commands nor governs the subject of the small clause.[12]

To summarize, Kayne's (1984) argument for (5) based on (22)–(24) is inconclusive, since it relies on the assumption that sisterhood, rather than θ-marking, is the crucial property distinguishing between a true direct object and the subject of a small clause with respect to Subject Condition effects. If L-marking is the relevant notion, then the Subject Condition effects simply show that the subject of the small clause is not governed by the adjectival head that θ-marks it.

2.6 Reflexive Clitics in Italian

Rizzi (1986) provides clear evidence that small clause raising structures like those in (2) are derived by NP-movement, based on the behavior of reflexive clitics in French and Italian. The basic observation is that a reflexive clitic may never intervene between NP-trace and its antecedent. This effect serves as a diagnostic for NP-movement, and small clause raising structures behave just like their infinitival counterparts in this respect:

(26) a. *Gianni$_i$ si$_i$ sembra [t$_i$ non fare   il suo dovere].
    Gianni to-himself seems   not to-do his duty
    'Gianni seems to himself not to do his duty.'

  b. *Gianni$_i$ si$_i$ sembra [t$_i$ intelligente].
    Gianni to-himself seems   intelligent
    'Gianni seems intelligent to himself.'

Rizzi suggests that the problem involves the existence of a local binding relation between the reflexive clitic and the trace of the NP-moved subject. Since the clitic is bound by the subject, it in turn binds the subject's trace. Now if each link in an A-chain must involve local binding, as in *LGB*, it follows that the reflexive clitic in (26a–b) must head the chain of the subject's trace, since it locally binds that trace. This excludes the matrix subject NP from the A-chain containing its trace, thus depriving it of a θ-role, in violation of the θ-Criterion. (Although the clitic is adjoined to V, it still c-commands and binds the NP-trace, given May's (1985) theory of domination, since it is dominated by just a single segment of the V-node and therefore does not count as being dominated by V.)[13]

Abstracting away from the details of Rizzi's theory, its central empirical claim is that a reflexive clitic may not intervene between an NP-trace and its antecedent and that this serves as a diagnostic for the presence of NP-trace. Hence, some factor must force the presence of NP-trace in (26b). The clausal theory of predication has this effect: the adjectival predicate must form a constituent with its subject, and that subject can only be a trace of the matrix subject. Williams's looser c-command condition on predication allows the VP-internal AP to be predicated of the subject of IP directly, so it cannot account for the obligatory presence of the trace in (26b).

Note that (26b) cannot be captured by Williams's theory simply by assuming that the AP is obligatorily predicated of the closest preceding NP (that is, the clitic), thereby depriving the subject of a θ-role; this is because nonreflexive clitics may freely intervene between the AP and the matrix subject, without any effect on θ-marking of the subject. Thus, it seems clear that the problem with (26b) is due to the presence of the NP-trace. This supports the clausal theory of predication and, by extension, the existence of small clauses.

2.7 Summary of the Evidence for Small Clauses

We have seen that small clause subjects behave like true structural subjects in several respects. Some of these similarities turn out to be theory-neutral for the small clause controversy, given a certain latitude in formulating other assumptions. The Subject Condition effects can be captured by either theory if Chomsky's (1986a) theory of movement is assumed, and the binding data can be captured by either theory given judicious adjustments in the definition of *governing category*.

Safir's subject small clauses and Chung and McCloskey's Irish small clauses simply show that small clauses *may* exist as constituents; they do not conclusively show that all predicate phrases must be sisters of their subjects. Thus, they support the possibility of (5) without excluding the possibility of (8). Only the data involving interpolation of matrix adverbs and the Italian reflexive clitic facts provide unambiguous support for the clausal theory of predication.

3   Evidence for a Complex Predicate

3.1   Cliticization and Small Clause Restructuring

3.1.1   Cliticization out of Small Clauses in Italian   Rizzi (1986) observes that a clitic corresponding to the complement of an adjective in a small

clause may not attach to the governing matrix verb in structures like (27):

(27) a. ?I nostri amici gli$_i$ hanno reso   [[Maria piu
          our   friends to-him have   rendered   Maria more
          affezionata [e]$_i$].
          affectionate
          'Our friends have rendered Maria more affectionate to him.'

       b. ??Gli$_i$ ritenevo   [tua   sorella affezionata [e]$_i$].
           to-him believed(1SG) your sister   affectionate
           'I believed your sister (to be) affectionate to him.'

He points out that if clitic traces are anaphors subject to Condition A of the *LGB* binding theory, then the ungrammaticality of (27) follows from the fact that the small clause is the governing category for the complement of the adjective; this mirrors the situation in English.

(27) is also excluded by Borer's (1983) theory of cliticization, according to which a clitic must govern its trace in order to identify its features. Borer assumes that both the clitic and its "trace" are base-generated, but her analysis translates directly into a movement theory, where clitics are incorporated heads in the sense proposed by Baker (1988). A clitic may not govern its trace if a barrier intervenes, and this is the source of the problem in (27). AP is not a barrier to government by the clitic, since AP is L-marked by V; but Chomsky's (1986a) Minimality Condition on government prevents the clitic from governing its trace, since the trace is locally governed by the intervening head A within A'. Rizzi (1990) proposes a more restricted Relativized Minimality Condition, whereby intervening heads block government by other heads but not antecedent government by maximal projections. But even Relativized Minimality blocks government by the clitic in (27) if clitics are treated as incorporated (X^0) heads.

However, it happens that cliticization is possible if no overt subject intervenes between the adjective and the matrix verb:

(28) a. Gianni$_i$ gli$_j$ è [t$_i$ affezionato e$_j$].
          Gianni to-him is   affectionate
          'Gianni is affectionate to him.'

       b. Gli$_j$ ritenevo   [t$_i$ affezionato e$_j$ anche tua   sorella$_i$].
           to-him believe(1SG)   affectionate   also   your sister
           'I believe your sister also (to be) affectionate to him.'

       c. Maria$_i$ gli$_j$ era   ritenuta [t$_i$ affezionata e$_j$].
           Maria to-him was believed   affectionate
           'Maria was believed (to be) affectionate to him.'

Rizzi suggests that (28) reflects the application of a V-A reanalysis rule, which enables the matrix verb to govern the clitic trace. Then the trace has the main clause as its governing category, within which it is bound by the clitic, as Condition A requires. He suggests that reanalysis is subject to a condition of string adjacency, so that it is permitted in (28) but blocked in (27), the desired result. This account translates directly into Borer's theory of clitics, provided that reanalysis extends the clitic's domain of government (and not just the verb's); then the clitic governs and identifies the features of its trace in (28), but not in (27).

3.1.2 Reanalysis as Restructuring   Rizzi suggests that V-A reanalysis involves no actual restructuring; instead, A is assigned a "government index" by V, as proposed by Rouveret and Vergnaud (1980). However, for reasons that will become apparent shortly, I will reinterpret reanalysis as a literal restructuring operation, producing an S-Structure representation where A is adjoined to V.

Rizzi's condition of string adjacency comes for free if V-A reanalysis involves actual adjunction of A to V. No condition of adjacency need be assumed; it is the application of restructuring that has the effect of making V and A adjacent. Suppose that restructuring applies optionally in the syntax of Italian. Then if V and A are overtly separated from each other, as in (27), restructuring cannot have applied; but if V and A are string-adjacent, as in (28), then restructuring *may* have applied. Thus, the examples in (28), unlike those in (27), are actually structurally ambiguous. They may have either the structure shown in (28), where a trace in the subject position of the small clause intervenes between the governing verb and the adjectival head of the small clause, or they may have a structure with A right-adjoined to V, preceding the subject trace. Henceforth we will be primarily concerned with the status of the second (restructured) representation of (28).

Note that restructuring must have the effect of allowing V (or the clitic attached to V) to govern the trace of the clitic. If restructuring is simply an instance of Move α, then the structure of AP remains intact, as in (29a), where the trace of A survives as an intervening governor, potentially preventing the clitic *gli* from governing its trace. Alternatively, restructuring might involve a radical structure-reducing rule of clause union, of the type proposed by Aissen and Perlmutter (1976). On this view, V-A restructuring entirely eliminates the phrase structure projected from A, and all arguments of A (including the trace of the subject NP and the trace of the clitic) are reanalyzed as structural complements of the derived complex

verb, as in (29b). (In both (29a) and (29b) I have abstracted away from the
effects of V-movement to Infl.)

(29) a.

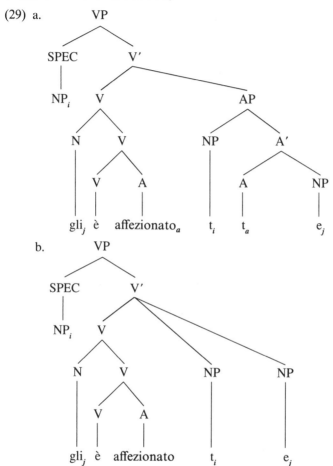

The clause union structure in (29b), unlike the structure derived by Move
α in (29a), potentially violates the *LGB* Projection Principle, which requires
that selectional properties be projected uniformly at D-Structure, S-Structure, and LF. However, this depends on how the Projection Principle is
interpreted.

   First, consider the selectional relation between V and AP. If V specifically selects AP as a complement at D-Structure but not as S-Structure,
then (29b) violates the Projection Principle. Suppose, however, that selectional relations hold between heads, as suggested by Baltin (1989), and that

the Projection Principle is restated as (30), essentially following Stowell (1989):

(30) *Revised Projection Principle*

If X selects Y as a lexical property, then X governs Y at D-Structure, S-Structure, and LF.

If V selects A, then by (30) V must govern A at every level. But the definition of government in (25) implies that V c-commands and governs A in (29b), so (30) is satisfied, both before and after restructuring.[14]

Next, consider the selectional relation between A and its complements in (29b). At D-Structure, the complements of A occur in A′, whereas at S-Structure they are complements of V in V′. But since A is dominated by just one V-segment, A continues to govern its complements, and this satisfies the Revised Projection Principle.

Finally, consider the selectional relation between A and its subject argument in (29b). Assuming that the subject is external to A′ at D-Structure, it follows that this selectional relation is not subject to the Projection Principle. However, the θ-Criterion requires that A θ-mark the "subject" argument at every level. Therefore, although the Projection Principle does not require this argument to be governed by either A or V at LF, the θ-Criterion forces it to occur as a complement in V′, since this is the only available A-position after restructuring.

Thus, a "clause union" version of restructuring is consistent with at least one interpretation of the Projection Principle. It is also consistent with all of the data considered below, and it must be considered a credible theory of restructuring. But restructuring might simply be an instance of Move α, a possibility to which I now turn.

3.1.3 Restructuring as Move α   If restructuring involves adjunction of A to V, it could be an instance of head-to-head movement (in the mode of adjunction), a subcase of Move α. This would imply that restructuring leaves the structure of the small clause intact, as in (29a). If so, the contrast between (27) and (28) implies that A-to-V movement neutralizes the status of A as an intervening head governor for the Minimality Condition.[15] For concreteness, I will adopt Rizzi's (1990) Relativized Minimality Condition, mentioned above:

(31) X α-governs Y only if there is no Z such that
      a. Z is a typical potential α-governor for Y, and
      b. Z c-commands Y and does not c-command X.

An intervening head has no effect on antecedent government by XP; it only affects government by another head. In (27) the unincorporated head A corresponds to Z in (31); A is a potential (and actual) head governor of the clitic trace, and A fails to c-command the clitic. Hence, (31) prevents the clitic from head-governing its trace. (The matrix head V does not block head government by the clitic, since V and the clitic are in a mutual c-command relation.)

In (29a) A is adjoined to V, and the clitic is adjoined to the derived $[_V \ V + A]$ (see note 13). Since the adjoined clitic is dominated by just one segment of the V-node, both V and A c-command the clitic (and vice versa). Thus, neither V nor A in (29a) corresponds to Z in (31). But the trace of A within A' does not c-command the clitic, so it should count as an intervening governor for Relativized Minimality. Evidently it does not. This suggests that (31) should be restated in terms of chain theory:

(32) a. X α-governs Y only if there is no Z such that
     a. Z is a typical potential α-governor for Y, and
     b. the α-chain containing Z c-commands Y and does not c-command X.
   b. An α-chain C c-command X if and only if any element of C c-commands X.

This has the desired result; although the head chain consisting of A and its trace c-commands the trace of the clitic, this head chain also c-commands the clitic in (29a), and so there is no Minimality effect.

Actually, clitic placement motivates a revision of Relativized Minimality along the lines of (32), independently of small clause constructions. I have followed the literature in assuming that Romance pronominal clitics are adjoined to V, but in finite clauses they precede the finite main verb or auxiliary and therefore must be assumed to be adjoined to INFL. This implies that the head V inside V' is a potential intervening governor. But V moves to INFL in finite clauses in Romance,[16] so the clitic is actually adjoined to [V + INFL]. This explains the lack of Minimality effects, if Relativized Minimality is restated in terms of chain government as in (32).

3.2   Scope Effects and LF Restructuring in English

3.2.1   The Scope Asymmetry   Williams (1983) observes that whereas (33a) is ambiguous, permitting either a matrix or an embedded scope construal for the subject QP, (33b) is unambiguous, allowing only a matrix scope construal:

(33) a. Someone$_i$ seems [t$_i$ to be angry at John].

    b. Someone$_i$ seems [t$_i$ angry at John].

According to May (1985), the raised QP in (33a) may adjoin either to the matrix IP or to the subordinate IP at LF. If QP adjoins to the matrix IP, it locally $\bar{A}$-binds its trace in the matrix subject position as a variable and takes scope over the matrix verb *seem*. But if QP adjoins instead to the subordinate IP, it locally $\bar{A}$-binds the NP-trace as a variable and does not take scope over the matrix verb.

As Williams observes, the lack of a narrow scope construal in (33b) is surprising if small clauses exist. The QP ought to have undergone NP-movement in (33b), leaving NP-trace in the subject position of the small clause. The QP should be able to adjoin to the small clause and locally $\bar{A}$-bind the NP-trace, yielding a narrow scope construal. The fact that this construal is unavailable represents a fundamental difference between small clauses and infinitives, which the theory of these constructions must not ignore.

3.2.2 The Issue of NP-Movement   Williams attributes the failure of quantifier lowering in (33b) to two factors. First, he wishes to argue against the small clause structure (5); second, he wishes to argue that constructions like (33b) are not derived by NP-movement. Either factor would be sufficient to block the narrow scope construal. In this section I address the issue of NP-movement and its significance for the scope facts.

Since Williams's rule of predication allows the VP-internal AP in (33b) to be directly predicated of the matrix subject, it does not need to posit a trace for that subject. On this view, the subject of a raising verb is not necessarily a non-θ-position, even though the raising verb does not itself θ-mark it.

Note that passive verbs behave like raising verbs in this respect; (34) only allows a broad scope construal:

(34) Someone$_i$ is considered t$_i$ angry at John.

This contrasts with infinitival complements to passive verbs, where a narrow scope construal is possible:

(35) Someone$_i$ is believed t$_i$ to be angry at John.

If Williams excludes the narrow scope construal in (33b) on the grounds that there is no VP-internal trace, then the same must be true for passives like (34).

We have already seen that the distribution of reflexive clitics in Italian supports the (obligatory) occurrence of an NP-trace in small clause raising and passive constructions like (33b) and (34). But it turns out that this issue is beside the point, since the analogous narrow scope construal is unavailable even with ECM-type small clauses, where the existence of a VP-internal NP is not in dispute. In (36a) the QP must take broad scope over the matrix predicate, whereas a narrow scope construal is possible with the infinitive in (36b):

(36) a. John proved two assumptions false.

b. John proved two assumptions to be false.

Plainly the application of quantifier raising (QR) will leave a VP-internal trace in (36a), so the unavailability of the narrow scope construal must hinge on the exclusion of the small clause as a possible domain of quantification at LF, rather than on the presence or absence of a trace. However (36a) is explained, the solution will presumably extend to the raising and passive structures in (33b) and (34).

3.2.3 Small Clauses as Domains of Quantification Suppose that quantifier scope is determined by (37):

(37) QP takes scope over XP if and only if QP c-commands XP at LF.

Williams maintains that the absence of the narrow scope construal indicates the nonexistence of small clauses as syntactic constituents; there is no small clause XP for QP to adjoin to. But since we have seen evidence that small clauses do exist as constituents at S-Structure, a more conservative conclusion is warranted. Scope is based on LF representations, and this leaves open the possibility that small clauses at S-Structure differ from small clauses at LF. In other words, the lack of the narrow scope construal might be explained even if small clause complements have the structure in (5) at S-Structure, provided that they undergo restructuring at LF, even in English.

Before examining this possibility, I will consider a different sort of approach that is consistent with the structure in (5) at LF. Suppose that QP is subject to the general condition on adjunction proposed by Chomsky (1986a), such that maximal projections may adjoin only to maximal projections that are not arguments. Small clause complements are arguments of the verbs that select them. Therefore, they are not possible adjunction sites for QP at LF, and QP must adjoin to the matrix VP, which is a nonargument complement of INFL, yielding the broad scope construal.

The viability of this solution obviously rests on the assumption that LF movement (and QR in particular) must observe the prohibition against adjunction to arguments. Note, however, that this same prohibition prevents QP from adjoining to an IP infinitival complement. The narrow scope construal with infinitival complements like (33a), (35), and (36b) would therefore have to involve adjunction of QP to the infinitival VP. If the subject of IP originates within VP as in Koopman and Sportiche 1988, then the VP-internal trace could serve as the variable bound by the VP-adjoined QP. But if the subject originates in IP, then the VP-adjoined QP would not c-command the trace in the subject position of IP, since QP is dominated by I'.[17]

If QR is permitted to adjoin QP to an argument at LF, then a different explanation for the scope facts is needed, and small clause restructuring can play a role in this account. If restructuring is the radical operation of clause union considered in section 3.1.2, then the desired result is trivially obtained, since the small clause is assumed to be eliminated on this view, as in (29b).

But if restructuring is a subcase of Move α, then the AP headed by the trace of the incorporated A must somehow be neutralized as a possible domain of quantification for its subject. Suppose that the following principle holds at LF:

(38) *Predicate Scope Principle*

    a. A quantifier phrase QP must take scope over a predicate P.

    b. For any predicate head P appearing in a chain of head positions $(P, t_i, \ldots, t_n)$, QP takes scope over P if and only if QP c-commands P.

In structures where no head movement occurs, (38b) amounts to a standard definition of scope in terms of c-command. But in structures where V moves to INFL, (38b) requires that QP must appear at LF in a position that c-commands INFL if it is to take scope over V.

If small clauses did not undergo restructuring, it would be possible for QP to satisfy (38) by adjoining to the small clause, thus taking (narrow) scope over the adjectival predicate. But LF restructuring forces the QP to adjoin to the matrix clause in order to satisfy (38). In order to take scope over the adjective, QP must adjoin to an XP dominating A. But then QP must also take scope over the matrix verb, since every XP dominating A also dominates V after the former adjoins to the latter. Thus, the hypothesis that small clause complements must undergo LF restructuring plays a crucial role in accounting for the small clause/infinitival scope asymmetry, if LF adjunction to arguments is permitted.

3.3 The Null Operator Asymmetry and LF Restructuring

3.3.1 Head Government and Identification The distribution of traces in parasitic gap and *tough*-movement constructions provides further evidence that small clauses undergo restructuring at LF. Here we find another asymmetry between infinitives and small clauses: the trace of a null operator may occur as the subject of a small clause but not as the subject of an infinitive.

My interpretation of this asymmetry draws on the analysis of null operator movement and the Empty Category Principle (ECP) in Stowell 1985, 1986, which I will translate here into a modified version of Chomsky's (1986a) barriers framework. The theory claims that traces are subject to two distinct licensing conditions: they must be *head-governed* at S-Structure, and they must be *identified* at LF, where identification is defined as in (39):[18]

(39) α identifies β if and only if

α θ-governs β, or α antecedent-governs β.

The disjunctive definition of identification can be simplified in terms of coindexation with the governor, given the theory of θ-grids in Stowell 1981, but I will ignore this here.

Although the S-Structure Head Government Condition plays an important role in capturing certain traditional ECP effects (including *that*-trace effects), it is the LF Identification Condition that we will be concerned with here. An object trace is normally identified by the verb that θ-governs it, whereas a subject or adjunct trace must be identified by its antecedent (that is, it must be antecedent-governed).

3.3.2 Null Operators and Identification In *tough*-movement and parasitic gap constructions, a null operator (NO) undergoes syntactic movement to the SPEC of CP position, as in Chomsky 1986a. The NO-trace may never occur in a subject or adjunct position, even if this position is accessible to normal *wh*-movement. This pattern suggests that the Identification Condition is at work. Suppose that the definition of *identification* is modified so as to require that the identifying category be a member of a chain with an overt head:

(40) α identifies β if and only if

a. α is in a chain with an overt head, and

b. α θ-governs β, or α antecedent-governs β.

Given (40a), an NO is incapable of identifying its trace, so NO-trace should be confined to positions that are identified under θ-marking—that is, to direct object positions. This comes close to matching the facts, with one exception: small clause subjects behave like objects with respect to the Identification Condition. I suggest that this is an effect of small clause restructuring at LF.

Let us now take a closer look at the facts. First consider the exclusion of an adjunct NO-trace:

(41) a. *Yesterday$_i$ was easy to catch the bus t$_i$.
     b. *There$_i$ was fun to have a vacation t$_i$. [referential *there*]

Adjuncts are not θ-governed; unlike objects, they must be identified by antecedent government. But the NO fails to satisfy (40a), so nothing identifies the NO-trace, which violates the Identification Condition.[19]

Consider next an NO-trace in the subject position of IP. Though *tough*-movement is generally impossible out of finite IPs, it is marginally acceptable if the IP is headed by a modal, as in (42a). Nevertheless, subject extraction in (42b) is completely impossible:

(42) a. ?This book$_i$ is impossible [O$_i$ to believe
        [(that) John could have written t$_i$]].
     b. *John$_i$ is impossible [O$_i$ to believe
        [(that) t$_i$ could have written this book]].

This effect is also visible in parasitic gap constructions, where object extraction from a tensed clause is more acceptable:

(43) a. Which man$_i$ did you interview t$_i$
        without [O$_i$ knowing [that John had already spoken to e$_i$]]?
     b. *Which man$_i$ did you interview t$_i$
        without [O$_i$ knowing [(that) e$_i$ had already spoken to John]]?

This subject-object asymmetry is not a *that*-trace effect, since it persists even if the complementizer is absent. The same asymmetry shows up with extraction from ECM infinitives, where *wh*-trace is possible:

(44) a. These diaries$_i$ are easy [O$_i$ to believe
        [Hitler to have written t$_i$]].
     b. *Hitler$_i$ is easy [O$_i$ to believe
        [t$_i$ to have written these diaries]].
(45) a. Which diaries$_i$ did you read t$_i$
        without [O$_i$ believing [Hitler to have written e$_i$]]?
     b. *Which author$_i$ did you read about t$_i$
        without [O$_i$ believing [e$_i$ to have written any diaries]]?

Object extraction is allowed in (42)–(45) because the object trace is θ-marked by the governing verb and does not need to be identified by the NO; it only needs to be $\bar{\text{A}}$-bound by it. But subject extraction is impossible, since the NO-trace violates the Identification Condition; the verb that θ-marks the NO-trace does not govern it, and the NO is ineligible as an identifying category, given (40a).

But the subject position in a small clause behaves differently. It may harbor the trace of an NO in a *tough*-movement construction:

(46) a. John is easy [O$_i$ to consider [e$_i$ intelligent]].
   b. Frank was impossible for the jury [O$_i$ to find [e$_i$ innocent]].

This contrast between small clause subjects and infinitival subjects is not specific to English. It also shows up in French and Italian, as noted by Cinque (1984), who attributes the observation to Kayne:

(47) a. *Cet homme est facile à croire être intelligent.
      *Quest' uomo è facile da ritenere essere intelligente.
      'This man is easy to consider to be intelligent.'
   b. ?Cet homme est facile à croire intelligent.
      ?Quest' uomo è facile da ritenere intelligente.
      'This man is easy to consider intelligent.'

The same is true of NO-traces in parasitic gap constructions, although the improvement over infinitival subjects is not as great as with *tough*-movement, for reasons I do not understand:[20]

(48) a. ?Which man$_i$ did you interview t$_i$
      without [O$_i$ considering [e$_i$ foolish]]?
   b. ?Which defendant$_i$ did the jury meet t$_i$
      before [O$_i$ finding [e$_i$ guilty]]?

If an NO is incapable of identifying its own trace, then the NO-traces in (46), (47b), and (48) must be identified under θ-government by the adjectival head of the small clause.

In section 2 I argued that the existence of Subject Condition effects with extraction from the subject of a small clause shows that it is not L-marked at S-Structure. This implies that the small clause subject is not governed by the category that θ-marks it (the adjectival head of the small clause predicate). This conclusion is supported by the fact that PRO may occur as the subject of an adjunct small clause, but not as the subject of a complement small clause—an asymmetry that is explained if the subject of a small clause may be governed only by an external category that L-marks the small clause.[21]

But this seems to be contradicted by the absence of Identification Condition effects with NO extraction, which suggests that the subject of the small clause *is* θ-governed (hence L-marked). This apparent contradiction can be resolved if we assume that the subject of a complement small clause is *not* θ-governed at S-Structure in English, but *is* θ-governed at LF—as a result of small clause restructuring.

It is clear that the Identification Condition holds at LF, since LF movement of subjects and adjuncts requires antecedent government (see Huang 1982; Lasnik and Saito 1984). If the adjectival head of a small clause complement must be adjoined to the matrix verb at LF, then A should θ-govern the NO-trace from the V-adjoined position, explaining the absence of Identification Condition effects:

(49)

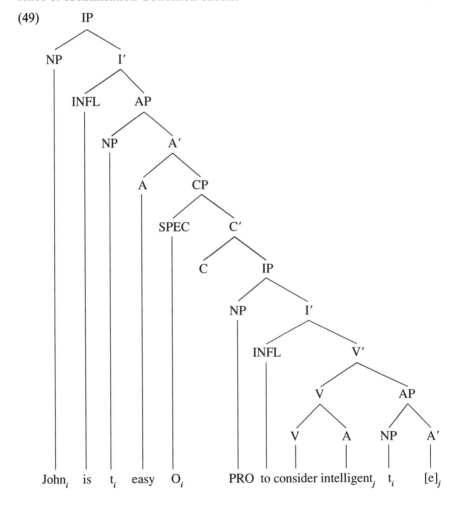

In (49) AP is L-marked by V and hence is not a barrier. Furthermore, A c-commands and governs the trace of the NO from its derived V-adjoined position. A governs and θ-marks the subject position of AP, and the Identification Condition is satisfied.

On the other hand, the Subject Condition is a Subjacency effect and thus serves as a reliable negative diagnostic for L-marking at the point in the derivation where movement applies. These effects arise with syntactic extraction from small clause subjects in English because restructuring does not apply prior to S-Structure. But Italian allows restructuring prior to S-Structure, and so Subject Condition effects should not arise in that language if restructuring has applied. Longobardi (1986) provides evidence supporting this:

(50) a. *Maria, con cui$_i$ ritengo [[parlare t$_i$] del tutto inutile]
        Maria with whom I believe   talking   completely useless
     b. *Maria, di cui$_i$ considero [[dubitare t$_i$] inammissibile]
        Maria of whom I consider   doubting   inadmissible

(51) a. Maria, con cui$_i$ ritengo del tutto inutile [parlare t$_i$]
     b. Maria, di cui$_i$ considero inammissibile [dubitare t$_i$]

Thus, there turns out to be no conflict between the distribution of Subject Condition effects and Identification Condition effects with NO-traces, provided that small clauses originate with the D-Structure representation in (5) and undergo restructuring prior to LF. Only at S-Structure do English and Italian differ, with both structures available in Italian.

3.4 Subject Small Clauses Revisited

My last argument for small clause restructuring at LF is based on the fact that small clauses may not in general function as subjects of other predicates. This argument is inspired by one of Baker's (1988) arguments for incorporation as an instance of Move α.

Suppose that small clauses must undergo restructuring at LF if and only if they function as arguments. Suppose further that small clause restructuring is a subcase of Baker-style incorporation (that is, Move α). Such movement is possible only if the incorporated head originates in an L-marked complement of the higher head, and subjects are generally not L-marked. Therefore, restructuring should be impossible if the small clause is itself a non-L-marked subject. Then if restructuring is both necessary and impossible with argument small clauses, they should never occur as subjects. We have already seen that this is correct:

(52) a. *[The workers angry] displeases me.

   b. *John believes [[the workers angry] to displease me].

(53) a. *[t$_i$ angry] seems the workers$_i$.

   b. *The workers$_i$ seem [[t$_i$ angry] to displease me].

Up to this point I have relied on Chomsky's (1986a) barriers theory to explain this. If the subject of the small clause is overt (52), then nothing assigns Case to it, since the non-L-marked small clause is a barrier. The raising-type small clauses in (53) are also impossible as subjects, for familiar reasons, including the fact that the barrierhood of the small clause blocks government of the trace in (53b).

But there is a gap in this account so far. It treats subject small clauses on a par with adjunct small clauses: in each case the small clause AP is a barrier to government and Case marking of its subject. But this should still allow for such small clauses to exist, if they contain (ungoverned) PRO subjects. Though this is true of adjuncts, it is not true of subjects:

(54) a. *[PRO$_i$ happy] would please me$_i$.

   b. *John believes [[PRO$_i$ happy] to please me$_i$].

My previous discussion failed to exclude these examples. But the hypothesis that small clauses must undergo LF restructuring when they function as arguments would explain why (54) is impossible: the adjectival head cannot adjoin to the matrix verb, since it would be unable to govern its trace across the small clause barrier. This would also (redundantly) explain the impossibility of (52) and (53).

Consider how this affects Safir's (1983) examples of small clauses functioning as the subjects of *be*, as in (13) above. I have suggested that these small clauses are θ-governed and L-marked by *be*. This predicts that such small clauses should disallow PRO subjects (which is correct). It also allows for the possibility of restructuring at LF; if A adjoins to *be*, it governs its trace across the L-marked small clause boundary. This allows such clauses to exist.[22]

4   Residual Problems

4.1   The Cause of Restructuring

Since D-Structure is a pure projection of thematic structure, it analyzes QPs as normal arguments; it is blind to their quantificational properties. But LF, where quantification is interpreted, requires *wh*-phrases and other QPs to bind variables and to take scope over a particular syntactic domain.

This conflict between the structural requirements imposed by D-Structure and LF motivates the *wh*-movement and QP-movement operations mapping between them.

There is no established corresponding explanation for the necessity of small clause restructuring. If small clauses function as arguments of verbs in the same way that infinitives and tensed clauses do, then they should be able to occur as complements of verbs at LF. But if our interpretation of the data in section 3 is correct, there must be some hitherto unrecognized principle of LF that forces the head of a small clause complement to adjoin to the governing verb.

In seeking to determine what principle might be at work here, we must take into account the precise effects of restructuring. These include the following:

(55) a. A is adjoined to V;
     b. A is no longer the head of AP;
     c. A is governed by the category governing V.

If restructuring is a subcase of Move α, then a further effect is

d. A binds a trace in the head of AP.

If restructuring is a structure-reducing process of clause union, then instead of (d) we have

e. V does not govern an AP complement.

Presumably one of the effects in (55) is responsible for resolving some problem with the structure in (5) at LF, but with so many choices it is hard to decide among them. It is also far from clear what principle(s) might be sensitive to these effects.

Restructuring might be due to a requirement that AP cannot be the complement of V at LF. This could be derived from a more general principle such as (56a) or (56b):

(56) a. A predicative category may not function as an argument.
     b. Only a referential category may function as an argument.

The small clause structure in (5) would violate such a principle, motivating LF restructuring as a means of eliminating the offending AP or VP argument. But this would be compatible only with the clause union view of restructuring; if restructuring is a subcase of Move α, the AP complement is preserved, and restructuring would be of no help in satisfying (56). A variation on (56a) would be compatible with the Move α theory, however:

(57) A lexical predicate may not be the head of an argument.

This allows AP to be an argument, but the lexical predicate A may not be its head; therefore, A must adjoin to V, leaving a trace as the head of the argument AP.

Neither (56) nor (57) has any effect on APs functioning as adjunct small clauses and NP-internal modifiers, since these APs are not arguments. This is fortunate, since if restructuring were necessary in such structures, they could not exist; the head of XP may be incorporated into Y only if Y θ-governs (and L-marks) XP.

On the other hand, both principles would force restructuring with small clauses functioning as subject arguments. But restructuring is not possible out of a (non-L-marked) subject, so a small clause should not occur as a subject. I have already pointed out the empirical advantages of this line of reasoning in section 3.4.

Neither (56) nor (57) has any effect on VP predicates functioning as the structural complements of functional categories such as INFL, since such complements are not true arguments of any predicate. If V-to-INFL movement is a subcase of the same process as small clause restructuring (as the Move α analysis implies), then it is tempting to attribute the necessity of both types of incorporation to the same principle. (56) and (57) implicitly reject this, however.

Of course, there are other imaginable ways of forcing small clause restructuring at LF. For instance, one might exploit the fact that as a result of restructuring, the incorporated head A is governed by the category governing V (namely, INFL), since V is no longer an intervening governor for Minimality. This might be forced by an LF principle such as (58):

(58) A predicate head must be governed by a referential category.

The intuitive basis for (58) is that every instance of predication must be linked to some reference point that is independent of the inherent reference of its subject. If we assume that INFL counts as a referential category on a par with N (or perhaps D), then (58) would force small clause restructuring as a means of allowing INFL to govern A. This has roughly similar effects to (56)/(57), although it encounters certain problems in accounting for adjunct small clauses, which I will not go into here.

4.2   Predicate Phrase Movement

It is to be expected that the relatively simple picture of small clause restructuring presented here will give way to a more complex set of possibilities when a wider set of languages is considered. For instance, Horvath

(1986) observes that in Hungarian, small clause predicates typically undergo movement to the preverbal FOCUS position at S-Structure. (This movement is blocked if the FOCUS position is occupied by a *wh*-phrase, in which case the predicate shows up in its D-Structure position.) Even in English, small clause predicates may themselves undergo syntactic *wh*-movement, as Williams (1983) observes:

(59) How foolish$_i$ do you consider Bill t$_i$?

If the small clause predicate is a nonmaximal (X′) projection, as in (5), then syntactic theory must permit movement of nonmaximal projections, contrary to Chomsky (1986a).

There is some independent evidence that nonmaximal X′ projections may undergo movement. Perhaps the best-known example of this is Rouveret and Vergnaud's (1980) V′-movement in French causatives, although other analyses of these constructions are possible. But other instances of V′-movement are attested in the literature. Cline (1986) accounts for Verb-Object-Subject constituent order in Hixkaryana in terms of V′-fronting, which (as he points out) allows for other constituents of the VP to be "stranded" to the right of the subject.

But if movement of X′ categories must be excluded, then obviously (59) indicates that small clause predicate phrases are XPs. This would entail revising the D-Structure representation in (5) along the lines suggested by Koopman and Sportiche (1988), according to which the subject position in a small clause occupies a position adjoined to a predicate phrase XP. This would leave other aspects of our analysis unaffected.

A more serious problem posed by examples like (59) concerns the mechanics of reconstruction and its relation to restructuring. To handle such cases, our theory must assume that some sort of literal reconstruction is available, so as to permit the *wh*-moved small clause predicate in (59) to occur inside VP at LF, as input to the restructuring. If this sort of literal reconstruction is not really possible, then a rather more abstract version of the restructuring hypothesis would have to be assumed. Specifically, one would have to assume either that the trace of a small clause predicate may itself be incorporated into the matrix verb, or else that "restructuring" involves some sort of nonstructural connection being established between the matrix verb and the small clause predicate, in the spirit of proposals by Rouveret and Vergnaud (1980) and Rizzi (1986). But this would have to be formulated so as to capture the LF effects that we have interpreted in section 3 in terms of head-to-head adjunction.

5   Conclusion

We have seen that small clause constructions exhibit a pattern of syntactic behavior suggesting that they originate as true clausal constituents at D-Structure. But small clauses exhibit other properties suggesting that they undergo restructuring of some sort. This restructuring is restricted to small clauses functioning as complements, and it seems to be required only at LF—although it may take place prior to S-Structure in some languages, such as Italian.

The fact that restructuring must apply somewhere in the mapping from D-Structure to LF implies that these levels impose contradictory requirements on small clause constructions. I have considered a couple of ways of capturing this, based on one or another of the putative LF principles discussed in section 4.1. This part of the theory is highly speculative, and the nature of the relevant LF requirement is an open question. On the other hand, the general picture of small clause constructions that emerges from this treatment has some interesting implications for the nature of the levels of D-Structure and LF, and for the rules mapping between them. Viewed from this perspective, the analysis has significance beyond the specifics of the small clause phenomena under discussion.

First, it supports the existence of LF as a genuine level of syntactic representation with its own distinctive properties. If these properties are not confined to matters of quantifier scope and proper government of traces, then LF must be more than just an enriched version of S-Structure annotated with scope assignments, and it would be unwise to assume that LF can be eliminated simply by adopting more complex rules for interpreting quantifier scope at S-Structure.

Second, it suggests that the basic approach to parametric variation underlying Huang's account of *wh*-movement has a broader applicability. If we confine our attention to the study of S-Structure and its relation to D-Structure, we are led to conclude that many syntactic rules are language-specific: *wh*-movement seems to apply in English but not in Chinese, and small clause restructuring seems to apply in Italian but not in English. But a more optimistic appraisal of the universality of syntactic rules is in order if a large number of apparently language-specific rules turn out to be motivated in the mapping from S-Structure to LF in those languages where they have not applied in the mapping from D-Structure to S-Structure. If the relevant cross-linguistic variation can be confined to whether S-Structure projects the input or output of individual rules, the rules themselves can be taken to be universal, as can the D-Structure and LF representations that they connect.

This provides a useful analytical tool for comparative syntax. If two languages exhibit different structures for a given construction at S-Structure, then there is a good chance that one language is projecting the D-Structure form of the construction at S-Structure, while the other language is projecting the LF form, and we should expect to find evidence for both structures at the relevant levels in each case. Of course, this research strategy is already motivated by Huang's treatment of *wh*-movement, but its usefulness in explaining the properties of small clause constructions suggests that it is a viable approach to many other types of cross-linguistic variation, including aspects of the theory of complementation that are usually thought to be unrelated to the theory of LF.[23]

Notes

1. The structure in (6) is suggested in Stowell 1981, but with the category label "S" taking the place of "I":

(i)

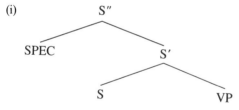

2. I assume that the small clause predicate harbors no null head corresponding to INFL, contrary to Kitagawa (1986).

3. Schein (1981) allows for (8) by reinterpreting the argument structure of verbs taking small clause complements. He proposes that these verbs select a *predicate* as their internal argument and that the predicate is responsible for forcing the presence of a VP-internal NP in order to satisfy the θ-Criterion. Schein, like Williams, requires that subjects be external to the lexical XP that θ-marks them. In section 2 I argue against this view.

4. Small clauses like that in (12) should not be confused with referential NPs containing adjectival modifiers. Since all clauses (including small clauses) trigger singular agreement, I use a small clause with a plural subject to avoid confusion.

Note that small clauses with PRO subjects are also excluded from subject position:

(i) *[PRO sick] would bother John.
   "To be sick would bother John"

In section 3 I attribute this to the fact that argument small clauses must undergo restructuring at LF. This leads to a violation of the Empty Category Principle (ECP) if the small clause is a subject, as in (i).

5. Examples like (13) are worse when *be* takes a small clause raising complement (see Stowell 1978):

(i) ??[Workers angry about the pay]$_i$ is [t$_i$ unfortunate].

This makes sense if dyadic (identificational) *be*, unlike raising *be*, θ-marks and L-marks its subject.

6. Intervening time adverbials seem to allow a matrix construal more readily in these contexts. This might indicate that the time adverbial receives a matrix construal because of the anaphoric temporal relation between the matrix and subordinate INFL positions. Campbell (1989) shows that temporal adverbs may not occur in small clause complements; this follows if temporal adverbs must modify an event variable in INFL, which is absent in small clauses.

7. Examples like (i) and (ii) are acceptable:

(i) ?John$_i$ considers [Mary smarter than himself$_i$].

(ii) ?The boys$_i$ find [Sally similar to each other$_i$].

Safir (1988) attributes this to the fact that the lexical semantics of the small clause predicate prevents the small clause subject from binding the anaphor. See also Keenan 1988.

8. In order for the floated anaphor to be subject to Condition A, it should be governed; see the PRO theorem of *LGB*. It is unclear what governs the reflexive in (20), other than the NP subject.

9. See Koopman and Sportiche 1988, Fukui and Speas 1985, Kuroda 1986, and Kitagawa 1988.

10. As Longobardi (1985) notes, Kayne's (1984) Connectedness Condition is unable to capture Huang's (1982) Condition on Extraction Domains (CED) effects in a unified fashion, since right-branch adjuncts yield CED effects. Chomsky's (1986a) account builds the CED into the definition of barriers in terms of L-marking, thus avoiding the problem.

11. Here I adopt the more restrictive version of L-marking in Chomsky 1986a, where Case government alone is insufficient to sanction L-marking.

12. As it stands, (25b) may be too restrictive, since it prevents a verb from c-commanding (and governing) categories adjoined to X'. We can allow this by revising (25b) as follows:

b. α *c-commands* β if and only if
   every category dominating α includes β.
c. α *dominates* β if and only if every segment of α dominates β.
   α *includes* β if and only if some segment of α dominates β.
   α *excludes* β if and only if no segment of α dominates β.

13. Since pronominal clitics precede the finite verb, even if it is an auxiliary verb, they must be VP-external; I assume that they are in fact adjoined to INFL. But then if clitics must govern their traces, it must be possible for a clitic adjoined to INFL to govern across the intervening verb. This follows if V adjoins to INFL in finite clauses, as proposed in section 3.

14. This revision is motivated in Stowell 1989 to account for the distribution of inherent Case. My use of it here is partly inspired by Marantz's (1984) version of the Projection Principle, which allows selectional requirements to be satisfied by morphological merger.

15. This has the same effect as Baker's (1988) *Government Transparency Corollary* (GTC), which states that a lexical category X that has an item Y incorporated into it governs everything that Y governed in its original structural position. It is natural to derive the GTC from the interaction of incorporation with the Minimality Condition, as in the text discussion.

16. See Taraldsen 1983 and Pollock 1989 for arguments that V moves to finite INFL in Romance; compare Emonds 1978.

17. The narrow scope construal would still be possible if scope were defined in terms of *m-command*, as in May 1985.

18. The idea that the ECP consists of two distinct conditions of head government and identification was first suggested by Jaeggli (1981). See also Aoun et al. 1987, Stowell 1985, 1986, and Rizzi 1990.

19. It is hard to show conclusively that NOs may not bind adjunct traces in parasitic gap constructions, since adjuncts and parasitic gaps are both optional.

20. Acceptability improves if the two verbs governing the licensing trace and the parasitic gap are thematically similar. Also, for some reason eventive verbs like *prove* seem better than stative verbs like *consider*:

(i)   ??Who$_i$ did you criticize t_i without considering e_i stupid?

(ii)   ?Who$_i$ do you consider t_i crazy without considering e_i stupid?

(iii) Which theory$_i$ did you attack t_i without proving e_i false?

21. Small clauses with PRO subjects may not themselves occur as subjects because of the necessity of restructuring; see section 3.4.

22. It is unclear how to exclude raising and ECM structures like (i) and (ii) if Safir's small clauses are L-marked:

(i)   *The workers$_i$ seem [[t$_i$ angry] to be the sort of situation we want to avoid].

(ii) *John believes [[the workers angry] to be the sort of situation we want to avoid].

Perhaps this shows that *be* governs the subject position of IP only when it occurs in a finite IP; this would follow if V-to-INFL movement only applies with finite clauses.

23. Other examples of parametric variation of this sort are discussed in the literature. For instance, possessor raising, which applies in the syntax of some languages (Carden, Gordon, and Munro 1982) may apply at LF in languages like English (Campbell and Martin 1989). Likewise, QR with universal QPs applies at LF in languages like English (see, for example, May 1985) but in the syntax in languages such as KiLega (Kinyalolo 1990).

References

Aissen, J., and D. Perlmutter (1976). "Clause Reduction in Spanish." In *Proceedings of the Second Annual Meeting, BLS*. Berkeley Linguistics Society, University of California, Berkeley.

Aoun, J., N. Hornstein, D. Lightfoot, and A. Weinberg (1987). "Two Types of Locality." *Linguistic Inquiry* 18:537–577.

Baker, M. (1988). *Incorporation: A Theory of Grammatical Function Changing*. University of Chicago Press, Chicago.

Baltin, M. (1989). "Heads and Projections." In M. Baltin and A. Kroch, eds., *Alternative Conceptions of Phrase Structure*. University of Chicago Press, Chicago.

Borer, H. (1984). *Parametric Syntax*. Foris, Dordrecht.

Bresnan, J. (1982). "Control and Complementation." *Linguistic Inquiry* 13:343–434.

Campbell, R. (1989). "The Grammatical Structure of Verbal Predicates." Doctoral dissertation, UCLA.

Campbell, R., and J. Martin (1989). "Sensation Predicates and the Syntax of Stativity." In J. Fee and K. Hunt, eds., *Proceedings of the Eighth West Coast Conference on Formal Linguistics*. Stanford Linguistics Association, Stanford University.

Carden, G., L. Gordon, and P. Munro (1982). "Raising Rules and the Projection Principle." Ms., University of British Columbia, Washington State University, and UCLA.

Chomsky, N. (1973). "Conditions on Transformations." In S. Anderson and P. Kiparsky, eds., *A Festschrift for Morris Halle*. Holt, Rinehart and Winston, New York.

Chomsky, N. (1975). *The Logical Structure of Linguistic Theory*. Plenum, New York. (Also 1985, University of Chicago Press, Chicago.)

Chomsky, N. (1980). "On Binding." *Linguistic Inquiry* 11:1–46.

Chomsky, N. (1981). *Lectures on Government and Binding*. Foris, Dordrecht.

Chomsky, N. (1986a). *Barriers*. MIT Press, Cambridge, Mass.

Chomsky, N. (1986b). *Knowledge of Language: Its Nature, Origin, and Use*. Praeger, New York.

Chung, S., and J. McCloskey (1987). "Government, Barriers, and Small Clauses in Modern Irish." *Linguistic Inquiry* 18:173–237.

Cinque, G. (1984). "A-bar Bound *pro* vs. Variable." Ms., Università di Venezia.

Cline, D. (1986). "Constituent Order in Hixkaryana." Master's thesis, UCLA.

Emonds, J. (1978). "The Verbal Complex V′–V in French." *Linguistic Inquiry* 9:151–175.

Fukui, N., and M. Speas (1985). "Specifiers and Projection." In *MIT Working Papers in Linguistics* 8. Department of Linguistics and Philosophy, MIT.

Horvath, J. (1986). *FOCUS in the Theory of Grammar and the Syntax of Hungarian.* Foris, Dordrecht.

Huang, C.-T. J. (1982). "Logical Relations in Chinese and the Theory of Grammar." Doctoral dissertation, MIT.

Jaeggli, O. (1981). *Topics in Romance Syntax.* Foris, Dordrecht.

Kayne, R. (1984). *Connectedness and Binary Branching.* Foris, Dordrecht.

Keenan, E. (1988). "Complex Anaphors and Bind Alpha." In *Papers from the twenty-fourth Regional Meeting, CLS.* Chicago Linguistic Society, University of Chicago.

Kinyalolo, K. (1990). "Syntactic Dependencies and the Spec-Head Agreement Hypothesis in KiLega." Doctoral dissertation, UCLA.

Kitagawa, Y. (1986). "Subjects in Japanese and English." Doctoral dissertation, University of Massachusetts, Amherst.

Koopman, H., and D. Sportiche (1988). "Subjects." Ms, UCLA.

Kuroda, S.-Y. (1988). "Whether We Agree or Not: Rough Ideas about the Comparative Grammar of English and Japanese." *Lingvisticae Investigationes* 12: 1–47.

Lasnik, H., and M. Saito (1984). "On the Nature of Proper Government." *Linguistic Inquiry* 15, 235–289.

Longobardi, G. (1985). "Connectedness and Island Constraints." In J. Guéron, H.-G. Obenauer, and J.-Y. Pollock, eds., *Grammatical Representation.* Foris, Dordrecht.

Longobardi, G. (1986). "The Theoretical Status of the Adjunct Condition." In T. Taraldsen, ed., *Proceedings of the Tromsø Round Table on Comparative Romance Syntax.* Tromsø University Press.

Marantz, A. (1984). *On the Nature of Grammatical Relations.* MIT Press, Cambridge, Mass.

May, R. (1985). *Logical Form: Its Structure and Derivation.* MIT Press, Cambridge, Mass.

Pollock, J.-Y. (1989). "Verb Movement, Universal Grammar, and the Structure of IP." *Linguistic Inquiry* 20: 365–424.

Rizzi, L. (1986). "On Chain Formation." In H. Borer, ed., *The Syntax of Pronominal Clitics (Syntax and Semantics* 19). Academic Press, New York.

Rizzi, L. (1990). *Relativized Minimality.* MIT Press, Cambridge, Mass.

Rothstein, S. (1983). "The Syntactic Forms of Predication." Doctoral dissertation, MIT.

Rouveret, A., and J.-R. Vergnaud (1980). "Specifying Reference to the Subject: French Causatives and Conditions on Representations." *Linguistic Inquiry* 11:97–202.

Safir, K. (1983). "On Small Clauses as Constituents." *Linguistic Inquiry* 14:730–735.

Safir, K. (1989). "Implied Non-Coreference and the Pattern of Anaphora." Ms., Rutgers University.

Schein, B. (1981). "Small Clauses and Predication." Ms., MIT.

Stowell, T. (1978). "What Was There before There Was There." In D. Farkas et al., eds., *Papers from the Fourteenth Regional Meeting, CLS*. Chicago Linguistic Society, University of Chicago.

Stowell, T. (1980). "Subjects across Categories." Ms., MIT.

Stowell, T. (1981). "Origins of Phrase Structure." Doctoral dissertation, MIT.

Stowell, T. (1983). "Subjects across Categories." *The Linguistic Review* 2, 285–312. (Revised version of Stowell 1980.)

Stowell, T. (1985). "Null Operators and the Theory of Proper Government." Ms., UCLA.

Stowell, T. (1986). "Null Antecedents and Proper Government." In S. Berman et al., eds., *Proceedings of the Sixteenth Annual Meeting, NELS*. GLSA, University of Massachusetts, Amherst.

Stowell, T. (1989). "Raising in Irish and the Projection Principle." *Natural Language and Linguistic Theory* 7:317–359.

Taraldsen, T. (1983). "Parametric Variaton in Phrase Structure: A Case Study." Doctoral dissertation, University of Tromsø.

Williams, E. (1983). "Against Small Clauses." *Linguistic Inquiry* 14:287–308.

Chapter 9

A Directionality Parameter   Knut Tarald Taraldsen
for Subject-Object Linking

In this paper I will examine some properties of three construction types: (1) the Scandinavian "*la*-causatives," (2) the particle construction, and (3) the analytic past tense construction (temporal auxiliary + past participle). The relevant data concerning (1)–(2) will be found in Scandinavian. The discussion of (3) will also lead to examining certain properties of Romance. My goal in sections 1–3 will be to establish that these three construction types share properties that are reflected in their similar behavior with respect to certain phenomena of parametric variation. I will also propose a partial interpretation of the variation patterns. In sections 4–5 I will develop the initial idea in a way that leads me to postulate a directionality parameter for a certain type of licensing rule.

1   Three Cases of Cross-Linguistic Variation in Scandinavian

I will begin by describing the three instances of cross-linguistic variation in Scandinavian that I will ultimately argue to reflect a single phrase structure parameter.

1.1   Word Order in the *La*-causative Construction
The verb *la* 'let' occurs in sentences like (1), where the embedded infinitive has a subject NP bearing its external θ-role, in all three Scandinavian languages:

(1) Vi *lar* vokteren   henge fangene.
     we let the warden hang the prisoners

This construction seems similar to the one found with perception verbs:

(2) Vi *ser* vokteren   henge fangene.
     we see the warden hang the prisoners

However, with the meaning of 'cause, make', *la* may also occur with an embedded infinitive that lacks a (subject) NP bearing its external θ-role. Thus, (3) is a grammatical sentence in Swedish (modulo choice of morphemes):

(3) Vi lar henge fangene.
    we let hang the prisoners
    'We let the prisoners be hanged.'

Notice that the infinitival verb in (3) has the same morphological shape as in (1); that is, it is an "active" form. In this respect the construction in (3) is similar to the Romance "passive" causative construction illustrated in the (4), the French counterpart of (3):

(4) Nous faisons pendre les prisonniers.
    we   make   hang   the prisoners
    'We make the prisoners be hanged.'

However, we will see later that the parallelism between (3) and (4) is not complete. In (3) (and (4)) the thematic object of the infinitive follows it. This word order is not permitted in Danish. In this language the thematic object of the infinitive must precede the infinitive in *la*-causatives, as in (5):

(5) Vi lar *fangene*   henge.
    we let the prisoners hang
    'We let the prisoners be hanged.'

(Again, there is no "passive morphology" on the infinitive.) Conversely, the word order illustrated by (5) is illicit in Swedish, so that we have the following picture at this point:

(6)   Swedish   Danish
    (3)   OK   *
    (5)   *   OK

In Norwegian, however, both word orders are available in the *la*-causatives, so that (3) and (5) are both grammatical in that language.

1.2 Word Order in the Particle Construction
In Swedish, sentences like (7), where the particle precedes the NP, are grammatical:

(7) Vi släpte *ut* hunden.
    we let   out the dog

If the particle has a complement, the particle may follow the NP, as in (8) (= (12a) in Holmberg 1984):

(8) Han kastade boken   *ut* genom   fönstret.
    he   threw   the book out through the window

However, a "bare" particle may not follow the NP in Swedish, so that (9) is ungrammatical in that language:

(9) *Han släpte hunden *ut*.
    he   let   the dog out

In Danish, on the other hand, (9) is grammatical, but (7) is not; in other words, the particle must follow the NP in Danish. We now see a pattern emerging. Just as the infinitive must precede the object NP in the *la*-causative construction in Swedish, so the particle must precede the NP in that language. In Danish the infinitive must follow the object NP, and the particle must also follow the NP. Assuming that the particle construction is to be grouped with the *la*-causatives with respect to word order variation, we now expect that Norwegian should have both word order options in the particle construction. Since (7) and (9) are both grammatical in Norwegian, this seems correct.

A caveat is required, however. When the NP is an unstressed pronoun, the word order in (7) ceases to be available in Norwegian (as in English):

(10) *Vi slapp *ut*   den.
     we let   out it

(11) Vi slapp den *ut*.
     we let   it   out

But in Swedish (10) is also grammatical (and (11) is ungrammatical).

Ignoring this complication, we can summarize our findings as follows:

(12)

	Swedish	Danish	Norwegian
la V NP	OK	*	OK
la NP V	*	OK	OK
V PRT NP	OK	*	OK
V NP PRT	*	OK	OK

1.3 Auxiliary Selection

In all Scandinavian languages analytic past tenses (the perfect and pluperfect) are formed with the temporal auxiliary *ha* 'have' in the active mood, and with *bli* 'become' or *være* 'be' in the passive. Thus, (13)–(16) are grammatical in all three languages:

(13) Per *har* kysset Kari.
     Per has kissed Kari

(14) Per *har* sunget.
      Per has sung

(15) Kari *er/blir*   kysset (av Per).
      Kari is/becomes kissed by Per

(16) Det *er/blir*   sunget.
      it   is/becomes sung

In Swedish the auxiliary *hava* 'have', but not the auxiliary *vara* 'be', is also used to form the analytic past tenses of unaccusative verbs:

(17) Per *har* kommit.
      Per has come

In Danish, on the other hand, ergative participles combine only with the auxiliary *være* 'be', not with the auxiliary *have* 'have':

(18) Per *er* kommet.
      Per is come

We can summarize these findings as follows:

(19)   Swedish   Danish
      (17)   OK   *
      (18)   *   OK

Assuming the same parameter to underlie both the two instances of word order variation described above and the variation depicted in (19), we now predict that Norwegian again should have both the Swedish and the Danish option. This expectation is fulfilled, since (17) and (18) are both possible (with no difference of meaning) in Norwegian. This fact—that auxiliary selection shows the same kind of cross-linguistic variation within Scandinavian as the word order in *la*-causatives and particle constructions —provides the initial impetus to group the analytic past tense construction together with the other two construction types. However, we will encounter more cogent evidence that supports this grouping.

2 Hierarchical Structure

2.1 *La*-Causatives

We will start by looking at Swedish (and Norwegian) word order—namely, the type ... *la- V NP*, where V is an infinitival V, and NP is the thematic subject of V. (3) is an example of this sort:

(3) Vi lar henge *fangene*.
     we let hang the prisoners
     'We let the prisoners be hanged.'

There are two main hypotheses to consider, each of which has two major variations. The first question is whether or not the embedded V in a sentence like (3) has a subject NP. There are two ways of representing the structure of (3) if the embedded V has a subject:

(20) vi lar [$_S$ NP [$_{VP}$ henge fangene]]

(21) vi lar [$_{XP}$ henge [$_S$ fangene [$_{VP}$ V t]]]

First consider (20). Obviously, NP must be some sort of empty category (EC). There are four possibilities within Government-Binding (GB) Theory, taking the set of ECs to be defined in terms of the binary features [±pronominal] and [±anaphoric]:[1]

(22)   PRO   pro   trace   variable
      pronominal   +   +   −   −
      anaphoric   +   −   +   −

We can presumably eliminate the interpretation of the embedded subject EC of (20) as a trace or a variable, since there is no antecedent binding it, as would be required by the following two conditions on anaphors and variables:[2]

(23) a. A trace must be locally argument-bound (A-bound).
      b. A variable must be locally operator-bound.

In order for the embedded subject EC to be PRO, it must be ungoverned. But the structure given in (20) is isomorphic to the structure of (1) (repeated below), which is given in (24):

(1)   Vi lar vokteren   henge fangene.
      we let the warden hang the prisoners

(24) vi lar [$_S$ vokteren [$_{VP}$ henge fangene]]

In (24) the matrix V must govern the embedded subject position, since the embedded subject would otherwise fail to be assigned Case. Thus, it seems likely that the matrix V should govern the embedded subject position in (20) as well, implying that the embedded subject EC is not an instance of PRO. Notice also that PRO must in general bear a θ-role. Thus, sentences like (25), with the structural analysis in (26), are ungrammatical, since the infinitive, an ergative V, fails to assign a θ-role to its subject:

(25) *It would be fun to arrive many people.

(26) it would be fun [$_S$ PRO to [$_{VP}$ arrive many people]]

However, the subject EC in (20) must be like an expletive subject rather than a θ-marked external argument, since it cannot control reflexives or infinitival adverbials. Compare (27)–(28) to (29)–(30):

(27) Vi lar vokteren$_i$ henge fangene   i ferien sin$_i$.
      we let the warden hang the prisoners during his (REFL) holidays

(28) Vi lar vokteren   henge fangene   efter å ha spist sin frokost.
      we let the warden hang the prisoners after having had breakfast

(29) *Vi lar henge fangene   i ferien sin.
      we let hang the prisoners during his (REFL) holidays

(30) *Vi lar henge fangene   efter å ha spist sin frokost.
      we let hang the prisoners after having had breadfast

In (27) the possessive reflexive *sin* is licitly bound by the embedded subject NP (*vokteren*). If the embedded subject EC in (20) were an argument (θ-bearing constituent), then we would expect *sin* to be licitly bound in (29) as well. But the ungrammaticality of (29) contradicts this expectation. Similarly, the embedded subject NP controls the infinitival adverbial after *å ha* ... in (28) (by virtue of controlling its subject PRO). Again, if the embedded subject EC in (20) were an argument, we would expect that the infinitival adverbial in (30) could also be controlled by the subject EC; but this construal is unavailable. (Consequently, (30) is ungrammatical, because the third person reflexive *sin* requires the PRO subject of the infinitival adverbial to be controlled by a third person NP, but no such controller is available, if the embedded subject EC of (20) is not a controller—control by the nonsubject *fangene* being excluded for independent reasons.) The lack of parallelism between (27)–(28) and (29)–(30) is therefore compatible with the analysis in (20), just in case the subject EC of (20) is not an argument but an expletive element, since expletive elements can plausibly be considered to be inappropriate antecedents for reflexives and infinitival adverbials (or, more accurately, their PRO subjects). However, we have seen that PRO must bear a θ-role; that is, it cannot be an expletive element (see (25)–(26)). Hence, we are led to exclude the possibility that the embedded subject EC in (20) is PRO, independently of whether the embedded subject positon is governed in (20).

The remaining possibility in terms of (22) is that the embedded subject EC postulated in (20) is an occurrence of pro. (Notice, however, that even though pro appears to support an expletive function, it can also in general be an argument (see Rizzi 1986). Hence, the contrast between (27)–(28) and (29)–(30) remains unexplained, unless we have some independent reason why the embedded subject position in (20), but not in (27)–(28), cannot be assigned a θ-role.) However, there is no independent evidence that Scandinavian allows pro (governed by V). In particular, it contrasts with Italian in the same way as English with respect to the diagnostics employed by Rizzi (1986) to show that Italian has pro (governed by V). Therefore, we are ultimately led to discard the anlysis in (20).

The analysis in (21) draws on the existence (in Danish and Norwegian) or *la*-causatives in which the thematic object of the infinitive precedes the infinitive itself. (5) (repeated here) is an example of this kind:

(5) Vi lar fangene   henge.
    we let the prisoners hang
    'We let the prisoners be hanged.'

I will argue that the thematic object of the infinitive is moved into the subject position of a clausal constituent in (5). If the infinitive is fronted in such a structure, (21) results (with XP = S' or S depending on whether this instance of V-fronting is movement of COMP or adjunction to S). In Swedish this V-fronting must then be obligatory, whereas it should be optional in Norwegian and impossible in Danish. This analysis predicts that the postinfinitival NP (*fangene*) in (3) should have the same set of "subject properties" that the preinfinitival NP has in (5). However, we will see that this is not the case. Whereas the preinfinitival NP in (5) does behave like a subject with respect to certain phenomena, this not true of the postinfinitival NP in (3). Therefore, we are also led to discard analysis (21).

Having eliminated both possibilities for analyzing sentences like (3) as having an embedded subject position, we must consider the options available on the view that there is no embedded subject position. One possibility is to assign the structure in (31):

(31) vi lar [$_{VP}$ henge fangene]

The other is to assume that there is not even an embedded VP. Assuming binary branching,[3] this means that the structure must be as in (32):

(32) vi [$_{VP}$ [$_V$ lar henge] fangene]

The latter alternative seems to be at odds with the fact that the string *lar henge* is not treated like a unit (= V) with respect to the "verb-second" phenomenon (V2). Under V2, the tensed V *lar* is obligatorily separated from the cooccurring infinitive:

(33) Derfor   *lar* vi *henge* fangene.
      therefore let we hang the prisoners

(34) *Derfor *lar henge* vi fangene.

Hence, we will tentatively adopt the conclusion that a sentence like (3) has the (S-Structure) analysis in (31).[4]

Turning now to the analysis of (5), we find two initially plausible options. Either the D-Structure object NP is moved to a nonargument position

(Ā-position), the VP-adjoined position, or it is moved to the subject position of a clausal structure. (35) represents the first of these options, and (36) represents the second:

(35) vi lar [$_{VP}$ fangene [$_{VP}$ henge t]]

(36) vi lar [$_{SC}$ fangene [$_{VP}$ henge t]]

In (36) I have chosen to label the constituent *fangene henge t* SC (= "small clause"). This should be regarded as shorthand for a clausal constituent whose exact categorial status remains to be determined.

One consideration that favors (36) over (35) concerns the binding of reflexives in Scandinavian. The pair (37)–(38) illustrates the general fact that only subjects can bind reflexives:[5]

(37) *Vi arresterte *spionen* like før *sin* avreise.
we arrested   the spy just before his (REFL) departure

(38) *Spionen* ble arrestert like før   *sin*   avreise.
the spy was arrested just before his (REFL) departure

Crucially, movement to Ā-positions does not turn nonsubjects into possible antecedents for reflexives:

(39) **Hvilken spion* arresterte vi like før   *sin*   avreise?
which   spy   arrested   we just before his (REFL) departure

(40) **Spionen* arresterte vi like før   *sin*   avreise.
the spy   arrested   we just before his (REFL) departure

(39) is an instance of *wh*-movement, and (40) is an instance of topicalization. In each case the moved object NP remains ineligible for binding the reflexive. It may be that "cliticization" of unstressed pronouns across underlyingly preverbal adverbs involves movement to the VP-adjoined position, so that a sentence like (41) should be analyzed as in (42) (see Christensen 1985; Holmberg 1984):

(41) Derfor   arresterte vi *ham* ikke tidligere.
therefore arrested   we him not   earlier
'Therefore, we did not arrest him earlier.'

(42) derfor arresterte [$_S$ vi [$_{VP}$ ham [$_{VP}$ ikke V t tidligere]]]

However, leftward movement of an unstressed object pronoun does not enable the pronoun to act as antecedent of a reflexive:

(43) *Derfor   arresterte vi *ham* ikke før   *sin*   avreise.
therefore arrested   we him not   before his (REFL) departure

Based on these observations, we see that (35) predicts that the preinfinitival

NP in (5) may not be the antecedent of a reflexive, whereas (36) predicts that it may. As the grammaticality of (44) shows, the latter prediction is correct:

(44) Vi lot *spionen* arrestere like før   *sin*   avreise.
     we let the spy arrest   just before his (REFL) departure
     'We made the spy the arrested just before his departure.'

Hence, we conclude that a sentence like (5) is to be analyzed as in (36), with the preinfinitival NP as the subject of an embedded clausal structure.[6] Notice that the ungrammaticality of the following sentence supports our earlier decision to discard (21) as a possible analysis of (3): *Vi lot arrestere* spionen *like før* sin *avreise* 'we let arrest the spy just before his departure'. Thus, we reach the conclusion that (3) is to be analyzed as in (31), and (5) as in (36):[7]

(3) Vi lar *henge* fangene.
    we let hang the prisoners
    'We let the prisoners be hanged.'

(5) Vi lar fangene   *henge*.
    we let the prisoners hang
    'We let the prisoners be hanged.'

(31) vi lar [$_{VP}$ henge fangene]

(36) vi lar [$_{SC}$ fangene [$_{VP}$ henge t]]

2.2 Particle Constructions

Let us first consider which structural analysis to assign to a particle construction in which the NP precedes the particle. Following in part Kayne (1985a), we will assume that the NP and the particle form a separate constituent, as indicated in (45):

(45)

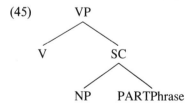

(For the time being I leave undetermined the internal structure of the PARTP.)

The evidence supporting this assumption (beyond what Kayne adduces) is discussed in Taraldsen 1983a. For example, the preparticle NP behaves like a left-branch constituent with respect to extraction from a complex

NP. Compare (46), which groups with (49)–(50), to (47)–(48):

(46) *en mann som vi ikke slipper [noen   som kjenner ____] inn
     a man that we not let   anybody that knows   in

(47) en mann som vi ikke slipper noen   inn [som kjenner ____]
     a man that we not let   anybody in   that knows

(48) en mann som vi ikke slipper inn [noen   som kjenner ____]
     a man that we not let   in   anybody that knows

(49) *en mann som [ingen   som kjenner ____] arbeider her
     a man that nobody that knows   works   here

(50) *en mann som vi ikke anser   [noen   som kjenner ____]
     a man that we not consider anybody that knows
     lykkelig
     happy

The parallel behavior of (46) and (49)–(50) in this paradigm will follow from Kayne's (1984:8) Connectedness Condition or Chomsky's (1986a) formulation of the Subjacency Condition, provided the preparticle NP is on a left branch.

Next let us consider the particle construction in which the NP follows the particle. I diverge from Kayne's (1985a) analysis by taking the NP to be base-generated in the postparticle position. Thus, we will not assume that the postverbal NP is adjoined to VP or the PARTP, leaving a trace in the preparticle position. Some evidence supporting this position is given in Taraldsen 1983a. Notice also that the possibility of extracting from a postparticle NP (see (48)) may indicate that the NP is in an argument position rather than in an adjoined position (see Chomsky 1986a; Cinque 1985; Huang 1982; Longobardi, forthcoming).

We will assume that the postparticle NP is generated under the PARTP node, as a complement to the particle; see section 4.4 for more discussion. If this is correct, the hierarchical structures that are assigned to particle constructions are isomorphic with the ones attributed to la-causatives in the preceding subsection.

2.3 Auxiliary Selection and Clitic-Participle Agreement

We have previously found reason to believe that the auxiliary alternation in Scandinavian is controlled by the same parameter that controls the word order variation in la-causatives and particle constructions. In fact, comparison of the Romance languages offers a stronger argument.

Some Romance languages show (morphological) agreement between a past participle cooccurring with auxiliary *have* and a preceding clitic pronoun. Thus, we find sentences like (51) in Italian and (52) in French:

(51) Paolo *li*   ha già   lett*i*.

  Paolo them (MASC.PL) has already read (MASC.PL)

(52) Ces   tables, il *les*   a   repeint*es*.

  these tables he them (FEM.PL) has repainted (FEM.PL)

Kayne (1985b) argues that agreement always is with a local subject, so that (51)–(52) must have the form (53), where $V + to$ is a participle:

(53) ...Cl$_i$ have [$_{SC}$ e$_i$ [$_{VP}$ V + *to* e$_i$...

Thus, a language that for some reason allows auxiliary *have* to appear only with a bare VP, but not with an SC as in (53), will never show clitic-participle agreement. Notice, however, that the structure in (53) is isomorphic with the structure we have been led to assume for Scandinavian *la*-causatives and particle constructions. For instance, (53) must share with the *la*-causatives of the form (36) the property of containing an SC with a non-θ-marked subject position. This strongly suggests that the same parameter that determines whether a language may have *la*-causatives or particle constructions in which the NP precedes the infinitive or the particle also determines whether clitic-participle agreement is possible.[8]

Notice now that we seem to have the following correlation: Exactly those Romance languages have clitic-participle agreement that also have an alternation between the auxiliaries *have* and *be* in the compound past tenses. Thus, both clitic-participle agreement and auxiliary alternation are found in French and Italian, but not in Portuguese, Spanish, or Romanian.[9]

This suggests that auxiliary selection and participle agreement are controlled by the same parameter. But since we have seen that the parameter controlling auxiliary selection is the same as the one controlling the word order variation in Scandinavian *la*-causatives and particle constructions, we now conclude that participle agreement and the Scandinavian-type word order variation also are determined by the same parameter.

3 Government and the Internal Structure of SC

In order to determine the factors controlling the word order variation seen in *la*-causatives and particle constructions, I will first consider evidence supporting a theory of government where a minimality condition replaces the condition that certain projection types are barriers to government. Then I will show that this theory of government imposes a strict requirement on the internal structure of the SC that I will take to occur in *la*-causatives and in particle constructions where the NP precedes the infinitive or the particle. Finally I will suggest that the internal structure of the SC interacts with predication in a way that leads to preliminary formulation of a parameter.

3.1   The Minimality Condition on Government

Government is thought of as a relation between some nonphrasal constituent X (the governor) and a phrase Z (the governee) c-commanded by X.[10] However, it is well known that in many instances c-command is not sufficient for government to obtain. The following are three examples of this kind:

(54) ... V [$_{NP}$ NP$_i$ ... N ...] ...

(55) ... V [$_{PP}$ P NP] ...

(56) ... INFL [$_{VP}$ V ... NP ...] ...

We do not want to say that V governs NP$_i$ in (54), since various incorrect predictions with respect to Case marking and extraction of NP$_i$ would then ensue. For the same reason, we will want to prevent V or INFL from governing the NP in (55)–(56), although the c-command requirement is satisfied.

Chomsky (1980) proposes that certain constituent types be considered impregnable to government from the outside. In particular, X would not govern Z in the configuration (57):

(57) ... X ... [$_\alpha$ ... Z ...]
$\quad$ α = S or NP

Chomsky (1981) generalizes this approach so that all maximal projections become "barriers" to government. Empirically, this presents the obvious advantage of extending the account to (55)–(56) (assuming VP to be a maximal projection). There is also a conceptual bonus, since the question "Why are just S and NP barriers?" does not arise.[11] Yet both empirical and conceptual problems remain.

The main empirical problem, from our point of view, comes from the recognition that S is a maximal projection (for instance, of INFL); see, in particular, Chomsky 1986a. But the Standard GB Theory analyses of raising and "accusative-with-infinitive" presuppose that a matrix V can govern the subject of S, as indicated in (58)–(59):

(58) John$_i$ seems [$_S$ t$_i$ to understand]

(59) we believe [$_S$ him to understand]

Chomsky (1986a) makes a special stipulation to exempt S from barrier status (in the cases relevant for government). The major conceptual problem of the generalized barriers approach is simply that it remains unexplained why maximal projections should be barriers to government (perhaps, only under the special conditions formulated in Chomsky 1986a).

Another, quite different type of condition has been imposed on government, namely, the "minimal c-command requirement." A definition of government incorporating such a requirement could run as follows (see Chomsky 1980):

(60) A governs B $=_{\text{def}}$ (a) A $= X^0$, (b) A c-commands B, and (c) there is no C (distinct from A) c-commanding B but not A.

As Chomsky (1986a) notes, the minimal c-command requirement excludes government of NP by V or INFL in (55)–(56) independently of the barriers proviso, since the P in (55) and the V in (56) c-command NP, but not V or INFL.

Notice that clause (c) of (60) would also prevent V from governing NP_i in (54), if the definition of c-command includes the following:[12]

(61) A c-commands B $=_{\text{def}}$ the least constituent C containing both A and B (a) immediately dominates A or (b) is a projection of A.

Since the constituent labeled NP in (54) is a projection of N, it follows from clause (b) of (61) that N c-commands NP_i. But it does not also c-command V. Therefore, (60) implies that V does not govern NP_i.

Combined with (61), the minimality condition on government subsumes the proposal that maximal projections are barriers to government.[13] Hence, we have a solution to the conceptual problem arising from the original barriers idea: maximal projections are barriers simply because they have heads. In fact, we can draw the stronger conclusion that all headed constituents—in other words, all projections—are barriers.

This leads us back to the major empirical problem for the barriers approach. We have seen that S, being a maximal projection, should also be a barrier to government, but isn't. With respect to the combination of minimal c-command and (61), the problem seems even harder, since S should now be a barrier, even if not maximal. However, it turns out, as we will see after a brief detour, that the analysis based on minimal c-command offers an interesting solution to this problem, one that is not open to the barriers approach.

What we want to do is extend the minimal c-command approach in the spirit of Reuland (1981, 1983). The intuitive idea is that the domains of distinct governors must not intersect (where the "domain of governor X" is understood as the set of all constituents governed by X). Thus, the minimal c-command condition expressed as clause (c) in (60) should really be restricted to those cases where C actually governs B—that is, where C minimally is a (lexical) X^0 element. This leads to the following formulation:

(62) A governs B $=_{def}$ (a) A $= X^0$, (b) A c-commands B, and (c) if C (distinct from A) c-commands B, but not A, then C must not govern B.

This definition has the unusual feature that the term to be defined—namely, *governs*—occurs in clause (c) of the definition, making it appear circular. However, (62) can always be applied in a stepwise fashion such that clause (c) does not come into play in the initial steps. To illustrate, consider how (62) is applied to the structure in (54) (assuming (61) to hold):

(54) ... V $[_{NP}$ NP$_i$ ... N ...] ...

First, consider the pair (NP$_i$, N). Taking N as A with respect to (62), we see that there is no Y^0-element (other than A) that c-commands B ($=$ NP$_i$), but not A. Hence, N is determined to govern NP$_i$ on the basis of clauses (a)–(b) alone. Next, consider the pair (V, NP$_i$). Clearly, V taken as A meets both clause (a) and clause (b) with respect to B $=$ NP$_i$. But now clause (c) also comes into play. Since N c-commands NP$_i$ (by virtue of (61)), but not V, the antecedent part of clause (c) holds true with C $=$ N. Therefore, N must not govern NP$_i$. But we have already established that it does. Hence, clause (c) does not hold, and we conclude that V does not govern NP$_i$ in (54).

Notice, incidentally, that V does govern N, since there is no other X^0-element that c-commands N, but not V. More generally, it will normally be the case that the head of a projection X^i can be governed by an element outside of X^i, since the head is normally not c-commanded by a Y^0-element within its own projection. Thus, the approach to government proposed here needs no special stipulation to accommodate Belletti and Rizzi's (1981) observation that if A governs a (maximal) projection B, it also governs the head of B.

I will illustrate and develop this account of government by applying it to a few illustrative cases, including government into S.

3.2 Some Applications

First let us consider three cases where maximal projections fail to be barriers to government. They turn out to have a common structural characteristic, and we will see how the proposed definition of government, suitably extended, predicts the lack of barrier status from this shared characteristic.

French exhibits the alternation illustrated in (63)–(64):

(63) J'ai lu   beaucoup de romans policiers.
     I have read many   (of) mysteries

(64) J'ai   beaucoup lu   de romans policiers.
     I have many   read (of) mysteries
     'I have read many mysteries.'

The separation of a quantificational determiner from the rest of the NP it modifies is possible with all quantifier words that occur in the structure Q de N^i (such as *trop* 'too much/many', *pas mal* 'quite a bit/few'). But it is not possible with quantifier words that are not followed by *de*:

(65) J'ai lu   plusieurs romans policiers.
     I have read several   mysteries

(66) *J'ai plusieurs lu romans policiers.

We will assume that the separation is effected by a movement rule (possibly the one that relates (?*)*J'ai compris tout* and *J'ai tout compris*, both 'I have understood everything') that leaves a trace in the determiner position of the postverbal NP; but see Kayne 1975 for alternative views.

A related case is the extraction of determiners of NP under *wh-*movement. In French, for example, *combien* 'how much/many' can be extracted from the containing NP:

(67) Combien as-tu   lu   de romans policiers?
     how many have you read (of) mysteries
     'How many mysteries have you read?'

Again, *combien* occurs in the context Q de N^i. Determiners that do not occur in this context cannot undergo *wh-*movement separately:

(68) *Quels as-tu   lu   romans policiers?
      which have you read mysteries

Norwegian provides a similar case, when *hva* 'what' occurs in NPs of the form *hva for en* N^i 'which N^i' (literally 'what for a N^i'). (Dutch and German exhibit the same phenomenon.) Both (69) and (70) are possible:

(69) Hva for en bok   har du lest?
     what for a   book have you read
     'Which book have you read?'

(70) Hva har du lest for en bok?
     what have you read for a   book
     'Which book have you read?'

This alternation is not found with *wh*-determiners that are not followed by a preposition:[14]

(71) Hvilken bok   har   du   lest
      which   book have you read

(72) *Hvilken har du lest bok?

Finally, extraction of *wh*-determiners from AP in Romanian provides a case similar to *combien*-extraction in French, but with AP rather than NP as the containing category. In Romanian the *wh*-word *cît* 'how (much/many)' occurs in the context Q *de* A^i, as in (73), and can be separated from the rest of the AP under *wh*-movement:

(73) Nici nu ştii   cît   de norocit am   fost.
     even not you-know how lucky   I-have been
     'You don't even known how lucky I have been.'

(74) Nici nu ştii   cît   am   fost de norocit.
     even not you-know how I-have been lucky
     'You don't even known how lucky I have been.'

Other adjectival *wh*-modifiers are not followed by *de* and also do not extract. Even more strikingly, *cît* also occurs as a nominal modifier, but it is not followed by *de* in NPs and also does not extract from NP:

(75) Nici nu ştii   cîte   fete am   văzut.
      even not you-know how many girls I-have seen
      'You don't even know how many girls I have seen.'

(76) *Nici nu ştii cîte am văzut fete.

Assuming that the determiner leaves a trace in the determiner position of the containing NP/AP, the well-formedness of the extraction structures raises a question with respect to the Empty Category Principle (ECP). In particular, let us assume that government by the head N or A does not make the determiner position properly governed in the sense of the ECP.[15] Then proper government will obtain just in case the V governing the NP or AP in (64), (67), (70), and (74) also governs its determiner position. But this should be impossible, if maximal projections are always barriers to government.

Government into NP and AP should also be impossible, if (62) were correct as formulated. Ideally, our definition of government should be such that government into AP and NP would be allowed just in case there is a preposition following the determiner position, as in all the grammatical cases reviewed above, and in none of ungrammatical ones. But (62) should actually be modified for independent, conceptual reasons, and the required revision turns out to give just the desired result.

We formulated (62) to reflect the intuitive idea that domains of distinct governors may not intersect. Yet, clause (c) says only that government cannot go into the domain of a separate governor. To reflect our leading idea more accurately, clause (c) should also say that government cannot go out of the domain of a separate governor. This is achieved in the following formulation, which henceforth replaces (62) as our definition of government:

(77) A governs B $=_{def}$ (a) A = X^0, (b) c-commands B, (c) if C (distinct from A) c-commands B, but not A, then C must not govern B, and (d) if C (distinct from B) c-commands A, but not B, then C must not govern A.

The addition of clause (d) has the effect that the head X does not govern the DET(erminer) position in the configuration (78):

(78) ... $[_X{}^{max} DET ... [_{X^i} P [_{X^{i-1}} ... X ...]]]$ ...

Consider first the pair (P, X). Clauses (c) and (d) do not come into play, since there is no third Y^0 c-commanding one of P, X, but not the other. Consequently, setting A = P, we determine that P governs X by virtue of clauses (a)–(b) alone. Suppose now that we take the head X to govern its determiner position in (78). Setting now A = X and B = DET, we see immediately that clauses (a)–(b) are met. But now there is a third element C, also a Y^0-element, c-commanding one of A and B, but not the other. P c-commands X (= A), but not DET (= B) (because it can only c-command by clause (a) of definition (61), not being a head). Thus, with C = P, the antecedent part of clause (d) is not satisfied, and we conclude that the head X does not govern the determiner position of its projection in (78).

This means that when a construction of the form (78) is embedded under a Y^0-element Y, as in (79), Y will govern the determiner position of X^{max}:

(79) ... Y ... $[_{X^{max}} DET ... [_{X^i} P [_{X^{i-1}} ... X ...]]]$ ...

Suppose A = Y and B = DET. Clauses (a)–(b) both hold. Does clause (c) hold? Clearly, there is a Y^0-element distinct from Y that c-commands DET (= B), but not Y(= A), namely, X. So the antecedent part of clause (c) is true. Hence, it must also be true that X(= C) does not govern DET(= B). But as we have seen, this is true: X does not govern DET in (79). Therefore, clause (c) is met, and since clause (d) does not come into play, we conclude that Y indeed governs DET in (79).

From the present point of view, examples (64), (67), (70), and (74) are just special instances of (79), with Y = V, P = *de* or *for*, and X = N or A. Thus, once we generalize the definition of government to exclude all cases where the domains of distinct goverors intersect, we automatically have an account where the transparency to government of NP and AP depends on the existence of a preposition like *de* or *for*. Since a comparable result does not appear available on the barriers analysis, we take it that the data discussed above provide empirical support for our account of government.

Government into S can be treated in the same way. There are three relevant construction types to consider: raising, "exceptional Case marking," and English *for-to* construction. In terms of the account just proposed, it is revealing that in languages like Norwegian or English these constructions are possible only if the infinitival complement contains a so-called infinitival marker, such as *to*. I will claim that this is because the infinitival marker functions in the same way as the prepositional elements studied above. In its absence, the head of S governs the embedded subject. But when the infinitival marker occurs, it governs the head of S, so that the head of S does not govern the embedded subject, which is therefore ungoverned within the embedded S. Only then may an element outside the embedded S (the matrix V, or *for*) govern the embedded subject.[16,17]

3.3 Projection Composition
Returning to the question of formulating a parameter to control the three types of cross-linguistic variation discussed earlier, we will now see that the previous observations about government provide a clue. Initially we will look only at the *la*-causatives. In particular, we will see that the proposed view of government leads to a very specific requirement for structures like (36):

(36) vi lar [$_{SC}$ fangene   [$_{VP}$ henge t]]
     we let   the prisoners   hang

We assume that the preposed NP *fangene* must be Case-marked in its S-Structure (argument-) position. This is true regardless of whether its trace is Case-marked or not. Data from languages like Icelandic, where an NP with inherent Case moved to the subject position of an infinitival clause may appear only in "exceptional Case marking" contexts, indicates that a (nonnull) NP must appear in a Case-marked position at S-Structure even if it is part of a Case-marked chain anyway.

But since Case (other than nominative) is only assigned left to right in Scandinavian, the subject position of the SC in (36) is Case-marked only if it is Case-marked by the matrix V *lar*. Therefore, *lar* must govern the subject of the SC.

Taking into consideration the conclusions reached in the preceding subsections, we see that the infinitive *henge* must not govern the subject of the SC. Given the lack of any prepositional element that could have the effect of preventing *henge*, taken as the head of the SC, from governing the subject, we are therefore led to conclude that the infinitive must not be the head of the SC. (The SC is either headless or headed by some "defective" element incapable of governing the subject position.)

Suppose now that in Swedish, where (36) is ill formed, each V must project to some V^i predicated of a subject. Superficially, it might appear that this condition would already be contradicted by the well-formedness of (31) in Swedish:

(31) vi lar [$_{VP}$ henge fangene]

In (31) the embedded VP does not seem to be paired with a subject. Suppose, however, that we introduce the following convention for *projection Composition* (p-composition):

(80) If X^i is a projection of X and immediately dominates Y^j, a projection of Y categorially nondistinct from X, then each X^h, for $h \geqslant i$, is a projection of both X and Y.

If (80) is correct, the matrix VP in (31) is also a projection of the infinitive, since it immediately dominates a projection of the infinitive (which, obviously, is categorially nondistinct from V), as shown in (81):

(81)

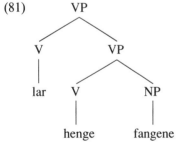

In the next section we will see a piece of Swedish data that supports the contention that (80) applies in all well-formed instances of the general form illustrated in (31). If this contention is correct, then the infinitive does indeed satisfy the requirement that it project to some V^i predicated of a subject. In (31) the relevant subject is the subject of the matrix VP, which is also a projection of the infinitive.

Having seen that (80) makes (31) compatible with the assumption that each V in Swedish must head some V^i predicated of a subject, we may now investigate the consequences of this assumption with respect to the structure in (36). We see immediately that p-composition, as defined in (80), may not take place in the substructure given in (82), unless the node labeled SC is in fact also a projection of the infinitive:

(82)

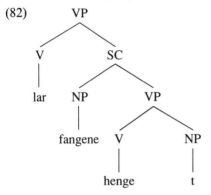

But we have previously determined that (36) is ill formed if SC $= V^j$, since the matrix V will then be unable to assign Case to the NP *fangene*. Therefore, p-composition cannot take place in (36), which for this reason will violate a requirement that each V heads a projection predicated on a subject. Since (36) is in fact ill formed in Swedish, we might therefore take Swedish to be subject to such a requirement.

Notice that we have been assuming throughout that the embedded VP is not predicated of the SC subject in (36). This is because whenever a VP headed by an active form of a transitive V is predicated of some NP, it always assigns it an "external" θ-role. But in (36) no θ-role is assigned to the subject position of the SC—if it had been, the θ-Criterion would have been violated, since *fangene* "inherits" the object θ-role. However, the embedded VP probably *is* predicated of the SC subject in examples like (83):

(83) Vi lar vokteren   henge fangene.
      we let the warden hang the prisoners

Interestingly, such sentences are grammatical in Swedish as well, which is expected if we take the view that the only thing ruling out (36) is the requirement about predication, as discussed above.

Thus, we may consider the parameter we are looking for to be partially related to the question whether, in a given language, each V must project to V^j predicated of a subject or not. In Swedish this restriction holds. In

Danish and Norwegian it does not. I will explore this idea at greater length below.

4 Linking Asymmetries

In this section I will develop further the preliminary formulation of the parameter controlling word order in Scandinavian causatives and particle constructions, clitic-participle agreement in Romance, and auxiliary alternation. I will argue that the parameter is to be formulated in terms of processes relating predicates and arguments.

I will begin by presenting the basic idea and by showing its applicability to word order facts concerning Scandinavian causatives and to particle constructions. In section 5 I will demonstrate that the auxiliary alternation is accounted for by the interplay of the proposed parameter and some fairly standard assumptions about the morphology of participles. I will also show that some contrasts between Spanish and Italian with respect to Case marking in absolute participle constructions fall under the analysis.

4.1 The Basic Idea

A VP is typically involved in two different predication relations: it is the locus of the predication on an object NP (henceforth, the *internal predication*), and it is itself predicated on the subject (henceforth, the *external predication*); see Marantz 1984, Chomsky 1981. Predication may be reflected by θ-role assignment. But we want to use the notion "predication" also to refer to the relationship between an ergative V and its subject. This too will be counted as an instance of external predication in what follows (compare Rothstein 1983). Similarly, an intransitive V lacking an object will nevertheless be considered to support internal (0-place) predication. The main idea that will be exploited is that there is an asymmetric dependency between the two predication relations such that the existence of one may depend on the existence of the other, but not vice versa. Moreover, we will take it that Universal Grammar does not determine which predication relation (external or internal) will be "dominant," giving rise to a parameter.

To implement this idea, we first define *canonical predication for V* in the following way: The relation between V and a sister constituent X^m of V' is canonical external predication, if and only if either V is transitive or intransitive and X^m is θ-marked, or V is ergative and X^m is not θ-marked. Then X^m is a *canonical subject* of V. V supports canonical internal predication if and only if V is intransitive and there is no sister X^m, V is transitive and governs a Case-marked X^m, or V is ergative and governs a Caseless X^m. Then X^m is a *canonical object* of V.

We will assume that in every language either canonical internal predication is licensed by canonical external predication, or the other way around. Thus, every language is subject to (84) or (85):

(84) A canonical subject of V_i is licensed only if V_i supports canonical internal predication.

(85) Canonical internal predication is licensed for V_i only if V_i has a canonical subject.

In languages where (84) holds, each time a transitive or ergative V has a canonical subject, it must be able to find a canonical "object" (in the extended sense). In a sense, it must link its subject to an object. We will therefore say that such languages have *subject-driven linking*.

In languages where (85) holds, each time a transitive or ergative V has a canonical "object" (in the extended sense), it must be able to project to a VP ($= V'$) with a canonical subject. We will say that such languages have *object-driven linking*.

I will illustrate the properties of this analysis in the course of applying it to the Scandinavian *la*-causatives.

4.2 Deriving the Word Order in Swedish Causatives

Let us begin by considering causatives with the word order shown in (86):

(86) Vi lar henge fangene.
we let hang the prisoners
'We let the prisoners be hanged.'

We have previously argued that the structure should be represented as in (87):

(87) vi [$_{VP}$ lar [$_{VP}$ henge fangene]]

Suppose now that the language in question has object-driven linking. We will assume that the transitive V *henge* remains a Case assigner in (87) and, moreover, that Case assignment applies obligatorily whenever it can. The embedded V, then, has a canonical "object," in the sense of (85). Consequently, it must project to a VP-node having a subject that is canonical for the embedded V—that is, a subject in a θ-position, since the embedded V is transitive.

Clearly, the embedded VP has no subject at all in (87). Therefore, (85) will exclude the structure, unless the embedded V can be said to project to the matrix VP. Since the subject of the matrix VP is in fact in a θ-position (bearing the external θ-role induced by the causative V), it would be appropriate for the embedded V, and (85) would be satisfied. This means that (87) will be characterized as well formed in a language with object-driven linking just in case the process of p-composition (80) (repeated here as (88)) is available:

(88) If X^i is a projection of X and immediately dominates Y^j, a projection of Y categorially nondistinct from X, then each X^h, for $h \geqslant i$, is a projection of both X and Y.

Assuming (88) to hold, we will conclude that (87) is well formed in a language with object-driven linking. However, (90), the structure we have attributed to causatives with the word order in (89), will fare differently:

(89) Vi lar fangene   henge.
      we let the prisoners hang
      'We let the prisoners be hanged.'

(90) vi [$_{VP}$ lar [$_{SC}$ fangene$_i$ [$_{VP}$ henge t$_i$]]]

Again, our assumptions regarding Case assignment imply that Case is assigned to the object of the infinitive, the trace of *fangene*. If linking is object driven, then (85) implies that the embedded V, a transitive V, must be the head of a VP with a subject in a θ-position. Clearly, the subject of the SC is not in a θ-position (since its chain would otherwise receive two distinct θ-roles) and therefore is not in this case appropriate in the sense of (85). As in (87), only the matrix subject will make linking terminate successfully. However, in order for the matrix subject to be analyzed as the subject of a VP headed by the embedded V, the projection of the embedded V must be compounded with the projection of the matrix V, just as in (87). But (88) allows p-composition in (90) just in case SC is analyzed as a further projection of the infinitive. That, on the other hand, would mean that the infinitive governs the subject position of SC, so that the matrix V would be prevented from also governing this position, with ensuing failure of Case assignment.[18] Hence, there is no way for (90) to be grammatical in a language with object-driven linking.

Since (90) must be ill formed and (87) well formed in Swedish, we will assume that Swedish has object-driven linking. From the point of view of section 1, object-driven linking can be seen as the reason why Swedish Vs are subject to the licensing condition that they head a predication on an external argument. For transitive and unaccusative Vs, this now follows from the necessity of linking the object to an appropriate subject. With transitive Vs, this requires the V to head a predication on an external argument in the standard sense of "predication." Given our extension to the relation between a subject position and a VP headed by an unaccusative V, it follows for all dipositional Vs.[19]

This analysis of the *la*-causative construction in Swedish makes the same predictions about sentences like (91)–(92), where a θ-role is assigned to the subject position of SC, as the preliminary formulation in section 1:

(91) Jeg lar Per rive   huset.
     I   let Per demolish the house

(92) De   lot barna   sove.
     they let the children sleep

(93) jeg lar [$_{SC}$ Per [$_{VP}$ rive huset]]

(94) de lot [$_{SC}$ barna [$_{VP}$ sove]]

The analysis also makes a more subtle prediction. Suppose that we replace the transitive infinitive in (87) with an unaccusative one:[20]

(95) vi [$_{VP}$ lot [$_{VP}$ omkomme fangene]]
             die

No element can assign (structural) Case to the object of the infinitive in (95). The matrix V is a Case assigner but fails to govern the embedded object position, which is "already" governed by the infinitive. Moreover, the embedded object NP is not adjacent to the matrix V. The embedded V, on the other hand, is an unaccusative V and therefore does not assign (structural) Case.[21] Hence, the embedded V has a Case-free object NP, which is an appropriate object for an unaccusative V. If linking is object driven, it therefore follows from (85) that the embedded V must head a VP with an appropriate subject position. Since the embedded VP has no subject at all, our sole candidate is the matrix subject. As before, we can therefore assume that the projections of the matrix and the embedded V are compounded, so that the embedded V also is a head of the matrix VP. But in (95) this is not sufficient for satisfaction of (85). Since a θ-role (the "causer role") is assigned to the subject of the matrix VP, this subject is not appropriate for the embedded V, which is now unaccusative. Hence, we must conclude that (95) is ill formed, even though the quite similar structure in (87) is well formed.

This prediction is borne out. Sentences like (96) are in fact ungrammatical in Swedish (and Norwegian), contrasting minimally with sentences like (86):

(96) *Vi lar omkomme fangene/mange fanger.
     we let die   the prisoners/many prisoners

(86) Vi lar henge fangene.

        we let hang the prisoners

Notice also that (96) becomes grammatical, even in Swedish, when the object of the unaccusative infinitive is moved to the subject position of SC:

(97) Vi lar fangene   omkomme.

        we let the prisoners die

(98) vi [$_{VP}$ lar [$_{SC}$ fangene$_i$ [$_{VP}$ omkomme t$_i$]]]

This is because the non-θ-marked subject position of the SC provides an appropriate subject for the embedded unaccusative to link to; in other words, from our point of view, (97) is like (91)–(92).

4.3   Deriving the Word Order in Danish Causatives

Let us now consider the status of (87) in a language with subject-driven linking, that is, a language subject to (84):

(87) vi [$_{VP}$ lar [$_{VP}$ henge fangene]]

The embedded V raises no problem with respect to (84). If its projection is not compounded with the matrix VP (assuming p-composition to be optional, perhaps erroneously), it has no (appropriate) subject, and (84) is simply irrelevant. If, on the other hand, p-compositon takes place, then (84) dictates that the embedded V, being transitive, govern a Case-marked NP, which it does, given previous assumptions about Case assignment.

The matrix V, however, is also transitive.[22] Since it heads a VP whose subject is in a θ-position, (84) requires that it too govern a Case-marked constituent. We have already observed that the matrix V does not govern the object of the infinitive in (87), given clause (c) of definition (77) of government. The only constituent governed by the matrix V in (87) is the embedded VP. But Case cannot in general be assigned to VP, since its head, V, cannot bear Case features. Hence, the matrix V has no appropriate "object" in (87), and (84) is violated. Therefore, (87) is illformed in a language with subject-driven linking, and correspondingly, sentences like (86) are ungrammatical in such languages:

(86) Vi lar henge fangene.

        we let hang the prisoners

Conversely, sentences like (89) will be characterized as well formed in languages where (84) (rather than (85)) holds:

(89) Vi lar fangene henge.

To see this, consider again (90), the structure assigned to (89):

(90) vi [$_{VP}$ lar [$_{SC}$ fangene$_i$ [$_{VP}$ henge t$_i$]]]

Here, the matrix V does govern an appropriate "object"—namely, the NP in the subject position of SC—provided SC is not a projection of the infinitive. Since we are considering a language with subject-driven linking, (85) does not hold, and the fact that the embedded transitive V has a Case-marked object does not force it to link to an appropriate subject, so that p-composition with the matrix VP, requiring $SC = V^n$, is not forced in (90). Hence, (90) is well formed in a language with subject-driven linking, and (89) is therefore expected to be grammatical.

Since in fact (86) is impossible in Danish, but (89) is grammatical, we will take it that Danish has subject-driven linking.

Finally, we will assume that linking has no fixed direction in Norwegian —in other words, that licensing of a predication relation can proceed either from internal to external, as in Swedish, or the other way around, as in Danish. Therefore, both (86) and (89) are available in Norwegian. Similarly, both the Swedish and the Danish option will be available in particle constructions and compound past tenses.

4.4 Particle Constructions

The most straightforward way to extend this analysis to particle constructions consists in analyzing sentences like (99)–(100) as shown in (101)–(102) and stipulating that bare particles are like transitive Vs with respect to Case assignment and conditions (84)–(85):

(99) Hun sendte ut *maten.*
      she   sent   out the food

(100) Hun sendte *maten*   ut.
      she   sent   the food out

(101) hun sendte [$_{PrtP}$ ut *maten*]

(102) hun sendte [$_{SC}$ *maten$_i$* [$_{PARTP}$ ut t$_i$]]

If so, we have an immediate account in terms of (84) and (85) for the fact that Swedish accepts (99), but not (100), and that the judgments in Danish are the other way around.

However, this account does not extend to sentences where particles combine with unaccusative Vs:

(103) Det kom inn *en hund.*
      it   came in   a dog
      'There came in a dog.'

(104) Det kom *en hund* inn.
      it   came a dog   in

In particular, if the particle is like a transitive V in the causative construction, then (105), the structure underlying (103), would be ill formed not only in Danish but also in Swedish:

(105) det [$_{VP}$ kom [$_{PARTP}$ inn en hund]]

The reason is that the matrix subject position obviously is not a θ-position in (105), so that the matrix subject is not appropriate, in the sense of (85), for the particle, which we have assumed to be like a transitive verb. Hence, (85) is violated.

Conversely, if the particle is treated like an unaccusative V in (103)–(104), so that (105) is well formed in Swedish, we have no way of explaining why (104) is not also well formed in Swedish. Consider (106), its underlying structure:

(106) det [$_{VP}$ kom [$_{SC}$ en hund$_i$ [$_{PARTP}$ inn t$_i$]]]

If *inn* is unaccusative with respect to the application of (85), then the particle can in fact satisfy (85) by linking to the SC subject, which, being in a non-θ-position, is appropriate for an unaccusative element. Then there would be no need for p-composition with the matrix VP, and SC would not need to be analyzed as a projection of the infinitive, so that the matrix V could govern the subject position in SC.[23]

To accommodate these observations, we will tentatively assume that particles assimilate to the matrix V under p-composition but are otherwise like transitive Vs with respect to (84)–(85). Thus, the particle is unaccusative like the matrix V in (105), where p-composition applies, so that (105) now conforms to (85). But in (106), where p-composition cannot apply with impunity (but see note 23), the particle is transitive with respect to (84)–(85), and (85) therefore characterizes (106) as ill formed in Swedish, as desired.

Perhaps this hypothesis can be formulated in such a way as to receive independent support from the contrasts seen in the following Swedish sentences.[24]

(107) Hon har jagat   bort hunden.
         she   has chased away the dog

(108) *Hunden blir jagad   bort.
          the dog is   chased away

(109) Hunden blir bortjagad.
         the dog is   awaychased
         'The dog is chased away.'

On the one hand, the ungrammatical passive sentence in (108) contrasts with the active one in (107). On the other hand, incorporation of the particle into the V restores grammaticality to the passive sentence, as seen in (109). Suppose that p-composition only allows a particle to assimilate to the lexically given specification of the matrix V with respect to the transitive/unaccusative opposition. Thus, although a past participle comes to behave like an unaccusative V in the passive construction with respect to external θ-role assignment, it nevertheless counts as a transitive, as determined by the lexical root, with respect to assimilation. Then the particle is transitive in (110) (the structure underlying (108)), even if p-composition takes place, triggering assimilation:[25]

(110) hunden$_i$ blir [$_{SC}$ t$_i$ [$_{VP}$ jagad [$_{PARTP}$ bort t$_i$]]]

But since not even the matrix subject (that is, the trace subject of SC) is in a θ-position in (110), the "transitive" particle has no appropriate subject, and (110) accordingly conflicts with (85), thus accounting for the ungrammaticality of (108) in Swedish. (In (109) we assume that a complex V is formed, so that there is no particle projection falling under the scope of (85).)

As we should expect, the ungrammaticality of (108) in Swedish contrasts with the grammaticality of the corresponding sentence in Danish:

(111) Hunden bliver jaget   bort.
      the dog is   chased away

On the proposed analysis, (111) can have the structure in (112), falling under (84), since linking is subject driven in Danish:

(112) hunden$_i$ bliver [$_{SC}$ t$_i$ [$_{VP}$ jaget [$_{SC}$ t$_i$ [$_{VP}$ bort t$_i$]]]]

In (112) the particle is also "transitive" (since the impossibility of applying p-composition entails nonapplication of assimilation), but because linking is not object driven, the presence of the NP governed by the particle does not induce linking. Moreover, since the SC subject is not in a θ-position and is therefore not appropriate for the "transitive" particle, subject-driven linking is not induced either. In other words, the particle does not fall under the scope of (84), and we expect (112) to behave like a simple passive sentence with respect to (84).

5 Linking and the Auxiliary Alternation

We will now turn to the alternation between auxiliary *have* and *be*. Our task is to implement the idea defended in sections 1–3 that the same parameter controls both word order in particle constructions and Scandinavian causatives, on the one hand, and auxiliary alternation, on the other. Since the primary motivation for attempting this unification was the co-variation holding between auxiliary alternation and clitic-participle agreement, let us begin by exploring whether the proposed analysis extends straightforwardly to clitic-participle agreement.

5.1 Clitic-Participle Agreement

Following Kayne (1985b), we have previously assumed that a sentence with clitic-participle agreement, like the Italian (113), must have a structure like (114), with an embedded SC whose subject position is not a θ-position:

(113) Mario li   ha letti
      Mario them-MASC has read-MASC.PL
      'Mario has read them.'

(114) Mario [$_{VP}$ li$_i$ ha [$_{SC}$ t$_i$ [$_{VP}$ letti t$_i$]]]

In this respect, the structure required for clitic-participle agreement is just like the structure underlying *la*-causatives with the infinitive following its thematic object and particle constructions with the particle following the NP. Therefore, as noted in section 3, a property of a language L excluding these construction types is also likely to rule out (114) in L. This is indeed the case with respect to the analysis proposed in section 4.

Consider (114), assuming a language L with object-driven linking. Since we consider a participle based on a transitive root to remain transitive, the participle must then link to a θ-marked subject position, if its object is Case-marked. We will assume that a past participle must assign Case to its object in (114), returning to this question below in connection with passives. On this assumption, (85) requires that the participle be the head of a VP whose subject is in a θ-position. The subject position of SC is not a θ-position. Hence, the participle must link to the matrix subject, which is assigned a θ-role by the matrix VP (see next section 5.2). For this to be possible, however, p-composition must put the projection of the participle together with the projection of the matrix V. But this is only possible, as we have seen, if SC is a projection of the participle, with the consequence that the matrix V (the auxiliary) does not govern the SC subject. Assuming, as before (section 2), that only government by the matrix V would qualify as proper government in the sense of the ECP in (114), it follows that (114) is ill formed in a language with object-driven linking.[26] Correspondingly, we account for the lack of clitic-participle agreement in Spanish, Portuguese, and Romanian by stipulating that these languages go by (85)—in other words, that they have object-driven linking.

Suppose now that linking is subject driven in L. Then the fact that the SC subject is not in a θ-position—in other words, that it is not "appropriate" for a transitive participle—simply means that no linking is induced with respect to the participle. In particular, there is no need to analyze SC as a projection of the participle, and therefore no obstacle to having the matrix V govern the SC subject, as required by the ECP. As for the matrix V, we will assume that auxiliary *have* is like the main V *have* stripped of semantic content. In particular, it is transitive and a Case assigner. As such, it interacts successfully with (85) in (114). The presence of a subject in a θ-position must be matched by a governed Case-marked constituent. This constituent is the trace in the subject position of SC, governed and Case-marked by the auxiliary. In this respect, then, (114) is quite analogous to causative structures like (90) or particle constructions like (102), where the SC subject is also the Case-marked constituent the matrix V links to.

We will consider French and Italian, languages with clitic-participle agreement, to have subject-driven linking.

5.2 Auxiliary *Have* + Past Participle

We must now show that the property of having subject-driven linking also induces the auxiliary alternation, whereas a language with object-driven linking cannot have such an alternation. The problem decomposes into two questions: (1) Why is the combination *have* + unaccusative participle licit in a language with object-driven linking, but not in a language with subject-driven linking? (2) Why is the combination *be* + unaccusative participle licit in a language with subject-driven linking, but not in a language with object-driven linking? Let us begin by addressing question (1).

It seems clear that the structure of a sentence like *John has read the books* should be like (115) rather than like (116) (with NP empty):

(115) John [$_{VP}$ has [$_{VP}$ read the books]]

(116) John [$_{VP}$ has [$_{SC}$ NP [$_{VP}$ read the books]]]

Suppose first that NP is not coindexed with *John*. Then, NP cannot be an anaphoric trace, since it has no c-commanding antecedent. Nor can it be a variable, since there is no corresponding operator. Hence, it would have to be PRO or pro. The first of these two options is presumably ruled out by the requirement that PRO be ungoverned: in (116) the subject of SC is governed either by the participle or by the auxiliary. Moreover, since the external θ-role corresponding to the embedded VP is in fact assigned to the subject of the matrix VP (see below for discussion), there is no available θ-role for the subject position of SC, so that NP must have the properties of an expletive. But PRO does not in general appear to be interpretable as an expletive, judging from sentences like *It is nice to be read many books.*[27] This leaves the possibility that NP = pro. But pro that is not "identified" (for example, by a clitic, according to Chomsky (1982)) is in general interpreted as generic and animate, not as an expletive. Hence, the null NP in (116) does not correspond to any of the established types of empty category, if it is not coindexed with *John*.

Suppose now that NP and *John* are coindexed. Then NP could be analyzed as an anaphoric trace without violating Principle A of the binding theory. However, we have assumed that the subject of the matrix VP is a θ-position, although the auxiliary lacks semantic content and therefore cannot induce an external θ-role. Hence, the external θ-role corresponding to the embedded VP must somehow be transferred to and assigned by the matrix VP. But then the subject of SC is not in a θ-position. Yet taking NP as an (anaphoric) trace of *John* implies that there is a chain with *John* as its head and NP as its foot. If a chain is interpreted either as a record of the head's "history of movement" or as entailing θ-marking of the head on the basis of the foot, then the argument *John* is (116) will fail to be associated with a θ-role at some level of representation and will therefore violate the θ-Criterion. Thus, we conclude that the null NP in (116) is a source of ill-formedness even if co-indexed with the matrix subject.[28] Therefore, (116) cannot be the correct representation of *John has read the books*. Rather, the representation must be as in (115).

This means that the auxiliary *have* is like the Scandinavian causative *la* 'let, make' in that it is free to take either an SC or a "bare" VP as its "complement" provided general conditions are met. In a language with object-driven linking, only the structure with the bare VP is possible, the SC analysis being excluded not only in the case represented by (116) but also in the case represented by (114), where the empty SC subject is licit as the trace of the clitic. Clearly, the structure in (115) satisfies (85) the same way the isomorphic *la*-causatives and particle constructions do: the participle, analyzed as a transitive V with a Case-marked object NP, links to the θ-marked matrix subject position via p-composition.

Incidentally, the notion of p-composition also provides a way of accounting for the assignment of an external θ-role to the subject of the matrix VP in compound past tenses. Since we take the auxiliary *have* to lack semantic content, the external θ-role cannot originate from the matrix V. Instead, it must come from the embedded V, a conclusion that is supported by the meaning. If the embedded V in fact is also head of the matrix V, by p-composition, then this apparent "transfer" of θ-role to the matrix VP turns out to be a subcase of regular external θ-role assignment by VP, determined by a head of the VP.[29]

Turning now to languages with subject-driven linking, we notice that the arguments for analyzing *John has read the books* as in (115) remain valid. Hence, auxiliary *have* must be able to embed a bare VP in these languages, too, although *la* 'make' cannot cooccur with a bare VP. Why the total parallelism between *la*-causatives and compound past tenses breaks down here, is the first question to be addressed.

Going back to previous discussion, we recall that (87) is ill formed with respect to (84), because the transitive matrix V fails to govern a Case-marked constituent:

(87) vi [$_{VP}$ lar [$_{VP}$ henge fangene]]

This, in turn, is due to the fact that the head of VP, the only constituent governed by *lar* in (87), cannot bear Case features. Now, the head of the embedded VP in (115) has a morphological property not shared by the embedded V in (87): it incorporates the participial affix (here, -*t*), an element that elsewhere manifests a capacity to bear nominal features (that is, number and gender features):

(115) John [$_{VP}$ has [$_{VP}$ read the books]]

It seems reasonable to assume that -*t* may also bear Case features.[30] Then the embedded VP in (115) may actually be Caxe-marked, since its head can bear Case features; therefore, (115) is well formed with respect to (84), the embedded VP being the Case-marked constituent that the transitive auxiliary is required to govern. From this point of view, a Danish sentence like (117) can consistently receive the analysis in (118), even though Danish must have subject-driven linking, and similarly for the French and Italian sentences (119) and (121):

(117) Jon har lest   bøgerne.
       Jon has read the books

(118) Jon [$_{VP}$ har [$_{VP}$ lest bøgerne]]

(119) Jean a   dormi.
       Jean has slept

(120) Jean [$_{VP}$ a [$_{VP}$ dormi]]

(121) Gianni ha   baciato sua madre.
       Gianni has kissed his mother

(122) Gianni [$_{VP}$ ha [$_{VP}$ baciato sua madre]]

Thus far we have seen that both languages with object-driven linking and languages with subject-driven linking accept auxiliary *have* governing a bare participial VP in the general case. Let us now consider the special case where the participle is based on an unaccusative V.

We know that auxiliary *have* combines with an unaccusative participle in Swedish, Spanish, Portuguese, and Romanian, but not in Danish, French, or Italian. Taking previous conclusions into account, we therefore want it to be the case that auxiliary *have* can combine with an unaccusative participle only in languages with object-driven linking. We will now see that this result can be obtained, given a fairly plausible assumption concerning the linking process.

Consider first the status of (124), the structure assigned to the Spanish sentence (123), in a language with object-driven linking (like Spanish):

(123) Pedro ha llegado.

    Pedro has arrived

(124) Pedro$_i$ [$_{VP}$ ha [$_{VP}$ llegado t$_i$]]

Since the participle is an unaccusative V in (124), the presence of a Caseless object NP induces linking to a non-θ-marked subject position, under (85). Given p-composition, the linking process terminates successfully at the matrix subject, a non-θ-marked position, since neither the auxiliary nor the participle induces an external θ-role. Hence, (123) is well formed in a language with object-driven linking.[13]

Suppose now that linking is subject driven. Then, assuming p-composition, *Pedro* is the subject of an unaccusative V, the participle. Since *Pedro* is in a non-θ-position, (84) requires linking to a Caseless subject, a requirement satisfied by the object of the participle. However, *Pedro* is obviously also the subject of the matrix V, the auxiliary *ha*. Suppose we have the following condition, requiring the linking process to apply uniformly with respect to all X that the triggering subject/"object" is a subject/"object" of:

(125) Linking induced by A terminates successfully just in case linking applies with respect to every B that A bears the linking-inducing relation to.

(125) stipulates that the linking induced by the subject *Pedro* in (124) cannot terminate successfully unless it can also apply with respect to the auxiliary. But the auxiliary *have* is like the main verb *have* except for its lack of semantic content. In particular, it is transitive. Therefore, it cannot link the non-θ-marked subject position of (124) to an "object" (the em-

bedded VP). For this reason, (125) has the effect that (124) is excluded in languages with subject-driven linking. Notice that the ultimate cause of its ungrammaticality is an intuitively plausible one, namely, that auxiliary *have* is transitive.

The transitive nature of auxiliary *have* is irrelevant in a language with object-driven linking. Although p-composition, by making the matrix VP a joint projection of both verbs, has the effect of rendering the matrix subject analyzable as the subject both of the auxiliary and of the participle, the embedded VP remains the projection of the participle only, and the object of the participle is consequently not also the object of the auxiliary, nor even governed by it. Therefore, (125) does not require that the linking process induced by the object of the participle also apply with respect to the auxiliary (which it could not do, since a transitive V cannot link to a non-θ-marked subject position).

It follows that the correct cross-linguistic acceptability pattern for auxiliary *have* + unaccusative participle can be seen as a consequene of taking Swedish, Spanish, Portuguese, and Romanian to have object-driven linking and Danish, French, and Italian to have subject-driven linking. Thus, the cross-lingusitic distribution of *have* + unaccusative in Scandinavian is linked to the word order variation in *la*-causatives and particle constructions and its distribution in Romance is correctly linked to the distribution of clitic-participle agreement.

5.3 Auxiliary *Be* + Past Participle

We now turn to the question why the combination auxiliary *be* + unaccusative participle is grammatical in languages with subject-driven linking (such as Danish, French, and Italian), but not in languages with object-driven linking (such as Swedish, Spanish, Portuguese, and Romanian). Let us begin by considering the implications of the fact that in both types of language, *be* combines with past participles based on transitive verbs, forming passives.

Notice first that a past participle always agrees with the subject of the auxiliary in passives in all Romance languages. Keeping to Kayne's (1985b) proposal that agreement is always with a local subject, this means that auxiliary *be* can be followed only by an SC, not by a bare VP. Thus, a Spanish sentence like (126) is uniquely analyzable as (127) (where the subject of SC triggers agreement in the participle):

(126) La playa sera   destruida.
      the beach will-be destroyed

(127) la playa$_i$ [$_{VP}$ sera [$_{SC}$ t$_i$ [$_{VP}$ destruida t$_i$]]]

Clearly, the subject position of the SC is not θ-marked. Otherwise, it could not contain an element binding a trace in the object position, given the θ-Criterion. Therefore, linking induced by the object of the participle could not terminate at the SC subject, given our earlier assumption that a transitive verb remains transitive under participle formation. In fact, not even the matrix subject would be appropriate for a transitive V to link to, since the matrix subject position is not θ-marked in (127). (For reasons familiar from the preceding discussion, the participle could not link to the matrix subject in (127) even if it were θ-marked: this would presuppose p-composition, so that SC = V^m, with the effect that the auxiliary could not govern the subject trace, as required by the ECP; see the discussion of (114).) Therefore, we would initially expect (127) to be ill formed in a language with object-driven linking, contrary to fact.

However, this expectation arises only if the object of the participle in (127) actually is an *appropriate* "object" for the participle, in the sense of (85). Since we consider the participle to inherit transitivity from its root, we have an appropriate "object" just in case the object NP is Case-marked. However, since we have previously stipulated that the participle also retains the Case-assigning capacity of the root and that Case assignment must apply when applicable, it would appear to follow that the object of the participle must be Case-marked by it. On the other hand, we have also claimed that the participial affix -t is capable of being Case-marked. We may now use this idea again. Suppose that the obligatoriness of Case assignment is satisfied if a given Case assigner assigns Case once and is associated with the lexical root.[32] Then the obligatoriness requirement can be met if the Case associated with the verbal root is assigned to -t in (127), leaving the object NP not Case-marked. Hence, (127) has an analysis on which the object of the participle is not Case-marked and is therefore not an appropriate "object" for a transitive participle. Correspondingly, (85) does not apply, and linking is not induced. Therefore, (127) is well formed even in a language with object-driven linking, as required.

This analysis appears to presuppose a special view on the relationship between Case marking by V and external θ-role assignment. Crucially, we do not want the root to satisfy the obligatoriness condition on Case assignment by assigning Case to -t in (114):

(114) Mario [$_{VP}$ li$_i$ ha [$_{SC}$ t$_i$ [$_{VP}$ letti t$_i$]]]

Otherwise, we would be unable to maintain our previous argument showing (114) to be ill formed in languages with object-driven linking.

The crucial difference between (127) and (114), from the point of view adopted here, is that only in (127) is there an external θ-role corresponding to the embedded VP (but assigned by the matrix VP).[33] My hypothesis is that the embedded VP induces this external θ-role, only if the embedded V (the participle) assigns Case to its object NP. More generally, I will assume that Case assignment to the object NP reflects the process of creating a (compositional) external θ-role; see Marantz 1984:23–41. Hence, the participle must assign Case to the object NP, rather than to -t, in (114), but not in (127), where nonassignment to the object NP leads to lack of an external θ-role (that is, to the passive meaning).

We have seen that the subject of the SC is not an appropriate subject for the transitive participle in (127), because it is not in a θ-position. However, there is some reason to think that it is in a certain sense not the subject of the participle at all, although we will continue to maintain that it is immediately dominated by SC. Consider that (128) is impossible in Spanish, with the "raising" analysis in (129):

(128) *Los turistas seran   destruidos la   playa.

       the tourists will-be destroyed the beach

(129) los turistas$_i$ seran [$_{SC}$ t$_i$ [$_{VP}$ destruidos la playa]]

In order to exclude (129) as a legitimate analysis of (128), it seems necessary to prevent the embedded VP from assigning a θ-role to the SC subject, even in contexts where such assignment would not contradict the θ-Criterion, as it would in (127). This, however, seems equivalent to preventing the embedded VP from being analyzed as a predication on the subject of an SC embedded under auxiliary *be* (or, perhaps, any temporal auxiliary). But if the theory must be formulated so as to achieve this result, then the SC embedded under *be* will never be the locus of an external predication relation that could license an internal one, in other words, the subject of SC would always be an "inappropriate" subject with respect to (85) even for unaccusative participles, for which a non-θ-marked subject would otherwise be appropriate.

This conclusion immediately makes it clear why auxiliary *be* does not combine with unaccusative participles in languages where linking is object driven. Consider (131), the structure of the ungrammatical Spanish sentence (130):

(130) *Pedro *es* llegado.

       Pedro is arrived

(131) Pedro$_i$ es [$_{SC}$ t$_i$ [$_{VP}$ llegado t$_i$]]

Given that linking is object driven in Spanish, the presence of the Caseless object NP forces the unaccusative participle to link to a non-θ-marked subject position. But although the SC subject certainly is not θ-marked, it does not count as an appropriate subject for the participle, because no relation of external predication holds between the participle VP and the subject of an SC embedded under auxiliary *be*. Therefore, the matrix subject is the only NP that can make the linking terminate successfully. But the matrix subject cannot be analyzed as the subject of the participle unless p-composition takes place, and then the SC must be a projection of the participle, so that the auxiliary cannot govern the subject trace of SC, as would be required for the ECP to hold. Hence, (131) is ill formed in a language with object-driven linking.

Unlike what happens in (127), the possibility of having the root of the participle assign Case to -*t* doesn't help here. Even if the unaccusative root could assign Case at all, preventing Case from being assigned to the object NP of the participle in (131) does not prevent linking from being induced, since the participle is unaccusative and it is precisely Caseless NPs that induce linking with unaccusative verbs (in languages with object-driven linking).

In a language with subject-driven linking the structure in (131) is well formed. Since the presence of the object of the participle does not induce linking, the status of the SC subject (with respect to predication) simply does not play any role. Only the matrix subject induces linking, if we consider auxiliary *be* as an unaccusative V, so that a non-θ-marked subject position is appropriate for it. The auxiliary will then link either to the SC or to the subject NP of SC, both being Caseless constituents governed by the auxiliary.

This completes the demonstration that languages with subject-driven linking will have the auxiliary alternation in the sense that auxiliary *have* can and must be "replaced" with auxiliary *be* with unaccusative participles, whereas languages with object-driven linking lack the alternation in the sense that auxiliary *have* neither can nor must be "replaced" with *be* with unaccusative participles.

5.4 Case Assignment in Absolute Participle Constructions

Striking support for the analysis just presented can be found in absolute participle constructions in Italian (as in (132)) and Spanish (as in (133)).

(132) *Distrutto il villaggio,* i   soldati se ne andarono.
     destroyed the village   the soldiers left
     'Having destroyed the village, the soldiers left.'

(133) *Destruido el pueblo*, los soldados se fueron.
      destroyed the village the soldiers   left
      'Having destroyed the village, the soldiers left.'

If absolute participle constructions have the form of SCs, then their (empty) subjects cannot be θ-marked, given the ungrammaticality of (134)–(135), with intransitive participles:

(134) *Dormito, i   soldati se ne andarono.
       slept   the soldiers left
       'Having slept, the soldiers left.'

(135) *Dormido, los soldados se fueron.
       slept   the soldiers left
       'Having slept, the soldiers left.'

The contrast between (132)–(133) and (134)–(135) follows if the subject position of the participle must not be θ-marked, since it then reflects the contrast between passives from transitive verbs and passives from intransitive verbs in these languages:

(136) Il villaggio sarà   distrutto (dai   soldati).
      the village   will-be destroyed by-the soldiers

(137) El pueblo sera   destruido (por los soldados).
      the village will-be destroyed by the soldiers

(138) *Sarà   dormito (dai   soldati).
       will-be slept   by-the soldiers

(139) *Sera   dormido (por los soldados).
       will-be slept   by the soldiers

Looking next at how the object of the participle is Case-marked, we note first that in both languages nominative Case can be assigned to this position in the absolute participle construction, as shown by the morphological form of personal pronouns: *Distrutto io,* ... (Italian), *Destruido yo,* ... (Spanish) 'Destroyed I, ...' (that is, 'Having destroyed me, ...'). In Italian, however, accusative Case can also be assigned, judging from the fact that a pronominal object may cliticize onto the participle as an accusative clitic (see Belletti 1988).[34]

(140) Distruttolo, i   soldati se ne andarono.
      destroyed-it the soldiers left
      'Having destroyed it, the soldiers left.'

The double option is compatible with the proposed analysis. Consider the structure (141), on the assumption that an external θ-role is not assigned to the SC subject:

(141) [$_{SC}$ NP [$_{VP}$ distrutto il villaggio]] i soldati ...

Since linking is subject driven in Italian, the fact that the non-θ-marked subject of the SC is not appropriate for the transitive participle means that linking is not induced in (141). In particular, no consideration related to linking determines the Case marking of the object of the participle. It may either be not Case-marked by the participle (with the Case assigned to -t) or marked accusative.

For Spanish, however, the proposed anlaysis makes a clear prediction about the Case marking of the object of the participle. Since linking is object driven in Spanish, a Case-marked object will induce linking to an appropriate subject in Spanish. But the subject of SC in a structure like (141) is not θ-marked and therefore is inappropriate for a transitive participle. Hence, linking could not terminate successfully, and therefore it must not be induced. Consequently, we are led to predict that the object of an absolute participle cannot be marked with accusative Case in Spanish, and the correctness of this prediction is confirmed by the ungrammaticality of (142), the Spanish counterpart of (140):

(142) *Destruidolo, los soldados se fueron.
      destroyed-it the soldiers   left

In order for this to count as support for our analysis, we must resolve two problems that the extension to absolute participle constructions gives rise to. The first concerns the claim that an external θ-role cannot be assigned to the SC subject in an absolute participle construction. Earlier we used the observation that an external θ-role is not assigned to the subject of a participial SC embedded under auxiliary be as a basis for the claim that external predication does not hold between the SC subject and the embedded VP. However, it would now seem that we are forced to make the same claim about the subject of the SC in absolute participle constructions. Though this does no harm in the cases where the participle is transitive, it leads to the incorrect prediction that there are no absolute participle constructions based on unaccusative participles in languages with object-driven linking. For instance, in Spanish the following sentence is grammatical:

(143) Llegado Pedro, Maria se fue.
      arrived Pedro Maria left
      'Pedro having arrived, Maria left.'

Given the structural analysis in (144), (143) would contradict (85), unless the empty subject of the SC is canonical for the participle:

(144) [$_{SC}$ NP [$_{VP}$ llegado Pedro]] Maria se fue

Clearly, the non-Case-marked subject of the SC in (144) is appropriate for the unaccusative participle, but only if external predication holds at all.

To arrive at a coherent position, we must attribute the lack of external predication in an SC embedded under an auxiliary (*be*) to factors that treat transitive and unaccusative participles alike, whereas the lack of external predication in absolute participle constructions should be forced just when necessary to prevent a θ-role from being assigned to the subject (in other words, not with unaccusative participles). Without taking a stand on why θ-assignment to the subject should create ill-formedness, I would suggest that external predication does not obtain in an SC embedded under auxiliary *be* because the SC subject functions as the "object" of the auxiliary. Recalling the earlier suggestion to consider auxiliary *be* as an unaccusative V, let us assume that *be* in fact selects the subject of SC as its "object."[35] Assuming a principle requiring uniqueness of grammatical relations, this would be sufficient to guarantee that the structural subject of SC embedded under *be* would never be the subject of external predication. In a participial SC not embedded under an auxiliary—for example, in an absolute participle construction—this would not hold, however. Here, the structural subject would be free to be the subject of external predication as long as this does not lead to a conflict with a requirement that no θ-role may be assigned to the subject.

The second problem concerns the status of the empty subject NP postulated in structures like (144). Being unbound, it could not be a trace (either variable or anaphoric). Given its expletive character, it could not easily be analyzed as an occurrence of PRO either. Therefore, it must be an occurrence of pro. But it is not "identified" in the appropriate way unless the agreement features on the participle can identify it.

5.5 Romance Causatives

An obvious question arises from the proposed analysis. Romance languages have causatives in many ways similar to the Scandinavian *la*-causatives. In particular, a sentence like (145) is grammatical in all Romance languages except Romanian (which lacks infinitival causatives altogether):

(145) Nous faisons pendre les prisonniers.

      we   make   hang   the prisoners

This observation contradicts the proposed analysis, if (145) has the same structure as superficially similar Swedish sentences like (87), since such a structure ought to be ill formed in French and Italian, languages with subject-driven linking, for exactly the same reason they are ill formed in Danish. Thus, we are forced to assume that the structure of (145) is not like (146) (isomorphic with (87)), but rather like (147), at least in French and Italian:

(146) nous [$_{VP}$ faisons [$_{VP}$ pendre les prisonniers]]

(147) nous [$_{VP}$[$_V$ faisons pendre] les prisonniers]

If the causative and the infinitive constitue a complex V, as in (147), then condition (85) will apply only with respect to this V, in effect treating (144) as a simple sentence like *John ate the apple*. In particular, (85) is satisfied because the only VP in the sentence is headed by a transitive V, *faisons pendre*, which governs a Case-marked NP. Obviously, we must also assume that it is not possible to analyze *la* and its infinitive as one V in Scandinavian.

This conclusion, to which we have been forced by our analysis, correctly predicts certain differences between Romance causatives and their Scandinavian counterparts. First, we now understand why a causative can be formed on an ergative infinitive in Romance, but not in Scandinavian—in other words, why (148) is grammatical in all Romance languages, whereas (96) is ungrammatical in all Scandinavian languages:

(96) *Vi lar omkomme fangene/mange fanger.
     we let die   the prisoners/many prisoners

(148) Nous faisons mourir les prisonniers/beaucoup de prisonniers.
      we   let   die   the prisoners/many prisoners

In section 4.2 we attributed the ungrammaticality of (96) to the fact that the ergative infinitive fails to satisfy condition (84), since the θ-marked matrix subject is not a canonical subject for it. That account presupposes a structure like (149) for (96):

(149) vi [$_{VP}$ lar [$_{VP}$ omkomme fangene/mange fanger]]

If the causative V and the infinitive cannot be analyzed as a complex V in Scandinavian, this is indeed the only analysis available. But in Romance the causative V and the infinitive *can* be analyzed as a complex V, giving (150) as a possible analysis of (148):

(150) nous [$_{VP}$[$_V$ faisons mourir] les prisonniers/beaucoup de prisonniers]

Since the ergative infinitive is only a proper subpart of a lexical item in (150), it is simply not subject to condition (85), which instead takes effect with respect to the whole complex V—a transitive V, if we take the causative to determine the syntactic properties of the complex V.

Furthermore, the availability of the complex V analysis in Romance, and its unavailability in Scandinavian, implies that Romance may have "active" causatives of the type illustrated in (151)–(152), although Scandinavian may not:

(151) Nous faisons chanter Jean.
       we   make   sing   Jean

(152) Nous faisons lire un livre à   Jean.
       we   make   read a   book (to) Jean

(153) *Vi lar synge Jens.
       we let sing Jens

(154) *Vi lar lese en bok   (til) Jens.
       we let read a   book (to) Jens

The ungrammaticality of (153) is a consequence of Case theory. In the structure (155) no V can assign Case to *Jens*—the infinitive, because it is intransitive, and the matrix V, because it is not adjacent to *Jens*:

(155) vi [$_{VP}$ lar [$_{SC}$[$_{VP}$ synge] Jens]]]

Similary, (154) will be excluded if a "dative" preposition like Romance *à* in (152) can only be inserted in front of an NP that is the sister of a direct object, since *Jens*, the "external argument," must be outside the V'-projection of the infinitive:[36]

(156) vi [$_{VP}$ lar [$_{SC}$[$_{VP}$ lese en bok] Jens]]

Since Romance allows the causative and the infinitive to be analyzed as one V, (151)–(152) can still be assigned structures consistent with Case theory:

(157) nous [$_{VP}$[$_V$ faisons chanter] Jean]

(158) nous [$_{VP}$[$_V$ faisons lire] un livre à Jean]

In (157) *Jean* is governed by and adjacent to a Case assigner (the complex V), assuming again that the complex V inherits syntactic properties from the causative verb. In (158) the "dative" preposition is inserted in front of a sister of the direct object, as required.[37]

Finally, none of the Romance languages allow the word order found in Danish (and Norwegian) *la*-causatives illustrated in (89):

(89) Vi lar *fangene*   henge.
     we let the prisoners hang
     'We let the prisoners be hanged.'

Thus, (159) is ungrammatical in French, contrasting with (145):

(159) *Nous faisons *les prisonniers* pendre.
       we   let   the prisoners   hang

Within the proposed analysis, the ungrammaticality of (159) in French cannot have the same source as the ungrammaticality of (89) in Swedish, since French should have subject-driven linking, like Danish. But we nevertheless predict the ungrammaticality of (159) in all Romance languages, if the single V analysis of the causative verb and the infinitive is not only possible, but in fact obligatory, in Romance. Then (159) is impossible because its derivation requires the object NP to move into a lexical item (the complex V)—something that is standardly assumed to be forbidden by general principles.

Thus, various contrasts between Scandinavian and Romance causatives are explained, if Romance, but not Scandinavian, analyzes the causative verb and the infinitive as a single V—an assumption that our general analysis forces us to make. In other words, the Romance/Scandinavian contrasts discussed above can be viewed as further evidence in favor of the proposed analysis.

6 Conclusion

In the preceding sections I first presented a set of syntactic phenomena, showing cross-linguistic covariation: word order in Scandinavian *la*-causatives, word order in particle constructions, and clitic-participle agreement and auxiliary alternation in past tenses. I argued that the cross-linguistic variation manifested in each domain is controlled by a single parameter. I also sketched an analysis that would induce the word order restrictions on Swedish *la*-causatives as a consequence of a requirement to the effect that every Swedish V must head a predication.

The final formulation of the parameter incorporates a slightly more specific version of this idea. It says that in Swedish, internal predicaton (by V) must be licensed by external predication (by VP). It also induces the word order restrictions in Danish by taking Danish to be subject to the condition that external predication must be licensed by an internal one. Norwegian permits either predication relation to license the other one, so that Norwegian will share the word order possibilities of Swedish and Danish.

I also demonstrated how fixing the direction of the asymmetric dependency between the predication relations predicts whether a language can have clitic-participle agreement and whether it will exhibit alternation between the auxiliaries *have* and *be* in compound past tenses. (Again, attributing no fixed directionality to the dependency between the predication relations in Norwegian predicts that Norwegian will share the possibilities of Danish and Swedish or of Italian and Spanish.)

I then offered a somewhat speculative extension of the analysis to account for a contrast between Italian and Spanish with respect to Case marking (and cliticization) of the direct object in absolute participle constructions.

Finally, I showed that the analysis forces an independently justified claim about the structure of Romance counterparts to *la*-causatives, given the lack of any parallel to the Swedish/Danish word order contrast in Romance.

I think that my analysis is in the spirit of the general enterprise of current generative grammar. In particular, if this analysis is correct, language-specific phrase structure rules are not needed to account for the word order variation in Scandinavian, eliminating a potential obstacle to the total suppression of phrase structure rules. Rather, I have been able to rely on general licensing rules for features. With respect to the nascent study of such rules, these results suggest that the direction of the dependency expressed by statements of the form "A licenses B" may not in general be fixed by Universal Grammar.

Notes

1. See Aoun 1985 for a different analysis.

2. See Taraldsen 1983b for an argument that these definitions are to be preferred to definitions using the concepts "argument-position-bound" (A-bound) and "non-argument-position-bound" ($\bar{\text{A}}$-bound); and see Cinque 1985 for a related view.

3. See Kayne 1984:chap. 7. Notice, however, that one suggestion we will consider in section 5.5 concerning *à*-insertion in Romance causatives will be inconsistent with strict binary branching.

4. However, the strength of the text argument is weakened if we are correct in claiming, in section 5.5, that Romance causatives analyze the causative verb and the infinitive as a lexical unit, since French may also have V-fronting (giving rise to (complex) subject-clitic inversion (see Den Besten 1983; Kayne 1984: chap. 10) separating the causative verb from the infinitive:

(i) Quand fera-t-il   publier ton livre?
     when   will make he publish your book
     'When will he have your book published?'

(ii) *Quand fera publier-il ton livre?

However, the motivation for adopting this analysis for Romance would disappear if we were to adopt it for Scandinavian as well. Hence, we retain an argument for the text conclusion.

5. Including subjects of SC:

(i) Vi anser   Jens$_i$ trofast mot sitt$_i$ kall.

   we consider Jens true   to his (REFL) vocation

6. The fact that nonreflexive *hans* 'his' also is possible in (44) is consistent with our analysis, although (i) is ungrammatical with coreference.

(i) *Spionen ble arrestert like før   hans   avreise.

   the spy was arrested just before his (nonrefl) departure

In (44) the temporal adverb might be attached in the matrix clause, in which case the pronoun would not be c-commanded by the embedded subject NP.

7. Although I claim that the infinitive and its thematic object form a constituent both in (3) and in (5), the relevant string does not seem to behave like a unit under movement. Thus, (i)–(ii) are both ill formed:

(i) *Henge fangene   lar vi aldri.

    hang   the prisoners let we never

(ii) *Fangene   henge lar vi aldri.

    the prisoners hang let we never

In other cases a V-projection may be topicalized:

(iii) Hengt fangene   har vi ikke.

    hanged the prisoners have we not

The ungrammaticality of (ii) can be viewed as an effect of Case theory. That is, Case fails to be assigned to the preinfinitival NP when it is no longer governed by the matrix V:

(iv) *John smart, we did not consider.

As for (i), where one might plausibly take Case to be assigned to *fangene* by the infinitive, I will propose an explanation in section 4.2.

8. The prediction that a language like Danish might also have clitic-participle agreement is not verifiable, because Scandinavian "clitics" attach to the participle rather than to the auxiliary, so that an empty subject of the participle would not have a c-commanding antecedent.

9. Catalan is problematic with respect to the descriptive generalization adopted in the text. The auxiliary alternation is extinct in modern Catalan, but clitic-participle agreement survives. Catalan could conceivably be somewhat like Norwegian, combining the options of Spanish and French.

10. The standard definition of c-command (one of many considered by Reinhart (1976)) is essentially as follows:

(i) A c-commands B $=_{def}$ the least constituent containing A, B dominates A immediately.

Below, I suggest that this is only one clause in the complete definition of c-command.

11. NP and S (or, perhaps, S′) may constitute a natural class in several respects (for instance, θ-marking) and may share the property of being potential argument. What remains to be determined, from this point of view, would be why such a property should induce barrierhood.

12. This definition combines the one given in note 10 with a definition akin to the one given by Chomsky (1981) (clause (b) of (61)). Having only clause (b) would require a separate notion of c-command for binding, in addition to being incompatible with the analysis in the following subsection, where various prepositional nonheads are required to be governors.

13. However, its predictions remain distinct from those made by the version of the barriers analysis described by Chomsky (1986a), where maximal projections θ-marked by an X^0-element are not always barriers.

14. Notice also that a possessive *wh*-phrase can be separated from the rest of the NP in the construction (i) in Norwegian, but not in (ii):

(i)   Hvem sin bok   er det?
       who   his book is that
       'Whose book is that ?'

(ii)   Hvem er det sin bok?
       who   is that his book
       'Whose book is that?'

(iii) Hvis bok er det?
       whose book is that

(iv)   *Hvis er det bok?
       whose is that book

Fiva (1987:48–72) shows that the contrast between (ii) and (iv) falls under an analysis similar to the one given in the text, with *sin* 'his (REFL)' having the same effect as the prepositions in the examples discussed here.

15. If this assumption were incorrect, there could be no ECP account of the contrast in extractability between determiners and complements to N or A. Why determiners should not be properly governed by heads, although governed by them, is unclear. Perhaps a constituent B that is properly governed by A in addition to being governed by A must also either itself be θ-marked "directly" by A or else be the specifier (= determiner or subject) of a constituent C that is directly θ-marked by A.

16. With respect to languages (such as the Romance languages) where no infinitival marker appears in raising and exceptional Case marking contexts, we could say either that S is headless, or else that its head (for instance, INFL) only governs left to right (assuming that the subject precedes the head). See Taraldsen 1984 for more discussion.

17. The infinitival marker will prevent the subject PRO from being governed by the head of the embedded S. At the same time, this makes the subject position accessible to government by the matrix V. We may take COMP to block the latter instance of government under a slight extension of definition (77): First assume that COMP may govern S, but never the subject of S, because it is not a structural

governor in the sense proposed by Kayne (1984: chap. 5); that is, COMP only governs sister constituents (except for *for*). Then replace clauses (c) and (d) of (77) with the following:

(c′) If C (an X^0 distinct from A) c-commands B, but not A, then C must not govern B or any D dominating B.

(d′) If C (an X^0 distinct from B) c-commands A, but not B, then C must not govern A or any D dominating A.

With the proviso (c′), PRO will be ungoverned by external governors in the configuration ... V [$_{S'}$ COMP [$_S$ PRO ...

18. See the discussion concerning the Case marking of the SC subject in (36) in section 2.1.

19. The fact that intransitive Vs fall outside the scope of this analysis has no adverse effect on our account of word order variation in Scandinavian *la*-causatives, since intransitives do not occur in this construction in any Scandinavian language:

(i) *Vi lot synge.
    we let sing
    'We let it be sung.'

Why this should be so is an interesting question, but independent of the problem under investigation

20. This particular verb *omkomme* 'die' is unaccusative in Swedish by the following criteria: (1) it takes an expletive subject (*Det omkom mange mennesker* 'There died many people') and (2) it does not passivize (**Det ble omkommet sjelden* 'There was died rarely'), unlike intransitive Vs (*Det ble danset sjelden* 'It was danced rarely'). In Norwegian and Danish *omkomme* is also to be classified as unaccusative, because it selects auxiliary *være* 'be' (optionally in Norwegian; see section 1.3).

21. Following Belletti (1988), we will assume that unaccusative V may assign a nonstructural Case (linked to θ-role assignment). NPs bearing only such Case will be considered Case-free with respect to (84)–(85)—that is, as appropriate object NPs for unaccusative Vs, but not for transitive Vs. If it is assigned nonstructural Case, the embedded object NP in (95) will meet the Case requirement on argument chains, so that the only reason for its ill-formedness is the one given in the text. (Possibly, assignment of the nonstructural Case requires the NP to be indefinite, as proposed by Belletti (1988). However, replacing *fangene* with indefinite *mange fanger* 'many prisoners' does not affect the status of (95); compare (96).)

22. This is indicated by the fact that *la* is a Case assigner.

23. Since the matrix V is an unaccusative, we cannot assume that structural Case assignment is the reason why the matrix V must govern the SC subject here. If the SC subject bears nonstructural Case (see Belletti 1988) assigned by the matrix V, it is sufficient to assume that nonstructural Case is assigned under government. If, on the other hand, the SC subject must be part of a Case-marked chain headed by *det* 'it' (see Chomsky 1981, 1986b), we could perhaps argue that the ECP holds for each link a_i, a_{i+1} of a chain, even when a_{i+1} is not empty.

24. Interestingly, the affixed reflexive *-s* can be used for "passivization" (compare Italian *si*) without forcing the particle to be incorporated, as in *Hunden jagas bort*

'The dog is chased away, suggesting that the external θ-role is assigned to -*s* and that -*s* can function as the subject with respect to the application of (85). Notice also that, surprisingly on the view adopted in the text, *Det ble jaget bort en hund* 'It was chased away a dog' (also ungrammatical in Swedish) is grammatical in Norwegian. (Also grammatical is the direct counterpart of (108), but this could be due to the existence in Norwegian of *De jaget hunden bort* 'They chased the dog away'.)

25. We assume that auxiliary *be* requires a full SC rather than a "bare" VP. The text argument could have been made exactly the same way without this assumption.

26. Government by the matrix V is also required, if the empty NP linked to a clitic (in Romance) is pro, which must be identified by being governed by X bearing the clitic; see Chomsky 1982. Notice also that the account given for the cross-linguistic distribution of clitic-participle agreement extends to *wh*-participle agreement on the analysis sketched in sections 1–3, with the "extra" trace in COMP/the SC-adjoined position being the one that must be (properly) governed by the matrix V.

27. On the reading 'It is nice for there to be read many books'.

28. Notice also that analysis in (116) with the SC subject coindexed with the matrix subject would incorrectly give rise to subject-participle agreement across auxiliary *have* when transposed to Romance or relevant Scandinavian dialects, for example, *I ragazzi hanno letti il libro* 'The children have read (PL) the book'.

29. However, it is not clear how to extend this analysis to structures where the auxiliary governs an SC, blocking p-composition, as required for clitic-participle agreement.

30. This assumption is common to many accounts of "Case absorption" by participles; see Jaeggli 1986, Fabb 1984, Baker 1988.

31. Notice, however, that this conclusion also presupposes that -*t* optionally may have the property of not being capable of bearing Case features (for instance, it presupposes the existence of both $+N$ and $-N$ -*t*), or else that the Case-bearing property only optionally percolates to the derived V-node. Otherwise, the obligatoriness of Case assignment would ensure that auxiliary *have* would have an appropriate ($=$ Case-marked) "object" ($=$ the embedded VP) in (124), so that (85) would require it to link to a θ-marked subject position.

32. One may, for instance, consider a Case-marking V to be provided with exactly one Case feature in the lexicon and stipulate that this feature must be assigned, if possible.

33. Exactly how the matrix VP "takes over" the external θ-role induced by the embedded VP is not clear in this case.

34. Notice, however, that in (140), but not in (132), the subject of the clause (*i soldati*) is necessarily identified with the agent of the absolute participle. Under the analysis proposed in the text, we cannot account for this by postulating a θ-marked obligatorily controlled PRO in the subject position of the SC. But we may assume that the participle may have an implicit agentive argument just in case it assigns accusative Case to its direct object; recall the claim in the text that a participle under auxiliary *have* with a θ-marked subject must Case-mark its object. Further-

more, we must assume that this implicit argument becomes identified with the subject by some process other than control.

35. The same could be true for the subject of an SC embedded under auxiliary *have*, causative *la*, and particle-taking V. In the first case the SC could not itself be the Case-marked "object" of the auxiliary, because the SC must not be headed by the V bearing -*t*. It is conceivable that the impossibility of combining auxiliary *be* and a bare VP is due to some principle precluding a non-NP from being the "object" of a V unless Case-marked by it.

36. I am assuming that only internal arguments may be immediately dominated by V'. Thus, the single V analysis of the causative verb and the infinitive must also induce "internalization" of the external argument of the infinitive (see Zubizarreta 1985).

37. Notice also that the proposal about *à*-insertion is inconsistent with the claim that all branching is binary. We could avoid this, if external arguments must be outside the maximal V-projection (as in Williams 1982 and contra Taraldsen 1983a), whereas *à*-insertion is possible only in a position immediately dominated by some V^i.

References

Aoun, J. (1985). *A Grammar of Anaphora*. MIT Press, Cambridge, Mass.

Baker, M. (1988). *Incorporation: A Theory of Grammatical Function Changing*. University of Chicago Press, Chicago.

Belletti, A. (1988). "The Case of Unaccusatives." *Linguistic Inquiry* 19:1–34.

Belletti, A., and L. Rizzi (1981). "The Syntax of *ne*: Some Theoretical Implications." *The Linguistic Review* 1:117–154.

Besten, J. den (1983). "On the Interaction of Root Transformations and Lexical Deletive Rules." In W. Abraham, ed., *On the Formal Syntax of the Westgermania*. Benjamins, Amsterdam.

Chomsky, N. (1980). "On Binding." *Linguistic Inquiry* 11:1–46.

Chomsky, N. (1981). *Lectures on Government and Binding*. Foris, Dordrecht.

Chomsky, N. (1982). *Some Concepts and Consequences of the Theory of Government and Binding*. MIT Press, Cambridge, Mass.

Chomsky, N. (1986a). *Barriers*. MIT Press, Cambridge, Mass.

Chomsky, N. (1986b). *Knowledge of Language: Its Nature, Origin, and Use*. Praeger, New York.

Christensen, K. K. (1985). "Subject Clitics and A'-Bound Traces." *Nordic Journal of Linguistics* 8:1–24

Cinque, G. (1985). "Bare Quantifiers, Quantified NP and the Notion of 'Operator' at S-Structure." Ms., University of Venice.

Fabb, N. (1984). "Syntactic Affixation." Doctoral dissertation, MIT.

Fiva, T. (1987). "Possessor Chains in Norwegian." Cand. philol. thesis, University of Tromsø.

Holmberg, A. (1984). "On Raising in Icelandic and Swedish." In *Working Papers in Scandinavian Syntax* 13. Linguistics Department, University of Trondheim.

Huang, C.-T. J. (1982). "Logical Relations in Chinese and the Theory of Grammar." Doctoral dissertation, MIT.

Jaeggli, O. (1986). "Passive." *Linguistic Inquiry* 17:587–622.

Kayne, R. S. (1975). *French Syntax*. MIT Press, Cambridge, Mass.

Kayne, R. S. (1984). *Connectedness and Binary Branching*. Foris, Dordrecht.

Kayne, R. S. (1985a). "Principles of Particle Constructions." In J. Guéron, H.-G. Obenauer, and J.-Y. Pollock, eds., *Grammatical Representation*. Foris, Dordrecht.

Kayne, R. S. (1985b). "L'accord du participe passé en français et en italien." *Modèles Linguistiques* 7:73–90.

Longobardi, G. (forthcoming). *Movement, Scope and Island Constraints*. MIT Press, Cambridge, Mass.

Marantz, A. (1984). *On the Nature of Grammatical Relations*. MIT Press, Cambridge, Mass.

Reinhart, T. (1976). "The Syntactic Domain of Anaphora." Doctoral dissertation, MIT.

Reuland, E. (1981). "Domains of Governors versus Boundaries for Government." Paper presented at the 1981 GLOW conference, Göttingen. Mimeograph, Groningen University.

Reuland, E. (1983). "Governing -*ing*." *Linguistic Inquiry* 14:101–136.

Rizzi, L. (1986). "Null Objects in Italian and the Theory of *pro*." *Linguistic Inquiry* 17:501–557.

Rothstein, S. (1983). "The Syntactic Forms of Predication." Doctoral dissertation, MIT.

Taraldsen, K. T. (1983a). "Parametric Variation in Phrase Structure: A Case Study." Doctoral dissertation, University of Tromsø.

Taraldsen, K. T. (1983b). "Som." In *Working Papers in Scandinavian Syntax* 1. Linguistics Department, University of Trondheim.

Taraldsen, K. T. (1984). "Some Phrase Structure Dependent Differences between Swedish and Norwegian." In *Working Papers in Scandinavian Syntax* 9. University of Trondheim.

Williams, E. (1982). "The NP Cycle." *Linguistic Inquiry* 13:277–295.

Zubizarreta, M.-L. (1985). "The Relation between Morphophonology and Morphosyntax: The Case of Romance Causatives." *Linguistic Inquiry* 16:247–289.

Chapter 10

The Derived Constituent Structure of the West Germanic Verb-Raising Construction	Anthony S. Kroch and Beatrice Santorini

1 Introduction

The analysis of the verb-raising phenomenon in West Germanic[1] poses an interesting and difficult problem for syntactic theory. Although verb raising is a productive process that gives rise to unbounded syntactic dependencies, it also appears to exhibit features associated with morphological processes, which are ordinarily considered more local. This mix of characteristics raises the question of whether verb raising should be treated as a case of morphological verb incorporation or given an entirely syntactic derivation. In order to forestall terminological misunderstanding, we note here that we

*Many people have helped us with this paper. For discussing with us the questions raised by our analysis, correcting our misconceptions, and providing us with native speaker judgments, we would like to thank Mark Baltin, Hans-Ulrich Block, Lori Davis, Dominique Estival, Liliane Evans, Robert French, Tilman Höhle, Gabriele Hoenigswald, Mark Johnson, Richard Kayne, Willy Kraan, Ann Langenakens, Elsa Lattey, Alec Marantz, Michael Moortgat, Anne Marie Musschoot, Susan Pintzuk, Gertrude Reichenbach, Henk van Riemsdijk, Kenneth Safir, Rex Sprouse, Therese Torris, and the participants in the Princeton Workshop on Comparative Grammar (1986) and the Fourth Workshop on Comparative Germanic Syntax (May 1987). We would also like to thank Mark Steedman for a number of helpful discussions and Jack Hoeksema for many discussions and native speaker judgments. We owe a particular debt of gratitude to Henry Hoenigswald, whose exceptionally clear and consistent judgments on many difficult examples and whose keen linguistic insight have contributed greatly to the analysis presented here. Finally, we must thank Annie Zaenen, whose linguistic analysis of the verb-raising construction we have adopted, and Aravind Joshi, who provided the formal meta-language in which we express our instantiation of that analysis. Of course, we alone are responsible for any remaining errors of fact or judgment in the analysis presented here. The work reported in this paper was funded in part by NSF grant DCR 84-11726, Aravind Joshi, Principal Investigator.

will use the term *morphological* in this paper in an extended sense to refer
to any analysis of the verb-raising construction that involves the formation
of a complex verb, whether in the lexicon or in the syntax. Generative
grammarians have almost unanimously assumed that a morphological
incorporation analysis of the verb-raising construction is correct. In this
paper we argue against the consensus and claim that a syntactic analysis
of verb raising is preferable to a morphological one on both empirical and
conceptual grounds. We begin by showing that the claim that verb raising
involves clause pruning or clause union cannot be maintained. We then
show that four of the five arguments that have been advanced in support
of the morphological incorporation analysis are incorrect and that the fifth
argument is inconclusive. From this, we conclude that one subcase of verb
raising—namely, the raising of *to*-infinitives—should not be described as
an instance of morphological incorporation. In the case of bare infinitive
raising, the empirical evidence from standard Dutch and German is consistent with either a morphological or a syntactic analysis, and we argue
on the basis of conceptual economy that bare infinitive raising in standard
Dutch and German should be given the same analysis as *to*-infinitives. In
support of this conclusion, we present comparative evidence from nonstandard and older varieties of West Germanic.

     In order to formulate our own analysis of the verb-raising construction,
we turn to the *tree-adjoining grammar* (TAG) formalism developed by
Joshi, Levy, and Takahashi (1975), Joshi (1983), and Kroch and Joshi
(1985). Joshi (1983) was the first to point out that the crossing dependencies
produced by verb raising in Dutch are amenable to a TAG analysis. We
present two syntactic analyses in the TAG formalism, the first of which
turns out to reconstruct certain undesirable aspects of the morphological
incorporation analysis and to assign a linguistically implausible structure
to at least one class of cases. Our second TAG analysis instantiates in a
natural way the syntactic analysis of verb raising proposed by Zaenen
(1979) and has many of the attractive features that one would expect to
find in a contemporary transformational account. We conclude with a brief
discussion of the open questions that remain concerning the status of verb
raising in the grammars of Dutch and German. We note here that since
the completion of this paper, a very interesting proposal has been advanced
according to which most cases of *to*-infinitive verb raising in Dutch are the
result of *to*-infinitive extraposition and leftward scrambling of complements (Den Besten et al. 1988; Den Besten and Rutten 1989). This work,
like the study presented here, relates verb raising to syntactic extraposition,
although, unlike our study, only for a subset of cases. Extending the

proposal to German, evaluating its validity, and relating it to other recent work on the verb-raising construction in the TAG framework (Joshi 1990) are at the focus of our current research on the topic.

The West Germanic verb-raising construction is illustrated in (1) and (2). As has become customary, we give examples as subordinate clauses in order to abstract from the effects of verb-second movement and constituent preposing, which apply to root clauses in Dutch and German.

(1) a. daß Hans Peter Marie schwimmen lassen sah (German)
       that Hans Peter Marie swim   make saw
       'that Hans saw Peter make Marie swim'
    b. daß Hans Peter Marie zu schwimmen zu zwingen verbot
       that Hans Peter Marie to swim   to force   forbade
       'that Hans forbade Peter to force Marie to swim'

(2) a. dat Jan Piet Marie zag laten zwemmen (Dutch)
       that Jan Piet Marie saw make swim
       'that Jan saw Piet make Marie swim'
    b. dat Jan Piet Marie verbood te dwingen te zwemmen
       that Jan Piet Marie forbade to force   to swim
       'that Jan forbade Piet to force Marie to swim'

The underlying structure associated with (1) and (2) is shown schematically in (3).[2]

(3)

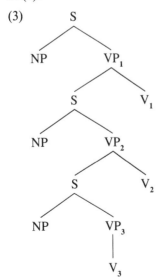

In the underlying sequence of verbs in (3), the verbs are ordered with the most deeply embedded verb leftmost and the matrix verb rightmost. In general, this word order is mapped directly onto derived structure in German, whereas the surface order of verb sequences in Dutch is the mirror image of the underlying order.

The analysis of verb raising currently accepted by most investigators treats the verb sequences in (1) and (2) as syntactically derived lexical items, known in the literature as *verb clusters*. The first and best-known attempt to formulate the verb cluster analysis in the framework of transformational grammar is due to Evers (1975). His treatment of the verb-raising construction embodies two independent claims: first, that movement of the verb and verb cluster formation occur as a single process and second, that this process of verb raising prunes the embedded clause boundaries of the structure to which it applies. More recent analyses (Zaenen 1979; Den Besten and Edmondson 1983; Haegeman and Van Riemsdijk 1986), though usually maintaining the verb cluster, have rejected the clause-pruning claim. In what follows, we present several empirical and conceptual arguments bearing on this claim that lead us to reject it as well.

2 Arguments for and against Clause Pruning

2.1 Scope of Negation

2.1.1 Evidence for Scope Ambiguity   Evers (1975) claims that in clauses with nonextraposed complements, negative operators that precede the verb sequence can take scope only over the matrix clause, but not over the underlying embedded clause.[3]

(4) weil sie   die Kraniche nicht zu fotografieren versuchen
    since they the cranes   not to photograph   try

That is, he claims that (4) is synonymous with (5a) only, rather than with (5b) or with both sentences in (5).

(5) a. weil sie   nicht versuchen, die Kraniche zu fotografieren
       since they not   try   the cranes to photograph
       'since they are not trying to photograph the cranes'
    b. weil sie   versuchen, die Kraniche nicht zu fotografieren
       since they try   the cranes not   to photograph
       'since they are trying not to photograph the cranes'

Evers assumes that the relationship between semantic scope and syntactic structure is constrained so as to allow sentence negation to take scope only over clauses that are present at derived structure, and he concludes that verb raising results in clause pruning, since the inability of negation to take scope over embedded clauses follows straightforwardly under the clause-pruning hypothesis but is difficult to reconcile with an analysis under which verb raising does not reduce the underlying biclausal to a derived mono-clausal structure.

Contrary to Evers's claim, however, the sentence in (4) is in fact ambiguous between the two readings in (5). The reversal of scope in the preferred readings of the two examples in (6), where sentence negation is in its canonical position between any NP arguments and any PP modifiers or complements of the verb, shows clearly that Evers's claim concerning the scope of negation is incorrect and that negation in an embedded clause can take scope either over its own clause, as in (6a), or over the matrix clause, as in (6b).

(6) a. daß ich die Arbeit nicht mit Verspätung einzureichen versuche
     that I the paper not with delay   in-to-hand   try
     'that I am trying not to hand in the paper late'
  b. daß ich die Arbeit nicht mit Verspätung einzureichen wage
     that I the paper not with delay   in-to-hand   dare
     'that I do not dare to hand in the paper late'

The example in (7) provides further evidence that sentence negation can take scope over an embedded clause.

(7) daß Julia ihren Spinat   nicht essen zu müssen versucht
    that Julia her   spinach not   eat   to have-to tries
    'that Julia is trying not to have to eat her spinach'

The narrow scope reading given in the gloss is by far the preferred reading of (7); the wide scope reading 'that Julia is not trying to have to eat her spinach' is virtually unavailable. Thus, if we accept Evers's assumption concerning the relationship between syntax and semantics, the facts of sentence negation actually cut against clause pruning.

Verb-raising sentences in West Flemish and Swiss German exhibit the same scope ambiguity that we have just noted for standard German (Lötscher 1978; Haegeman and Van Riemsdijk 1986). Thus, the sentences in (8) are ambiguous between a wide scope reading 'that Jan/Hans did not want to eat meat' and a narrow scope reading 'that what Jan/Hans wanted to do was not eat meat'.[4]

(8) a. da   Jan geen vlees hee willen   eten (West Flemish)
    that Jan no   meat has want-to eat
  b. das de Hans kä fläisch hät wele   ässe (Swiss German)
    that the Hans no meat   has want-to eat

2.1.2   Haegeman and Van Riemsdijk's Treatment of Scope Ambiguity Haegeman and Van Riemsdijk (1986) present a treatment of the ambiguity of negation and quantifiers that is based on their analysis of verb-raising construction. According to their treatment, which is essentially a variant of the analysis given by Evers (1975), verb raising consists of two separate processes: first, syntactic reanalysis of the sequence of verbs accompanied by clause union and second, inversion of the constituents of the reanalyzed verb sequence, which gives rise to variations on the word order of the underlying sequence of verbs. We illustrate Haegeman and Van Riemsdijk's rule of reanalysis using the West Flemish example in (8a), which is their example (52). Following their lead, we have replaced the present prefect tense in (8a) by the simple present in order to simplify the representation in (9); this replacement does not affect the scope ambiguity of negation.

(9) a.

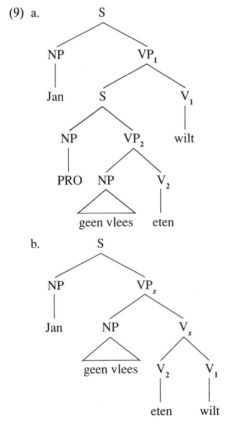

Reanalysis applies to the biclausal structure in (9a) to yield the monoclausal representation in (9b), which contains a complex lexical constituent V_x, the verb cluster. Note that Haegeman and Van Riemsdijk treat modals as control verbs in underlying structure. After reanalysis, the PRO subject of the modal may and must be unrealized in accordance with their formulation of the θ-Criterion. Inverting the constituents of the verb cluster yields the desired order of *wilt* and *eten*.

Haegeman and Van Riemsdijk extend their treatment to the dialectal variant of the verb-raising construction known as verb projection raising (Lötscher 1978; Den Besten and Edmondson 1983). In contrast to standard Dutch and German, certain West Germanic dialects, including West Flemish, allow NP arguments to occur within the sequence of verbs, as in (10a).

(10) a. da Jan wilt   geen vlees eten (West Flemish)
         that Jan wants-to no   meat eat
     b. da Jan geen vlees wilt   eten
         that Jan no   meat wants-to eat

(11) a. *dat Jan wil   geen vlees eten (standard Dutch)
          that Jan wants-to no   meat eat
     b. dat Jan geen vlees wil   eten
         that Jan no   meat wants-to eat

In order to account for the position of *geen vlees* within the verb sequence in (10a), Haegeman and Van Riemsdijk assumes that in West Flemish the matrix verb in the structure in (9a) can be reanalyzed not only with the embedded verb, but also with the embedded verb phrase. The resulting structure is shown in (12). Inversion of the immediate constituents of the verb cluster V_x yields the desired word order.

(12)

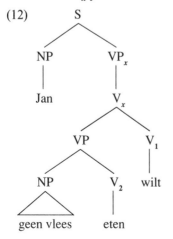

The rule of reanalysis proposed by Haegeman and Van Riemsdijk is not to be confused with a transformation that derives monoclausal from biclausal representations. Rather, reanalysis associates a set (generally a pair) of structures—namely, an unreanalyzed and one or more reanalyzed representations—with a given string. These multiple representations are then simultaneously available as input to syntactic processes such as movement. We would like to emphasize that a treatment of the West Germanic verb-raising construction that invokes reanalysis represents an unmotivated complication of the grammars of Dutch and German if an empirically equivalent treatment is available that does not require the multiple representations proposed by Haegeman and Van Riemsdijk. As we will show in section 4, such a simpler treatment can indeed be given. Moreover, even if certain constructions, notably the Romance and West Germanic subjectless causative constructions, should turn out to provide evidence for allowing the possibility of reanalysis as a descriptive device in Universal Grammar, it is clear that each particular appeal to the notion of reanalysis must be motivated on its own merits. We will show in the remainder of this section that the empirical evidence that Haegeman and Van Riemsdijk advance in support of their claim that verb raising involves clause union and reanalysis actually turns out to be problematic for their analysis.

Haegeman and Van Riemsdijk observe that (10b) is ambiguous with respect to scope of negation and propose the following analysis of the ambiguity. Given that the tensed verb *wilt* c-commands the negative NP *geen vlees* in the unreanalyzed representation in (9a) and that this c-command relation is reversed in the reanalyzed representation in (9b), they argue that the scope ambiguity of (10b) reflects the configurational difference between the two representations in (9).[5] In contrast to (10b), the sentence in (10a) allows only the narrow scope reading, a fact first noted by Lötscher (1978) for Swiss German. Haegeman and Van Riemsdijk attribute the absence of a wide scope reading to the fact that the negative NP *geen vlees* fails to c-command the tensed verb both in the unreanalyzed structure in (9a), which (10a) shares with (10b), and in the reanalyzed structure in (12). Thus, (10a) is not associated with any representation in which negation c-commands the modal.

If we take seriously Haegeman and Van Riemsdijk's proposal that scope relations directly reflect S-Structure configurations and that the basis for scope ambiguities is the availability of reanalyzed structures, as in (9b) and (12), then we are led to expect that sentences like (13) should be unambiguous in languages like English, in which verb sequences do not undergo reanalysis.

(13) The patient in ward four may eat nothing.

In particular, negation in such sentences should not take narrow scope over the modal, since the negative quantified NP *nothing* fails to c-command the tensed verb *may* at S-Structure.[6] Indeed, Haegeman and Van Riemsdijk claim that a wide scope interpretation of (13), their (88a), is unavailable, except under a marked intonation where *nothing* receives special stress. But in fact, sentences like (13) are perfectly ambiguous, as we show in (14). Note in particular that the wide scope reading in (14a) does not depend on intonational help, and that *nothing* in (14b) may receive stress without the wide scope reading being induced.

(14) a. Unless the doctor gives permission, the patient may eat nothing.
        'There is nothing that the patient is permitted to eat.'
     b. If the doctor gives permission, the patient may eat nothing.
        'The patient is permitted not to eat anything.'

Given the fact that negation can take wide scope in sentences like (13), the logic of Haegeman and Van Riemsdijk's argument dictates that the modal *may* must undergo reanalysis with the VP *eat nothing* in English. We are not aware of any independent evidence in favor of such an analysis, nor has such an analysis ever been suggested in the literature to our knowledge. Rather, we follow May (1985) in assuming that in English, scope relations are established at Logical Form (LF), an independently motivated level of syntactic representation derived from S-Structure by a rule of quantifier raising. This rule adjoins operators such as the negative quantifier *nothing* to the VP or the S in which they occur (May 1985:42). Under this approach, the adjunction of *nothing* at LF to the S that contains it at S-Structure results in the wide scope interpretation of negation illustrated in (14a), whereas its adjunction to VP gives rise to the narrow scope reading in (14b).

Since it is necessary to provide a treatment of scope ambiguities in English that is based on the rule of quantifier raising, a unitary treatment of the English and the West Germanic scope facts requires the extension of the quantifier-raising treatment to the West Germanic case, and re-analyzed structures like (9b) or (12) become irrelevant to the treatment of the scope facts, even if we continue to accept their existence. But then the fact that negative existential NPs that occur within the sequence of verbs take only narrow scope loses the explanation that Haegeman and Van Riemsdijk would give it, since the structures that they assign to (10a) and (10b) are identical prior to reanalysis. We conclude, therefore, that the treatment of scope proposed by Haegeman and Van Riemsdijk (1986) is conceptually weak and empirically inadequate.

2.1.3 A Quantifier-Raising Treatment of Scope Ambiguity   If we adopt May's rule of quantifier raising and extend it to negative operators like 'not' and 'never' in West Germanic, we are able to give an alternative treatment of the scope facts discussed by Evers (1975) and Haegeman and Van Riemsdijk (1986). Consider the scope facts for sentences containing nonextraposed clausal complements.

(15) a. daß er keinen Apfel zu essen versuchen darf
           that he no   apple to eat   try   may
    b. Er darf keinen Apfel zu essen versuchen.
          he may no   apple to eat   try

According to the generally accepted analysis of West Germanic clause structure, the main clause in (15b) is derived from an underlying verb-final structure essentially identical to that of (15a) by moving the tensed verb into COMP and by preposing exactly one maximal projection, here the subject *er*, to a clause-initial XP position. We give the S-Structure representations for the sentences of (15) in (16).

(16)

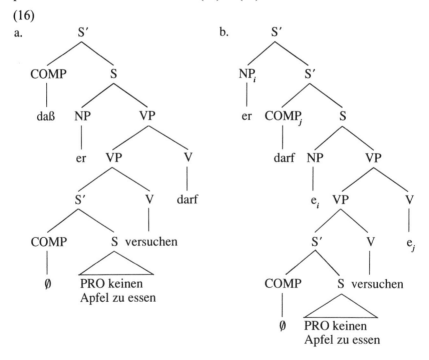

Both (15a) and (15b) are ambiguous between the narrow scope reading 'he is permitted to try not to eat an apple' and the wide scope reading 'he is not permitted to try to eat an apple'. In order to account for this scope ambiguity, we assume that quantifiers in German and Dutch can escape by quantifier raising out of untensed complement clauses when the clause is governed by the verb that subcategorizes for it.[7] Thus, the negative quantified NP *keinen Apfel* in (15) can adjoin to either the embedded or the matrix clause, giving rise to the narrow and the wide scope readings in (15), respectively. Quantified NPs containing the existential quantifier *ein* exhibit precisely the same scope ambiguity between a narrow and a wide scope interpretation.

(17) daß Hans eine Norwegerin heiraten will
     that Hans a   Norwegian marry   wants-to
     'that Hans want to marry a Norwegian'

The ambiguity in (17) is reflected in the existence of the two paraphrases 'that there is a certain Norwegian that Hans wants to marry' and 'that Hans wants to marry someone who is a Norwegian'. The negative operators *nicht* 'not', *nie* 'never', and *nicht mehr* 'not any more' behave in a way parallel to quantified NPs. We illustrate this parallelism by using examples with *nicht*, but analogous examples can readily be constructed with *nie* and *nicht mehr*. Thus, both sentences in (18) are ambiguous between a narrow scope reading 'he is permitted to try not to eat the apple' and a wide scope reading 'he is not permitted to try to eat the apple'.

(18) a. daß er den Apfel nicht zu essen versuchen darf
        that he the apple not   to eat   try   may
     b. Er darf den Apfel nicht zu essen versuchen.
        he may the apple not to eat   try

One difference between negative operators and quantified NPs is that the positioning of the former is somewhat freer. Thus, they are not restricted to their canonical position between NP complements of the verb and PPs but can also be generated as a sister of complement clauses, as in the preferred reading of (19).

(19) a. daß er nicht den Apfel zu essen versuchen darf
        that he not   the apple to eat   try   may
        'that he is not permitted to try to eat the apple'
     b. Er darf nicht den Apfel zu essen versuchen.
        he may not   the apple to eat   try
        'He is not permitted to try to eat the apple.'

The structure of (19a) on its preferred reading is given in (20).

(20)

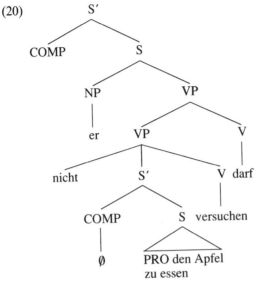

Since *nicht* in this position originates outside of the embedded clause and since adjunction of negation to the embedded S in LF would be ruled out by standard constraints on trace binding, the structure in (20) yields only a wide scope reading.

The treatment of sentence negation and outlined so far extends straightforwardly to sentences containing extraposed S′-complements.

(21) a. daß er versuchen darf, den Apfel nicht zu essen
        that he try   may the apple not   to eat
        'that he is permitted to try not to eat the apple'
    b. daß er nicht versuchen darf, den Apfel zu essen
        that he not   try   may the apple to eat
        'that he is not permitted to try to eat the apple'

The sentences in (21) are derived by extraposing the S′-complements in (18a) and (19a), respectively, and their S-Structure representations are given in (22).

(22) a.

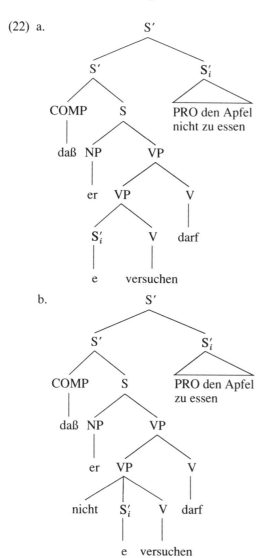

In (22a) *nicht* cannot escape out of its clause, since *versuchen* fails to govern the complement clause in its extraposed position. Hence, only the narrow scope reading is available in (21a). In (22b), on the other hand, negation is unable to escape out of the tensed matrix clause to a position from where it could c-command the extraposed clause. As a result, only the wide scope reading is available in (21b). Preposing the subject *er* or the tensed verb *darf* does not affect the configurational relations relevant for determining the scope of negation; hence, the matrix clauses in (23) are unambiguous in the same way as the corresponding subordinate clauses in (21) are.

(23) a. Er darf versuchen, den Apfel nicht zu essen.
        he may try   the apple not   to eat
        'He is permitted to try not to eat the apple.'
     b. Er darf nicht versuchen, den Apfel zu essen.
        he may not   try   the apple to eat
        'He is not permitted to try to eat the apple.'

The scope facts for quantified NPs in extraposed clauses are the same as for negation.

The scope facts that we observe in connection with verb projection raising in (10) are parallel to the facts for S'-extraposition. That is, sentences in which a verbal projection or a clause has not undergone movement are ambiguous, whereas sentences in which either verb projection raising or S'-extraposition has occurred permit only a narrow scope reading. We conclude from this parallelism that the facts in (10) are consistent with a syntactic analysis of verb projection raising and that they fail to provide evidence in favor of the analysis presented by Haegeman and Van Riemsdijk (1986).

The configurational relations relevant for determining scope are affected by instances of leftward movement such as constituent preposing in the same way as they are by instances of rightward movement such as clausal extraposition and verb projection raising. Consider the main clauses in (24), which are derived by preposing the clausal complements in the underlying structures associated with (18a) and (19a) and which have the derived structures in (25).

(24) a. Den Apfel nicht zu essen darf er versuchen.
        the apple not   to eat may he try
        'He is permitted to try not to eat the apple.'
     b. Den Apfel zu essen darf er nicht versuchen.
        the apple to eat may he not   try
        'He is not permitted to try to eat the apple.'

(25) a.

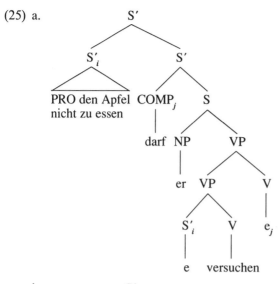

b.

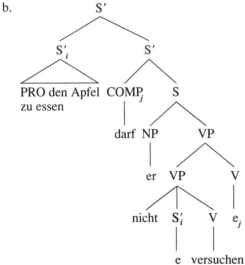

As in the case of extraposition, *nicht* in (25a) cannot escape out of the preposed clause and hence fails to c-command the matrix clause. In (25b), on the other hand, *nicht* cannot escape out of the matrix clause. As a result, only the narrow scope reading is available in (24a), and only the wide scope reading in (24b).

In summary, the approach to scope that we have outlined provides the basis for a uniform treatment of scope phenomena in English and West Germanic. In particular, it provides a uniform account of the fact that in

West Germanic the scope ambiguity of quantifiers and negative operators disappears when the constituents containing them are moved to nonargument positions, and it correctly predicts that only the narrow scope reading remains available after movement. Under Haegeman and Van Riemsdijk's approach, by contrast, the parallelism between the scope facts in the case of verb projection raising on the one hand and extraposition and constituent preposing on the other hand is not explained.

2.2 Clitic Movement

In this section we will show that the evidence based on clitic movement in Dutch and German that Evers (1975) and Haegeman and Van Riemsdijk (1986) adduce in favor of clause pruning actually cuts against it. Following Evers (1975), Zaenen (1979) observes that Dutch clitic direct objects are obligatorily preposed from their base-generated position to the position immediately following the subject.

(26) a. dat Jan Piet het kadootje gaf
          that Jan Piet the present   gave
          'that Jan gave Piet the present'
      b. *dat Jan Piet het gaf
          that Jan Piet it   gave
          'that Jan gave it to Piet'
      c. dat Jan het Piet gaf
          that Jan it   Piet gave
          (same as (26b))

Clitics that originate in bare infinitive complements are not clause-bound and can be preposed either to the position following the embedded subject or to the position following the matrix subject, as in (27a) and (27b), respectively.

(27) a. dat we de jongens het aan Piet hoorden vertellen
          that we the boys   it to Piet heard   tell
          'that we heard the boys tell it to Piet'
      b. dat we het$_i$ de jongens e$_i$ aan Piet hoorden vertellen
          that we it   the boys   to Piet heard   tell
          (same as (27a))

By constrast, clitics that originate in *to*-infinitives are clause-bound, as Zaenen (1979) points out.

(28) a. dat we de jongens het aan Piet verboden   te vertellen
          that we the boys   it to Piet prohibited to tell
          'that we prohibited the boys from telling it to Piet'

   b. *dat we het$_i$ de jongens e$_i$ aan Piet verboden te vertellen
      that we it   the boys   to Piet prohibited to tell
      (same as (28a))

The pattern in (28) is analogous to that in (29), where the entire clausal complement is extraposed.

(29) a. dat we de jongens verboden het aan Piet te vertellen
       that we the boys   prohibited it to Piet to tell
       (same as (28a))
    b. *dat we het$_i$ de jongens verboden e$_i$ aan Piet te vertellen
       that we it   the boys   prohibited to Piet to tell
       (same as (28a))

This parallelism shows that the S'-nodes dominating the *to*-infinitive complements in (28) and (29) have not been pruned. It is these nodes that block the movement of the clitic pronoun in (28b) and (29b) since Dutch, like many other languages, does not allow the raising of clitics out of full clausal complements.

The fact that clitics can move out of bare infinitive complements, as in (27b), has been interpreted as evidence for clause pruning. But the grammaticality of (27b) does not demonstrate that clause pruning has taken place, since it is consistent not only with clause pruning but also with an alternative analysis under which bare infinitive complements are dominated by VP or S, rather than S'. Under the latter analysis, clitic movement might be ruled out by Subjacency in (28b), but not in (27b). The clitic movement facts for German are more complicated than those for Dutch. First, there are two landing sites for clitic movement rather than just one: the standard Dutch position immediately following the subject and the position immediately following the COMP node.[8] Second, although some speakers allow clitic movement only in the case of bare infinitives just as in Dutch, many also accept clitic movement out of *to*-infinitives (Van Riemsdijk 1984; Haegeman and Van Riemsdijk 1986).

(30) daß uns$_i$ Hans e$_i$ seinen Wagen zu zeigen versucht hat
    that to-us Hans his   car   to show tried   has
    'that Hans tried to show us his car'

For such speakers, the facts of clitic movement provide no evidence against clause pruning, whether in the case of *to*-infinitives or in the case of bare infinitives. On the other hand, the facts in (30) also fail to demonstrate that the clause boundary in the case of nonextraposed *to*-infinitives has in fact been pruned. This is because clitic movement is acceptable even when the

S'-complement in which the clitic originates is extraposed and therefore cannot have undergone clause pruning (Kvam 1983). As the examples in (31) show, clitic movement out of extraposed clauses can take place to either landing site.

(31) a. Ich habe es$_i$ vorhin schon   versucht e$_i$ darzulegen.
     I   have it before already tried   to-explain
     'I have already tried to explain it before.'

   b. wenn ich Ihnen$_i$ versuchen darf, e$_i$ ein wenig zu helfen
      if   I   to-you try   may   a little to help
      'if I might try to help you a little'

   c. daß uns$_i$ Hans versuchte, e$_i$ seinen Wagen zu zeigen
      that to-us Hans tried   his   car   to show
      (same as (30))

   d. daß Hans uns$_i$ versuchte, e$_i$ seinen Wagen zu zeigen
      that Hans to-us tried   his   car   to show
      (same as (30))

In summary, the Dutch clitic movement facts in (28b) show that clause union cannot have taken place in the case of *to*-infinitives, even though verb raising has occurred. The German examples in (31) show the converse—namely, that clitic movement is possible even in the absence of verb raising, so that the clitic movement facts fail to bear on the existence of clause pruning in that language. Haegeman and Van Riemsdijk (1986) adduce the fact that clitics can be preposed out of *to*-infinitives in German, as in (30), as evidence for their claim that the West Germanic verb-raising construction is an instance of clause union. Their argument is vitiated, however, by their failure to recognize the eixstence of sentences like (31). Moreover, the fact that clitics can move out of *to*-infinitives in German actually turns out to be problematic for their analysis since they assume that "the effects of movement must be compatible with the structural constraints in all dimensions, not just in one" (Haegeman and Van Riemsdijk 1986:448). Thus, although clitic movement is licensed by the absence of a clause boundary in the monoclausal representation that results from reanalysis, the presence of an S' in the unreanalyzed, biclausal dimension should block clitic movement and (given their assumption) should rule it out in German just as in Dutch.

In this connection, a related difficulty for Haegeman and Van Riemsdijk's analysis should be pointed out. In standard Dutch and German, *to*-infinitives can undergo extraposition, but bare infinitives cannot.

(32) a. daß Hans versuchte, uns   seinen Wagen zu zeigen
         that Hans tried   to-us his   car   to show
         'that Hans tried to show us his car'
     b. *daß Hans wollte   uns   seinen Wagen zeigen
         that Hans wanted-to to-us his   car   show
         'that Hans wanted to show us his car'

Given Haegeman and Van Riemsdijk's assumption concerning movement,
the constrast between (32a) and (32b) is problematic since *to*-infinitive
complements are not dominated by S′ after reanalysis and hence cannot
undergo S′-extraposition. Rather, both bare infinitives and *to*-infinitives
are dominated by VP in the reanalyzed structure. Haegeman and Van
Riemsdijk's treatment would therefore lead us to expect (32a) to be ungrammatical, since verb projection raising in standard Dutch and German
is ruled out.

2.3 Binding of Reciprocal Pronouns
Reuland (1980) presents an argument against clause pruning based on the
intepretation of Dutch reciprocal pronouns. He notes that if verb raising
resulted in clause pruning, (33) would be expected to be grammatical since
the matrix subejct *de vrouwen* would be available as an antecedent for the
reciprocal pronoun *elkaar*.

(33) *dat de vrouwen de kamer   elkaar   vroegen te helpen
      that the women   the parliament each-other asked   to help
      'that the women asked Parliament to help each other'

But the ungrammaticality of (33) is expected if verb raising does not affect
the clausal status of the *to*-infinitive, as shown in (34).

(34) *dat de vrouwen de kamer$_i$ [$_{S′}$ PRO$_i$ elkaar$_i$ e$_j$] vroegen te helpen$_j$

Under the assumption that the movement of *te helpen* leaves a trace that
governs the reciprocal pronoun *elkaar*, the embedded clause is the domain
in which *elkaar* must be bound, according to the binding principles of
Government-Binding Theory (Chomsky 1981). The only potential antecedent for *elkaar* is the subject of the embedded clause, PRO. But since
PRO shares the number feature of its controller, the singular NP *de kamer*,
it fails to agree with the inherently plural reciprocal pronoun and (33) is
correctly ruled out. An analogous argument can be constructed on the
basis of the German counterpart of (33).

(35) *daß die Frauen den Bundestag einander   zu helfen baten
      that the women the parliament each-other to help   asked
      (same as (33))

Haegeman and Van Riemsdijk (1986) agree that the facts of binding argue against a clause-pruning analysis of the verb-raising construction and claim that their analysis is preferable to that of Evers (1975) because the binding facts can be stated on the unreanalyzed, biclausal representation of verb-raising sentences, in which subjects are configurationally defined. But since they fail to explain why the principles of the binding theory apply to the biclausal rather than to the monclausal structure in their two-dimensional representation, their analysis is stipulative. This conceptual weakness is compounded by the fact that they require syntactic movement to meet constraints on both the unreanalyzed and the re-analyzed representations, whereas they assume the interpretation of scope to be licensed by configurational relations in the reanalyzed representation only. Note that Reuland's argument against clause pruning is more highly theory-dependent than the first two arguments that we have presented. It hinges on the assumption, central to successive versions of transforma-tional grammar, that grammatical relations, in particular the notion of subject, are configurationally defined. If it turns out that the interpretation of reflexive and reciprocal pronouns must be established on the basis of thematic or grammatical relations rather than on the basis of syntactic configurations, then the argument will no longer go through.

2.4 The Projection Principle
In addition to these empirical arguments for rejecting the clause-pruning claim, we and others (Den Besten and Edmondson 1983; Kroch and Santorini 1985; Haegeman and Van Riemsdijk 1986) have noted that clause pruning is incompatible with one of the fundamental tenets of Government-Binding Theory, the Projection Principle, under which syn-tactic structure is constrained to reflect lexical argument structure at every syntactic level (Chomsky 1981, 1982, 1986b).

2.5 Verb Raising as Morphological Incorporation
In order to avoid the empirical and conceptual difficulties discussed above and in order to make the verb cluster analysis conceptually consistent with the principles of Government-Binding Theory, verb cluster formation must be formulated as a process distinct from clause pruning. A restatement of Evers's treatment of the verb-raising construction that does not involve clause pruning is presented by Den Besten and Edmondson (1983). Under their analysis, an underlying structure like (3) is related to a derived structure like (36a) in Dutch or (36b) in German.

(36) a.

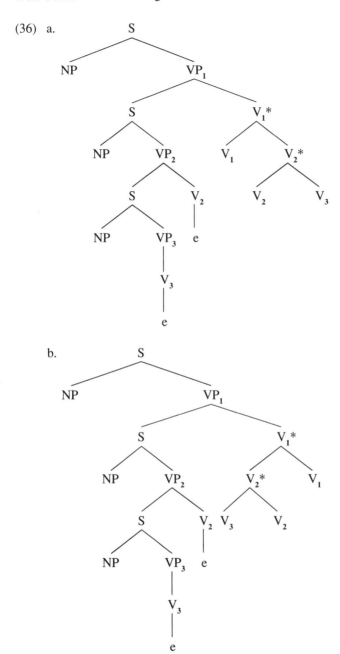

The structures in (36) are derived from the underlying structure in (3) by cyclic Chomsky-adjunction. The most deeply embedded infinitive V_3 adjoins to V_2, the verb minimally c-commanding it, and the resulting constituent in turn adjoins to the next higher verb, V_1. We have marked the constituents formed by adjunction with asterisks. The verb cluster is the constituent dominated by the node V_1^*. Dutch and German differ in the direction of adjunction so that verb cluster formation is string-vacuous in German, but not in Dutch.

The analysis of the verb-raising construction embodied in (36) is strikingly reminiscent of analyses of morphological causatives proposed by Marantz (1984) and others. Consider, for instance, the Chicheŵa causative construction in (37), for which Baker (1988) proposes the underlying and derived structures in (38).

(37) Mtsikana anau-gw-ets-a   mtsuko.
      girl   AGR-fall-make-ASP waterpot
      'The girl made the waterpot fall.'

(38)

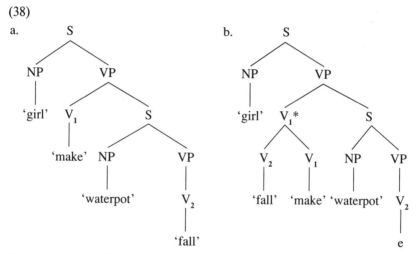

The structure in (38b) is derived from that in (38a) by morphological incorporation of the embedded verb into the matrix verb. Apart from the fact that the verb phrase is head-initial in Chicheŵa but head-final in West Germanic and that West Germanic verb raising applies to a greater embedding depth,[9] the structure derived by verb raising in (36) is identical to that derived by verb incorporation in (38). Given this remarkable coincidence of form, it is tempting to reformulate Den Besten and Edmondson's modified version of Evers's analysis as a claim that West Germanic verb raising is an instance of verb incorporation in Marantz's and Baker's sense. This way of looking at the verb cluster analysis is attractive because it makes that analysis stateable without ad hoc weakening of the theory of grammar. Furthermore, it makes the analysis of the verb-raising construction directly relevant to one of the most active areas of current research, the interface between morphology and syntax. As we will show in what follows, however, such a treatment of verb raising is untenable, at least in its most general form.

3   Arguments against the Verb Cluster

Having established that the verb-raising construction involves neither clause pruning nor clause union, we now turn to a discussion of the arguments bearing on the claim that the clause-final sequence of verbs forms a syntactically derived lexical constituent, the verb cluster, in West Germanic. Evers's original arguments for the verb cluster are based on evidence from nominalization, the position of sequence negation, and gapping. More recently (Evers 1981), he has proposed a further argument based on coordination. Finally, Den Besten and Edmondson (1983) have argued that the verb cluster hypothesis provides the basis for an elegant treatment of variations on the order of clause-final verbs in standard German. In this section we will discuss and refute each of these arguments in turn.

3.1   Nominalization

Evers (1975) observes that verbs in Dutch and German nominalize freely, so that corresponding to the verb in (39a) we have the nominal infinitive in (39b).

(39) a. daß meine Mutter singt
      that my   mother sings
      'that my mother sings'
   b. das Singen (meiner Mutter)
      the singing of-my mother
      '(my mother's) singing'

He then points out that verb sequences have corresponding complex nominalizations.

(40) a. daß meine Mutter singen lernen will
      that my   mother sing   learn wants-to
      'that my mother wants to learn to sing'
   b. das Singen-lernen- wollen   (meiner Mutter)
      the sing   learn   wanting-to of-my mother
      '(my mother's) wanting to learn to sing'

Assuming a parallel derivation for nominal infinitives like (39b) and complex nominalizations like (40b), Evers concludes that sequences of verbs like (40a) are complex derived lexical constituents. The structure of the complex nominalization in (40b) is shown in (41).

(41) [$_N$[$_V$[$_V$[$_V$ singen] lernen] wollen]]

Evers fails to observe, however, that verb sequences containing to-infinitives have no corresponding nominalizations even though they undergo verb raising. The crucial contrast is between (40b) and (42b).

(42) a. daß meine Mutter zu singen versuchte
         that my   mother to sing   tried
         'that my mother tried to sing'
     b. *das (zu-) singen-versuchen (meiner Mutter)
         the to   sing   trying   of-my mother
         '(my mother's) trying to sing'

Thus, the nominalization argument cuts against the verb cluster analysis of verb raising in the case of to-infinitives.

Though the grammaticality of bare infinitive nominalizations follows straightforwardly under Evers's treatment, his assumption that (40b) represents the nominalization of a verb cluster is not well founded. This is because the grammaticality of such nominalized forms is also consistent with an alternative analysis of complex nominal infinitives that treats nominalized bare infinitive sequences as lexical compounds of nominalized infinitives. It is well known that German and Dutch bare infinitives nominalize freely without changing form (except orthographically in German).[10]

(43) a. kleine   Katzen oft   streicheln
        small-ACC cats   often pet
        'to pet small cats often'
     b. das häufige Streicheln kleiner   Katzen
        the frequent petting   small-GEN cats
        'the frequent petting of small cats'

The distinction between the verbal infinitive in (43a) and the corresponding nominal infinitive in (43b) is reflected in the difference in the morphological case that is assigned to the NP argument of the infinitive and in the difference between the adverbial modifier *oft* and its adjectival counterpart *häufig*. As Höhle (1984) notes in discussing these examples, nominal infinitives cannot be modified by adverbs; hence, (44) is ungrammatical.

(44) *das oft- Streicheln kleiner   Katzen
     the often petting   small-GEN cats
     (same as (43b))

We attribute these differences between verbal and nominal infinitives to the fact that nominalization affects the categorial feature values of verbal infinitives. Thus, verbal infinitives are specified for the categorial feature values $[-N, +V]$, whereas nominal infinitives are specified for the converse values, $[+N, -V]$. This change in feature values has the syntactic consequence that nominal infinitives, like other nouns, are unable to assign Case. Thus, (45b) is ruled out by the Case Filter.

(45) a.   die Katzen   streicheln
          the cats-ACC pet
          'to pet the cats'
     b.   *das die Katzen   Streicheln
          the the cats-ACC petting
          'petting the cats'

Whereas the lexical projection of N cannot assign Case, the first phrasal projection of N—namely, N'—is able to assign structural genitive Case and the θ-roles of its head to the right, as in (46).

(46) [$_{NP}$ das [$_{N'}$[$_N$ Streicheln]] der Katzen]
          the   petting   the cats-GEN
     (same as (45b))

The facts for verbs that assign lexical Case (dative or lexically idiosyncratic genitive), like *helfen*, differ from those for *streicheln*. This is because the arguments of such verbs reject structural Case and must receive lexical Case.[11] The arguments of the nominalized infinitives of such verbs inherit this property. Thus, we find the pattern in (47), where (47c) is ungrammatical because structural genitive cannot be assigned to an argument that requires lexical Case.

(47) a.   den Kindern   helfen
          the childern-DAT help
          'to help the children'
     b.   *das den Kindern   Helfen
          the the children-DAT helping
          'helping the children'
     c.   *das Helfen der Kinder
          the helping the children-GEN
          (same as (47b))

A. S. Kroch & B. Santorini

We assme that nominalization does not affect other syntactic properties of the verbal infinitive, such as its argument structure or the direction of θ-role assignment. Thus, we expect, correctly, that the nominalized forms of verbal infinitives with PP arguments will be grammatical since PPs do not require Case.

(48) a. nach Paris reisen
        to   Paris travel
        'to travel to Paris'
   b. das nach-Paris-reisen
        the to   Paris traveling
        'traveling to Paris'

We assign the structure in (49) to the nominalization in (48b).

(49) $[_{NP}$ das $[_{N'}[_{PP}$ nach Paris] $[_N[_V$ reisen]]]]

    Nominalizations like (50b) are prima facie counterevidence to our claim that nouns cannot assign Case to their left.

(50) a. (kleine) Katzen streicheln
           small cats   pet
           'to pet (small) cats'
   b. das (kleine-) Katzen-streicheln
           the small   cats   petting
           'petting (small) cats'

The contrast between (50b) and (51b) shows, however, that the type of nominalization illustrated in (50b) is distinct from that in (48b).

(51) a. die kleinen Katzen streicheln
          the small cats   pet
          'to pet the small cats'
   b. *das die-kleinen-Katzen-streicheln
          the the small   cats   petting
          'petting the small cats'

Nominalizations like (50b) are derived by the morphological incorporation of nonmaximal nominal projections. Since the incorporation of maximal projections is ruled out, as one would expect, (51b) is ungrammatical. Of course, nominal phrases that undergo incorporation do not receive Case, and nominalizations like (52) are therefore ruled out by virtue of the constraint mentioned in connection with (47c), which requires that arguments of verbs that assign lexical Case must receive it.

(52) *das (kleinen)-Kindern-   helfen
     the small   children-DAT helping
     'helping (small) children'

Incorporation is extremely productive in Dutch and German, resulting in
derived verbs such as *Karten spielen* 'to play cards' and *Bier trinken* 'to
drink beer';[12] and the morphologically complex verbs it creates pattern
like simple verbs not only with respect to nominalization, but also with
respect to passive. This is shown in (53), where the tensed verb bears
singular agreement morphology in the impersonal passive construction,
demonstrating that the direct object has not been promoted to subject.
This promotion would have been obligatory had incorporation not applied.

(53) Es wurde oft   Karten gespielt, kleine Katzen gestreichelt.
     it was   often cards   played   small cats   petted
     'There was frequent card playing, petting of small cats.'

Thus, the internal structure of nominalizations like *Biertrinken* 'beer drink-
ing' or *Kartenspielen* 'card playing', given in (54), is distinct from the PP
case in (49).

(54) $[_{NP}$ das $[_{N'}[_N[_V[_N$ Bier$][_V$ trinken$]]]]]$

Nominal infinitives like (49) and (54) are free to undergo morphological
incorporation in the lexicon. Thus, under our analysis of bare infinitive
nominalizations, the derivation of the nominalizations in (55) is parallel
to that of the nominal infinitive *Kartenspielen* from the verbal infinitive
Karten spielen. The only difference between the two cases is that the
incorporated argument in *Kartenspielen* is the underived noun *Karten*,
whereas the incorporated nouns in (55) are nominal infinitives derived from
verbal infinitives. In the case of (55c), in fact, the incorporated nominal
infinitive *Segelschiffe-entwerfen* 'sailboat designing' is itself derived by
morphological incorporation of the noun *Segelschiffe*.

(55) a. dein $[_N[_V[_N[_V$ Singen$]]-[_V$ wollen$]]]$
        your   sing   wanting-to
        'your wanting to sing'
     b. dein $[_N[_V[_{N'}[_{PP}$ nach- Paris$]-[_N[_V$ reisen$]]]-[_V$ wollen$]]]$
        your   to   Paris   travel   wanting-to
        'your wanting to travel to Paris'
     c. dein $[_N[_V[_N[_V[_N$ Segelschiffe$]-[_V$ entwerfen$]]]-[_V$ müssen$]]]$
        your   sailboats   design   having-to
        'your having to design sailboats'

The recursive application of incorporation can give rise to even more complex bare infinitive nominalizations such as the one in (40).

In the Dutch counterpart of (40), both the order of the verbs in the verb sequence and that of the nominalized infinitives in the corresponding bare infinitive nominalization are mirror images of the German order.

(56) a. dat mijn moeder wil   leren zingen
        that my mother wants-to learn sing
        (same as (40a))

    b. het willen-   leren-zingen (van mijn moeder)
        the wanting-to learn sing   of my mother
        (same as (40b))

We attribute the parallel order of the verbs in (56a) and the constituents of the nominalized form in (56b) to the fact that the nominalized infinitives in (56b) inherit the direction in which they assign θ-roles from the underlying verbal infinitives in (56a). If we assume with Baltin (1989) that subcategorization is for heads rather than for maximal projections and extend his idea to say that θ-roles are also assigned to heads, then it is not surprising that the word order in the nominalization and the sentence are the same in (56).[13]

The analysis of bare infinitive nominalizations that we have just presented is consistent with the existence of verb sequences that have no corresponding nominalizations. Such verb sequences occur in German and very marginally in Dutch as a result of a rule of syntactic lowering. This rule moves quantified or emphatically stressed NPs into the VP. We illustrate syntactic lowering for simple clauses in (57b) and (58b).

(57) a. daß Hans allen Kindern das Buch zeigte
        that Hans to-all children the book showed
        'that Hans showed the book to all the children'

    b. daß Hans das Buch allen Kindern zeigte
        that Hans the book to-all children showed
        (same as (57a))

(58) a. daß keiner dem Hans das Buch gab
        that nobody to-the Hans the book gave
        'that nobody gave the book to Hans'

    b. daß dem Hans das Buch keiner gab
        that to-the Hans the book nobody gave
        (same as (58a))

Quantifier lowering is also possible in clauses in which verb raising has applied. We show this in (59) and (60), using an exceptional German sentence type in which the tensed verb occurs as the first verb in the verb sequence. Such sentences are one where modal verbs appear in a perfect tense, as in (59a) and (60a).[14] We return to these sentences in section 3.5 for other purposes. For the moment, however, their significance lies in the fact that the tensed verb delimits the sequence of verbs. As in the simple clause (58b), the subject of a clause in these sentences can occur inside the VP when stressed, as in (60b). In addition, it can occur inside the sequence of verbs, as in (60c).

(59) a. daß Hans Kindern   das Buch hätte   zeigen wollen
     that Hans to-children the book would-have show want-to
     'that Hans would have wanted to show the book to children'
   b. daß Hans das Buch Kindern   hätte   zeigen wollen
     that Hans the book to-children would-have show want-to
     (same as (59a))
   c. daß Hans das Buch hätte   Kindern   zeigen wollen
     that Hans the book would-have to-children show want-to
     (same as (59a))

(60) a. daß keiner gestern   hätte   kommen dürfen
     that nobody yesterday would-have come   be-allowed-to
     'that nobody would have been allowed to come yesterday'
   b. daß gestern   keiner hätte   kommen dürfen
     that yesterday nobody would-have come   be-allowed-to
     (same as (60a))
   c. daß gestern   hätte   keiner kommen dürfen
     that yesterday would-have nobody come   be-allowed-to
     (same as (60a))

In contrast to the verb sequences in (59c) and (60c), the corresponding nominalizations are completely unacceptable.[15]

(61) a. *dieses ewige Haben- Kindern-   zeigen-wollen (des   Buches)
     this   eternal having to-children show want-to of-the book
     'this constant having wanted to show children (the book)'
   b. *dieses ewige Haben- keiner- kommen-dürfen
     this   eternal having nobody come   be-allowed-to
     'this constant nobody having been allowed to come'

Under our analysis of bare infinitive nominalizations, the nominalized forms in (61) are both ruled out because the NP arguments fail to receive

Case from the nominal infinitives *zeigen* and *kommen* and because they cannot be derived by incorporation.[16]

Finally, our analysis of bare infinitive nominalization, in contrast to a verb cluster analysis, is consistent with the following facts from Swiss German (Henk van Riemsdijk, personal communication). Swiss German expresses the progressive aspect by means of the construction illustrated in (62), in which the copula is followed by the fused form *am* 'at-the' and a nominal infinitive.

(62) Er isch am   ruedere.
     he is   at-the row
     'He is rowing.'

The nominal infinitive need not be morphologically simple as it is in (62); rather, it can also be the nominalization of a verb derived by noun incorporation, as in (63a), or the nominalization of a bare infinitive sequence, as in (63b).

(63) a. Er isch am   klavierspile.
        he is   at-the piano-play
        'He is playing piano.'
     b. Er isch am   leere ruedere/autofaare.
        he is   at-the learn row   car-drive
        'He is learning to row/to drive a car.'

The facts in (62) and (63), in particular those in (63b), are consistent with a verb cluster analysis as well as with our analysis of bare infinitive nominalization. However, the two analyses make different predictions concerning the progressive of sentences in which verb projections are raised. Consider (64).

(64) das er wil   leere s   auto repariere
     that he wants-to learn the car   repair
     'that he wants to learn to repair the car'

We have seen in section 2.1 that the variant of the verb cluster analysis proposed by Haegeman and Van Riemsdijk would treat the sequence *leere s auto repariere* as a derived lexical constituent in a way parallel to the bare infinitive sequences *leere ruedere* and *leere autofaare* in (63b). The same is true of an alternative extension of the verb cluster analysis to verb projection raising proposed by Den Besten and Edmondson (1983), which we discuss in more detail in section 4.1. Under these analyses, one might therefore expect the progressive of the bare infinitive sequence in (64) to be grammatical. Under our nominal-compounding analysis, on the other hand, the progressive construction in question is predicted to be un-grammatical. This is because the status of *s auto* as a maximal projection prevents *s auto repariere* from being derived as a morphologically complex verb by noun incorporation. As a result, *s auto repariere* is unable to undergo nominalization and subsequent compounding with *leere*. As shown in (65), it is the prediction of the nominal-compounding analysis that is borne out.[17]

(65) *Er isch am   leere s   auto repariere.
       he is   at-the learn the car   repair
       'He is learning to repair the car.'

3.2 Sentence Negation

Evers's intuitively most appealing argument for the verb cluster is based on the position of *nicht* 'not' as a sentence negator. Objecting to the notion that negation can take scope over higher clauses from inside an embedded clause, Evers (1981:100) notes that "[t]he verb of the deepest embedded sentence [is] a strange place to negate the matrix structure." He observes further that sentence negation in clauses containing nonextraposed com-plements cannot occur immediately preceding the tensed verb.[18]

(66) a. daß meine Mutter dem   Mann das Buch nicht geben will
          that my   mother to-the man   the book not   give wants-to
          'that my mother does not want to give the man the book'
      b. *daß meine Mutter dem   Mann das Buch geben nicht will
          that my   mother to-the man   the book give not   wants-to

From this, he concludes that negative operators like *nicht* are matrix constituents that precede the verb cluster. In order to maintain Evers's conclusion, given the collapse of the clause-pruning hypothesis, one would need to assume that in cases like (6b), repeated here as (67), the PP *mit Verspätung* undergoes string-vacuous incorporation into the verb cluster.

(67) daß ich die Arbeit nicht mit   Verspätung einzureichen wage
      that I   the paper not   with delay   in-to-hand   dare
      'that I do not dare to hand in the paper late'

Though it is true that PPs can occur within the sequence of verbs in many varieties of West Germanic, including standard German, the verb sequence in standard German and Dutch cannot in general contain NP arguments. Therefore, the example in (68) shows clearly that *nicht* can take matrix scope from within the lowest embedded clause.[19]

(68) daß meine Mutter dem   Mann nicht das Buch geben will
     that my   mother to-the man   not the book give wants-to
     (same as (66a))

Note further that negation in (7), repeated here as (69), takes scope over the clause containing *müssen* even though *nicht* precedes the most deeply embedded verb *essen* and not *müssen*.

(69) daß Julia ihren Spinat nicht essen zu müssen versucht
     that Julia her spinach not eat   to have-to tries
     'that Julia is trying not to have to eat her spinach'

We attribute the unacceptability of (66b) to the fact that *nicht* originated historically as a morphologically complex negative element that occupied an argument position within the VP, just as *not* did in English. But whereas *not* in Modern English has come to be a true sentence negator associated with INFL, *nicht* continues to behave syntactically in a way that reflects its historical origin. Thus, although *nicht* is morphologically simple from the synchronic point of view, its scope behavior is parallel to that of the morphologically complex *nothing*; that is, it is a constituent of VP and undergoes quantifier raising, as we saw in section 2.1. In Old English, on the other hand, where sentence negation was expressed by the precursor of *not*, the morphologically simple sentence-negating proclitic *ne*, sentence negation immediately precedes the matrix verb in a clause-final verb sequence, as in (70) (Van Kemenade 1985).

(70) þæt nan hæthen cyning ær   gedon ne dorste
     that no heathen king before do   not dared
     'that no heathen king had dared to do before'

3.3 Gapping

Evers (1975) notes that gapping affects sequences of verbs in the same way as it does simple verbs and concludes from this fact that verb sequences are lexical constituents of category V.

(71) a. daß Hans Gedichte schreibt und Heike Romane
        that Hans poems   writes and Heike novels
        'that Hans writes poems and Heike novels'
     b. daß Hans Gedichte zu schreiben beginnen wird und Heike
        that Hans poems   to write   begin   will and Heike
        Romane
        novels
        'that Hans will begin writing poems and Heike novels'

This argument assumes that the possibility of gapping reliably indicates the status of a string as a constituent. But as Evers himself points out, gapping can delete discontinuous strings like *bei diesem Tanz ... schaute.*

(72) daß Hans bei diesem Tanz zu mir schaute und ich zu ihm
     that Hans at this dance to me looked and I   to him
     'that Hans looked at me during this dance and I at him'

We know that the VP in (72) has the binary-branching structure [*bei diesem Tanz* [*zu mir* [*schaute*]]] and that the deleted sequence *bei diesem Tanz schaute* is not a constituent since permuting the order of the PPs *bei diesem Tanz* and *zu mir* results in the ungrammatical sequence **daß Hans zu mir bei diesem Tanz schaute.*

Thus, gapping in German, as in English, does not always delete constituents. Indeed, in English gapped sentences, the deletion of nonconstituent sequences like *will sing* in (73a) is generally more natural than the deletion of only parts of such sequences, even when the deleted elements are constituents.

(73) a.   John will sing the recitativos and Mary the arias.
     b.   ?John will sing the recitativos and Mary may the arias.
     c.   ?John will sing the recitativos and Mary play the harpsichord.

Even if gapping were constrained to delete constituents, however, the verb cluster hypothesis would give rise to incorrect predictions concerning the deletion of substrings of the verb sequence. Consider (74), where the bracketing indicates the derived constituent structure of the verb sequence under the verb cluster hypothesis.

(74) daß Hans Gedichte [[[schreiben] können] möchte]
     that Hans poems   write   be-able would-like
     'that Hans would like to be able to write poems

     a.   *... und Heike Romane muß
           and Heike novels   has-to
        and Heike has to novels'
     b.   ... und Heike Filme drehen
           and Heike films turn
        and Heike to make films'

Under the assumption that gapping deletes constituents, the verb cluster hypothesis leads one to expect that deleting the sequence *schreiben können*, which forms a derived constituent, should be preferable to deleting the nonconsitutent sequence *können möchte*. But this prediction is not borne out; and in fact, as we indicated in (74), the actual acceptability pattern of the sentences produced by deleting these sequences is precisely the reverse of that expected under the verb cluster hypothesis.

3.4 Coordination

Evers (1981) argues that sequences of verbs behave like simple verbs with respect to what he terms emphatic coordination.

(75) a. daß wir die Kinder   entweder hören oder sehen
        that we the children either   hear or   see
        'that we either hear or see the children'
     b. daß wir die Kinder   entweder tanzen sehen oder singen hören
        that we the children either   dance see   or   sing   hear
        'that we either see the children dance or hear them sing'

Moreover, he claims that emphatic coordination on matrix verbs is not acceptable.

(76) *daß wir die Kinder   tanzen entweder sehen oder hören
       that we the children dance either   see   or   hear
       'that we either see or hear the children dance'

This argument is unsatisfactory in at least two respects. First, the German and Dutch sentences in (77) are incorrectly ruled out.[20]

(77) a. daß wir die Kinder   entweder spielen oder tanzen sehen werden
        that we the children either   play   or   dance see   will
        'that we will see the children either play or dance'
     b. dat we de kinderen ofwel kunnen ofwel moeten zien spelen
        that we the children either be-able or   have-to see play
        'that we are either can or must see the children play'

Second, the argument depends on the assumption that the possibility of coordination is evidence that the conjoined strings are constituents. That this assumption is not valid is shown by sentences such as (78), where there is no reason to believe that the sequence consisting of the indirect and the direct object forms a constituent.[21]

(78) Hans wird entweder Heike das Buch oder Bernd die Platte schenken.
     Hans will either   Heike the book or   Bernd the record give
     'Hans will either give Heike the book or Bernd the record.'

3.5 Word Order

Den Besten and Edmondson (1983) present an argument for the verb cluster based on the standard German word order illustrated in (79), which we mentioned above in connection with the quantifier-lowering examples in (59) and (60).

(79) daß ich Anne hätte   besuchen müssen
     that I   Anne would-have visit   have-to
     'that I would have had to visit Anne'

According to their analysis, the order of the verbs in (79) is the result of a stylistic inversion rule that permutes the two immediate constituents of the verb cluster. The underlying and derived structures they assign to the verb sequence in (79) are shown in (80); V_2* and V_1 are the constituents that permute.

(80) a.

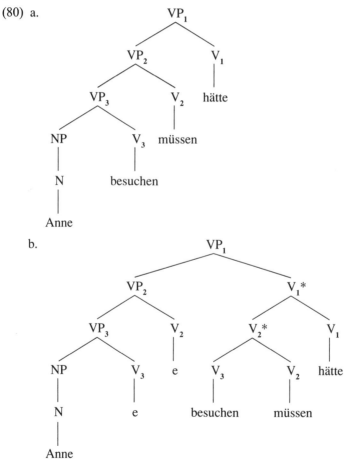

b.

In other varieties of West Germanic—for instance, in Swiss German—the mirror image of V_1 V_3 V_2 verb sequences occurs. Such sequences can be derived by inverting the immediate constituents of V_2*, yielding the word order in (81) (Lötscher 1978).

(81) wil   er en   gsee choo hät (Swiss German)
     since he him see   come has
     'since he saw him come'

However, Den Besten and Edmondson's inversion analysis of the verb orders in (79) and (81) is open to the objection that the permutation of constituents of morphologically complex lexical items is an otherwise unparalleled phenomenon in West Germanic, if not universally. Moreover, they fail to note that there are two actually occurring verb sequences that cannot be derived by inverting (sub)constituents of the verb cluster. These are the $V_2\ V_1\ V_3$ sequence in (82), which is possible in Swiss German, and its mirror image in (83), which occurs generally in Southern German dialects—for example, in Franconian (Lötscher 1978).[22]

(82) wo   s aagfange hät rägne (Swiss German)
     when it started   has rain
     'when it started to rain'

(83) daß er singen hat müssen (Franconian)
     that he sing   has have-to
     'that he had to sing'

4   A Syntactic Analysis of Verb Raising

4.1   The Uniform Derivation Hypothesis

We have demonstrated that the arguments that have been advanced in favor of the verb cluster are either incorrect or inconclusive. The evidence that we have presented shows clearly that verb raising must be syntactic in the case of *to*-infinitives. First, nominalizations of *to*-infinitives are ungrammatical. Second, it appears from a survey of cross-linguistic facts that verb incorporation occurs only with modals, causatives, and perception verbs—that is, with verbs that subcategorize for VPs or small clauses rather than for S′-complements (Baker 1988).[23] If this restriction is correct, then the raising of *to*-infinitives cannot be an instance of morphological incorporation, since *to*-infinitives undergo raising freely despite the fact that they originate in S′-complements in underlying structure. In the case of bare infinitive raising, the empirical evidence from nominalization and clitic placement in standard Dutch and German is consistent with either a morphological incorporation analysis or a purely syntactic treatment. In this paper we will adopt what we will refer to as the *uniform derivation hypothesis*; that is, the hypothesis that verb raising is a syntactic process that affects bare infinitives and *to*-infinitives in a parallel manner. This hypothesis is attractive since it results in a unitary analysis of the word order facts in those varieties of West Germanic that exhibit verb raising. If it should turn out, however, that the proper analysis of bare infinitive raising involves the formation of a derived lexical constituent in the syntax, the TAG analysis that we present will have to be revised to take advantage of an extension of the TAG formalism that is independently motivated by facts concerning extraposition (Kroch and Joshi 1987), and we would be led to formulate an analysis of bare infinitive raising similar to that proposed by Heycock (1987) for the Japanese causative construction, which clearly is morphological in our sense.

Comparative evidence for the uniform derivation hypothesis comes from the possibility of verb projection raising in many varieties of West Germanic (Lötscher 1978; Den Besten and Edmondson 1983). Thus, West Flemish and Swiss German permit bare infinitive constructions like those in (84) and (85), respectively.

(84) En ge   zoudt nog moeten uw   eigen pintje betalen.
     and you would yet have-to your own beer pay
     'And you would even have to pay for your own beer.'

(85) a. Mer händ em   Hans welen   es velo schänke.
        we   have to-the Hans want-to a bike give
        'We wanted to give Hans a bike.'

     b. Mer händ welen   em   Hans es velo schänke.
        we   have want-to to-the Hans a bike give
        (same as (85a))

In order to account for these facts, Den Besten and Edmondson (1983) suggest that the projection level to which verb raising applies varies parametrically across dialects. In both West Flemish and Swiss German, the projection dominating the verb and its direct object can be raised, in contrast to standard Dutch, which permits only the raising of the verb itself. In Swiss German, in addition, the entire VP can become part of the verb sequence. Den Besten and Edmondson then extend the verb cluster analysis to the phrasal raising constructions in (84) and (85). Their treatment results in a lexical constituent, the verb cluster, that dominates a phrasal projection of V. Since such constituents, which are anomalous with regard to X-bar theory, are not required elsewhere in West Germanic and since a syntactic analysis of verb raising is available, as we will show, the verb cluster analysis of verb projection raising results in an unwarranted weakening of the constraints on possible phrase structures in Dutch and German.[24]

It might be objected that what appear to be phrasal projections of V in (84) and (85) are in fact complex lexical items derived by the process of morphological incorporation discussed in section 3.1. The constituents dominated by the verb cluster would then be morphologically complex lexical constituents, rather than phrases. There are two difficulties with this attempt to salvage a morphological analysis of verb projection raising. First, the sequences *uw eigen pintje betalen* and *es velo schänke* in (84) and (85) cannot be derived by incorporation since they contain maximal projections. Second, treating the sequence of verbs in (85b) as a lexically derived complex verb additionally violates the constraint mentioned in connection with (47c)—namely, that arguments of verbs that assign lexical Case must receive it—since *em Hans*, if incorporated, would not receive lexical dative Case. Thus, our revision of Den Besten and Edmondson's incorporation analysis of verb projection raising fares no better than their original proposal. We conclude that only a syntactic analysis of the verb-raising construction is able to capture that parallelism between lexical and phrasal raising in those dialects that allow verb projection raising and to provide a unitary analysis of bare infinitive raising across dialects.

Den Besten and Edmondson (1983:199f.) note that "[i]n 17th century Dutch ... direct objects (but not indirect objects) could be incorporated into verb raising." This is just the situation in modern West Flemish. Over the past three centuries, standard Dutch has innovated in comparison to West Flemish by gradually restricting verb raising to lexical projections of V. A similar development has taken place in standard German, where we find verb projection raising in the Early New High German of Luther:

(86) Die Mutter hätte   nicht gedurft   den Namen tragen.
     the mother would-have not   been-allowed-to the name   bear
     'The mother would not have been allowed to bear the name.'

We interpret the graduality of the historical drift toward the raising of smaller verbal projections as evidence for the unitary nature of phrasal and lexical bare infinitive raising, and hence for the conceptual desirability of a syntactic analysis of all bare infinitive raising.

4.2   Verb Raising as Infinitive Extraposition

Having adopted the uniform derivation hypothesis, we now address the problem of constructing a syntactic treatment of verb raising. Zaenen (1979) presents a syntactic analysis consistent with the evidence we have given, under which verb raising in short verb sequences (those consisting of two verbs) is the result of a process of infinitive extraposition.[25] If we extend her proposal to longer verb sequences such as the one in (2a), repeated here as (87), we predict the existence of derived structures like (88), where the S-nodes marked by asterisks are nodes resulting from Chomsky-adjunction.

(87) dat Jan Piet Marie zag laten zwemmen
      that Jan Piet Marie saw make swim
      'that Jan saw Piet make Marie swim'

(88)

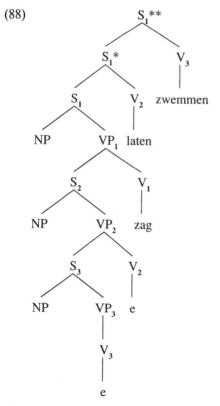

We assume that the untensed complement clauses S_2 and S_3 do not represent bounding nodes for Subjacency (Rizzi 1982); hence, the infinitives *laten* and *zwemmen* can be extraposed directly to S_1 and S_1* to give the desired $V_1\ V_2\ V_3$ order.

In the remainder of this paper we present two alternative instantiations of Zaenen's treatment of verb raising as infinitive extraposition, using the tree-adjoining grammar (TAG) formalism of Joshi, Levy, and Takahashi

(1975) and Joshi (1983).[26] Since the TAG formalism may be unfamiliar to many readers, we will first give a brief description of it before we present the two linguistic analyses that it makes possible. For a more detailed introduction to the formalism, we refer the reader to Joshi 1983 and Kroch and Joshi 1985. The linguistic relevance of the TAG formalism is discussed extensively in Kroch and Joshi 1985, 1987 and in Kroch 1987, 1989.

4.3 The TAG Formalism

The fundamental linguistic insight on which the TAG formalism is based is that local cooccurrence relations can be factored apart from the expression of recursion and unbounded dependencies. A TAG consists of a set of elementary trees on which local dependencies are stated and an adjunction operation, which composes elementary trees with one another to yield complex structures. In order to avoid confusion with the notion of adjunction familiar from Government-Binding Theory, we will make a terminological distinction between Chomsky-adjunction and tree-adjunction (or tree-adjoining). The elementary trees of a TAG are divided into initial trees and auxiliary trees, whose forms are illustrated in (89).

(89)

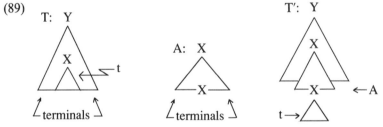

Initial trees have the form of the left-hand tree T. The root node of an initial tree is labeled S or S', its internal nodes are all phrasal categories, and its frontier nodes are all lexical categories. Auxiliary trees have the form of the center tree A. The root node of an auxiliary tree is a phrasal category, which we have labeled X. Its frontier nodes are all lexical nodes except for one phrasal node that bears the same category label as the root node.

We now define tree-adjunction as follows. Let T be an elementary tree with a nonterminal node labeled X, and let A be an auxiliary tree with a root node X. By definition, A will also have a foot node X. Tree-adjoining the auxiliary tree A at the node X of the elementary tree T then consists of the following steps.

1. The subtree of T dominated by X, t in (89), is excised, leaving behind a copy of its parent node X.

2. The auxiliary tree A is attached at X, and its root node is identified with the node X at which it attaches.

3. The subtree t is attached to the foot node of the auxiliary tree, and the node X that dominates t is identified with the foot node X of the auxiliary tree.

Thus, the result of tree-adjoining the auxiliary tree A in (89) at the node X of the initial tree T is the right-hand tree T′.

Using the TAG formalism, we can easily derive the German verb-raising examples in (1). For reasons of space, we illustrate only the derivation of (1a), repeated here as (90).

(90) daß Hans Peter Marie schwimmen lassen sah
     that Hans Peter Marie swim   make saw
     'that Hans saw Peter make Marie swim'

The derivation requires the initial tree and the two auxiliary trees in (91). Again, we omit S′, COMP, and INFL nodes to simplify the representation. Note carefully that the initial tree in (91) represents a special case of T in (89), namely, the case where Y and X coincide.

(91)   Initial tree

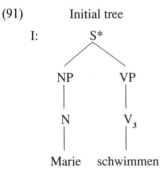

Auxiliary trees

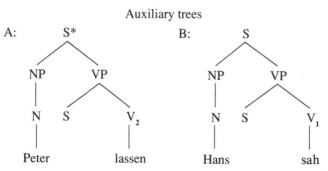

The sentence in (90) is derived by tree-adjoining the first auxiliary tree, A, at the designated node S* in the initial tree I, yielding A′ in (92). The second auxiliary tree, B, is then adjoined at the node S* in the subtree A of A′, yielding B′. Since tree-adjunction takes place at the root nodes of I and A, tree-adjunction here reduces to substitution; this is not the case in general, however.

(92)

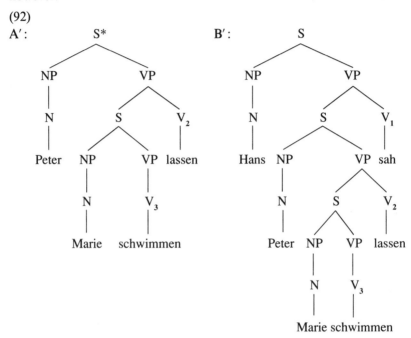

In order to derive the Dutch word order in (2), it is necessary to use elementary trees of a slightly different form—namely, ones in which an infinitive is extraposed and Chomsky-adjoined to the clause containing it. We will refer to such trees as trees with links, where *link* refers to the relationship between an empty category and the Chomsky-adjoined antecedent that binds it. The elementary trees required to derive (2a), repeated here as (93), are given in (94); they may be thought of as having been derived from the Dutch trees corresponding to the German ones in (91) by extraposing the infinitive verb.[27]

(93) dat Jan Piet Marie zag laten zwemmen
      that Jan Piet Marie saw make swim
      'that Jan saw Piet make Marie swim'

We follow Zaenen (1979) in assuming that only infinitives undergo extra-position; hence, the tensed verb in the second auxiliary tree, B, is not coindexed with a trace. But this is not dictated by the TAG formalism, and the Dutch word order in (93) could be derived by using auxiliary trees in which the tensed verb is extraposed as well.

(94)   Initial tree

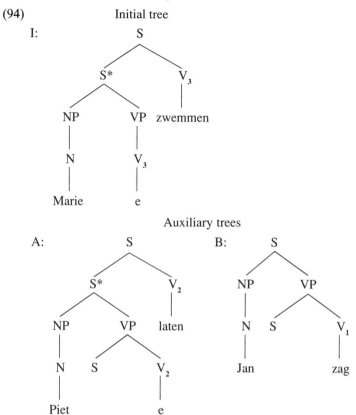

The derivation of (93) proceeds by tree-adjoining the auxiliary tree A at the designated node, S*, in the initial tree, and tree-adjoining B at S* in the subtree A of A'. Note that the derived constituent structure of the right-hand tree in (95) is identical to that in (88).

(95) A′:

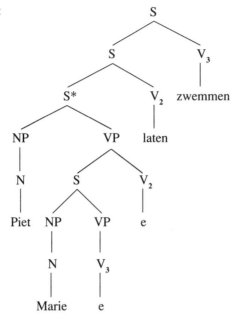

B′:

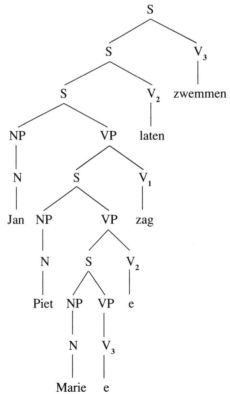

4.4   The String-Vacuous Raising Hypothesis

Except for the tree that contains that matrix verb, the elementary trees in (94) each have two structurally adjacent S-nodes. The derivation of Dutch verb sequences requires that each auxiliary tree be tree-adjoined at the lower S-node. It is formally possible in a TAG to derive the German verb sequences in (90) using trees that are structurally identical to those in (94) if one performs tree-adjunction at the higher S-node. Such a treatment instantiates a linguistic analysis under which German exhibits string-vacuous verb raising; thus, although it is a syntactic analysis, it reconstructs an important aspect of the verb cluster analysis. The trees resulting from the adjunction of A and B at the higher S-nodes in (94) (given the appropriate lexical changes) are given in (96) as A' and B', respectively.

(96) A' :

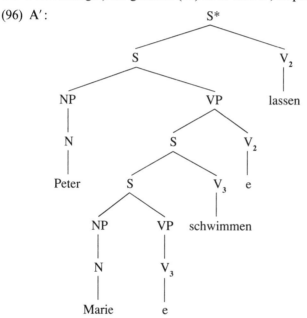

B′:

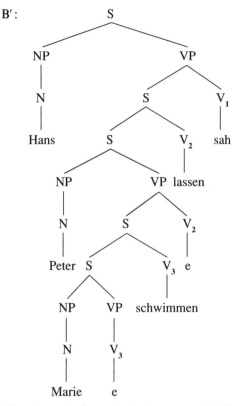

We will refer to the hypothesis that trees with links, as in (94), are used to derive verb-raising sentences in both German and Dutch as the *string-vacuous raising hypothesis*. According to this hypothesis, the difference between the two languages is reducible to a general constraint against tree-adjunction at the higher or lower of two structurally adjacent S-nodes in standard Dutch and German, respectively.[28] This constraint is the TAG equivalent of the constraint that governs the direction of Chomsky-adjunction under Den Besten and Edmondson's incorporation analysis of the verb cluster.

Verb sequences other than the standard German and Dutch ones illustrated in (90) and (93), respectively, can then be derived by relaxing this constraint, Consider the Franconian word order illustrated in (83) and repeated here as (97).

(97) daß er singen hat müssen
     that he sing   has have-to
     'that he had to sing'

The string-vacuous raising hypothesis requires the extraposition of *singen* in the initial tree. The form of the initial tree and the nature of tree-adjunction then dictate that modals must be lexically inserted into trees in which they govern clausal complements, just as in Haegeman and Van Riemsdijk's analysis. The trees that are required are given in (98).

(98)   Initial tree

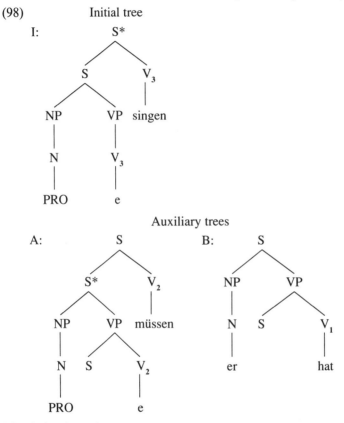

The derivation of (97) is shown in (99). The first and second auxiliary trees adjoin at the higher S-node of I and the lower S-node of A, respectively. We continue to omit S'-nodes to simplify the representation; hence, PRO is only apparently governed in the structures in (99).

(99) A′:

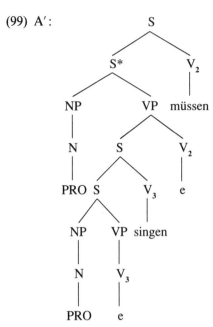

B′:

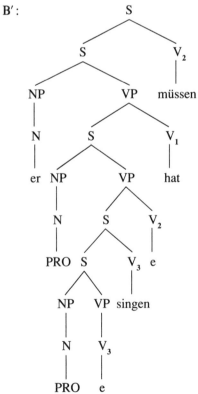

Performing tree-adjunction at the converse nodes as for Franconian inversion yields the mirror image of the verb sequences in (97), which we illustrated for Swiss German in (82) and repeat here as (100).

(100) wo   s aagfange hät rägne
       when it started   has rain
       'when it started to rain'

The trees required in the derivation are given in (101); since the derivation is straightforward, we will not give it in detail.

(101)   Initial tree

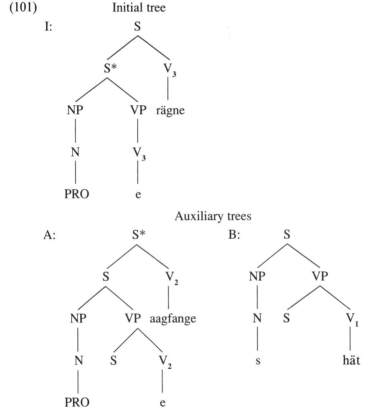

An analysis based on the string-vacuous raising hypothesis is attractive because it promises to reduce the variation in the word order of verb sequences to the choice of node at which auxiliary trees are adjoined as they enter the derivation. However, it fails to provide a plausible derived structure for examples like (102).

(102) daß sie hätte   schreiben können
      that she would-have write   be-able
      'that she could have written'

The trees required in the derivation of (102) are given in (103).

(103)   Initial tree

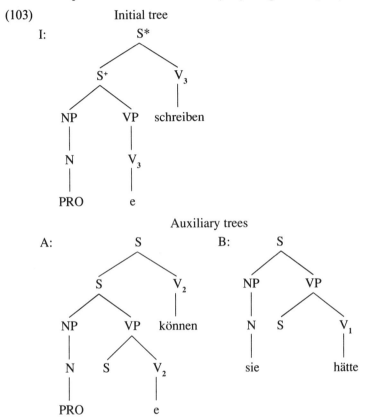

The auxiliary trees in (103) are simultaneously adjoined into the initial tree, with A and B adjoining at the higher and lower S-node, respectively. We illustrate the derivation of (102) in (104). For expository reasons, we present the derivation as if the adjunction of A into the initial tree preceded that of B.

(104)

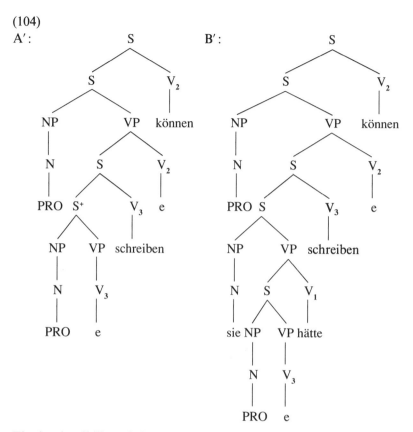

The implausibility of the derived structure in (104), in which the PRO subject of *können* c-commands its antecedent *sie*, leads us to reject the string-vacuous raising hypothesis.

4.5 An Analysis without String-Vacuous Verb Raising

We now present a TAG analysis of verb raising that is based on the assumption that there is no string-vacuous verb raising. This assumption has the formal consequence in a TAG that neither $V_3 V_1 V_2$ verb sequences nor their mirror image can be derived if modals are analyzed as subcategorizing for clausal complements. We therefore follow Den Besten and Edmondson (1983) in assuming that modals subcategorize for VP complement; accordingly, they are inserted into auxiliary trees with VP roots like the one in (105).

(105)

The Franconian example in (97) can then be derived using the elementary trees in (106).

(106)   Initial tree   Auxiliary trees

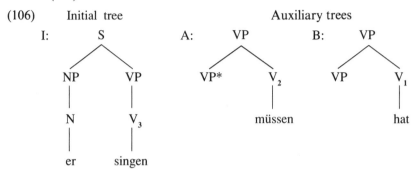

The first auxiliary tree adjoins at the VP-node of the initial tree to yield A', and the second auxiliary tree adjoins at the lower VP of the subtree A in A'.

(107) A':   B':

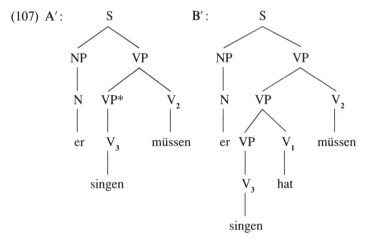

In certain varieties of Southern German, the word order corresponding to that in (97) is *singen müssen hat* (Den Besten and Edmondson 1983:182). Our TAG analysis reflects the minimal difference between the sequence without verb raising and the one in (97) quite simply: the sequence without verb raising is derived by using the same trees as in (106), but by adjoining the second auxiliary tree at the higher VP-node of A in A'.

The derivation of the Swiss German word order in (100) requires an initial tree with a link, corresponding to the extraposition of *rägne*, the infinitive complement of *aagfange*.

(108)

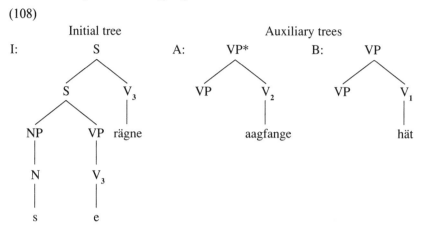

Initial tree   Auxiliary trees

The first auxiliary tree, A, adjoins at the VP of the initial tree, and the second auxiliary tree, which contains the matrix verb, then adjoins at the higher VP-node of the subtree A in A'.

(109) A':

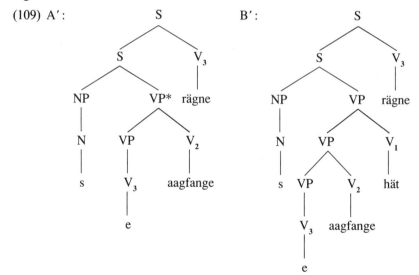

The V_1 V_2 V_3 counterpart of the sequence in (100) would be derived by tree-adjoining B at the lower VP-node of A in A'.

The derivation of the remaining two verb sequences discussed in section 3.5—namely, V_1 V_3 V_2 and its mirror image V_2 V_3 V_1—requires the

Chomsky-adjunction of infinitives to VP. The trees needed to derive the verb sequence in (102) are given in (110).

(110)   Initial trees

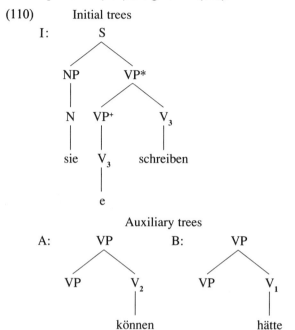

Both auxiliary trees adjoin simultaneously in the initial tree at VP* and VP$^+$, respectively. For expository reasons, we again illustrate the derivation as if the adjunction of A preceded that of B.

(111)

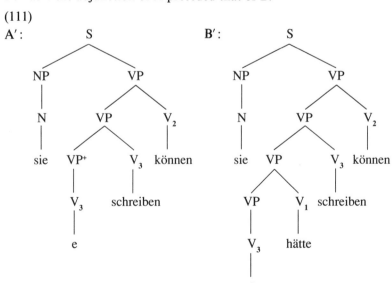

As the reader can easily verify, the mirror image of the verb sequence in (102), which is illustrated for Swiss German in (81), can be derived by performing adjunction at the converse nodes of the initial tree.

Under a TAG analysis without string-vacuous verb raising, it is not possible to reduce the variation in the word order of verb sequences to a single difference, as under the string-vacuous raising hypothesis. Rather, there are two sources of such variation, which are a result of the fundamental distinction that is drawn in a TAG between the expression of local relations on the one hand and recursion on the other. The first source of word order variation is the choice between elementary trees with or without extraposed infinitives, and the second is the choice between different nodes as sites for tree-adjunction. Note that from the point of view of learnability, a syntactic analysis without string-vacuous verb raising is preferable to one with it. Under the string-vacuous raising hypothesis, the language learner would need to postulate the existence of trees with links in the absence of positive string evidence. An analogous learnability problem arises when a morphological analysis is maintained for German, as Evers (1981) notes. A syntactic analysis without string-vacuous verb raising, on the other hand, requires the language learner to posit trees with links only when faced with relevant string evidence.

We conclude this section by reporting an interesting and subtle consequence of our TAG analysis. Given the small clause analysis of the complements of causatives and perception verbs that we have so far been assuming, a TAG analysis predicts the following contrast between German and Dutch.

(112) a. daß die Hitze Marie einschlafen wollen   ließ (German)
            that the heat Marie fall-asleep want-to made
            'that the heat made Marie want to fall asleep'
      b. *dat de hitte Marie deed willen   gaan slapen (Dutch)
            that the heat Marie made want-to go   sleep
            (same as (112a))

The derivation of (112a) is straightforward and requires that the first and second auxiliary trees in (113) adjoin simultaneously at VP and S of the initial tree.

(113)   Initial tree

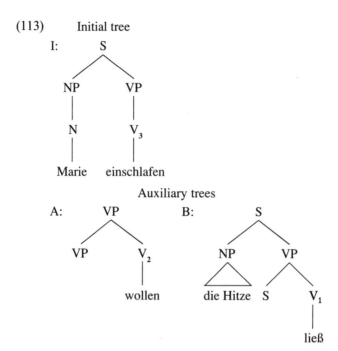

Now consider the derivation of (112b), which uses the trees in (114).[29]

(114)   Initial tree

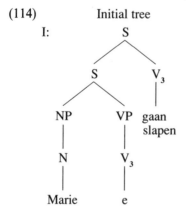

Auxiliary trees

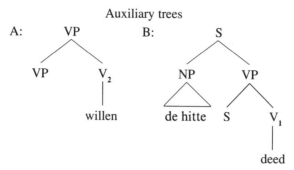

A: VP   B: S

As in the German case, the auxiliary trees would need to adjoin into the initial tree simultaneously. But whereas the auxiliary tree containing the modal can adjoin to the VP of the initial tree, yielding the tree in (115), the word order of the verb sequence in (112b) requires the auxiliary tree containing the causative to be adjoined at an S-node within the c-command domain of *willen*. But such a node does not exist, and hence (112b) cannot be derived using the trees in (114).[30]

(115)

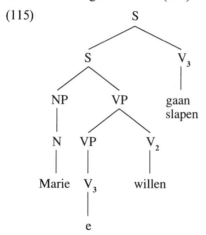

Though judgments concerning (112a) and (112b) are delicate, speakers of German and Dutch reacted differently to the corresponding sentences. The German speakers judged (112a) to be well formed, though some objected to its stylistic infelicity. By constrast, none of our Dutch informants accepted (112b), and one of them spontaneously cited the collocation of *deed* and *willen* as the source of unacceptability.[31]

4.6 Constituent Stranding in the Verb Sequence

We conclude the presentation of our TAG analysis of the verb-raising construction with a brief discussion of a further interesting class of verb-raising constructions. Lötscher (1978) and Haegeman and Van Riemsdijk (1986) note that Swiss German permits not only the raising of verbal projections, as in (116a), but also the stranding of NP arguments within the sequence of verbs, as in (116b).[32]

(116) a. das er em   Karajan wil   chöne en arie vorsinge
          that he to-the Karajan wants-to be-able an aria sing-for
          'that he wants to be able to sing an aria for Karajan'
      b. das er em   Karajan wil   en arie chöne vorsinge
          that he to-the Karajan wants-to an aria be-able sing-for
          (same as (116a))

Haegeman and Van Riemsdijk (1986) observe that analyses based on the cyclic adjunction of verbs or verbal projections, such as that proposed by Evers (1975) or Den Besten and Edmondson (1983), are unable to derive verb sequences that contain stranded constituents. Under Haegeman and Van Riemsdijk's analysis, sentences containing stranded constituents are derived by the multiple application of reanalysis to a given string.

In a TAG, the verb sequence in (116b) can be derived using an initial tree that encodes two instances of infinitive extraposition—namely, the extraposition of the phrasal projection that dominates *en arie vorsinge* to VP and the further extraposition of the lexical projection *vorsinge* to S. To simplify the representation in (117), we follow Haegeman and Van Riemsdijk in using the labels NP_1, NP_2, and NP_3 as abbreviations for *er, em Karajan*, and *en arie*, respectively.

(117)   Initial tree
     I: S

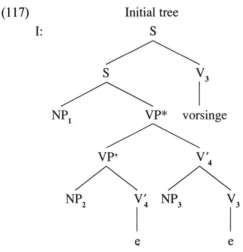

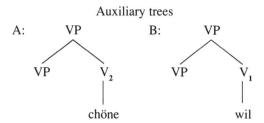

Auxiliary trees

The sequence in (116b) is derived by adjoining the auxiliary tree containing *chöne* at VP*, and the one containing *wil* at VP⁺. We illustrate the derivation as if the adjunction of the first auxiliary tree preceded that of the second.

(118)

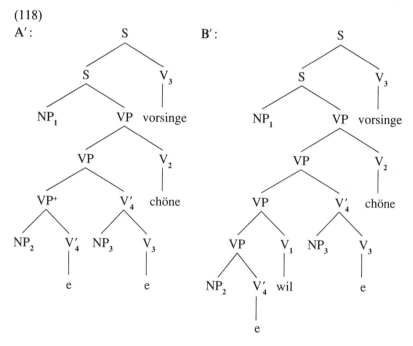

5 Conclusion

Not surprisingly, many important issues concerning the West Germanic verb-raising construction remain unresolved. Chief among these is the question of why verb raising is obligatory in so many West Germanic verb sequences. This is a particularly difficult problem for a morphological incorporation analysis. In a case like the Chicheŵa causative construction, the application of incorporation can be derived from the fact that the causative verb is an affix and hence cannot stand alone in derived structure. No such solution is available for the West Germanic case, where the elements in question are all full lexical items that can and do stand alone in other environments like simple tensed sentences and nominal infinitives. In an attempt to derive the obligatoriness of verb raising from principles of Universal Grammar, Evers (1981) proposes that verbs in Dutch and German must be aux-indexed according to the following recursive definition.

(119) A verb is aux-indexed if it incorporates $\langle + \text{tense} \rangle$ or $\langle - \text{tense} \rangle$ or if it is minimally and uniquely c-commanded by an aux-indexed verb.

According to Evers, *to*-infinitives either are unspecified for tense, like bare infinitives, or else bear the feature value [−tense]. When *to*-infinitives are unspecified for tense, they must undergo verb raising in order to acquire an aux-index just like bare infinitives, whereas *to*-infinitives that are specified for tense must undergo S'-extraposition just like tensed complement clauses. Evers's proposal is problematic in two respects. First, since he does not explain why aux-indexing is obligatory in Dutch and German, but not in other languages, his proposal is stipulative. Second, the aux-indexing proposal fails to explain why verb raising occurs even in environments in which bare infinitives are not c-commanded by an aux-indexed verb (Zaenen 1979).

(120) Jan naar die manifestatie   laten gaan doe ik nooit!
      Jan to   the demonstration let   go   do I never
      (standard Dutch)
      'I'll never let Jan go to that demonstration.'

In (120) *doe* functions as a carrier of tense, just like its English cognate *do*. The underlying structure associated with (120) is that in (121).

(121) ik nooit [$_{VP}$[$_S$ Jan naar die manifestatie gaan] laten] doe

The sentence in (120) is derived by preposing the bracketed VP in (121) to clause-initial position and moving *doe* to second position. The sequence *gaan laten* then undergoes verb raising, yielding the surface order in (120), in spite of the fact that *laten* is a bare infinitive and cannot aux-index *gaan*.[33]

Under a syntactic treatment of verb raising, on the other hand, it is natural to consider the obligatoriness of verb raising in certain syntactic environments as the grammaticization of infinitive extraposition, which serves to reduce the processing complexity associated with center-embedded structures. The extraposition of infinitives has thus become obligatory for the same reason that it is obligatory in the case of tensed complement clauses in Dutch and German and untensed complement clauses in Dutch, and preferred in the case of untensed complement clauses in German. Evidence that this approach is on the right track comes from at least three sources. First, Evers (1975:55) notes that the verb-raising construction is acceptable to a greater embedding depth and is used more frequently in Dutch than in German. Evers's observation is corroborated by the psycholinguistic study reported by Bach, Brown, and Marslen-Wilson (1987), according to which the verb-raising construction is processed more easily and accurately in Dutch, where it results in crossing dependencies, than in German, where the underlying nested dependencies are preserved at S-Structure. Second, Zaenen (1979) notes that short verb sequences can exhibit the underlying order of verbs in at least some dialects of Dutch if they consist of a single verb governing a bare infinitive. In sequences consisting of a single verb governing a *to*-infinitive or more than two verbs, verb raising is obligatory. In the nonstandard dialects of German that freely allow verb raising, such as Swiss German, verb raising also becomes obligatory once the sequence of verbs attains a certain degree of complexity, which Lötscher (1978) attempts to quantify. Third, many nonstandard dialects of German allow verb raising more freely than the standard language. Moreover, mixed crossing and nested dependencies like (122) are acceptable and fairly frequent in colloquial standard German (Kvam 1983; Hans-Ulrich Block, personal communication).

(122) daß Hans der Frau das Buch versucht hat zu geben
      that Hans to-the woman the book tried has to give
      'that Hans tried to give the woman the book'

As Lenerz (1984:177) notes, earlier stages of German also permitted verb raising more freely than the contemporary language, in which the superficial order of verbs in the verb sequence reflects their underlying order fairly strictly.[34] We attribute the aversion of the modern written language to verb raising to the fact that there has been a steady development in the written language dating from the Early New High German period toward strict verb-finality at S-Structure. Thus, though both Dutch and German are underlying verb-final languages (Koster 1975; Thiersch 1978), German, unlike Dutch, does not allow PP extraposition as freely as Dutch and does not require the extraposition of untensed complement clauses.

The question of how the grammaticization of infinitive extraposition is to be expressed formally in a synchronic grammar remains open. One approach that seems to us to be promising is to argue that to varying extents in the various dialects of West Germanic, the directionality of θ-role assignment by matrix verbs to complement verbs has become decoupled from basic phrase structure order. Thus, whereas West Germanic verb phrases continue to be head-final and to assign Case and θ-roles to the left for nominal arguments, they have come to assign θ-roles to the right for complement verbs and clauses. Under such conditions, a complement verb or clause might have to extrapose in order to receive its θ-role. This would then account for why tensed clauses in German and all complement clauses in Dutch must extrapose. Further, if we accept that θ-roles are assigned to the heads of phrases rather than to maximal projections as we proposed in section 3.1, then verb raising, interpreted as infinitive extraposition, becomes simply a way of satisfying the directionality requirement of θ-role assignment for verbal complements. Needless to say, these remarks are largely speculative and should be taken only as suggestive of a possible line of investigation for future research.

We conclude this paper by briefly recapitulating our findings. In section 2 we presented four arguments against the claim that verb raising involves clause pruning or clause union, and we reformulated the currently accepted verb cluster analysis of the verb-raising construction as the claim that verb raising is the result of morphological incorporation. In section 3 we showed that all of the arguments that have been proposed in support of this analysis are incorrect or inconclusive. We then drew the conclusion in section 4 that an incorporation analysis of verb raising is not tenable in the case of *to*-infinitives, basing our finding on evidence from two sources. First, the facts of clitic placement in Dutch show that verbs undergo raising out of full S'-complements. If verb raising were incorporation, these facts would be surprising in view of the constraints on incorporation familiar from other languages. Second, the contrast between complex nominalizations of bare infinitives, which are grammatical, and of *to*-infinitives, which are not, shows that verb sequences containing *to*-infinitives cannot be complex verbs. Given that the empirical evidence in the case of bare infinitives is consistent with either a morphological or a syntactic analysis of bare infinitive raising, we then proposed the uniform derivation hypothesis, according to which a syntactic analysis of verb raising extends to bare infinitives. This extension is concpetually desirable since it results in a unitary analysis of the word order facts in Dutch verb sequences. The comparative data we presented from Flemish and Swiss German and earlier stages of Dutch and German lent empirical support to the uniform derivation hypothesis.

Adopting Zaenen's analysis of verb raising as infinitive extraposition, we presented two TAG instantiations of her syntactic analysis. Though the first of these turned out to be conceptually inadequate, our second TAG analysis accounted straightforwardly for the range of word order variation that we find in West Germanic, including a class of examples that are underivable under a morphological analysis since they contain constituents that are stranded within the sequence of verbs. The fact that it is possible to formulate two alternative linguistic analyses in the TAG formalism illustrates the important methodological point that although the TAG formalism allows us to instantiate linguistic analyses in a natural way, it does not in itself provide a linguistic analysis and hence is not itself a theory of grammar. Instead, it is a metalanguage that enforces precise statements of linguistic analyses in which it is possible to trace exactly how the consequences of each linguistic decision ramify throughout the grammar. Finally, we suggested that West Germanic verb raising might represent the gramaticization of the process of infinitive extraposition, which, like other instances of extraposition, reduces the processing complexity associated with the underlying center-embedded structures to which it applies.

Notes

1. In this paper we use *West Germanic* as a convenient cover term for standard Dutch and German and their nonstandard varieties rather than in its traditional sense, in which it also includes English.

2. We have omitted S', COMP, and INFL nodes in order to simplify the representation in (3); no theoretical point is intended.

3. Following Evers, we will give standard German examples from now on, unless an argument depends on word order facts specific to other varieties of West Germanic.

4. When governing an infinitive, the expected past principle of a modal suppletes to the infinitive in all varieties of West Germanic except Frisian. We make no attempt here to explain this phenomenon, which goes by the names of *Ersatzinfinitiv*, *infinitivus pro participio*, or *double infinitive construction*. (For discussion, see Hoeksema 1980, 1988; Lange 1981; Den Besten and Edmondson 1983 and references therein).

5. Given the parallel word order of the West Flemish example in (10b) and its standard Dutch equivalent in (11b), we would expect both examples to exhibit the same scope ambiguity. The narrow scope reading may not be available in standard Dutch, however—a fact for which we would have no explanation.

6. We assume that the different syntactic status of modals in English and in the West Germanic languages is irrelevant to the issue at hand.

7. Note that the escape of quantifiers is governed by the same condition as verb raising itself. Thus, neither quantifier raising nor verb raising is possible out of tensed complement clauses, which are obligatorily extraposed in German and Dutch. Furthermore, verb raising out of subject complement clauses is ruled out, even when these are not extraposed (Evers 1975:40).

(i)   daß die Kraniche zu sehen mich erschüttert
       that the cranes   to see   me   upsets
       'that it upsets me to see the cranes'

(ii)   *daß die Kraniche mich zu sehen erschüttern
       that the cranes   me   to see upset
       (same as (i))

In a parallel way, negation cannot escape out of the subject complement clause in (iii).

(iii) daß die Kraniche nicht zu sehen mich erschüttert
       that the cranes   not to see   me   upsets

Thus, (iii) means only 'that is upsets me not to see the cranes' and not 'that it does not upset me to see the cranes.' The extreme unacceptability of (ii) suggests that it is due to a violation of the Empty Category Principle or the Condition on Extraction Domains (Huang 1982) rather than to a Subjacency violation. If this is the case, then the asymmetry between subject and object clauses with respect to verb raising and quantifier raising provides evidence for the existence of VP in German.

8. Certain Dutch dialects pattern with German in this respect (Weijnen 1966:327). Clitic movement to the position immediately following COMP is subject to a constraint that clitic objects must not precede pronominal subjects.

9. Baker (1988) observes that in principle, the multiple application of verb incorporation is grammatical in Chicheŵa. However, double causatives are awkward and triple causatives are completely unacceptable since verb incorporation gives rise to center-embedded structures that are extremely difficult to parse. West Germanic verb raising remains acceptable to a greater embedding depth than the Chicheŵa causative construction, perhaps because it is not restricted lexically to the complements of a single verb.

10. Since even simple *to*-infinitives do not nominalize in Dutch and German, the analysis of bare infinitive nominalizations that we present below correctly and straightforwardly rules out the unacceptable *to*-infinitive nominalizations in (42b). We attribute the inability of *to*-infinitives to nominalize to the fact that, containing INFL, they are necessarily phrasal.

11. The personal passive construction in (i) is ruled out for this reason, in contrast to the impersonal passive in (ii).

(i)   *Die Kinder   wurden geholfen.
       the children-NOM were   helped
       'The children were helped.'

(ii) Den Kindern   wurde geholfen.
      the children-DAT was   helped
      (same as (i))

12. In contrast to the spelling of the nominalizations of these derived verbs, which are spelled as one word, the spelling of the verbs themselves is misleading since it suggests that they are phrases.

13. The analysis of bare infinitive nominalizations presented in the text does not account for, and in fact predicts to be ungrammatical, complex nominalizations like (i), which are accepted by many speakers (Höhle 1984).

(i) a. dein ewiges (den)- Kindern- Schokolade-geben
         your eternal to-the children chocolate   giving
         'your constant giving chocolate to (the) children'
     b. dein ewiges (den)- Kindern-die-Schokolade-geben
         your eternal to-the children the chocolate   giving
         'your constant giving the chocolate to (the) children'

The fact that in such cases speakers accept direct objects that are maximal projections as well as incorporated direct objects suggests to us that the nominalizations in (ia) and (ib) are derived by a linguistically marginal process of nonce-nominalization that results in complex nominalized forms that correspond to VPs and that is distinct from the nominalization processes discussed in the text. In contrast to the nominalized forms derived by these latter processes, which decline in acceptability as they become more complex, nonce-nominalizations tend to become slightly more acceptable as they gain in complexity. They remain quite awkward, however, and seem similar to English cases like *This looks like a hunker-down-and-wait-out-the-storm situation.*

The distinction between linguistically well integrated nominalization processes on the one hand and nonce-nominalization on the other permits us to account for the following pattern of acceptability, noted by Höhle (1984: fn. 16c).

(i) a. dein den-Ball-in-die-Ecke- werfen
         your the ball in the corner throwing
         'your throwing the ball into the corner'
     b. dein ewiges den- Kindern-süße- Bonbons- schenken
         your eternal to-the children sweet candies   giving
         'your constant giving the children sweet candies'

(ii) a. dein in-die- Ecke- werfen   des   Balls
         your in the corner throwing of-the ball
         (same as (ia))
     b. *dein ewiges den- Kindern-schenken süßer   Bonbons
         your eternal to-the children giving   of-sweet candies
         (same as (ib))

The nonce-formations in (i) are equally acceptable. But whereas the thematic structure of the underlying verbs is expressed in an apparently parallel manner in (ii), with the theme argument occurring in postnominal position in both cases, there is a marked contrast in the acceptability of (iia) and (iib). Under our analysis, this contrast is due to the fact that the derivations of (iia) and (iib) are not parallel.

The form in (iia) is derived by nominalizing the verbal infinitive *werfen*. The PP argument can precede the nominal infinitive since it does not require Case, whereas the NP argument must appear in the postnominal position, where it receives structural genitive Case. The nominalization in (iib), on the other hand, cannot be derived by the first two nominalization processes discussed in the text nor is it a possible nonce-formation, since *den Kindern schenken* is not a VP.

14. Recall that the expected participle of the modal *wollen* suppletes to the infinitive, just as in the West Flemish case in (8).

15. For some speakers, all bare infinitive nominalizations containing *haben* are unacceptable.

16. The forms in (61) are also not possible nonce-formations since the verb sequences in (59c) and (60c) are not VPs.

17. *Leere* 'learn' takes both bare infinitive and *to*-infinitive complements. The *to*-infinitive variant of (65) given in (i) is independently ruled out by the fact that *to*-infinitive sequences contain INFL, as mentioned in note 10.

(i) *Er isch am   leere s   auto z repariere.
    he is   at-the learn the car to repair
    (same as (65))

18. In the preverbal position, *nicht* can express only constituent negation of the verb.

19. NP arguments that occur within the verb sequence as a result of syntactic lowering are either quantifiers or require special stress, unlike *das Buch* in (68).

20. Emphatic coordination appears to be acceptable only on the first position of a sequence of verbs; thus, the translation equivalents of (77a) in Dutch and (77b) in German are unacceptable.

21. Arguments for the verb cluster based on coordination are given quite often (Bresnan et al. 1982; Steedman 1985). In the absence of a satisfactory linguistic theory of conjunction, however, their strength is hard to evaluate (but see Steedman 1989). In this paper we will have nothing further to say on the analysis of conjoined verb sequences, though we recognize that ultimately a convincing account of them will be required.

22. For sequences like (82), Lötscher (1978) suggests that the participle *aagfange* and the auxiliary *hät* are rebracketed as a single constituent, which then permutes with the most deeply embedded verb *rägne*. His rebacketing proposal, however, does not extend to the Franconian word order in (83).

23. The formulation of this generalization is ours; Baker himself uniformly assigns the category S' to all infinitival complements.

24. Even if we follow Chomsky (1986a) in interpreting X-bar theory as a constraint on D-Structure only, an incorporation analysis of verb projection raising violates the Like-Attracts-Like Constraint proposed by Baltin (1982). We thank Lori Davis for this point.

25. Haegeman and Van Riemsdijk (1986:432) argue for a distinction between verb (projection) raising and extraposition. They claim that if verb (projection) raising

were subsumed under extraposition, the ungrammaticality of raising constituents of category S, illustrated in (i) for Swiss German, "would remain quite mysterious."

(i) *das er wil   laa sini chind   mediziin studiere
     that he wants-to let his children medicine study
     'that he wants to let his children study medicine'

They go on to interpret the ungrammaticality of (i) as evidence against analyses under which S is a projection of V in the Germanic languages other than English. But both their distinction between verb (projection) raising and extraposition and their interpretation of the ungrammaticality of (i) are vitiated by the fact that (i) is ruled out for independent reasons. Since verbs cannot assign Case rightward in West Germanic, the subject of the complement of the causative *laa*—namely, *sini chind*—fails the Case Filter. Thus, the ungrammaticality of (i) fails to bear on the status of S as a projection of V, nor does it bear on the existence of VP as a maximal projection of V in German and Dutch. Our alternative analysis of the ungrammaticality of (i) is supported by the constrast between leftward and rightward movement of small clauses, as illustrated in (ii) and (iii), respectively.

(ii) ?Meinen Mann   mit einer anderen tanzen würde ich nie   lassen.
      my   husband with an   other   dance would I   never let
      'I would never let my husband dance with another woman.'

(iii) *Ich würde nie   lassen meinen Mann   mit einer anderen tanzen.
       I   would never let   my   husband with an   other   dance
      (same as (ii))

26. We will not give the TAG derivations of the LF representations discussed in section 2.1, although more than one implementation is possible in a TAG analysis.

27. Verb sequences that contain NP constituents, like those discussed in section 3.1 and 4.1, can be derived by using elementary trees in which phrasal projections of the verb are extraposed.

28. The different types of constraints on tree-adjunction and their consequences for the generative power of TAG are discussed in detail in Joshi 1983 and Kroch and Joshi 1985.

29. For expository convenience, we treat *gaan slapen* as a simple lexical item.

30. Deriving the converse embedding of causatives of perception verbs under modals is unproblematic in both German and Dutch.

31. Linguistically trained speakers of Dutch hesitate to rule out (112b) on syntactic grounds, pointing out that its unacceptability might be due to a violation of the selectional restrictions of the causative. If this turns out to be correct, the derivation of (112b) in a TAG would require an analysis under which causative subcategorize not for small clauses but rather for an NP VP sequence. The hypothesis that selectional restrictions are responsible for the difference in the judgments of Dutch and German speakers seems implausible to us, however, since one would expect the same selectional restrictions to hold in both languages.

32. In standard Dutch, particle verbs such as *inleveren* 'hand in' may be split, with the particle ending up stranded within the sequence of verbs (Lange 1981:77).

(i) omdat- ie   het boek heeft in willen   leveren
   because you the book have in want-to hand
   'because you wanted to hand in the book'

33. Alternatively, verb raising could precede constituent preposing if it is assumed to be cyclic. Constituent preposing would then have to apply to the derived constituent, as in (i).

(i) [$_{VP}$[$_{VP}$[$_S$ Jan naar de manifestatie e$_i$] laten] gaan$_i$]

34. Note that the freer application of verb raising in Middle High German continues to be reflected in the order of the elements in the nominalization *Hörensagen* 'hearsay.'

References

Bach, E., C. Brown, and W. D. Marslen-Wilson (1987). "Crossed and Nested Dependencies in Dutch and German: A Psycholinguistic Study." *Language and Cognitive Processes* 1:249–262.

Baker, M. (1988). *Incorporation: A Theory of Grammatical Function Changing*. University of Chicago Press, Chicago.

Baltin, M. (1982). "A Landing Site Theory of Movement Rules." *Linguistic Inquiry* 13:1–38.

Baltin, M. (1989). "Heads and Projections." In M. Baltin and A. S. Kroch, eds., *Alternative Conceptions of Phrase Structure*. University of Chicago Press, Chicago.

Besten, H. den., and J. A. Edmondson (1983). "The Verbal Complex in Continental West Germanic." In W. Abraham, ed., *On the Formal Syntax of the Westgermania*. Benjamins, Amsterdam.

Besten, H. den, and J. Rutten (1989). "On Verb Raising, Extraposition and Free Word Order in Dutch." In D. Jaspers, ed., *Sentential Complementation and the Lexicon*. Foris, Dordrecht.

Besten, H. den, J. Rutten, T. Veenstra, and J. Veld (1988). "Verb raising, extrapositie en de derde constructie." Ms., University of Amsterdam.

Bresnan, J. W., R. M. Kaplan, S. Peters, and A. Zaenen (1982). "Cross-serial Dependencies in Dutch." *Linguistic Inquiry* 13:613–635.

Chomsky, N. (1981). *Lectures on Government and Binding*. Foris, Dordrecht.

Chomsky, N. (1982). *Some Concepts and Consequences of the Theory of Government and Binding*. MIT Press, Cambridge, Mass.

Chomsky, N. (1986a). *Barriers*. MIT Press, Cambridge, Mass.

Chomsky, N. (1986b). *Knowledge of Language: Its Nature, Origin and Use*. Praeger, New York.

Evers, A. (1975). "The Transformational Cycle in Dutch and German." Doctoral dissertation, University of Utrecht. Distributed by the Indiana University Linguistics Club, Bloomington.

Evers, A. (1981). "Two Functional Principles for the Rule 'Move V.'" *Groninger Arbeiten zur germanistischen Linguistik* 19:96–110.

Haegeman, L., and H. van Riemsdijk (1986). "Verb Projection Raising, Scope, and the Typology of Verb Movement Rules." *Linguistic Inquiry* 17:417–466.

Heycock, C. (1987). "The Structure of the Japanese Causative." Technical report MS-CIS-87-55, Department of Computer and Information Sciences, University of Pennsylvania.

Höhle, T. N. (1984). "On Composition and Derivation: The Constituent Structure of Secondary Words in German." In J. Toman, ed., *Studies in German Grammar*. Foris, Dordrecht.

Hoeksema, J. (1980). "Verbale verstrengeling ontstrengeld." *Spektator* 10:221–249.

Hoeksema, J. (1988). "A Constraint on Governors in the West Germanic Verb Cluster." In M. Everaert, A. Evers, M. A. C. Huybregts, and M. Trommelen, eds., *Morphology and Modularity. In Honour of Henk Schuttink*. Foris, Dordrecht.

Huang, C.-T. (1982). "Logical relations in Chinese and the Theory of Grammar." Doctoral dissertation, MIT.

Joshi, A. K. (1983). "Tree Adjoining Grammars: How Much Context-Sensitivity Is Required to Provide Reasonable Structural Descriptions?" In D. Dowty, L. Karttunen, and A. Zwicky, eds., *Natural Language Processing: Psycholinguistic, Computational and Theoretical Perspectives*. Cambridge University Press, New York.

Joshi, A. K. (1990). "Processing Crossed and Nested Dependencies: An Automaton Perspective on the Psycholinguistic Results." *Language and Cognitive Processes* 5:1–27.

Joshi, A. K., L, Levy, and M. Takahashi (1975). "Tree Adjunct Grammars." *Journal of the Computer and System Sciences* 10:136–163.

Kemenade, A. van (1985). "Verb Raising in Old English." In *Proceedings of the Fourth Amsterdam Conference of English Historical Linguistics*. Benjamins, Amsterdam.

Koster, J. (1975). "Dutch as an SOV Language." *Linguistic Analysis* 1:111–136.

Kroch, A. S. (1987). "Unbounded Dependencies and Subjacency in a Tree Adjoining Grammar." In A. Manaster-Ramer, ed., *Mathematics of Language*. Benjamins, Philadelphia.

Kroch, A. S. (1989). "Asymmetries in Long Distance Extraction in a Tree-Adjoining Grammar." In M. Baltin and A. S. Kroch, eds., *Alternative Conceptions of Phrase Structure*. University of Chicago Press, Chicago.

Kroch, A. S., and A. K. Joshi (1985). "The Linguistic Relevance of Tree Adjoining Grammars." Technical report, Department of Computer and Informtion Sciences, University of Pennsylvania.

Kroch, A. S., and A. K. Joshi (1987). "Analyzing Extraposition in a Tree Adjoining Grammar." In G. Huck and A. Ojeda, eds., *Discontinuous Constituency*. Academic Press, New York.

Kroch, A. S., and B. Santorini (1985). "Questioning the West Germanic Verb Cluster." Paper presented at the Annual Winter Meeting of the Linguistic Society of America, Seattle, Wash.

Kvam, S. (1983). *Linksverschachtelung im Deutschen und Norwegischen*. Niemeyer, Tübingen.

Lange, K.-P. (1981). "Warum Ersatzinfinitiv?" *Groninger Arbeiten zur germanistischen Linguistik* 19:62–81.

Lenerz, J. (1984). *Syntaktischer Wandel und Grammatiktheorie*. Niemeyer, Tübingen.

Lötscher, A. (1978). "Zur Verbstellung im Zürichdeutschen und in anderen Varianten des Deutschen." *Zeitschrift für Dialektologie und Linguistik* 45:1–29.

Marantz, A. (1984). *On the Nature of Grammatical Relations*. MIT Press, Cambridge, Mass.

May, R. (1985). *Logical Form: Its Structure and Derivation*. MIT Press, Cambridge, Mass.

Reuland, E. (1980). "V-Raising in Dutch: Anomalies Explained." In *Papers from the Sixteenth Regional Meeting, CLS*. Chicago Linguistic Society, University of Chicago.

Riemsdijk, H. van (1984). "On Pied-Piped Infinitives in German Relative Clauses." In J. Toman, ed., *Studies in German Grammar*. Foris, Dordrecht.

Rizzi, L. (1982). *Issues in Italian Syntax*. Foris, Dordrecht.

Steedman, M. (1985). "Dependency and Coordination in the Grammar of Dutch and English." *Language* 61:523–568.

Steedman, M. (1989). "Constituency and Coordination in a Combinatory Grammar." In M. Baltin and A. S. Kroch, eds., *Alternative Conceptions of Phrase Structure*. University of Chicago Press, Chicago.

Thiersch, C. (1978). "Topics in German Syntax." Doctoral dissertation, MIT.

Weijnen, A. A. (1966). *Nederlandse dialectkunde*. Van Gorcum, Assen.

Zaenen, A. (1979). "Infinitival Complements in Dutch." In *Papers from the Fifteenth Regional Meeting, CLS*. Chicago Linguistic Society, University of Chicago.

Chapter 11

Parameters of Phrase Structure and Verb-Second Phenomena

Lisa deMena Travis

In the spirit of Borer (1983), I explore in this paper the range of grammatical domains that may be affected by parametric variation. Borer suggests that "all parametric variaton can be reduced to the properties of the inflectional system" but notes that although this is attractive, word order variation provides a quite spectacular counterexample. Certainly, beyond the choice of lexical items, the most noticeable difference from language to language is the arrangement of these lexical items. Here I explore the possibility that parameters of word order, though not due only to properties of lexical items, may at least be restricted to certain domains.

There should be no question whether there is a need to restrict parameters. Just as in a system of rules, linguists sought to restrict the power of these rules, in a system of parameters, the power of parameters must also be limited. Without such a goal, familiar problems of acquisition and impossible language types will surface. The more ways in which languages may vary, the greater the burden on the child, and the wider the variation expected in natural languages of the world. There is also a more practical methodological reason to restrict parameters. If the range of possible analyses for a given set of data is limited for the child, it will also be limited for the linguist.

In Standard Theory, language-specific word order was represented in the system of phrase structure rules. These rules represented many different

This paper is basically a reworking of the account of verb-second phenomena given in Travis 1984 and benefits from discussions over the years with various members of the Germanic linguistics community such as Harald Clahsen, Molly Diesing, Jean duPlessis, Anders Holmberg, Tony Kroch, Maíre Noonan, Christer Platzack, Eric Reuland, Ken Safir, Beatrice Santorini, Sten Vikner, and Fred Weerman. I will probably regret not paying more heed to their comments. I would also like to acknowledge FCAR grant 88EQ3630 and SSHRCC grant 410-87-1071, which support continuing research on this topic.

relations, however, and I will argue that only certain of these relations may be parameterized, the others being uniform across languages or belonging to the lexicon. For example, rules of the type given in (1) encode both precedence and dominance relations.

(1) V′ → V (NP) (PP) (CP)

This rule states not only that a V′ will dominate a V and an optional NP, PP, and CP but also that the V precedes the NP, both of these precede the PP, and these three all precede the CP. More recently, these relations have been teased apart. First, principles such as X-bar theory restricted the dominance relations of phrase structure rules. Then word order parameters such as headedness, the direction of θ-role assignment, and the direction of Case assignment (see Koopman 1983; Travis 1984) accounted for the precedence relations of phrase structure. The principles of X-bar theory deal only with dominance relations, whereas precedence relations are determined by parameters. I will claim that this is not accidental and that, in fact, parameters may affect only precedence relations and that dominance relations are universal, varying only through complementation as indicated in the lexicon.[1]

For several theoretical reasons one might suspect that dominance relations should not be allowed to vary from language to language. This intuition comes from the fact that many of the notions of syntactic theory are defined on dominance relations. These notions range from the definition of subject as [NP, S] and object as [NP, VP], to the definition of c-command, which itself underlies the definitions of government and of binding. If dominance relations could vary from language to language, we might expect wild variations in the hierarchical position of subject or the effects of binding. Movement regularities further argue for a restriction on the variation of dominance relations. Chomsky (1986) restricts structure-preserving movement of maximal projections to specifier positions, and movement of heads is movement to other head positions (see also Travis 1984; Baker 1988). As we will see, such notions of movement often cannot be upheld in a system that allows parameterization of certain dominance relations. Barring any evidence of variation in this direction, I will make the strongest claim by assuming that dominance relations are constant.

The use of universal constituency as an argument for a particular analysis is not new to the literature. One clear case in point concerns Verb-Subject-Object (VSO) languages. Though it has been proposed that such languages have flat structures at some level of representation (see, for example, Chung 1983), this raises problems in other parts of the grammar such as the binding theory. If subject and object were both sister to V, we would not expect binding asymmetries since the subject and object NPs would c-command each other. Many linguists (see, for example, Emonds 1980, Sproat 1985), assuming that VPs are universal, have argued that VSO word order cannot arise through base generation of a flat structure. Rather, an S–VP order is generated, the surface word order being the result of V-movement. This line of argumentation may be extended by assuming that IP dominates NP and I′ and that I′ dominates INFL and the VP universally, further restricting the possibilities of VSO languages. Now (2a) is a possible structure for VSO languages, whereas (2b) is not.

(2) a.   b.

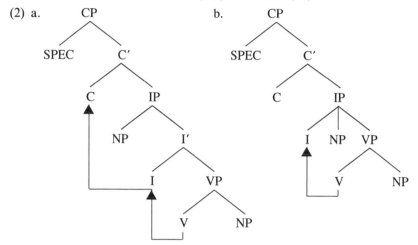

As (2a) indicates, head movement of the V into INFL and of INFL into COMP will account for the surface VSO word order.

In this paper I will be particularly concerned with the problem of word order parameters in several Germanic languages. There has been a general consensus among Germanic linguists (see, for example, Toman 1984) that German and similar languages do not have an INFL node that is separate from COMP. Such an account depends on the possibility that parameters may affect the dominance relations in a phrase marker. As a representative of this viewpoint I will use Platzack 1983 which gives a detailed explication of how these parameters could be used to account for a wide variety of word order facts in Germanic languages. Since the account depends on the so-called COMP-INFL parameter that alters the position and function of the COMP and INFL nodes, I will refer to this analysis as the *COMP/INFL account*.

Since the COMP/INFL account is not available in the system I have sketched above, I will propose a different account for the same word order facts that assumes one phrase structure tree in which only precedence relations vary. This second account (developed from Travis 1984) relies on the assumption that under the Empty Category Principle (ECP), empty heads must be identified. I will refer to this analysis as the *ECP account*.

First I will show that the ECP account explains the same range of facts as the COMP-INFL account, arguing that the former is at least as adequate as the latter. Next I will show that when the two accounts make different predictions concerning additional facts, it is the ECP account that makes the correct predictions.

The parameters that I propose will involve (i) the headedness of the VP, (ii) the exact nature of COMP (for instance, whether or not it contains the appropriate features), and (iii) whether a language has adjunction to IP. I will argue that these are all parameters that are needed independently in the description of other languages and that they are well within the limits of parametric possibilities. Since these parameters are needed independently and can account for the data, I argue that not only are the mechanisms introduced in the COMP/INFL account unnecessary, they introduce an unwanted complication into the grammar, providing both linguists and language learners with two possible grammars for the same range of data.

1   The COMP/INFL Account (Platzack 1983)

In his article, Platzack (1983) gives three possibilities for the position of COMP and INFL, thereby dividing the Germanic language family into three subtypes.[2]

(3) a. *English*   b. *German/Swedish*

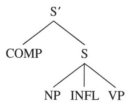

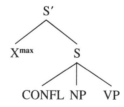

c. *Icelandic*

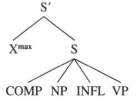

Note that COMP has three different functions. In English it is the daughter of S'; in German and Swedish it is part of the conflated category CONFL, which is the daughter of S; and in Icelandic both it and a separate category INFL are daughters of S. Though German/Swedish and Icelandic do not have a COMP that is a daughter of S', they do have an X^{max} category in this position.

Platzack's proposal neatly accounts for a variety of facts concerning word order in Germanic languages. These are listed in (4) and will be discussed in more detail in the following sections.

(4) a. German/Swedish and Icelandic have verb-second (V2) effects.
   b. There are no V2 effects in English.
   c. There is a complementary distribution of lexical complementizers and V2 effects in German/Swedish but not in Icelandic.
   d. There is V-movement in clauses with lexical complementizers in Icelandic.

1.1   V2 Effects (German/Swedish and Icelandic)

One of the more remarkable characteristics of Germanic languages is that the inflected verb in root clauses must always appear as the second constituent of the sentence. In the German examples in (5), for instance, the inflected verb *haben* appears in the second position independently of whether the first position is occupied by the subject as in (5a) or an adverb as in (5b). Similarly in the Icelandic examples: the subject is first in (5c) and an adverb is first in (5d), but in both cases the inflected verb *hafði* appears in second position. As (5e) and (5f) show, any deviation from this order results in an ungrammatical string.

(5) a. Die Kinder *haben* das Brot heute gegessen.   (G)
        the children have the bread today eaten
        'The children have eaten the bread today.'
   b. Heute *haben* die Kinder das Brot gegessen.   (G)
   c. Helgi *hafði* trúlega   keypt bókina.   (I)
        Helgi had   probably bought the book
        'Helgi had probably bought the book.'
   d. Trúlega *hafði* Helgi keypt bókina.   (I)
   e. *Heute die Kinder *haben* das Brot gegessen.   (G)
   f. *Trúlega Helgi *hafði* keypt bókina.   (I)

In Platzack's account, the fact that only one constituent may precede the inflected verb is captured by the phrase structure allowed for German/Swedish and Icelandic.

(6) a. *V2 in German/Swedish*   b. *V2 in Icelandic*

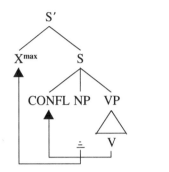
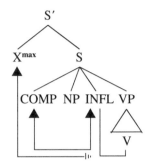

In German and Swedish the inflected verb appears in the CONFL node dominated by S, having moved there from the V-position. One constituent and only one constituent, then, may move to the X^{max} position that precedes CONFL and is dominated by S'. Whether this constituent is the subject or a nonsubject, its sentence-initial position will be due to movement to the X^{max} position dominated by S'. In Icelandic the inflected verb first moves to INFL and then to COMP, where, as in German and Swedish, it may be preceded by one and only one constituent that has moved to the X^{max} position dominated by S'.

1.2   No V2 Effects (English)

In English the pattern just described for the Germanic languages does not hold. Though the inflected verb is in second position when the subject is sentence-initial, if an adverb precedes the subject, the inflected verb will be in third position, as in (7a). In fact, the V2 word order results in an ungrammatical string, as in (7b).

(7) a.   Today the children *have* eaten the bread.

    b.   *Today *have* the children eaten the bread.

Again, the reason for these facts is clear from the phrase structure that Platzack proposes for English. Two elements precede INFL, the position in which the inflected verb is found, and it is this configuration that makes it possible for the finite verb to appear in third position. The subject is base-generated in a position before the inflected verb, and the adverb will have moved to the COMP position dominated by S'.[3]

(8)

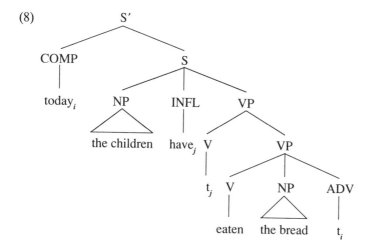

1.3   Lexical Complementizers and V2 (German/Swedish)

Another property of many V2 languages is that V2 effects do not appear when the clause has a lexical complementizer. Although the inflected verb appears in second position in the root clause in (9a), it appears sentence-finally when it is in an embedded sentence (9b) with the lexical complementizer *daß*. In (9c), where *haben* appears in the embedded clause but where there is no lexical complementizer, the inflected verb is again in second position.

(9) a. Die Kinder *haben* das Brot gegessen.   (G)
        the children have   the bread eaten
        'The children have eaten the bread.'

    b. Ich weiß, daß die Kinder das Brot gegessen *haben*.   (G)
        I   know that
        'I know that the children have eaten the bread.'

    c. Ich weiß, die Kinder *haben* das Brot gegessen.   (G)

This complementary distribution is accounted for by the fact that, in German and Swedish, COMP and INFL are a conflated category. When COMP is already filled by a lexical complementizer, the verb has no place to move to and remains in the sentence-final position.

(10)

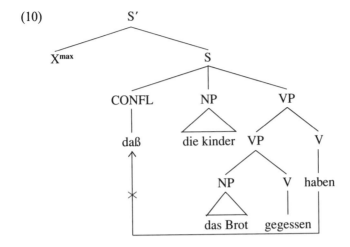

1.4 V-Movement in Embedded Clauses (Icelandic)

Unlike German and Swedish, Icelandic does have V-movement when a lexical complementizer is present. Assuming that negative-particles and certain adverbs are generated in a position just before the VP, the examples in (11) illustrate that although both Swedish and Icelandic have V2 in root clauses, Swedish verbs remain in base-generated position in embedded clauses whereas Icelandic inflected verbs still move to a position in front of the adverb.

(11) a. Hann *kemur*   <u>ekki</u> hingað. (I)
    he   come(FUT) NEG here
    'He will not come here.'
  b. Jan *kommer*   <u>inte</u> hit. (S)
    Jan come(FUT) NEG here
    'Jan will not come here.'
  c. Eg veit að hann *kemur*   <u>ekki</u> hingað. (I)
    I   know that he   come(FUT) NEG here
    'I know that he will not come here.'
  d. Jag vet   att han <u>inte</u> *kommer*   hit. (S)
    I   know that he NEG come(FUT) here
    'I know that he will not come here.'

In Platzack's model, this difference arises because Icelandic has separate COMP and INFL nodes and Swedish has a conflated category. The presence of a lexical complementizer in embedded clauses prevents movement to COMP, but the inflected verb still may move to the INFL node.

(12) a. *Swedish*

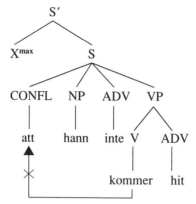

b. *Icelandic*

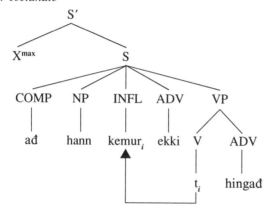

2 The ECP Account (Travis 1984)

Although the COMP/INFL proposal accounts for an array of facts concerning the word order differences in Germanic languages, it must resort to variations in the phrase structure tree that affect dominance relations. This solution is not possible, however, in a system that constrains parametric variation to precedence relations. The ECP account claims that the following tree is constant for all of the three subgroups of the Germanic family, consistent with the thesis put forth here.

(13) *English, German, Swedish, Icelandic*

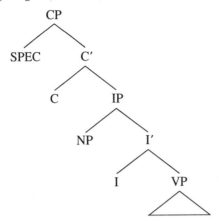

The only variation will be found in the ordering of elements within the VP. As we will see, English, Icelandic, and Yiddish VPs are head-initial, whereas German and Swedish VPs are head-final. Differences in the position of the inflected verb will be accounted for through head-to-head movement.

In section 2.1 I will show that all the possible verb positions can be described in terms of the tree in (13). In section 2.2 I will present an account that explains what forces V-movement. Finally, in section 2.3 I will propose parameters that will account for word order variations within the Germanic language family.

2.1   Verb Positions

2.1.1   English   As the examples in (14) illustrate, certain verbs in English may appear in three different positions.[4]

(14) a. The children should *have* eaten the bread.
    b. The children *have* eaten the bread.
    c. Why *have* the children eaten the bread?

In (14a) the verb *have* is in its base-generated V-position (the head of VP); in (14b) it appears in the INFL-position (the head of IP); and in (14c), it appears in the COMP-position (the head of CP). Taking the tree for English, it is easy to see how these three positions can be accounted for through head movement.

(15)

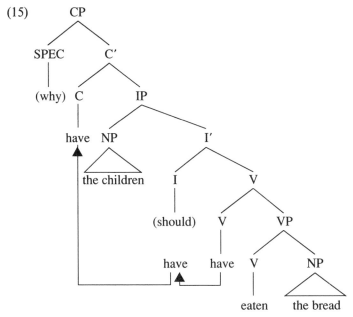

At the heart of my proposal for Germanic word order is the assumption that V2 languages account for verb positioning the same way. Either the verb appears in the base-generated V-position, or it moves to INFL, or it moves through INFL to COMP. The generalizations to be made concerning the placement of the verb in English are the following:

(i)   The auxiliary verb appears as the head of VP when INFL is already filled.

(ii) The auxiliary verb appears as the head of IP when INFL is not already filled.[5]

(iii) The auxiliary verb appears as the head of CP when the SPEC of CP is filled by movement or by an abstract Q morpheme.

In the following sections I discuss head movement in the other two languages types characterized in the COMP/INFL account.

2.1.2   German/Swedish   The following examples illustrate the three positions in which a verb may appear in German and Swedish.[6]

(16) *German*

Head of VP
a. Ich weiß, daß die Kinder [_{VP} das Brot gegessen *haben*].

Head of IP

    b. [$_{IP}$ Die Kinder *haben*$_i$ [$_{VP}$ das Brot gegessen t$_i$]].

    Head of CP

    c. [$_{CP}$ Heute$_j$ *haben*$_i$ [$_{IP}$ die Kinder t$_i$ [$_{VP}$ das Brot t$_j$ gegessen t$_i$]]].

(17) *Swedish*

    Head of VP

    a. Jag vet att Jan inte [$_{VP}$ *kommer* hit].

    Head of IP

    b. [$_{IP}$ Jan *kommer* inte [$_{VP}$ t$_i$ hit]].

    Head of CP

    c. [$_{CP}$ Sannolikt *kommer* [$_{IP}$ Jan t$_i$ inte [$_{VP}$ t$_i$ hit]]].
       probably

The generalizations to be made about this language type are the following:

(i)   The inflected verb appears as the head of VP when INFL is already filled or when there is a lexical COMP.

(ii) The inflected verb appears as the head of IP when the sentence is subject-initial and there is no lexical COMP.

(iii) The inflected verb appears as the head of CP when the SPEC of CP is filled either by movement or by an abstract Q morpheme (the assumption being that nonsubjects have moved to SPEC of CP).

2.1.3 Icelandic   In the Icelandic type of Germanic language, the verb will only appear in the V-position if INFL is otherwise filled. When INFL is not filled, the verb will move to INFL, and if SPEC of CP is filled, the verb will move to COMP.

(18) *Icelandic*

    Head of VP

    a. [$_{IP}$ Hann má   ekki [$_{VP}$ *koma* hingað]].
       he   may not   come here

    Head of IP

    b. [$_{IP}$ Hann *kemur*$_i$ ekki [$_{VP}$ t$_i$ hingað]].
       he   come not   here

    Head of CP

    c. [$_{CP}$ Trúlega   *kemur*$_i$ [$_{IP}$ hann t$_i$ ekki [$_{VP}$ t$_i$ hingað]].
       probably come   he   not   here

The generalizations to be made about this language type are the following:

(i)   The verb appears as the head of VP only when INFL is otherwise filled.

(ii)   The verb appears as the head of IP when the sentence is subject-initial.

(iii) The verb appears as the head of CP when the SPEC of CP is filled either by movement or by an abstract Q morpheme (the assumption being that nonsubjects are in the SPEC of CP).

Though V-movement may explain why verbs *may* appear in the positions in which they appear, it is not yet clear either why they *must* appear in these positions or what produces the differences between the language types. The first question will be discussed in section 2.2 and the second in section 2.3.

2.2   Theory of V-Movement

2.2.1   Identification   The use that I make of the ECP is actually a development of Platzack's suggestion that empty heads must be properly governed in order to explain why *wh*-movement does not trigger subject-aux inversion in English embedded clauses. Platzack assumes that an empty COMP in English may either be filled with [+wh] by the matrix V (as in (19d)) or be filled through movement of the verb (as in (19a)). V-movement will be blocked in (19c) since the COMP is filled by the [+wh] feature.

(19) a.   What [$_{COMP}$ will] the children eat?
      b.   *What [$_{COMP}$ e] the children will eat.
      c.   *I wonder what [$_{COMP}$ will] the children eat.
      d.   I wonder what [$_{COMP}$ +wh] the children will eat.

Since I assume a modified view of the ECP with specific consequences for its application to empty heads, I will discuss both the ECP and the behavior of heads below.

In a slight variation on the current view of the ECP, I assume that empty categories, including heads, must be identified.

(20) *Empty Category Principle*
      Empty categories must be identified.

(21) *Identification*
      An empty category is identified if and only if
      a. the gap is properly governed, and
      b. the features of the gap are recoverable.

(22) *Proper government*
      A properly governs B if and only if A governs B and
      a. B is a complement or the head of a complement of A, or
      b. A is an antecedent for B.

The definition of proper government that I assume is similar to the one proposed by Stowell (1981) in that the relevant relation is not simply one of structure but also one of function. In other words, the empty category not only must be governed by a head but also must be in a certain relation with that head. I take this relation to be the complement relation, which includes θ-marking of a lexical head (see Stowell 1981) and licensing by a functional head (see Abney 1986).

The intuition behind this version of the ECP is as follows. An empty category requires a two-part identification: its position must be identified, and its content must identified. Its position is identified through proper government, and its contents are identified through some manner of feature retrieval.

The problem of feature retrieval raises questions of its own. This idea of recoverability is an extension of suggestions made by Kayne (1981) and Bouchard (1983). The obvious way by which features may be recovered is through binding. When a maximal projection moves, it leaves a coindexed trace, creating a chain through which the necessary features are retrieved. As we will see, however, feature retrieval for heads is not achieved through chains, thereby explaining some very basic differences between the behavior of heads and that of maximal projections.

2.2.2 Behavior of Heads
It has already been noted in the literature that heads behave in some respects very differently from maximal projections. This difference is particularly evident in the transformational component. In Travis 1984 I pointed out that head movement appears to be more restricted than movement of maximal projections and I proposed the Head Movement Constraint to describe this apparent locality condition on the movement of heads.

(23) *Head Movement Constraint*
An X^0 may only move into the Y^0 that properly governs it.

Though this constraint may describe the facts, an explanation is still needed (see Koopman 1983 and Baker 1988 for different accounts). I propose that heads, unlike maximal projections, do not leave coindexed traces under movement. Cosubscripting has become part of two components of the grammar: movement and reference. When an element moves, it is assumed that it leaves behind a coindexed trace (as in (24a)). It is also assumed that two elements that corefer are coindexed (as in (24b)).

(24) a. Mary$_i$ was seen t$_i$.
  b. Mary$_i$ is proud of herself$_i$.

One might wonder whether one type of cosubscripting might be reduced to the other. Since it is not clear how coreference could be reduced to movement, the only possibility is that coindexing of movement be reduced to that of coreference. Since the two NPs (24a) might be said to corefer, this is not an unlikely assumption. I would conclude, therefore, that since heads cannot refer (only maximal projections may be referential), they cannot bear indices even when left empty through movement.

If head movement does not leave coindexed traces, however, some other means must be found for features to be transmitted from the moved element back to the empty category. Such a means in fact exists. Independently we need a mechanism whereby a head may transmit features to a head that it properly governs (see Fabb 1984). This mechanism can be used for affix-hopping structures as well as for Case assignment.

(25) *Head feature transmission*

   They should have been watching him.

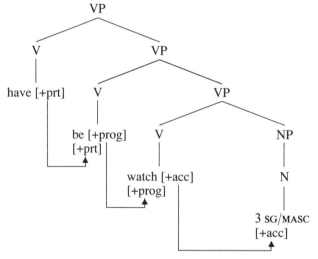

The same mechanism may be used to recover the features of an empty head. In fact, since (by assumption) head movement does not leave a coindexed trace, features *must* be recovered through feature transmission. Because of this, the restriction on head movement can in fact be reduced to a restriction on head feature transmission. In the structure shown in (25) features are always transmitted from a head A to a head B whose maximal projection is a sister to A. The assumption is that the features are assigned to the maximal projection and then percolate to the head of this maximal projection.

(26) *Restriction on head feature transmission*[7]
Head features may only be transmitted from a head to its sister.

If features may be transmitted only under such conditions, the Head Movement Constraint will follow. In the tree in (27) we want to allow the head Z to move to position Y, while disallowing movement to position X.

(27) a.   b.

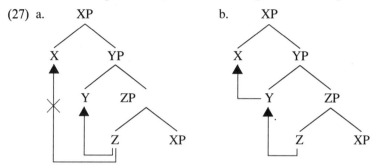

Since any features in position Y may be transmitted to position Z by head feature transmission, if Z has moved to Y, the features are recoverable for the identification of the contents of Z. However, if Z moves to position X, the relevant features may not be transmitted back to Z since the maximal projection of Z is not a sister to X. The empty category left in position Z would then violate the ECP, since its contents would not be identified. The contents of Z may appear in X, however, if movement has occurred through the intermediate position of Y.[8] In this case, for Y to be identified, the features of X would have to be transmitted to Y. Since these features would include those of Z, now the features of Z could be transmitted from Y to the empty category in Z.

Another peculiarity of heads is that they may be base-generated empty in positions that are not identified. My assumption here is that the functor nodes (in the sense of Abney 1986) may be generated phonetically empty (though they might carry features). As such, they are subject to the ECP. If an empty head is base-generated in a position where it is not identified, it must be filled by head movement to avoid a violation of the ECP. It is this assumption that will force head movement under certain conditions. (28) illustrates such a case for English.

(28) $[_{CP}$ why $[_{C'}$ e $[_{IP}$ the children $[_{I'}$ e $[_{VP}$ have eaten the bread]]]]]

Movement of *why* to the SPEC of COMP indicates that a CP has been generated and that an empty head is present—namely, COMP. Since the empty head is not identified (it is not properly governed), the structure will be ruled out as it stands. However, through head movement, *have* may move through the empty INFL position into the empty COMP, giving the following S-Structure representation.

(29) [$_{CP}$ why [$_{C'}$ have [$_{IP}$ the children [$_{I'}$ e [$_{VP}$ e eaten the bread]]]]]

Now the only empty categories are INFL and V. INFL is identified since IP is the complement of COMP and this COMP has the appropriate features to be transmitted to the head of IP. Once these features are transmitted to INFL, V is similarly identified. VP is the complement of INFL and INFL has the appropriate features to transmit to V.

The next step is to see how the base generation of empty heads and head movement may be used to explain the problems of V2 languages and what parameters account for the variations noted in the COMP/INFL proposal.

2.3 V2 and the Identification of Heads
In this section I will review the facts accounted for by the COMP/INFL proposal and discuss the parameters necessary to account for the same facts within the ECP proposal.[9] One parameter that both proposals share is the headedness parameter.

Parameter 1
VPs are head-initial/final.
    English, Swedish, Icelandic: head-initial
    German: head-final

2.3.1 V2 (German/Swedish and Icelandic) Within the ECP account, it is assumed that root clauses are generated differently depending on whether the constituent that precedes the inflected verb is a subject or a nonsubject. In instances where the subject is sentence-initial, it is assumed that only in IP has been generated. The D-Structure representation would then be as follows. I will illustrate using German examples, but Swedish and Icelandic would be treated similarly, the main difference being that VPs are head-initial in these two languages.

(30) [$_{IP}$ die Kinder [$_{I'}$ e [$_{VP}$ das Brot gegessen *haben*]]]

Since INFL is empty and is not identified (it is not properly governed), *haben* will be forced to move out of its base-generated V-position into INFL via head movement. This results in the following S-Structure representation.

(31) [$_{IP}$ die Kinder [$_{I'}$ *haben* [$_{VP}$ das Brot gegessen e]]]

The empty category in V will be identified since it is properly governed by being the head of the complement of INFL, and it will retrieve its features from the INFL node, which properly governs it.

When a nonsubject is sentence-initial, it appears in SPEC of CP, creating the following structure after maximal projection movement.

(32) [$_{CP}$ heute$_j$ [$_{C'}$ e [$_{IP}$ die Kinder [$_{I'}$ e [$_{VP}$ das Brot t$_j$ gegessen *haben*]]]]]

Since neither the empty category in COMP nor the one in INFL is identified, head movement of *haben* is forced through INFL to COMP, creating the following representation at S-Structure.

(33) [$_{CP}$ heute$_j$ [$_{C'}$ *haben* [$_{IP}$ die Kinder [$_{I'}$ e [$_{VP}$ das Brot t$_j$ gegessen e]]]]]

The empty categories in INFL and V are identified in the same way as those in the English example in (29).

2.3.2 No V2 (English)   The second parameter deals with whether or not a language allows adjunction to IP. This parameter is needed independently to account for varieties of movement in languages of the world. For example, this parameter may be used to account for the following distinction in Spanish (Torrego 1984).

(34) a. ¿Qué querían esos dos?
            what want   those two
            'What did those two want?'
      b. *Qué esos dos querían?
      c. ¿Por qué Juan quiere salir antes que los demás?
            why   Juan want   leave before   the others
            'Why does Juan want to leave before the others?'

In Spanish [+wh] arguments must move to SPEC of CP position; [+wh] nonarguments may either move to the SPEC of CP position or adjoin to IP.

The assumption, then, is that whereas English does allow adjunction of nonarguments to IP, German/Swedish and Icelandic do not. Thus, in the following string *today* has been adjoined to the IP, an option not open to German.

(35) [$_{IP}$ Today [$_{IP}$ the children have eaten the bread]].

Since *today* does not appear in the SPEC of CP position, there is no empty COMP that must be filled by V-movement in order to avoid a violation of the ECP. This accounts for the lack of V2 effects in English.

Parameter 2
Adjunction to IP for fronting rules
    German/Swedish, Icelandic: no
    English: yes

It is important to note that such adjunction can be used only for certain elements in certain languages. As we have seen, Spanish allows this for

[+wh] nonarguments but *not* for [+wh] arguments. In English this is possible for [−wh] nonarguments; however, [+wh] must move to SPEC of CP, accounting for the V2 effects in these structures.

(36) a. On Tuesday Mary *will* go to the store.
b. When *will* Mary go to the store?

2.3.3 Complementary Distribution of V-Movement and COMP (German/Swedish)

In terms of the ECP account, the question here is why the verb in languages such as German and Swedish remains in its base-generated position whenever a complementizer appears. The relevant S-Structure representation would be as follows.

(37) ich weiß [$_{CP}$ daß [$_{IP}$ die Kinder [$_{I'}$ e [$_{VP}$ das Brot t$_j$ gegessen *haben*]]]]

It would appear that (37) contains an empty category in INFL that is not properly governed.

If INFL is allowed to remain empty, it must be identified. The gap will be identified by virtue of being the head of the complement of a lexical complementizer. In order to identify the contents of the gap, however, we must assume that complementizers in certain languages carry features that are sufficient to identify the contents of the empty head.

A further point must be made. If an empty category is identified (in other words, if its gap and features are identified), then it may no longer be a landing site for movement. One might think of this in terms of a feature complex. If the feature complex of a node is complete (as it must be in order to be identified), the node is "filled." This prevents movement from occurring in (37). This also can be used to explain the lack of movement in English embedded questions. In (19d) the empty category is identified by being the head of the complement of V. The feature [+wh] also is recoverable from the verb.[10]

Parameter 3
COMP can identify contents of INFL.
German/Swedish: yes
English, Icelandic: no

2.3.4 V-Movement in Embedded Clauses (Icelandic)

No further parameter is needed to explain the presence of V-movement in Icelandic. Since Icelandic does not have complementizers that are able to identify the contents of an empty INFL, V-movement will always take place to fill this position.

2.4 Additional Facts

2.4.1 Subject/Nonsubject Asymmetry in Icelandic/Yiddish   Though Plat-
zack does not mention this, the COMP/INFL account can explain certain
subject/nonsubject asymmetries that occur in languages of the Icelandic
type. Yiddish is similar to Icelandic in all of the ways discussed above. Its
VPs are head-initial, it does not allow adjunction to IP, and its COMP
cannot identify features of an embedded INFL.

(38) a. Di kinder   musn onheybm zeyr heymarbet.
          the children must PFX-start their homework
      b. Di kinder   heybm on zeyr heymarbet.
          the children start   PFX their homework
      c. Zeyr heymarbet heybm di kinder on.
      d. *Haynt di kinder heybm on zeyr heymarbet.
          today
      e. Ikh gloyb az   di kinder heybm on zeyr heymarbet.
          I   believe that

V-movement is most remarkable in verbs with separable prefixes. (38a) illustrates the infinitival form of the verb *onheybm*. There is no V-movement
since the INFL is filled with *musn*. In (38b) V-movement has occurred into
the empty INFL-position, and the verb *heybm* is separated from its prefix
on. In (38c) the object *zeyr heymarbet* has moved to the SPEC of CP
position, and the verb has moved through INFL into the COMP-position.
(38d) shows that there is no IP adjunction in Yiddish, and (38e) shows that
V-movement occurs even in embedded clauses.

The need for allowing a base-generated subject-first clause is clearest in
embedded questions. In [+ wh] clausal complements, V-movement must
occur but the element preceding the inflected verb must be the subject.[11]

(39) a. Ikh veys nit far vos *di kinder*   heybm on zeyr heymarbet
          I   know NEG why   the children start   PFX their homework
          haynt.
          today
          'I don't know why the children start their homework today.'
      b. *Ikh veys nit far vos *haynt* heybm di kinder on zeyr heymarbet.

2.4.2 Subject/Nonsubject Asymmetry in German/Swedish   The COMP/
INFL and ECP accounts differ on how subject-first root clauses in Ger-
man/Swedish are treated. In the COMP/INFL account, whether the clause
is subject-first or non-subject-first, the sentence-initial element is always in

the X^{max} position and the inflected verb in second position is in COMP. In the ECP account, however, only nonsubjects are accounted for through movement to SPEC of CP with subsequent V-movement to the head of CP. Subject-first sentences have the option of undergoing no maximal projection movement. The subject may remain in its base-generated position. If this is the case, the V moves, but only into INFL. Since there is no movement into SPEC of CP, there is no need for the CP projection, and only an IP is generated. The different bracketings are given in (40) and (41).

(40) *COMP/INFL account*

    a. [$_{S'}$ Die Kinder$_j$ [$_S$ haben$_i$ t$_j$ [$_{VP}$ das Brot heute gegessen t$_i$]]].

    b. [$_{S'}$ Heute$_j$ [$_S$ haben$_i$ die Kinder [$_{VP}$ das Brot t$_j$ gegessen t$_i$]]].

(41) *ECP account*

    a. [$_{IP}$ Die Kinder [$_{I'}$ haben$_i$ [$_{VP}$ das Brot heute gegessen e]]].

    b. [$_{CP}$ Heute$_j$ [$_{C'}$ haben$_i$ [$_{IP}$ die Kinder [$_{I'}$ e [$_{VP}$ das Brot t$_j$ gegessen e]]]]].

In fact, the ECP account makes German look similar to Icelandic/Yiddish and would suggest that there should be similar subject/nonsubject asymmetries in these languages. Certainly, if there were such asymmetries, the COMP/INFL proposal would not be able to account for them. In fact, I claim that there are such asymmetries in German, arguing that, theoretical issues aside, there are empirical reasons for preferring the ECP account over the COMP/INFL account. This asymmetry is shown in (42).

(42) a.   Das Kind hat das Brot gegessen.
        the child has the bread eaten
        'The child has eaten the bread.'

    b.   Es   hat das Brot gegessen.
        it (the child) has the bread eaten
        'He/she has eaten the bread.'

    c.   Das Brot haben die Kinder gegessen.
        the bread have the children eaten
        'It's the bread that the children have eaten.'

    d.   *Es   haben die Kinder gegessen.
        it (the bread) have   the children eaten

When the sentence-initial subject is replaced by the neuter pronoun *es*, the resulting string is grammatical. However, when the sentence-initial object is replaced by the same neuter pronoun, the resulting string is ungrammatical. Whatever accounts for this (perhaps only pronouns that can bear focal stress may be moved to SPEC of CP), there must be some way to distinguish between sentence-initial subjects and sentence-initial nonsubjects. This structural distinction is available only to the ECP account.

2.5 Residual Problems

Certain questions arise in this account, two of which I will address here.

2.5.1 English Merger

In English, only auxiliary verbs and modals can appear in INFL, as the following data show.

(43) a. The children must (n't/not) go.
      b. The children have (n't/not) gone.
      c. The children go (*n't/*not).

What happens when the clause contains only a main verb, as in (43c)? It would appear that INFL was empty; but since the structure is grammatical, the string does not appear to violate the ECP. What I am assuming is that English allows adjacent INFL and V to undergo morphological merger of the type described by Pranka (1983). Evidence that this occurs comes from the fact that if adjacency is disturbed in any way, the empty INFL must be filled through *do*-support, as the following example shows.[12]

(44) a.   the child [$_{INFL}$ +pres] [$_V$ go]
      a'. the child [$_{INFL/V}$ goes]   (after merger)
      b.   the child [$_{INFL}$ +pres] not [$_V$ go]
      b'. the child [$_{INFL}$ does] not [$_V$ go]   (cannot undergo merger)

2.5.2 Sentential Adverbs

Although the COMP/INFL account explains the following distinction, it is not clear how the ECP account would predict it.

(45) a.   John probably will come late.
      b.   *Johann wahrscheinlich wird spät kommen.
           Johann probably   will late come

English allows sentential adverbs to appear between the subject and the inflected verb; German does not. If, as the ECP account suggests, both strings are simply Subject-ADV-INFL-VP, there should be no difference between the two. In the COMP/INFL account, however, since (45b) would have the structure X^{max}-ADV-S, (45b) could be ruled out in the same way as (46).

(46) *Why did probably John come late?

However, a closer look at the facts across the language groups shows that a distinction has to be sought independently for movement to a topic position (X^{max} in the COMP/INFL account, SPEC of CP in the ECP account). In Yiddish and Icelandic embedded clauses, where there is a consensus that the subject is in its base-generated position, the same distinction holds.

(47) *Ikh veys vos er efsher   vet esn.
     I   know what he probably will eat
     'I know what he probably will eat.'

The fact that the English translation is grammatical and the Yiddish equivalent is not cannot be explained through topicalization of the subject since in this structure we know that the subject is not in the topic position. Whatever the explanation, then, it is independent of V2 phenomena.[13]

3 Conclusion

I have used two arguments to support the ECP account of word order variation in Germanic languages. The first argument is theoretical. I have proposed that parameters of phrase structure be restricted to precedence relations such as headedness and direction of Case assignment and θ-role assignment. Given this, dominance relations would remain constant and structural notions that are built on dominance relations would remain fairly constant cross-linguistically. If such a restriction holds, accounts of Germanic word order that assume that languages like German and Swedish have no separate INFL nodes could not be maintained. Since the ECP proposal is able to account for the facts of Germanic word order without resorting to such a conflation of categories, it is the preferred solution.

The second argument is empirical. A COMP/INFL type account does not distinguish sentence-initial subjects from sentence-initial nonsubjects since both are moved to topic position. In the ECP account, sentence-initial subjects are in base-generated position, whereas sentence-initial nonsubjects are in the SPEC of CP. Since facts concerning German pronouns argue that some distinction must be made in these cases, the ECP account finds further support.

Finally, there is the question of learnability. If the COMP/INFL account is the "correct" one, an acquisition issue is raised. I have argued that all of the parameters and mechanisms proposed in the ECP account are needed independently of the problems of Germanic word order. Headedness of VPs distinguishes Japanese from French. The possibility of adjunction to IPs distinguishes [+wh] arguments from [+wh] nonarguments in Spanish. Proper government of empty heads distinguishes root questions from embedded questions in English. If all of these distinctions are available in the grammar, the introduction of the conflation of COMP and INFL is redundant. Such proliferation of possible accounts makes the linguist's task more difficult, but, more importantly, it presents an acquisition problem. How would the child know which analysis to choose? Although it is not provable, the common assumption is that for any given set of data there is only one possible account. Therefore, given the theoretical and empirical arguments above, the ECP proposal is the most likely.

Notes

1. For example, the English verb *look* subcategorizes for a PP, whereas the French verb *regarder* selects an NP. It may also be (following a proposal in Rochette 1988) that verbs that select propositional complements may determine whether the proposition is a CP, an IP, or a VP.

2. Platzack (1986) proposes a revised version of word order variation within German languages. Though this newer view avoids some of the problems addressed here, other problems remain and still others are raised. I will, however, be referring to the 1983 article, which more accurately represents the type of account against which I am arguing.

3. I am assuming that the auxiliaries *have* and *be* are base-generated in V-position.

4. The position of *have* can be seen clearly in (14a) and (14b) through placement of the negative clitic *n't*.

(i)   The children shouldn't *have* eaten the bread.

(ii) The children *have*n't eaten the bread.

5. In English, only auxiliaries and modals may appear in INFL for independent reasons (see Lightfoot 1979 for a historical account). In section 3 I will discuss the problem of main verbs in more detail.

6. Though head movement in these examples has left coindexed traces, I will argue later that the empty element left behind by head movement does not bear a subscript.

7. For more details on head feature transmission and an explanation of how this might be used to account for adjacency conditions in syntax, see Lamontagne and Travis 1986.

8. One could also say that movement may occur directly to X if Y is empty. In other words, it would be difficult to distinguish movement through Y and movement directly to X with an empty Y since no coindexed traces are left.

9. Since parameters should account for a cluster of properties, to call each of these language differences a parameter is not quite accurate. It is assumed that the "parameters" described in this chapter will eventually be subsumed under larger, more explanatory parameters.

10. It was this observation that prompted Platzack to propose that the empty COMP would violate the ECP unless it was filled either by V-movement (as in root questions) or by the [+wh] feature from the verb.

11. Diesing (1990) reports different judgments for data of the type given in (39b).

12. Note that adverbs such as *never* and *usually*, which have the option of appearing on either side of INFL, will be able to avoid blocking such merger, as in *They never go to school, They usually go to school.*

13. In Travis 1988, I propose that adverb generation and distribution are explained by assuming that adverbs in most situations do not project to XPs and as defective categories are licensed by features on a head.

References

Abney, S. (1986). "Functional Elements and Licensing." Talk presented at GLOW, Gerona, Spain.

Baker, M. (1988). *Incorporation: A Theory of Grammatical Function Changing.* University of Chicago Press, Chicago.

Borer, H. (1983). *Parametric Syntax.* Foris, Dordrecht.

Bouchard, D. (1983). *On the Content of Empty Categories.* Foris, Dordrecht.

Chomsky, N. (1986). *Barriers.* MIT Press, Cambridge, Mass.

Chung, S. (1983). "The ECP and Government in Chamorro." *Natural Language and Linguistic Theory* 1:207–244.

Diesing, M. (1990). "Verb Movement and the Subject Position in Yiddish." *Natural Language and Linguistic Theory* 8:41–80.

Emonds, J. (1980). "Word Order in Generative Grammar." *Journal of Linguistic Research* 1:33–54.

Fabb, N. (1984). "On Syntactic Affixation." Doctoral dissertation, MIT.

Kayne, R. (1981). "ECP Extensions." *Linguistic Inquiry* 12:93–133.

Koopman, H. (1983). *The Syntax of Verbs.* Foris, Dordrecht.

Lamontagne, G., and L. Travis (1986). "The Case Filter and the ECP." *McGill Working Papers in Linguistics* 3.2. Department of Linguistics, McGill University.

Lightfoot, D. (1979). *Principles of Diachronic Syntax.* Cambridge University Press, Cambridge.

Platzack, C. (1983). "Germanic Word Order and the COMP/INFL Parameter." In *Working Papers in Scandinavian Syntax* 2. Linguistics Department, University of Trondheim.

Platzack, C. (1986). "COMP, INFL, and Germanic Word Order." In L. Hellan and K. K. Christensen, eds., *Topics in Scandinavian Syntax.* Reidel, Dordrecht.

Pranka, P. (1983). "Syntax and Word Formation." Doctoral dissertation, MIT.

Rochette, A. (1988). "Semantic and Syntactic Aspects of Romance Sentential Complementation." Doctoral dissertation, MIT.

Sproat, R. (1985). "Welsh Syntax and VSO Structure." *Natural Language and Linguistic Theory* 3:173–216.

Stowell, T. (1981). "Origins of Phrase Structure." Doctoral dissertation, MIT.

Toman, J., ed. (1984). *Studies in German Grammar*. Foris, Dordrecht.

Torrego, E. (1984). "On Inversion in Spanish and Some of Its Effects." *Linguistic Inquiry* 15:103–129.

Travis, L. (1984). "Parameters and Effects of Word Order Variation." Doctoral dissertation, MIT.

Travis, L. (1988). "The Syntax of Adverbs." In *McGill Working Papers in Linguistics: Special Issue on Comparative Germanic Syntax*. Department of Linguistics, McGill University.

Chapter 12

| On the Nature of Lexical Government | Norbert Hornstein and David Lightfoot |

1 Introduction

Chomsky (1981) has argued that nonpronominal empty categories at Logical Form (LF) should be properly governed and that proper government should be defined disjunctively (1). Thus, an empty category must be either lexically governed (1a) or antecedent-governed (1b).

(1) *a* properly governs *b* if and only if *a* governs *b* and

   either

   a. *a* is a lexical category (that is, an X^0 in the X-bar system, but not $INFL^0$)

   or

   b. *a* is a phrasal category X'' locally coindexed with *b*.

Lasnik and Saito (1984) (henceforth L&S) explore the range of proper government, investigating several devices that are needed in order for (1) to have appropriate effects. They reformulate the Empty Category Principle (ECP) as an LF filter (2), whereby a trace is illicit at LF if it fails to have the feature $[+\gamma]$. $[+\gamma]$ may be assigned in the syntax or at LF under conditions of proper government, as in (1).

(2) *[... t ...]
      $[-\gamma]$

If one asks where the balance between lexical and antecedent government lies, one finds that $[+\gamma]$ features are assigned under antecedent government

Thanks to Jean-Roger Vergnaud for helpful discussion. This paper was written in 1986 and has been revised only to the extent of updating references. Consequently, it does not deal with the extensive body of work developing the barriers framework of Chomsky 1986. For discussion of that framework, see Lightfoot and Weinberg 1988, which was written after this paper.

(1b) for the vast majority of cases that L&S discuss. Lexical government, however, is relevant for traces in complement positions, for subject positions in Chinese, and perhaps for exceptional Case marking contexts. So the traces in (3) are lexically governed, not antecedent-governed, there being no local coindexed phrasal category.

(3) a. What$_i$ did Fay say [that Kay INFL bought e$_i$]?

    b. Zhangsan xiangxin [shei mai-le   shu]?

       Zhangsan believe   who buy-ASP book

       'Who does Zhangsan believe bought books?'

    c. [[shei$_i$] [Zhangsan xiangxin [e$_i$ INFL mai-le shu]]]

The trace in (3a) is lexically governed by *bought* and consequently does not need a local antecedent; this permits long-distance movement from direct object positions generally. The fact that *shei* 'who' may have wide scope in (3b) leads L&S to follow a suggestion made by Huang (1982) that INFL may act as a (marginal) lexical governor in Chinese; hence, the trace in the LF representation (3c) is lexically governed by the INFL.

We will argue here that L&S have underestimated the role of lexical government and that (1a) plays an extensive role on the Phonetic Form (PF) side of the grammar (section 1). This will suggest moving the lexical government requirement to PF (section 2) and adapting the antecedent government restriction on LF representations (section 3). We adopt an alternative and simpler model in section 3 and show that that model more than fulfills the goals of L&S and, moreover, explains some of the apparently unmotivated features of their analyses (section 4). In section 5 we will review the apparatus that the two models invoke.

2 Lexical Government at PF

In this section we will briefly consider some phenomena that L&S do not discuss, which motivate a lexical government condition on empty elements at PF. The facts and their analyses are discussed in more detail in Aoun, Hornstein, Lightfoot, and Weinberg 1987 (henceforth AHLW).

First, Chomsky (1981) and Stowell (1981) have shown that the deletion of complementizers is subject to lexical government. They take COMP to be the head of a clause and show that the governed complementizers in (4) may be deleted, but not the ungoverned complementizers in (5). Since these complementizers are not coindexed with NPs, antecedent government cannot make the relevant distinctions.

(4) a.   It was apparent (that) Kay left.
    b.   The book (that) Kay wrote arrived.
    c.   It was obvious (that) Kay left.

(5) a.   It was apparent yesterday *(that) Kay left.
    b.   The book arrived yesterday *(that) Kay wrote.
    c.   *(That) Kay left was obvious to all of us.
    d.   Fay believes, but Kay doesn't, *(that) Ray is smart.

The same requirement extends to *wh*-words in COMP. Assuming that nonrestrictive relatives have the structure of (6a), where the relative clause is outside the head NP, and that restrictive relatives have the structure of (6b), we account for the nondeletability of *wh*-words in nonrestrictive relatives by claiming that a deletion site in COMP must be lexically governed, in this case by the head noun.[1] So the ungoverned *wh*-word in (7a) may not be deleted, unlike the governed *who* in a restrictive relative (7b). Similarly, the relative pronoun in restrictive relatives like (8) may not be deleted because it is not governed by the head noun: an extra maximal projection (the PP and NP indicated) separates the head from the wh word.

(6) a.   [NP] S′
    b.   [DET [$_{N'}$ N′ S′]]

(7) a.   Fay saw Kay, who I admire.
    b.   Fay saw a guy (who) I admire.

(8) a.   the guy [$_{S'}$[$_{PP}$ to whom] I wrote]
    b.   the guy [$_{S'}$[$_{NP}$ whose house] I bought]

Exactly the same restriction holds for a trace in COMP. Just as a *that* is not deletable in an extraposed construction because it is not lexically governed, so a trace will also not be properly governed. The ungrammaticality of (9) suggests that an intermediate trace in COMP is subject to a condition of lexical government.

(9) *Who$_i$ was it apparent yesterday [$_{S'}$[e$_i$ that] Kay saw e$_i$]?

Similarly, if we follow Aoun (1985), Kayne (1981a), and Stowell (1981) in taking nonbridge verbs not to properly govern into a lower COMP, a condition of lexical government explains not only the inability to delete a complementizer (10a) but also the inability to have a trace in such a COMP (10b). Bridge verbs like *think*, on the other hand, do govern into COMP and so (10c) is well formed.

(10) a.   Fay quipped *(that) Kay left.
     b.   *Who$_i$ did Fay quip [[e$_i$ that] Kay met e$_i$]?
     c.   Who$_i$ did Fay think [$_{S'}$[e$_i$ that] Kay met e$_i$]?

A condition of lexical government also distinguishes some ill-formed gapping structures if one assumes that an empty verb, indicated here by "GAP," may not lexically govern. This makes the relevant distinctions in (11), where the ungrammatical structures have an empty NP, e_j, which is not lexically governed.

(11) a.   Fay introduced Kay to Ray and Jon introduced Don to Ron.
　　 b.   Fay introduced Kay to Ray and Jon GAP Don to Ron.
　　 c.   *Which man$_i$ did Fay introduce e$_i$ to Ray and which woman$_j$ (did) Jon GAP e$_j$ to Ron?
　　 d.   *Fay wondered what$_i$ Kay gave e$_i$ to Ray and what$_j$ Jon (did) GAP e$_j$ to Ron.
　　 e.   *Fay admired e$_i$ greatly [her uncle from Paramus]$_i$ but Jon (did) GAP e$_j$ only moderately [his uncle from New York]$_j$.
　　 f.   Fay gave her favorite racket to Ray and Jon GAP his favorite plant to Ron.
　　 g.   *Fay gave e$_i$ to Ray [her favorite racket]$_i$ and Jon (did) GAP e$_j$ to Ron [his favorite plant]$_j$.

The same assumptions also explain the facts of (12), where the ungrammatical structures have a deleted complementizer (12b) and a trace in COMP (12c) that are not lexically governed.

(12) a.   Fay thought Kay hit Ray and Jon GAP that Don hit Ron.
　　 b.   *Fay thought Kay hit Ray and Jon GAP [$_{S'}$ ∅ Don hit Ron].
　　 c.   *Who$_i$ did Fay think Kay hit e$_i$ and who$_j$ (did) Jon GAP [$_{S'}$ [e$_j$ (that)] Don hit e$_j$]?

A "gapped" verb does not involve movement and is unindexed at PF, receiving its index (the index of the antecedent overt verb) at LF. In this regard, such a verb contrasts with a verb moved in the syntax, which does act as a lexical governor. So Dutch has structures like (13), where the trace of the moved verb licenses the empty NP.

(13) Wie$_i$ doodde$_j$ je   [$_{VP}$ e$_i$ e$_j$]?
　　 who killed   you
　　 'Who did you kill?'

The distinction between gapped and moved verbs suggests that a condition of lexical government holds on the PF side of the grammar, where the trace of a moved verb is indexed but the trace of a gapped verb is not. There is a good deal of evidence for this position.[2]

First, we can adapt an argument that Saito (1984) offers on the basis of a dialect of Japanese. Right node raising (RNR) leads to structures like

(14), where the complement clause has been raised to a position where it is no longer governed by the verb and *that* cannot be deleted.

(14) Fay believes and Kay asserted publicly [that the dean lied].

This shows that the condition that controls the deletability of complementizers (the condition of lexical government) applies to the output of RNR; before RNR applies, *that* would be governed and hence deletable. However, RNR does not affect binding relations: thus, in (15) *him* must be interpreted as disjoint from *John* and from *Jim*.

(15) Jim wants and John expects [him to win].

This follows if the binding theory (requiring pronouns to be free in their Domain; see below) applies to the structure preceding RNR, where *him* is c-commanded by *Jim* and *John*. Whether the binding theory holds at S-Structure or at LF, then, there needs to be a condition of lexical government that determines the deletability of complementizers and applies to a level of representation after S-Structure and after RNR has applied— namely, at PF. This, of course, is not to say that the condition holds of a purely phonetic representation, but rather at some appropriate level of abstraction on the PF side of the grammar on the basis of which the phonetic representation is determined.

Second, we have shown that the deletion of complementizers is subject to a condition of lexical government, a condition that distinguishes between (16a) and (16b).

(16) a. The reason [$_{S'}$[why$_i$] Fay left e$_i$] disturbed us all.
      b. The reason he gave [$_{S'}$[why$_i$] Fay left e$_i$] seemed specious.

Why may be deleted in (16a), but not in (16b), where it is not lexically governed. In both (16a) and (16b), however, the trace of the adjunct e$_i$ must be locally bound in its clause (for reasons to be discussed below). Consequently, *why* must be present at S-Structure in order for the LF requirements to be met, being deleted in (16a) *after* S-Structure. Therefore, the condition on deletability must also apply after S-Structure, hence at PF.

A third reason to take the condition of head government to apply at PF and not at S-Structure relates to preposition stranding, which occurs freely at LF but is generally not possible in the syntax. Syntactic stranding in modern English must involve some marked property, as noted by many writers: perhaps a reanalysis process along lines suggested by Hornstein and Weinberg (1981) or a process extending government across a PP-node along lines suggested by Kayne (1981a), so that the trace is lexically governed. Whatever that process is, it must apply after stylistic rules that can affect government relations—for example, the permutation rule relating *speak to Fay tomorrow* and *speak tomorrow to Fay*. If the V governs the PP after these stylistic rules apply, then the marked process permits the V to govern the NP object of the preposition, permitting (17a) but not (17b–c).[3]

(17) a.   Who$_i$ will you speak to e$_i$ tomorrow?
     b.   *Who$_i$ will you speak tomorrow to e$_i$?
     c.   *Which concert$_i$ did you sleep during e$_i$?

This shows not only that a condition of lexical government must apply after at least some stylistic rules, hence after S-Structure, but also that imposing a condition of lexical government at LF leads to some complications. Since prepositions may be stranded freely at LF, their traces would have to be lexically governed at LF under L&S's view (because the trace in *Who$_i$ did Fay say [that Kay spoke to e$_i$]?* is analogous to the trace in (3a) and is not antecedent-governed). That would entail saying that prepositions are proper governors at LF but not at PF.[4]

We began by noting that L&S make limited use of lexical government as part of their LF condition, and we have shown here that a condition of lexical government is needed at PF to determine the distribution of phonetically empty complementizers and NPs. We have also noted that making lexical government an LF property entails an asymmetrical view of prepositions: that they are proper governors at LF but not at PF. This raises the question of whether we can eliminate an apparent redundancy and make lexical government exclusively a property of the PF side of the grammar. In that case we will need some other account to permit long-distance movement from direct object position at LF and an alternative analysis for the Chinese facts that lead L&S to make INFL a (marginal) governor in that language.

3   An Alternative to Antecedent Government at LF

The fundamental reason why L&S postulate the disjunctive definition of proper government is to permit long movement from a direct object position in structures like (3a) and many others. Presence of *that* means that the trace cannot be locally coindexed with a c-commanding element and therefore some other notion is needed to license the object trace; lexical government suffices in this case.

An alternative approach might build on the similarity between L&S's antecedent government and the binding theory. L&S define antecedent government (their (55)) as (18). They adopt Reinhart's (1979) definition of c-command, that *a* c-commands *b* if neither *a* nor *b* dominates the other and the first branching node dominating *a* dominates *b*.

(18) *a* antecedent-governs *b* if
   a. *a* and *b* are coindexed
   b. *a* c-commands *b*
   c. there is no *c* (*c* an NP or S′) such that *a* c-commands *c* and *c* dominates *b* unless *b* is the head of *c*.

So antecedent government calls for coindexing with a c-commanding element within the local NP or S′, and thus is very similar to Principle A of Chomsky's (1981) binding theory, which required an anaphor to be coindexed with a c-commanding element within its governing category (which could be NP or S). The virtual identity of these notions suggests that there is some redundancy. Since proper government is a condition specifically holding for empty elements, L&S's account requires some version of the binding theory in addition to antecedent government for overt anaphors, although this plays no role in their discussion.[5]

AHLW propose a model (19) that incorporates a "generalized binding theory" (20) at LF, in which the traces of *wh*-movement are treated as anaphors.

(19)

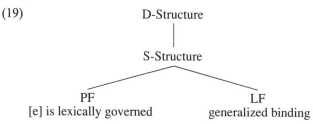

(20) For X = A or Ā
   A. An X-anaphor must be X-bound in its Domain.
   B. An X-pronoun must be X-free in its Domain.
   C. R-expressions must be A-free.

Traces of *wh*-items are treated as both anaphors and R-expressions, hence are subject to both Principle A and Principle C of (20). This permits long-distance movement from direct object positions, AHLW follow Chomsky's notion of an accessible SUBJECT (modifying slightly the definition of accessibility) and define a Domain for an element as the first NP or clause containing an accessible SUBJECT; as in Chomsky's (1981) account, a SUBJECT might be either a c-commanding NP or AGR.

Generalizing Principle A of (20) to apply to *wh*-traces entails that a *wh*-trace in object position would have no accessible SUBJECT, hence no Domain, and therefore would not be subject to the locality condition imposed by the binding theory. A *wh*-trace in subject position, however, would have an accessible SUBJECT in the local AGR, hence a Domain, and therefore would need to be bound (that is, coindexed with a c-commanding item) within that Domain.[6] So (21a) is well formed, the subject trace being bound within its Domain (the S') by the coindexed Comp. (21b) is ill formed because the subject trace is not bound in its Domain. (21c), however, is well formed even though the object trace is not bound within the local clause; this is because the trace has no accessible SUBJECT (see note 6), hence no Domain, and therefore is not subject to the binding theory.

(21) a.   Who$_i$ did Fay say [$_{S'}$[e$_i$]$_i$ [$_S$ e$_i$ AGR saw Kay]]?
     b. *Who$_i$ did Fay say [$_{S'}$[e$_i$ that$_j$]$_j$ [$_S$ e$_i$ AGR saw Kay]]?
     c.   Who$_i$ did Fay say [$_{S'}$[e$_i$ that$_j$]$_j$ [$_S$ Kay AGR saw e$_i$]]?

In (21) the COMP bears the index of one of the items that it contains. Just as L&S adopt the COMP-indexing convention of Aoun, Hornstein, and Sportiche (1981), so AHLW adopt a simplified version of the convention, permitting an index to percolate to COMP freely.[7] For AHLW an indexed COMP can act as a binder at LF and as a lexical governor at PF. AHLW also assume a version of the "Doubly Filled COMP Filter" for English, namely, that a COMP cannot contain phonetic material other than the head. Consequently, in (21b–c) the filter would be satisfied only if the index of *that* percolates to COMP, as indicated.

4   Explaining L&S's Account

If one ignores minor details, the only move made by AHLW that was not made by L&S was to take the trace of a *wh*-NP to be subject to Principle A of (20). This yields subject-object asymmetries at LF and enables one to dispense entirely with the notion of antecedent government. It also permits an explanation for some apparently unmotivated stipulations in L&S's account.

4.1   Status of VP

Though government generally may not take place across a maximal projection (see, for example, Chomsky 1981), L&S define antecedent government as being permitted across an intervening VP; thus, in (21a) the higher

COMP is said to antecedent-govern the head of the lower clause contained inside the VP. It is a mystery why this form of government should ignore just one of the maximal projections, VP. Under AHLW's model, government is not relevant at LF and is defined in the usual way: *a* governs *b* if they share all maximal projections, regardless of what the maximal projection might be. On the other hand, the reason why NPs and clauses but not VPs or PPs may be Domains at LF is that they are the categories with SUBJECTs; and Domains are defined in terms of accessible SUBJECTs, as in Chomsky 1981.

4.2   Lexical Government into COMP

Another oddity in L&S's account that now becomes understandable is the fact that there is no lexical government into a COMP at LF. We have shown above that bridge verbs govern items in their lower COMP at PF, but L&S argue that lexical government must not be allowed to license traces in COMP at LF. They take (23) to be the LF representation of the Japanese (22) (their (83) and (84)).

(22) *[$_{NP}$[$_{S'}$ Hanako-ga [$_{S'}$ Taroo-ga naze sore-o te-ni ireta tte]   itta]
      Hanako-NOM Taro-NOM why it-ACC obtained COMP said
      koto]-o sonnani okotteru no?
      fact-ACC so much be angry Q
      'Why$_i$ are you so angry about the fact that Hanako said that Taro obtained it t$_i$?'

(23) [$_{S'}$[$_{S}$[$_{NP}$[$_{S'}$[$_{S}$ Hanako-ga [$_{S'}$[$_{S}$ Taroo-ga e$_i$ sore-o te-ni ireta] tte e$_i$] itta]
      koto]]-o sonnani okotteru] naze$_i$] no

They argue that the initial trace in (23) is antecedent-governed and that the ill-formedness is due to the intermediate trace, which is not antecedent-governed within the S'. This entails that "even a bridge verb like *itta* 'said' cannot govern a trace in the COMP of its S'-complement. Hence, it follows that a trace in COMP must be antecedent-governed" (p. 256; see also p. 246). So, although L&S adopt a disjunctive definition of proper government (1), they must stipulate that at LF a bridge verb may not govern a lower COMP, even though it may govern a lower COMP at PF, if our earlier demonstration is correct. They achieve this by stipulating that lexical government is possible only where either a θ-role or Case is assigned (thus, a verb may lexically govern its direct object or an NP to which it assigns Case by exceptional Case marking, but not in a raising context like *Fay$_i$ seems [e$_i$ to be happy]*, where the trace is antecedent-governed; see pp. 277–278). This complication is an artifact of permitting lexical government to apply at LF. Under AHLW's model, where lexical government is relevant only on the PF side, no stipulation is needed and one would not expect lexical government to license a trace at LF. For AHLW, the ungrammaticality of (22) and the ill-formedness of the LF representation (23) follow from the fact that the intermediate trace in (23) has an accessible SUBJECT (namely, the higher AGR), hence a Domain, and therefore must be bound in that Domain; because there is no binder in the Domain, the structure is ill formed. If the LF representation of (22) is (24), as L&S contemplate but reject (their (42)), then the highest trace fails to be bound in its Domain, the NP. (See below for why AGR acts as an accessible SUBJECT for 'why' but not for 'who' or 'what'.)

(24) $[_{S'}[_S[_{NP}[_{S'}[_S$ Hanako-ga $[_{S'}[_S$ Taroo-ga e_i sore-o te-ni ireta] tte $e_i]$ itta] $e_i]$ koto]-o sonnani okotteru] *naze$_i$* no

4.3 INFL in Chinese

Consider now what leads L&S to make INFL a lexical governor for a subject (but not for the adjunct 'why') at LF in Chinese. They note that (25) (their (33)) is ambiguous and may have the two LF representations (25a–b).

(25) Ni xiang-zhidao $[_{S'}$ shei mai-le sheme]?
     you wonder   who bought what
     a. $[_{S'}$ shei$_i$ $[_S$ ni xiang-zhidao $[_{S'}$ sheme$_j$ $[_S$ e_i mai-le $e_j]]]]$
     b. $[_{S'}$ sheme$_j$ $[_S$ ni xiang-zhidao $[_{S'}$ shei$_i$ $[_S$ e_i mai-le $e_j]]]]$

In (25a) e_i fails to be antecedent-governed in its S', and therefore L&S claim that it is licit by virtue of being lexically governed by INFL. The corresponding structure *who$_i$ do you wonder* $[[what_j]$ e_i *bought* $e_j]$ is ill formed because INFL is not a lexical governor in English. Now this is a curious claim because Chinese has a very impoverished verbal morphology, which manifests itself in the fact that there is no AGR in INFL, as indicated by the grammaticality of (26).

(26) Zhangsan$_i$ shuo $[_{S'}$ ziji$_i$ hui lai].
     Zhangsan say   self will come
     'Zhangsan said that himself will come.'

If Chinese lacks AGR, *ziji* has an accessible SUBJECT only in the higher clause, where it is bound by *Zhangsan*. So although Chinese INFL is weaker than its English counterpart in that it does not contain AGR, it is stronger insofar as it acts as a lexical governor, if L&S are correct. AHLW's model (19) *predicts* the well-formedness of (25a) given the well-formedness of (26) and the absence of AGR in Chinese. That is, since generalized binding treats both reflexives and traces of *wh*-items as subject to Principle A, both items are expected to uniformly reflect the absence of a local SUBJECT.

It is by no means clear what L&S mean by introducing the notion that INFL is a "marginal" governor at just one level (LF but not S-Structure; see p. 270), but they invoke it to explain not only clearly well formed structures like (25a) but also *Who thinks that who won the election?*, which they mark "??" but take to be grammatical. Here they claim that "INFL and Comp have a special relation at LF, a relation due to the LF movement of INFL into Comp" (p. 271). Once *that* deletes at LF, INFL, having moved to COMP, becomes the head of COMP and thus becomes the *antecedent* governor for an empty subject. L&S cite Den Besten (1978) and others who argue for a rule moving INFL to COMP, but they fail to observe that Den Besten's syntactic process is blocked by the presence of a complementizer and so is not parallel to what they need.

Conceptual and mechanical curiosities aside, there is compelling evidence not to take INFL as a governor in Chinese. It has generally been supposed for some time that Chinese has no syntactic *wh*-movement (Huang 1982). However, there is a movement process for topicalized expressions, and there is a clear subject-object asymmetry. Alongside (27a) one sometimes finds topicalized expressions like (27b), but never comparable cases where the subject is topicalized (27c).

(27) a.   John [$_{S'}$ dui Bill hen xihuan Mary] hen shangxin.
      John   to Bill very like   Mary very sorry
      'John is sorry that Bill likes Mary.'

   b. ?Mary$_i$, John [dui Bill hen xihuan e$_i$] hen shangxin.
       'Mary, John is sorry that Bill likes.'

   c. *Bill$_i$, John [du e$_i$ hen xihuan Mary] hen shangxin.
       'Bill, John is sorry likes Mary.'

If INFL is a governor, then the ungrammaticality of (27c) is mysterious. If, on the other hand, INFL is not a governor, then the ungrammaticality of (27c) follows naturally from a model like (19), where a trace must be lexically governed *at PF*. The possibility of the LF representation (25a) is due to the fact that Chinese lacks AGR, as shown by the grammaticality of (26); if there is no AGR, and if one generalizes the notion of an anaphor to include the trace of a *wh*-item, then e$_i$ has no accessible SUBJECT in (25a) and consequently is not subject to the locality condition imposed by the binding theory (20). The (relative) grammaticality of (27b) provides striking evidence that the PF/LF division of labor in (19) is along the right lines and that lexical government should be seen as a PF condition on empty elements. See AHLW for further discussion.

L&S make INFL a governor for a subject in Chinese but not for the adjunct 'why'. This is because a sentence like (28a) (their (34)) is unambiguous and has the LF representation (28b) but not (28c); they claim that (28c) is ill formed because e_j is neither antecedent-governed nor lexically governed.

(28) a. Ni xiang-zhidao [$_{S'}$ Lisi weisheme mai-le sheme]?
        you wonder   Lisi why   bought what
     b. [$_{S'}$ sheme$_i$ [ni xiang-zhidao [$_{S'}$ weisheme$_j$ [Lisi e$_j$ mai-le e$_i$]]]]
     c. [$_{S'}$ weisheme$_j$ [ni xiang-zhidao [$_{S'}$ sheme$_i$ [Lisi e$_j$ mai-le e$_i$]]]]

However, the ill-formedness of (28c) follows on other grounds, namely, that an adjunct like 'why' is generally nonreferential in all languages, hence not subject to Principle C of the bindng theory in (20). If e_j in (28) is only an anaphor, subject to Principle A of (20), then it has an accessible SUBJECT in *Lisi* and therefore must be bound in its local S', as it is in the well-formed (28b) but not in the ill-formed (28c). AHLW show that this is a productive analysis for the different behavior of 'why' and 'how' in Chinese, Dutch, English, French, and Japanese.

5 Some Methodological Objections

We have argued that there are empirical and theoretical reasons for preferring AHLW's version of the ECP to the theory proposed by L&S. In this section we will argue, somewhat more abstractly, that there are also methodological reasons for preferring our account. These reasons fall into three groups. First, L&S's theory makes crucial use of distinctions that are not at all perspicuous. In particular, a distinction between adjuncts and arguments lies at the heart of their account, but this distinction, we will argue, turns out to be fuzzy at best. Moreover, by taking adjuncts versus arguments as the relevant dichotomy, L&S suggest that the relevant considerations concerning the proper distribution of traces are structural. We will show that this is incorrect and suggest that the relevant distinction is one keyed to the content of the various adjuncts.

Second, L&S's theory makes heavy use of theoretical devices that are both idiosyncratic and not well motivated empirically. For example, ordering assumptions are crucial in obtaining their results. So too is their commitment to a "strongly" derivational theory. AHLW's account requires no ordering assumptions and can remain agnostic concerning the status of derivations. We consider this an advantage given the paucity of independent evidence that derivations, in the sense that L&S require, really are a central chracteristic of Universal Grammar (UG).

Third, L&S's theory involves three separate stipulations concerning *that*. It can be freely inserted, it can be freely deleted, and it can be the head of COMP and meet S-Structure selection requirements without bearing an index. This theory of UG entails complications for L&S's grammar of Polish; we will show that there is a simpler account.

5.1 What Is an Adjunct?

In L&S's account the central analytical distinction is the contrast between adjuncts and arguments. According to L&S, the grammar is organized as follows:

(29)

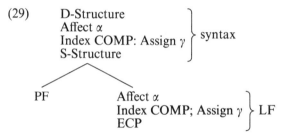

In their system adjunct traces must be γ-marked at LF and not before, even if they occur at S-Structure and could be γ-marked in the syntax. Argument traces, on the other hand, must be γ-marked at S-Structure if they can be, though it is possible to γ-mark argument traces at LF as well if they result from LF processes. In short, γ-marking for argument traces must occur at the level at which they are created, whereas adjuncts may be γ-marked only at LF.[8]

Both these assumptions are vital to L&S's approach. To see why, first consider (30), with an argument trace.

(30) *Who_i does John believe [[e_i that] e_i left]?

To explain the unacceptability of (30), L&S require that the subject e_i be γ-marked at S-Structure. However, it cannot be so marked because at S-Structure *that* is the head of COMP. Therefore, the intermediate trace in COMP is unable to γ-mark e_i. If γ-marking could be delayed until LF for the trace in subject position, then, in L&S's theory, it would be possible to delete *that* in LF, enabling the intermediate trace to become the head of COMP in LF. It could then percolate its index to COMP, and this would in turn allow the COMP to γ-mark the subject at LF. (30) would then be fully grammatical. To prevent this from happening, L&S require γ-marking for arguments to obligatorily apply at the *first* level where its structural description is met. In short, for L&S the rule of γ-marking applies obligatorily to argument traces as soon as it can apply.

For adjunct traces, however, things are different: they cannot be γ-marked at S-Structure even if they occur there.

(31) *Why$_i$ did John question [$_{NP}$ the fact [$_{S'}$ e$_i$ that [Bill left e$_i$]]]?

In (31), if γ-marking could apply to the adjunct trace at S-Structure, then we could not explain its "strong" unacceptability (it is worse than a "mere" Subjacency violation). L&S argue that sentences like (31) are ill formed because of the intermediate trace. The trace must be there to γ-mark the most deeply embedded trace of *why*. The unacceptability of (31) stems from the fact that the intermediate trace cannot in turn be γ-marked. Therefore, the sentence is rendered ungrammatical. However, if γ-marking for adjuncts were permissible at S-Structure, then (31) would be well formed. It would be possible to γ-mark the original trace and *delete* the intermediate trace in LF after it had γ-marked the most deeply embedded trace. To prevent this, L&S require that adjunct traces be γ-marked at LF and LF only.

Before we take up the objection to this proposal, it is worth observing that the theory we have outlined accounts for the data noted above without invoking γ-marking or any of the assumptions needed to make it function correctly. On our account, rules apply freely at any level to anything that meets the appropriate structural description at that level; we do not invoke rules that "must apply when they can apply." Binding applies in LF to all traces regardless of how they were formed. Similarly, in PF lexical government applies to all gaps regardless of their position.[9] It makes no difference in what order traces are accommodated. In (31) both the intermediate and the lowest trace fail to be bound within their domains (NP and S', respectively). In (30) the subject trace fails to be lexically governed at PF because the COMP is not coindexed with it (by virtue of containing *that*).

However, a basic objection can be raised against L&S's proposal. At the heart of their proposal lies the distinction between adjuncts and arguments. But what exactly is an adjunct? L&S (p. 241) suggest, following Huang (1982), that adjuncts are noncomplements, assuming tentatively that they are immediately dominated by S (their footnote 11). For L&S, then, adjuncts can be *structurally* distinguished from arguments and proper government is a structural well-formedness requirement with structurally distinguishable elements becoming subject to it at distinct grammatical levels. The problem arises once one considers the full range of adjuncts.

L&S observe that temporal *when* and locative *where* pattern quite differently from *why*. It is hard to see what structural reasons there are for distinguishing them, but L&S cite Huang (1982), who suggests two possible ways of distinguishing adjuncts. One way would distinguish them by their dominance relations; the other would distinguish them categorially.

On the first proposal, *where* and *when* would be dominated by different parts of the tree than *why*. However, L&S offer no evidence in favor of this assumption, and we can think of no evidence at least for English. If we assume that *wh*-words occupy the same positions as their corresponding "answers," then it is hard to see how temporal or locative phrases differ structurally from *because*-phrases. All three constitute islands to movement, as in (32).

(32) a. *What$_i$ did John meet Bill after e$_i$?
      b. *What$_i$ did John meet Bill three feet from e$_i$?
      c. *What$_i$ did John meet Bill because of e$_i$?

Since none of the three phrase types receives a θ-role or Case from the verb, none is lexically governed under L&S's account. Moreover, the three phrase types all seem to play analogous semantic roles in that they modify the S within which they are located.

Furthermore, all three phrase types can be fronted along with a VP in constructions like those in (33).

(33) a. John threatened to leave after the concert and leave after the concert he did.
      b. John threatened to leave for the airport and leave for the airport he did.
      c. John threatened to leave because of the heat and leave because of the heat he did.

In short, the evidence suggests that temporal and locative phrases have the same constituent structure as *because*-phrases. If *wh*-words occupy the same positions as their corresponding answers, this suggests that *why*, *where*, and *when* are all dominated by the same elements in the tree.

Huang's second suggestion for distinguishing *why* from *where* and *when* is that *why* is a PP whereas *where* and *when* are NPs, perhaps with an abstract preposition.[10] However, for English, the evidence for this is weak at best. *Where* and *when* are never preceded by prepositions, unlike their Chinese counterparts (see Huang 1982:529–530). Furthermore, all three question words seem to be surrogates for PPs in the sense that it is PPs that answer the corresponding questions.

(34) a. When did John leave? John left *(before) the concert.
     b. Where did John eat? John ate *(at) Gallagher's.
     c. Why did John leave? John left *(because of) the heat.

There is little independent evidence for the assumption that these *wh*-words differ in categorial status. Consequently, it seems unlikely that Huang's suggestions will really help to distinguish the various kinds of adjunct traces.

Given these observations, L&S's position begins to lose intuitive appeal. There is no evidence that the proper distinction is between elements in different structural configurations or of different syntactic categories. In that case, the difference must hinge on the sorts of entities the different variables range over. So, one might interpret Huang's distinction as a claim that *why*-variables are satisfied by different sorts of entities than *where*- or *when*-variables. We can mark the difference by saying that *why*-variables are placeholders for "properties," whereas *when*- and *where*-variables are satisfied by "objects." *Because*-phrases denote properties, whereas moments of time and places are objects. On this reading, *when* and *where* do differ from *why*, but the difference is an internal semantic difference pegged to the values of the variables that act as satisfiers rather than a structural difference pegged to the tree position or categorial content of the various phrases. The distinction between different variable types seems more appropriately attributed to the *binding* properties of the various operator-variable pairs than to the structural requirement that traces in certain configurations must be locally antecedent-governed. After all, the proper concern of binding encompasses the relation between operators and variables. Consequently, it is natural to link divergent behavior to the different binding requirements that distinct variable types are subject to.

So AHLW attribute the different behavior of traces left by *why* and *how* versus *when* and *where* to the fact that the traces differ in variable type: traces of *why* and *how* are subject to Principle A of the generalized binding theory, whereas traces of *where* and *when* are referential and are subject to both Principle A and Principle C. For the reasons outlined above, we find this a more natural approach than one that takes the central distinction to be that between adjuncts versus arguments, notwithstanding the lack of an appropriate definition of "adjunct."

5.2 Derivation

A second deep feature of L&S's model is that it employs ordering assumptions in deriving its results. This is so in two senses. L&S assume that operations are ordered within each component, and they must also assume that grammatical levels are ordered with respect to one another. To see this, let us look once again at their explanation for the *that*-trace effect.

Consider (35)–(37).

(35) *Who$_i$ do you think [e$_i$ that [e$_i$ left]]?

(36) you think [[who left]]

(37) [who$_i$ [you think [e$_i$ [e$_i$ left]]]]

L&S make two crucial assumptions to account for the unacceptability of (35). The first is that the rule Affect α applies before the rule of γ-marking. If these rules were freely ordered, it would be possible to derive the unacceptable (35) from (36): Affect α moves *who* to the matrix COMP to yield (37), and then the most embedded trace is γ-marked. Then Affect α is reapplied to delete the trace in COMP and to insert *that*.

Similarly, (35) could be derived if argument traces present at S-Structure could be γ-marked at LF, as we showed earlier. Thus, L&S must make a second assumption, that γ-marking applies "as soon as it can." However, the notion "as soon as it can" would make no sense if the levels were unordered with respect to one another. To phrase this differently, L&S must crucially assume not only that a sentence is a set of phrase markers but in fact that it is an *ordered* set of phrase markers. Without this stronger assumption it is impossible both to say that S-Structure "precedes" LF and to state the conditon that γ-marking must apply to an argument trace "as soon as it can apply."

This second assumption might not seem too exotic given the centrality of derivational notions in linguistic discussion. However, we would like to suggest that ordering assumptions are not really as central as commonly supposed, especially in the context of contemporary principle-based theories. As Chomsky (1983) has observed, recent work in the theory of grammar has shifted from rule-based theories that attempted to explain grammatical phenomena on the basis of interacting rules, to principle-based theories that attempt to account for linguistic phenomena on the basis of interacting principles. For our purposes, what is significant in this shift of focus is that it removes the notion of derivation, in the sense of an ordered sequence of phrase markers, as a critical notion of grammatical theory. Whereas it might make sense to ask in which order rules apply (given that application of one rule might feed another), it is less natural to order output principles (which can never feed each other). At least, no one to our knowledge has ever suggested that the order in which principles apply to phrase markers is an important feature of grammatical theory. Furthermore, there is little independent evidence in favor of constraints on derivations. Huang (1982), for example, argues convincingly that syntactic movement should be constrained by Subjacency but that LF movement should not be. He explains this difference by treating Subjacency as an S-Structure well-formedness condition rather than as a condition on the application of Move α. If one insists on treating Subjacency as a condition on rule application rather than on a type of representation, it remains something of a mystery why Subjacency does not constrain LF movement as well.[11] Phrase markers must meet certain consistency conditions if they all hold of the same sentence, but it does not follow from this that the phrase markers are sequenced or that UG places ordering requirements on grammatical levels. By this we do not mean that UG cannot make such demands; our point is that within current assumptions the requirement is not at all obvious and there is little empirical motivation for it. We consider it a virtue of our account that it does not assume a strong ordering hypothesis to derive ECP effects and that we need not assume that rules apply "as soon as they can." In short, our account requires neither interlevel nor intralevel ordering assumptions to derive the standard ECP data.

There is a further reason for dispensing with ordering assumptions. Within a theory that makes such assumptions, the question immediately arises why the rules are ordered the way they are and not some other way. One can always put such questions off by suggesting that they should be addressed to those who study evolution or molecular biology. But other things being equal, it is better to have a theory in which such questions are not given the chance to arise.[12] So a theory that dispenses with ordering, like ours, is better off in this regard than a theory that requires it, even if the ordering is universal.

As far as we can tell, L&S provide no evidence that derivational constraints are *superior* to output conditions. They show that if their approach is pursued, then it requires a rich conception of derivation and requires Subjacency to be treated as a constraint on derivations (p. 274) rather than on representations as Huang argues. This is because traces in COMP may be deleted in the course of a derivation, making Subjacency unstatable as an output condition. This in turn leads L&S to reintroduce Strict Cyclicity as an independent condition (p. 283), which can no longer be subsumed under Subjacency as Freidin (1978) argues. AHLW's analysis, on the other hand, does not delete traces in COMP and therefore undermines the empirical reasons for making Subjacency a condition on derivations. If there are no empirical reasons for taking such a strong derivational view, it is methodologically simpler to assume that *all* grammatical constraints are structural rather than derivational.

5.3 The Complementizer *That*

In this section we discuss the stipulations invoked by L&S to account for the behavior of *that*. L&S's account has three separate clauses that apply to the complementizer *that* and, in English, only to *that*: (i) *that* can be the head of COMP and meet selection requirements without having an index (p. 252), (ii) *that* can be deleted in LF because it alone lacks semantic content and is not required by other principles of grammar (p. 265), and (iii) *that* can be inserted anywhere in the derivation because it lacks semantic content (p. 282).[13] Presumably these conditions are quite general and it is accidental that only *that* falls under them in English. These stipulations at UG in turn entail further complications for L&S's treatment of Polish.

L&S point out that *that*-trace effects appear in Polish, as shown in (38).[14]

(38) a. Maria powiedziała, że   kto owiedza Janka?
        Maria said   that who visits   Janek-ACC
        'Who did Maria say visits Janek?'
    b. Co   Maria chce, żeby Janek kupił?
        what Maria want that Janek buy
    c. *Kto Maria chce, żeby kupił chleb?
        who Maria want that buy   bread

(38) reflects what L&S take as the usual case in Polish: movement is restricted to the embedded clause in the syntax. However, in certain *subjunctive* complements a *wh*-word may be extracted from the embedded clause and then the usual *that*-trace effects appear. To account for movement from such clauses and the usual *that*-trace data, L&S make three claims specific to Polish, all of which can now be dispensed with: that there is no syntactic movement from an Ā-position (their (159)), that therefore movement (for instance, in (38b)) can violate the Subjacency Condition in Polish (p. 280), and that, contrary to appearances, there is really only one element in COMP in (38a) (their (162), where *kto* is "adjoined to the embedded S").

We, on the other hand, need assume uncontroversially that only heads of phrases enter into selectional restrictions. In that case the S-Structure/ PF representations of the sentences in (38) are as shown in (39).

(39) a. Maria powiedziała, [[że kto$_i$]$_i$ e$_i$ owiedza Janka]
  b. co$_i$ Maria chce, [[zeby$_j$ e$_i$]$_j$ Janek kupił e$_i$]
  c. kto$_i$ Maria chce, [[zeby$_j$ e$_i$]$_j$ e$_i$ kupił chleb]

Chce selects the subjunctive complementizer *zeby* and consequently the
embedded COMP must bear the index of the complementizer, *zeby* being
the head. In that case the subject trace in (39c) cannot be head-governed,
violating the PF requirement on empty NPs. No such problem arises for
(39b), where the trace is governed by the embedded verb. Verbs like *chce*
that select subjunctive complementizers, unlike *powiedziała*, act as bridge
verbs and consequently properly govern into the lower COMP (section 2);
hence, the intermediate trace in (39b–c) is properly governed at PF. In the
case of indicative complements like the one in (38a), the matrix verb selects
only a [−wh] COMP, but not the complementizer *że* (which may, therefore, delete; compare *Jak myślisz, co Janek kupił?* 'What do you think Janek
bought?' or literally 'how do you think what Janek bought'). In (38a) *kto*
moves to COMP in the syntax and its index may percolate to the COMP,
as in (39a). We assume with L&S that at LF [+wh] items may not occur
in [−wh] positions and vice versa. Assuming, again with L&S, that traces
are always [−wh] (or, to put it differently, that the only elements that are
[+wh] are overt *wh*-words), we account for the occurrence of (38a): *kto*
moves in LF from the intermediate COMP (39a) and as a result the head
of the lower COMP is a trace (that is, a [−wh] word), conforming to the
LF requirement. Both of those LF requirements also hold on the PF side
for English, but for Polish PF requires only that there can be no [−wh]
item in a [+wh] position; unlike in English, it is not required that there be
no [+wh] item in a [−wh] position. The absence of this PF condition in
Polish would be "learnable" because the child would hear sentences like
(38a), in which a [+wh] word occurs in a [−wh] position.

In Polish *wh*-words must be in COMP at S-Structure. It also appears
that COMP can be multiply filled, and the order of the elements seems to
make no difference to acceptability.

(40) a. Zastanawiam się kto co   przyniesie.
      I wonder   who what will bring
      'I wonder who will bring what.'
   b. Zastanawiam się co kto przyniesie.
   c. *Zastanawiam sie kto przyniesie co.

This illustrates the familiar matter of complementizer selection. Certain
verbs select complementizers, and complementizers that are specially selected do not delete; deletion therefore is not keyed to any notion of

semantic content (see note 13).[15] For example, Polish *chce* selects *zeby*, just as *wonder* selects a [+wh] COMP, and the presence of *zeby* at PF is required because it is selected. This entails that *zeby* must percolate its index to COMP to meet the selectional restrictions, as is characteristic of languages with overt movement. Thus, (39c) is the PF structure of the unacceptable (38c). The trace in COMP cannot percolate its index to COMP because *zeby* must do so to meet selectional requirements. This leads to a violation because the embedded subject trace fails to be lexically governed by the COMP.

Consequently, we can dispense with the three devices L&S introduce for the Polish cases. We need no general prohibition against syntactic movement from $\bar{\text{A}}$-positions, we do not require movement in Polish to violate Subjacency, and we treat *wh*-movement at face value and assume that there can be many elements in COMP. The first of these stipulations is particularly costly. Most languages allow successive movement from $\bar{\text{A}}$-positions, and, indeed, Polish permits such movement if the lower clause has a subjunctive verb and is introduced by *zeby*; consequently, it is unclear how a child could learn that this is not possible from indicative clauses. It is also worth noting that the proposal is incompatible with the barriers framework proposed by Chomsky (1986), which is essentially an extension of the central ideas of L&S but where the widespread use of adjunction allows movement from $\bar{\text{A}}$-positions quite generally (see Lightfoot and Weinberg 1988 for discussion).

6 Conclusion

If we consider a wider range of data than L&S, including complementizer deletion, certain gapping phenomena, properties of intermediate traces, and so on, we find that these sorts of data strongly support the view presented by AHLW that lexical government must apply in PF so that all phonological gaps are properly governed. We have also argued that we can dispense with antecedent government at LF in favor of a version of generalized binding, which is independently needed and formally very similar to L&S's antecedent government. This eliminates obvious redundancy and has theoretical and conceptual advantages over L&S's approach. Finally, we suggested that the type of approach pursued by AHLW has certain important methodological advantages over the type of approach pursued by L&S. Thus, empirically, theoretically, and methodologically we believe that AHLW's approach to proper government is to be preferred to L&S's.

The notion of lexical government that we emply comes close to the claim that overt gaps occur only in *subcategorized* positions. Rouveret and Vergnaud (1980) argue that subcategorization relations should be expressed through coindexation; thus, a verb is coindexed with an NP that it subcategorizes. In that case the formal relationship between an indexed COMP and an empty subject would be identical to that between a verb and a subcategorized NP; this formal relationship constitutes what is usually called subcategorization. In each case an element is coindexed with something that governs it. Thus, we might say that COMP indexing is a way to subcategorize an empty subject and, generally, that empty NPs may only occur in subcategorized positions.

Another reason to view things in terms of subcategorization concerns the fact that verbs differ in terms of whether they allow bridge effects and deletion of complementizers, as noted earlier. Nouns, however, do not differ in this regard: any noun occurring as the head of a relative clause allows deletion of the complementizer: *the man* (*that*) *I met*. It is natural to assume that the head of a relative clause is coindexed with its lower COMP, as is required by the promotion analysis of Vergnaud (1974) or by an S-Structure predication process along the lines suggested by Williams (1980) (see Hornstein 1987 for independent arguments that this cannot be an LF process). In that case the COMP is subcategorized (on Rouveret and Vergnaud's definition) by the noun and may be empty. On the other hand, a noun followed by a complement clause (*our belief that the ECP must be split*) never allows deletion of the complementizer, presumably because it is not coindexed with the COMP and thus an empty COMP in this position would not be subcategorized. This is further evidence that indexical properties are crucial for licensing empty items at PF.

In raising constructions like *Fay$_i$ seems* [*e$_i$ to like ice cream*], it is sometimes assumed that *seem* does not subcategorize the lower subject because there are no selection effects between those two positions. However, there is no reason to equate subcategorization with selection domains. Selection is an S-Structure or LF process, but subcategorization (head government) is relevant at PF.

Prepositions constitute the one discrepancy between subcategorizing and lexically governing items: it is usually assumed that prepositions subcategorize for their complements (some prepositions may be followed by NPs, some by clauses, and some by both NPs and clauses), but they do not act as lexical governors at PF. Since prepositions are closed class items, unlike nouns, verbs, and adjectives, we can say that the requirement of lexical government for empty elements is essentially the condition that empty elements must be subcategorized by an open class item in PF, under Rouveret and Vergnaud's view that subcategorization is a formal relationsip and distinct from selection.

In any case, we have shown that lexical government plays an extensive role at PF. This in turn permits the elimination of antecedent government as an independent notion at LF. Having simplified UG in this way, we have also been able in many cases to adopt simpler and more perspicuous analyses than those of L&S.

Notes

1. This entails that a noun is a proper governor, contrary to some claims. Consequently, we cannot account for the nonoccurrence of *Fay$_i$'s appearance e$_i$ to leave* on the grounds that *appearance* cannot be a proper governor for the trace, in the fashion of Kayne (1981a). AHLW adopt a proposal of Bouchard (1982) and Chomsky (1986) that nouns assign inherent Case and that inherent Case assignment must be strictly parallel to θ-role assignment.

Observe, incidentally, that the structures in (6) suffice to explain why extraposition is permitted in restrictive relative clauses but not appositives. Only in the former case will the trace be properly governed.

2. The claim that an empty item at PF must be lexically governed by an indexed element explains other phenomena, as AHLW show. For example, the absence of the objective genitive reading in *each picture of Fay's* is due to the fact that the trace is not governed by an item that has an index at PF: *each picture of* [$_{NP}$ *Fay$_i$'s e e$_i$*]. Similarly in *the picture which is Fay's* and *this picture is Fay's*, which also lack the objective reading for *Fay*, which would contain a structure [$_{NP}$ *Fay$_i$'s e e$_i$*]. The PF condition also explains why *What is the crowd too angry to organize?*, discussed by Chomsky (1986), has only the reading where the subject of *organize* is *the crowd* and not some arbitrary referent; compare *The crowd is too angry to organize a meeting*, which is ambiguous. (See AHLW for discussion.)

Moreover, Williams (1981) points to the contrast between **John is known to have left but he$_i$ isn't GAP e$_i$ to have gone to the movies* and *It is known that John left but it isn't GAP that he went to the movies*. Under our account, the first sentence is ungrammatical because the trace of *he* is not lexically governed at PF.

3. Regardless of the structure, *speak* could not govern *to* in (17b) because adjacency is required for lexical government. This was noted by Saito (1984), who observed that an English complementizer may not be deleted if it is not adjacent to its governor: *It was believed by everyone *(that) Ray was a fool, Fay believed sincerely *(that) Ray was a fool*. This also explains why a *that*-complementizer at the front of the second of two relative clauses may not be deleted: *The story (that) Fay wrote *(that) The Nation published was about the FBI*.

4. Aoun (1985), Hornstein and Weinberg (1990), and Huang (1982) show that there is no pied piping at LF, so that prepositions are indeed followed by "traces" at LF. Bouchard (1982) argues that prepositions are not followed by "traces" at

LF because LF processes involve only copying, whereas syntactic processes involve copying and deletion and thus yield traces. However, if there is no "deletion" at LF, then what we and L&S have treated as [−wh] "intermediate traces" resulting from LF movement through COMP will be full-fledged *wh*-items, which will lead to selectional violations.

5. L&S do not discuss how quantifier scope is determined within their system. It is well known that different kinds of quantifiers are subject to distinct conditions on scope assignment. Aoun and Hornstein (1985) show that a theory of quantifier scope can be fashioned from the theory of generalized binding because it allows distinctions among types of variables. Since it is hard to imagine how antecedent government would permit distinctions among variable types, this constitutes independent motivation for a theory of generalized binding. If generalized binding is adopted, then antecedent government becomes redundant.

Furthermore, it is unclear whether antecedent government is empirically adequate even for a wider set of cases involving *wh*-movement at LF. To take one example, consider multiple questions like (i).

(i) Who said that books about who sold well?

Aoun and Hornstein (1985) and Hornstein and Weinberg (1990) show how such sentences can be accommodated within a theory of generalized binding, but they cause real difficulties for a theory like L&S's. At LF (i) has a structure like (ii), where e_j is not antecedent-governed.

(ii) $[_{S'}[\text{who}_i \text{ who}_j]_i [_S e_i \text{ said } [_{S'} \text{ that } [_S[_{NP} \text{ books about } e_j] \text{ sold well}]]]]$

This suggests that if one adopts a theory in which antecedent government plays a major role, then lexical government is also needed. In other words, one requires a *disjunctive* theory of proper governors at LF; AHLW provide several methodological and empirical reasons against such a disjunctive theory of proper government. Moreover, e_j will be lexically governed only if the definition of lexical government is greatly enriched. *About* is not a potential lexical governor, because it is a preposition. *Book* does not govern e_j, and as Kayne (1981b) has observed, reanalysis cannot apply within the NP to "extend" the government domain of *books*, because this sort of operation generally does not apply within NPs. The last possibility is that the LF representation of (i) is (iii), where pied piping has applied.

(iii) $[_{S'}[\text{who}_i \text{ about who}_j]_i [_S e_i \text{ said } [_{S'} \text{ that } [_S[_{NP} \text{ books } [_{PP} e_j]] \text{ sold well}]]]]$

In such a case *books* could properly govern the preposition trace e_j. However, Huang (1982), Aoun (1985), and Hornstein and Weinberg (1990) argue against permitting pied piping to apply in LF. Therefore, sentences like (i) pose real problems for a theory of the kind L&S are pursuing.

6. This is because if the index of AGR were to be assigned to a direct object, then the object would be A-bound, having the same index as the subject NP, which is necessarily coindexed with the AGR. Hence, AGR cannot be an accessible SUBJECT for a direct object. Assigning the index of AGR to a subject NP, however, does not entail that that NP is coindexed with any other A-position, and therefore AGR is an accessible SUBJECT for a subject NP.

7. Aoun, Hornstein, and Sportiche (1981) allow an index i to percolate to COMP if the COMP contains only i-indexed items. AHLW drop this condition.

8. It is not clear whether this requirement concerning argument traces is universal. We present data from Polish below indicating that γ-marking of argument traces might not always apply as soon as it can.

9. AHLW remain agnostic about whether or not lexical government is required of adjunct traces. To our knowledge, there is no great difficulty with either assumption. However, it is natural to think that lexical or "head" government is related to parsing considerations. Essentially, heads identify gaps that the parse must deterministically find in building the tree. As is well known, adjuncts are probably parsed "flat" and not attached to grammatical nodes on-line; see Marcus 1981 for discussion. This suggests that these positions are not identified via heads. If so, it is not clear that such gaps should fall under the requirement of lexical government.

10. It is unclear how the PP/NP distinction is supposed to account for the proper government data. It would appear that L&S are tacitly assuming that only antecedent government holds for PP-traces. However, this still leaves it unclear how the gaps due to movement of *when* and *where* are to be handled, and it seems to suggest that overt PP extraction should pattern with adjunct movement, which is incorrect: (i) is far better than adjunct extraction from *wh*-islands. Indeed, it seems on a par with sentences extracting *who* or *what*.

(i) To whom did John wonder whether Bill talked?

No doubt these problems can be dealt with. However, they will involve additional mechanisms that AHLW's approach can comfortably do without.

11. Hornstein and Weinberg (1987) argue that Subjacency cannot be construed as a condition on derivation. They show how one can slightly modify the notion of Subjacency so that it will explain the properties of parasitic gaps. However, within this account Subjacency must be construed as an output condition.

12. This methodological point is illustrated well by the following story about two physicists at the zoo. They are observing some camels, and the first physicist asks the second, "Why are there one-humped camels and two-humped camels but not N-humped camels where N > 2?" After some reflection, the second physicist replies, "You've misunderstood; there are concave camels and convex camels and that's all there can be!"

13. Strictly speaking, this is not correct. *That* can only be inserted in the syntax and LF. L&S's theory could not derive the *that*-trace effect if *that* insertion were allowed in PF. In that case the embedded subject trace could be γ-marked at S-Structure and then *that* could be inserted later in PF, leading to unacceptability. To prevent this, L&S must assume that *that* cannot be inserted in PF. This raises two questions: (1) As noted above, right node raising data first discussed by Saito (1984) suggest that complementizer deletion can occur in PF; why not *that* insertion as well? and (2) Why can *that* deletion occur everywhere but PF?

The notion of semantic content is not very clear. There are theories of indirect discourse that treat the complementizer *that* as similar to the demonstrative *that* (see Davidson 1969). The real point, however, is that unless L&S further specify what they take semantic content to be, it will always be ad hoc to decide whether a property is or isn't due to semantic content.

14. Thanks to Andrzej Skrzypiec and Tadeusz Zabrocki for discussion of the Polish data and for correcting an error in an earlier version.

15. See L&S and Aoun, Hornstein, and Sportiche 1981 for relevant discussion. These discussions indicate that in languages with overt movement the presence of an overt *wh*-element in the selected COMP is not a *semantic* requirement. There is a semantic selection requirement, but it is met at LF and is universal. However, there appears to be an additional requirement in overt movement languages that a phonetically realized [+wh] element must appear in the COMP of verbs such as *wonder*.

Such facts cause some difficulties for L&S's approach. The assumption that *that* and *that* alone can meet selection restrictions at S-Structure and be head of COMP when it lacks an index is crucial to their account. They show that in (i) (their (70)) *where* must take embedded scope.

(i) Who wonders where we bought what?

To capture this, they argue that *where* must percolate its index at S-Structure to meet the requirement, specific to languages with overt movement, that COMPs marked [+wh] or [−wh] have the appropriate heads at S-Structure. This means that at S-Structure *where must* percolate its index to COMP so that selection requirements are met, and it is this requirement that prevents *where* from moving again in LF. But this means that only *that* can satisfy selection restrictions without percolating an index. In AHLW's theory all elements in COMP, including *that*, can have indices that may percolate to COMP, with the result that selection requirements are met uniformly.

References

Aoun, J. (1985). *A Grammar of Anaphora*. MIT Press, Cambridge, Mass.

Aoun, J., and N. Hornstein (1985). "Quantifier Types." *Linguistic Inquiry* 16:623–637.

Aoun, J., N. Hornstein, D. Lightfoot, and A. Weinberg (1987). "Two Types of Locality." *Linguistic Inquiry* 18:537–577.

Aoun, J., N. Hornstein, and D. Sportiche (1981). "Some Aspects of Wide Scope Quantification." *Journal of Linguistic Research* 1:69–95.

Besten, H. den (1983). "On the Interaction of Root Transformations and Lexical Deletive Rules." In W. Abraham, ed., *On the Formal Syntax of the Westgermania*. Benjamins, Amsterdam.

Bouchard, D. (1982). "On the Content of Empty Categories." Doctoral dissertation, MIT.

Chomsky, N. (1981). *Lectures on Government and Binding*. Foris, Dordrecht.

Chomsky, N. (1983). "Some Conceptual Shifts in the Study of Language." In L. S. Cauman, I. Levi, C. Parsons, and R. Schwartz, eds., *How Many Questions?* Hackett, Indianapolis, Ind.

Chomsky, N. (1986). *Barriers*. MIT Press, Cambridge, Mass.

Davidson, D. (1969). "On Saying That." In D. Davidson and J. Hintikka, eds., *Words and Objections*. Reidel, Dordrecht.

Freidin, R. (1978). "Cyclicity and the Theory of Grammar." *Linguistic Inquiry* 9:519–549.

Hornstein, N. (1987). "Levels of Meaning." In J. Garfield, ed., *Modularity in Knowledge Representation and Natural-Language Understanding*. MIT Press, Cambridge, Mass.

Hornstein, N., and A. Weinberg (1981). "Case Theory and Preposition Stranding." *Linguistic Inquiry* 12:55–91.

Hornstein, N., and A Weinberg (1990). "The Necessity of LF." *The Linguistic Review* 7.2:129–167.

Hornstein, N., and A. Weinberg (1987). "Parasitic Gaps Revisited." Ms., University of Maryland.

Huang, C.-T. J. (1982). "Logical Relations in Chinese and the Theory of Grammar." Doctoral dissertation, MIT.

Kayne, R. (1981a). "ECP Extensions." *Linguistic Inquiry* 12:93–133.

Kayne, R. (1981b). "On Certan Differences between French and English." *Linguistic Inquiry* 12:349–371.

Lasnik, H., and M. Saito (1984). "On the Nature of Proper Government." *Linguistic Inquiry* 15:235–289.

Lightfoot, D. W., and A. Weinberg (1988). Review article on Chomsky 1986. *Language* 64:366–383.

Marcus, M. (1981). *A Theory of Syntactic Recognition for Natural Language*. MIT Press, Cambridge, Mass.

Reinhart, T. (1979). "Syntactic Domains for Semantic Rules." In F. Guenthner and S. J. Schmidt, eds., *Formal Semantics and Pragmatics for Natural Languages*. Reidel, Dordrecht.

Rouveret, A., and J.-R. Vergnaud (1980). "Specifying Reference to the Subject: French Causatives and Conditions on Representations." *Linguistic Inquiry* 11:97–202.

Saito, M. (1984). "Three Notes on Syntactic Movement in Japanese." Ms., MIT.

Stowell, T. (1981). "Origins of Phrase Structure." Doctoral dissertation, MIT.

Vergnaud, J.-R. (1974). "French Relative Clauses." Doctoral dissertation, MIT.

Williams, E. (1980). "Predication." *Linguistic Inquiry* 11:203–238.

Williams, E. (1981). "Argument Structure and Morphology." *The Linguistic Review* 1:81–114.

Chapter 13

Lexical Case Phenomena   Robert Freidin and
Rex A. Sprouse

1 Basic Assumptions

The analysis of Case phenomena presented in this paper is based on a
theory of Case structure in generative grammar that has been developed
over the past decade (see Chomsky 1986 for some general discussion and
Chomsky 1981 for more technical details of the basic theory). Central to
this theory of Case is the Case Filter (1), which plays a crucial role in
determining the distribution of lexical (that is, phonetically realized) versus
nonlexical NPs (trace[1] and PRO) in sentences.

(1) *Case Filter*
    *NP [+phonetic matrix] that is not Case-marked

The Case Filter designates as ill formed any lexical NP that is not marked
for Case. Under the well-motivated assumption that the infinitival subject
position in such constructions is not marked for Case, the Case Filter
excludes infinitival indirect questions with lexical subjects as in (2a) (in
contrast to (2b), where the infinitival has a nonlexical subject—in this
instance PRO—and to (2c), where the indirect question is a finite clause).

(2) a. *John wondered $[_{CP}$ what$_i$ $[_{IP}$ Mary to say e$_i$ to Bill]].
    b. John wondered $[_{CP}$ what$_i$ $[_{IP}$ PRO to say e$_i$ to Bill]].
    c. John wondered $[_{CP}$ what$_i$ $[_{IP}$ Mary said e$_i$ to Bill]].

Under this analysis, it must follow that the Case Filter does not apply to
D-Structure representations. If it did, then raising constructions such as
(3a) would be ruled out at D-Structure where the lexical subject is in an
infinitival subject position, illustrated in (3b).

We would like to thank Len Babby, Caroline Heycock, Joan Maling, and Halldór
Sigurðsson for helpful comments on this paper.

(3) a. Fred$_i$ seems [$_{IP}$ e$_i$ to be happy].
   b. [$_{NP}$] seems [$_{IP}$ Fred to be happy]
   c. *It seems [$_{IP}$ Fred to be happy].
   d. It seems [$_{IP}$ Fred is happy].

(3c) shows that a lexical subject cannot occur in the infinitival subject position of a raising construction at S-Structure, in contrast to the subject position of a finite complement (for example, (3d)). (3a) demonstrates that the Case Filter applies after movement transformations.[2]

If Case assignment applies after movement transformations and the Case Filter applies to syntactic representations derived via movement rules, there must be a mechanism for assigning Case to an NP that occurs in a Case-marked position at D-Structure and is moved to a position at S-Structure that is not Case-marked, as with the moved *wh*-phrase in (2). For the analysis of (2), we assume that the *wh*-phrase *what* inherits a Case marking via the trace that it binds in the complement object position. Thus, this mechanism for Case assignment in such representations derived by movement transformations can be construed as Case inheritance via trace binding.

Though Case inheritance holds generally for movements *from* a Case-marked D-Structure grammatical function position (for instance, object position) *to* an S-Structure position that is not a grammatical function position (for instance, the specifier position of CP), it does not seem to apply in constructions where movement is between two grammatical function positions. In (3a), for example, where movement occurs between two grammatical function positions (matrix subject and complement subject), the moved NP is assigned Case by virtue of moving into a Case-marked position from a position that is not Case-marked. This assumes that a verb like *seem* does not assign objective Case to the complement subject position —in contrast to a verb like *expect*, which does, as illustrated in (4).

(4) Bernie expects [$_{IP}$ Adam to win].

The difference between *seem* and *expect* that is thought to account for the difference in Case-marking possibilities is that *seem*, in contrast *expect*, does not assign a semantic function (or θ-role) to its subject. Given this correlation between θ-role assignment and Case-marking possibilities, it is assumed that a verb that does not assign a θ-role to its subject may not Case-mark an NP that it governs.[3] This correlation generalizes to passive constructions as well, where the passive predicate does not assign a θ-role to its subject.

(5) a. *It was expected [$_{IP}$ Adam to win].
     b. Adam$_i$ was expected [$_{IP}$ e$_i$ to win].

Thus, even though the passive predicate governs the infinitival complement subject, it does not assign objective Case to this NP, in contrast to the corresponding active predicate in (4). Thus, (5a) constitutes a Case Filter violation. In (5b) the D-Structure complement subject has moved into matrix subject position where it is marked for nominative Case in the normal fashion. This correlation between the inability of a verb to assign a θ-role to a subject and its inability to assign Case to an NP it governs is generally referred to in the literature as *Burzio's generalization* (see Chomskey 1986: 139–141 and Burzio 1986: sec. 3.1). It is standardly assumed that this failure of Case assignment results from a mechanism of "Case absorption," which is induced by passive morphology for passive predicates.[4] As we will show, this assumption requires some revision when we consider the fuller range of Case phenomena, which includes lexial Case—that is, Case marking that is determined as a lexical property of certain heads (for instance, V and P) in some languages, as opposed to Case marking determined solely in terms of syntactic configuration (henceforth configurational Case).

The Case-theoretic analysis of (2)–(5) given above, essentially the standard analysis, rests on several assumptions that we would like to examine in some detail in this and the following sections. Let us suppose that Case is assigned as an index to the maximal phrasal projection of N (designated as NP, in contrast to nonmaximal phrasal projections, which will be designated as N*). At this point two basic questions arise about the process of Case assignment: (i) What is the formulation of the rule of case assignment? and (ii) Where does this rule apply in relation to other rules of grammar (in other words, where is Case assignment located in the organization of a grammar)?

The formulation of the rule (or rules) of Case assignment crucially affects the interpretation of the Case Filter. Suppose the rule of Case assignment is stated in the optimally simple form (6).

(6) Assign Case to NP.

(Motivation for this formulation comes from lexical Case phenomena, as we will discuss in section 2.) If (6) is interpreted as an optional rule, then its particular behavior with respect to various constructions (when it must apply versus when it cannot apply) will be determined by general principles of grammar. For example, when the rule fails to apply to a lexical NP in a canonical Case-marked position (for instance, subject of a finite clause), then the resulting representation violates the Case Filter. When Case is assigned to a lexical NP in a syntactic position that is not licensed for Case (for instance, infinitival subject position in indirect questions, as in (2)), then the resulting representation violates the general principle of proper Case licensing stated in (7).

(7) *Principle of Proper Assignment*
   Each Case index must be properly assigned.[5]

A Case index will be *properly assigned* where it is governed by an appropriate element (for instance, accusative Case governed by V and nominative Case governed by agreement). (7) is independently needed to exclude instances where (6) assigns the wrong Case index to an NP (for instance, assigning accusative Case to the subject of a finite clause). Thus, under the formulation of Case assignment as (6), the explanation for why indirect infinitival questions in English may not have lexical subjects has two parts, one of which involves the Case Filter and the other, a principle of Proper Assignment.

An alternative to (6) would be a set of specific rules, each of which assigns a particular Case to an NP in a particular configuration. This is assumed in the standard analysis, where the lexical subject of an infinitival indirect question would never be assigned a Case and would therefore always constitute a Case Filter violation. This solution conflates Case assignment with Case licensing, which, we will argue, need to be distinguished for the analysis of lexical Case phenomena.

A third alternative would be to consider (6) as an obligatory rule in Universal Grammar (UG). Thus, every NP in a given phrase marker will be assigned Case. Under this analysis the Case Filter is essentially useless. To account for the "Case Filter effects" under the standard analysis, the principle of Case licensing would be restricted to phonetically realized NPs. Note that this is necessary in any event since PRO as well as lexical NPs will be Case-marked if (6) is obligatory, and presumably Case-marked empty categories are not subject to any particular Case principle. (Evidence that PRO must be Case-marked in some instances is discussed in section 5.)

2   Lexical versus Configurational Case in Russian

This section initiates an investigation of lexical Case phenomena that we hope to show has significant consequences for the theory of grammar as it has been formulated in the standard work on generative grammar (see Chomsky 1981, 1986). We begin with a discussion of lexical versus configurational Case in Russian as a striking illustration of the different syntactic properties of these two types of Case. In the following discussion *configurational Case* designates a Case marking that is licensed solely in terms of a canonical syntactic configuration (for instance, accusative Case on an NP governed by V or nominative Case on an NP governed by the agreement element). *Lexical case* designates a Case marking on an NP that is associated with a particular lexical head and that differs from the canonical configurational Case that would otherwise be assigned to the NP that bears the lexical Case.[6]

In Russian the lexical versus configurational Case distinction shows up clearly with respect to the verbal object.

(7). a. *Configurational Case*

   Ivan   poceloval [$_{NP}$ ètu   krasivuju devušku].
   Ivan-NOM kissed   that-ACC pretty-ACC girl-ACC
   'Ivan kissed that pretty girl.'

   b. *Lexical Case*

   i. Ivan   pomog [$_{NP}$ ètoj   krasivoj devuške].
      Ivan-NOM helped   that-DAT pretty-DAT girl-DAT
      'Ivan helped that pretty girl.'

   ii. *Ivan   pomog [$_{NP}$ ètu   krasivuju devušku].
       Ivan-NOM helped   that-ACC pretty-ACC girl-ACC

In both (7a) and (7bi) the verb governs its NP object. The verbs *poceloval* and *pomog* differ in that the latter requires that its object occur in the dative Case—thus, (7bii), where the object is Case-marked accusative, is ill formed even though the NP occurs in a syntactic configuration that licenses accusative Case. Note that in Russian Case is also morphologically realized on lexical modifiers of N (such as determiners and adjectives). This can be accounted for if Case marking of all such lexical elements of the NP results from propagation of the Case index on NP to the lexical constituents in the government domain of the lexical head N.

Russian exhibits a striking difference between lexical and configurational Case with respect to nouns modified by certain numerals.

(8). a. *Configurational Case*

   Ivan   poceloval [$_{NP}$ pjat'   krasivyx devušek].
   Ivan-NOM kissed   five-ACC pretty-GEN girls-GEN
   'Ivan kissed five pretty girls.'

b. *Lexical Case*
  i. Ivan   pomog [$_{NP}$ pjati   krasivym   devuškam].
      Ivan-NOM helped   five-DAT pretty-DAT girls-DAT
      'Ivan helped five pretty girls.'
  ii. *Ivan   pomog [$_{NP}$ pjati   krasivyx   devušek].
      Ivan-NOM helped   five-DAT pretty-GEN girls-GEN

In the "quantified" noun constructions in (8), when the NP is marked for configurational Case, the numeral manifests the appropriate configurational Case marking, whereas the remainder of the NP is obligatorily marked in the genitive. In contrast, a lexically Case-marked NP shows no such "Case splitting," as illustrated in (8bi) versus (8bii). (For further discussion of these constructions, see Freidin and Babby 1984 and Babby 1987.)

The failure of Case splitting in lexically Case-marked NPs can be accounted for by assuming that lexical Case marking involves a head-to-head relation (like selection). Thus, the verb *pomoc'* 'help' has a lexical property that imposes dative Case on the head of its NP object. This can be stated as a syntactic feature $+\_\_\_$ DAT that is interpreted like a selectional feature (for instance $+\_\_\_$ [+animate] for the verb *frighten*) and specifies a head-to-head relation between a verb and its object. Satisfaction of lexical properties where they exist in languages seems to be obligatory and to take precedence over structural properties where the latter conflict with the former. This follows if (9) is a principle of grammar.

(9) *Principle of Lexical Satisfaction*
    Lexical properties must be satisfied. (Freidin and Babby 1984)

Given that lexical Case properties must be satisfied, it follows from our assumption that Case is assigned to a maximal phrasal projection that there can be no Case splitting in lexically Case-marked NPs. In order for a lexical Case index to propagate from NP to its head, all projections of N will be lexically Case-marked and presumably all lexical constituents governed by N as well.

3 The Principle of Lexical Satisfaction

The Principle of Lexical Satisfaction (PLS) has several consequences for the distribution of Case in Russian. In general, it prohibits Case alternations that are possible with configurational Case from occurring when lexical Case is involved. For example, NPs bearing configurational Case may also be marked genitive (the so-called partitive genitive), as illustrated in (10).

(10) *Partitive genitive/configurational Case*
    a. Ja xoču vodu.
       I want water-ACC
       'I want water.'
    b. Ja xoču vody.
       I want water-GEN
       'I want some water.'

As (11) demonstrates, this kind of alternation is not allowed with lexically Case-marked NPs.

(11) *Partitive genitive/lexical Case*
    a. Ivan prišel [$_{PP}$ s   vodoj].
        Ivan arrived   with water-INST
        'Ivan arrived with water.'
    b. *Ivan prišel [$_{PP}$ s   vody].
        Ivan arrived   with water-GEN
        'Ivan arrived with some water.'

In (11a) the object of the preposition *s* 'with' is lexically Case-marked instrumental; thus, (11b) violates the PLS.

The genitive of negation is another phenomenon is Russian where a configurational Case alternates with genitive Case marking. For example, the subject of a negative finite clause may occur in the nominative or genitive, as in (12).[7]

(12) a. Pticy   bol'še   ne pojavljalis'.
       birds-NOM any-more NEG appeared
       'The birds didn't come again.'
    b. Ptic   bol'še   ne pojavljalos'.
       birds-GEN any-more NEG appeared
       'No birds came again.'

Since subjects in Russian never occur with lexical Case, this alternation is generally permissible. However, with objects of verbs the genitive of negation is only permissible when it alternates with configurational accusative Case. This alternation, which is similar in character to (12), is illustrated in (13).

(13) a. Oni   ne odobrjajut inostrannye metody.
       they-NOM NEG approve-of foreign-ACC methods-ACC
       'They do not approve of (the) foreign methods.'

b. Oni   ne   odobrjajut inostrannyx metodov.
they-NOM NEG approve-of foreign-GEN methods-GEN
'They do not approve of foreign methods.'

In contrast to configurational Case, lexical Case does not alternate with the genitive of negation—as predicted by the PLS. Thus, in (14) the genitive of negation is not allowed in alternation with the lexically Case-marked objects in the dative and instrumental Cases.

(14) a.   Oni   ne   podražajut inostrannym metodam.
they-NOM NEG imitate   foreign-DAT methods-DAT
'They do not imitate foreign methods.'

   b.   *Oni   ne   podražajut inostrannyx metodov.
they-NOM NEG imitate   foreign-GEN methods-GEN

   c.   Oni   ne   upravljajut inostrannymi mašinami.
they-NOM NEG drive   foreign-INST cars-INST
'They do not drive foreign cars.'

   d.   *Oni   ne   upravljajut inostrannyx mašin.
they-NOM NEG drive   foreign-GEN cars-GEN

As far as we can determine, the lack of a Case alternation between a lexical Case and the genitive of negation is a purely syntactic phenomenon and has no apparent explanation in terms of semantic differences between verbs that require lexically Case-marked objects and those that take configurationally Case-marked objects.

Passive constructions provide yet another instance where lexical and configurational Case are clearly distinguished. As is standard in so many of the world's languages, the accusative object in an active sentence shows up as the nominative subject of the corresponding passive sentence. (15) gives the paradigm for configurational Case active/passive constructions.

(15) a.   *Active*
Ivan   čitaet knigu.
Ivan-NOM reads book-ACC
'Ivan is reading the book.'

   b.   *Passive*
      i.   Kniga   čitaetsja   (Ivanom).
book-NOM is-being-read Ivan-INST
'The book is being read (by Ivan).'

      ii.   *Knigu   čitaetsja   (Ivanom).
book-ACC is-being-read Ivan-INST

      iii.   *Čitaetsja knigu (Ivanom).

In effect, (15a) and (15bi) illustrate an accusative/nominative Case alternation for the underlying object *knig-*. (15bii) shows that accusative Case is not licensed in subject position, and (15biii) demonstrates that the passive form *čitaetsja* does not allow a Case-marked lexical object. Thus, Russian passives appear to involve something like the " Case absorption" hypothesized for English passives.

The corresponding paradigm for a verb that imposes lexical Case on its underlying object is given in (16).

(16) a. *Active*
       Rabotnik   podražaet inostrannym metodam.
       worker-NOM copies   foreign-DAT methods-DAT
       'The worker is copying foreign methods.'
   b. *Passive*
       i. *Inostrannye metody   podražajutsja rabotnikom.
          foreign-NOM methods-NOM are-copied   worker-INST
          'Foreign methods are being copied by the worker.'
      ii. *Inostrannym metodam   podražajutsja rabotnikom.
          foreign-DAT methods-DAT are-copied   worker-INST
     iii. *Podražajutsja inostrannym metodam   rabotnikom.
          are-copied   foreign-DAT methods-DAT worker-INST

(16bi) violates the PLS under the assumption that the lexical property +___ DAT of *podražat'* is not affected by passive morphology. If passive morphology had the effect of canceling the lexical Case property of the verb, then (16bi) should be well formed, contrary to the facts. Under the assumption that the NP *inostrannym metodam* is a constituent of VP, (16biii) shows that the passive form of the verb does not allow a lexical NP in object position. Passive morphology therefore has the same effect on configurationally and lexically Case-marked objects. (16bii) demonstrates that the lexically Case-marked NP is not properly licensed in subject position. Thus, there is no possible way to satisfy both the lexical Case property of the verb and the Case properties of the passive construction in general.[8]

4 Lexical Case Phenomena in German

Like Russian, German also exhibits lexical Case marking on the objects of verbs. Though the vast majority of the transitive verbs in the German lexicon take NP objects with accusative Case marking in active clauses, there also exists a set of verbs taking NP objects with dative Case marking. This contrast is illustrated in (17).[9]

(17) a. daß der Polizist   [$_{VP}$[$_{V'}$ den Spion   beobachtete]]
       that [the policeman]-NOM   [the spy]-ACC observed
       'that the policeman observed the spy'
    b. daß der Polizist   dem Spion   half
       that [the policeman]-NOM [the spy]-DAT helped
       'that the policeman helped the spy'

In (17a) the NP object of the verb *beobachten* 'observe' occurs in the configurational accusative Case (hence *den Spion*), whereas in (17b) *helfen* 'help' selects a dative Case object (hence *dem Spion*).

German passive constructions exhibit an asymmetry in the behavior of configurational and lexical Case. A configurationally Case-marked object (that is, in the accusative) in an active construction occurs as a nominative in the subject position of a corresponding passive construction—as in English and Russian. In contrast, a lexically Case-marked object in an active construction remains in object position with the same lexical Case in the corresponding passive construction, as illustrated in (18b) as compared to (18a).[10]

(18) a. daß der Spion   beobachtet   wurde
       that [the spy]-NOM observed-PPP was
    b. daß dem Spion/*der Spion   geholfen   wurde
       that [the spy]-DAT/[the spy]-NOM helped-PPP was

In the two passive constructions, the D-Structure object of *beobachten* occurs with nominative Case marking, in contrast to the D-Structure object of *helfen*, which retains its dative Case marking in the passive, as required by the PLS. The grammaticality of *daß dem Spion geholfen wurde* demonstrates that German differs from Russian in that the selection of lexical Case seems to be sufficient to license the occurrence of Case in a position that is not licensed for configurational Case.

Given that German does not have lexically Case-marked subjects,[11] it should be expected that a lexically Case-marked object will not occur in subject position at S-Structure. The motivation for this assumption will become clear in the discussion of Icelandic that follows. For German, then, Burzio's generalization does not extend to lexical Case phenomena, though it remains valid for configurational Case phenomena.[12]

5 Lexical Case Phenomena in Icelandic

In this section we will examine the distribution of lexical Case in Icelandic, where unlike what happens in Russian and German, lexically Case-marked

NPs may occur in subject position as well as object position. This difference has important consequences for the analysis of passives whose corresponding active forms take lexically Case-marked objects, as we will discuss in section 5.2.

5.1   Verbs Selecting Lexically Case-Marked Subjects

Several studies[13] have presented tests for syntactic subjecthood in Icelandic. These tests involve a range of phenomena including the binding of reflexives and reciprocals for all speakers, coordination, expletive insertion (*það*), correspondence with PRO in control structures, and a number of superficially heterogeneous word order facts. Though these properties often coincide with the nominative Case NP with which finite verb forms must agree morphologically, this is not always the case. Here we mention only three of these properties as an illustration.

For many Icelandic speakers, reflexive binding is subject-oriented; thus, nonsubjects cannot serve as antecedents to reflexives.[14] (19a) gives the standard nominative subject case; (19b) shows that a nonnominative NP may also bind a reflexive.

(19) a. *Haraldur$_i$*   las   bókina sína$_i$.
        Harald-NOM read book   his (+ REFL)

    b. *Haraldi$_i$*   batnaði   veikin   hjá   bróður
        Harald-DAT recovered-from the-disease at-the-home-of brother
        sínum$_i$.
        his (+ REFL)

    c. **Haraldur$_i$*   drap Friðrik$_j$ hjá   bróður
        Harald-NOM killed Friðrik-ACC at-the-home-of brother
        sínum$_{i/*j}$.
        his (+ REFL)

It is assumed that this NP is also a structural subject, like its nominative counterpart. (19c) illustrates the fact that nonsubjects cannot bind reflexives. Note that although subject-oriented binding of reflexives is not observed in all idiolects of Icelandic, the fact that it holds in some is enough to establish the argument for lexically Case-marked subjects.

A second property of nominative subjects shared with certain lexically Case-marked NPs is that in yes/no questions, the NP immediately follows the finite verb. This parallelism follows if both *Haraldur* in (20a) and *Haraldi* in (20b) are structural subjects.

(20) a. Hefur *Haraldur*   lesið bókina?
        has   Harald-NOM read the-book

(27) a. Í gær   var hjálpað   barni.
          yesterday was helped-PPP a-child-DAT
      b. Það var hjálpað   barni.
          it   was helped-PPP a-child-DAT

In (27) *barni* (DAT) appears in object position at S-Structure, as in the corresponding active.[16] (27) demonstrates that passive morphology in Icelandic blocks neither the assignment nor the licensing of lexical Case with respect to object position. Thus, the movement of a lexically Case-marked object to subject position, as in (23b), is not forced by any Case Filter effect—again in contrast to its configurational Case counterpart.

Further evidence that passive predicates may license the occurrence of lexical Case in object positions comes from the analysis of ditransitive verbs, where the Case marking on one or both objects may be lexically selected.

With respect to passivization possibilities there are two distinct classes of ditransitive verbs in Icelandic: the *gefa*-class, where the unmarked order of objects in active sentences is DAT–ACC, and the *skila*-class, representing all other occurring Case patterns. In both classes the ±recipient NP precedes the theme NP. The classes may be summarized schematically as in tables 13.1 and 13.2.

With verbs of class I either object may move to subject position in the passive. This is illustrated in (28a–c).

Table 13.1

	± Recipient	Theme	Examples
Class I	DAT	ACC	gefa 'give,' syna 'show', meina 'refuse'
Class II a.	DAT	DAT	skila 'return', lofa 'promise'
b.	DAT	GEN	óska 'wish', synja 'deny'
c.	ACC	DAT	svipta 'deprive', sæma 'award'
d.	ACC	GEN	spyrja 'ask,' minna 'remind'

Table 13.2

gefa 'give'			skila 'return'		
θ_1	θ_2	θ_3	θ_1	θ_2	θ_3
agent	recipient	theme	agent	recipient	theme
	DAT			DAT	DAT

(28) a. Ég   syndi henni bílinn.
     I-NOM showed her-DAT the-car-ACC

   b. Bílinn   var syndur   henni.
     the-car-NOM was shown-PPP/NOM her-DAT

   c. Henni   var syndur   bílinn.
     her-DAT was shown-PPP/NOM the-car-NOM

In (28b–c) either NP object may occur in the subject position, while the other remains in postverbal object position. (28b), like (27), shows that passive morphology blocks neither the assignment nor the licensing of lexical Case on objects. (28c) illustrates how the lexically selected Case marking on the object must be preserved at S-Structure when the object is moved to subject position. The nominative Case marking on the object NP in (28c) cannot be an instance of lexical Case, since nominative alternates with accusative in active sentences.[17]

A different pattern obtains for class II ditransitives. In this class, only the ± recipient NP may move to subject position. Compare paradigms (28) and (29).

(29) a.   Egill   skilaði stelpunni   pennanum.
         Egill-NOM returned the-girl-DAT the-pen-DAT

   b.   Stelpunni$_i$ var skilað t_i pennanum.
       the-girl-DAT was returned-PPP   the-pen-DAT

   c.   *Pennanum$_i$ var skilað   stelpunni t_i.
       the-pen-DAT was returned-PPP the-girl-DAT

Given that passive morphology does not block Case assignment via selection of lexical Case and that an NP that is lexically Case-marked by a passive form may occur in syntactic subject position (as illustrated in (29b)), the ungrammaticality of (29c) is surprising. The most salient structural difference between the two passive constructions is that in the S-Structure representation of (29b) the lexically Case-marked trace is adjacent to the V that governs it, whereas in the S-Structure representation of (29c) it is not. We will suppose therefore that there is a general prohibition (30) against a lexically Case-marked trace that is not strictly adjacent to a governing lexical head.

(30) *Strict Adjacency for Lexically Case-Marked Trace*
     A lexically Case-marked trace must be strictly adjacent to a governing head.

(30) has the flavor of a locality condition; though why this particular condition holds remains to be explained.[18] In any event, the explanation

cannot be that the lexical antecedent of the lexically Case-marked trace is in some sense "too far away," because it is possible to raise such antecedents out of their clauses, as illustrated in (31a).

(31) a. Henni$_i$ eru taldir   [t$_i$ hafa   verið sýndir   t$_i$ bílarnir].
       her-DAT are believed   to-have been shown-PPP   the-cars

    b. Bílarnir$_i$ eru taldir [t$_i$ hafa   verið sýndir   henni   t$_i$].
       the-car-NOM are believed   to-have been shown-PPP her-DAT

(31) demonstrates that either underlying object NP of a class I ditransitive may be raised to a higher subject position with the familiar pattern of Case retention by the lexically Case-marked NP and Case alternation with the structurally Case-marked NP. Note that (30) would also hold for the intermediate trace in (31a) given that the matrix verb *taldir* governs the adjacent trace—which is plausible given that the familiar "exceptional Case marking" (ECM) constructions exist in Icelandic, as in (32).

(32) a. Þeir telja [$_{IP}$ henni$_i$ hafa   verið sýndur   t$_i$
       they believe   her-DAT to-have been shown-PPP/NOM
       bíllinn].
       the-car-NOM

    b. Þeir telja [$_{IP}$ bíllinn$_i$ hafa   verið sýndan
       they believe   the-car-ACC to-have been shown-PPP/ACC
       henni   t$_i$].
       her-DAT

As noted above, we assume that because Icelandic allows lexical Case selection for subjects, it is possible to move lexically Case-marked objects into subject positions under the proper conditions—one of which is the adjacency constraint (30), as (33)–(34) demonstrate.

(33) a. Þeir telja [$_{IP}$ stelpunni$_i$ hafa   verið skilað   t$_i$
       they believe   the-girl-DAT to-have been returned-PPP
       pennanum].
       the-pen-DAT

    b. *Þeir telja [$_{IP}$ pennanum$_i$ hafa verið skilað stelpunni t$_i$].

(34) a. Stelpunni   er talið [$_{IP}$ t$_i$ hafa   verið skilað   t$_i$
       the-girl-DAT is believe   to-have been returned-PPP
       pennanum].
       the-pen-DAT

    b. *Pennanum$_i$ er talið [$_{IP}$ t$_i$ hafa verið skilað stelpunni t$_i$].

Both (33b) and (34b) violate (30).[19]

Underlying subject NPs that involve lexical Case selection also occur in both ECM and raising constructions.[20] (35) provides three standard examples of lexical Case selection for subjects, one in each of the nonnominative Cases of Icelandic.

(35) a. Verkjanna   gætir   ekki.
       the-pains-GEN is-noticeable not
     b. Mér   batnaði   veikin.
       me-DAT recovered-from the-disease-NOM
     c. Mig   vantar peninga.
       me-ACC lacks   money-ACC

The corresponding ECM constructions are given in (36).

(36) a. Hann   telur   [IP mig   vanta   peninga].
       he-NOM believes   me-ACC to-lack money-ACC
     b. Hann   telur   [IP barninu   hafa   batnað
       he-NOM believes   the-child-DAT to-have recovered-from
       veikin].
       the-disease-NOM
     c. Hann   telur   [IP verkjanna   ekki gæta].
       he-NOM believes   the-pains-GEN not to-be-noticeable

Raising of the lexical Case selected subject is possible both in "seem"-type constructions and in the passive of ECM constructions. This is illustrated in (37) and (38), respectively.

(37) a. Mig   virðist vanta   peninga.
       me-ACC seems to-lack money-ACC
     b. Barninu   virðist hafa   batnað   veikin.
       the child-DAT seems to-have recovered-from the-disease-NOM
     c. Verkjanna   virðist ekki gæta.
       the-pains-GEN seems not to-be-noticeable

(38) a. Mig   er talið   vanta   peninga.
       me-ACC is believed to-lack money-ACC
     b. Barninu   er talið   hafa   batnað
       the child-DAT is believed to-have recovered-from
       veikin.
       the-disease-NOM
     c. Verkjanna   er ekki talið   gœta.
       the-pains-GEN is not believed to-be-noticeable

These paradigms demonstrate that lexical Case selected subjects in Icelandic have the same syntactic distribution and behavior as configuration-ally Case-marked subjects at S-Structure.[21]

6 Case Assignment versus Licensing

At the outset we suggested that Case assignment and Case licensing might well be distinct phenomena, which would lead to a very different view of the Case Filter than has standardly been supposed. We can now provide further evidence for this view based on a subject-object asymmetry with respect to lexical Case in Icelandic. As noted in section 5, the selection of lexical Case in object position can license the occurrence of a lexical NP in object position of a passive predicate, in contrast to the configurationally accusative Case-marked object, which is not licensed in the same position. With a lexical Case selected subject, however, selection is not sufficient to license the occurrence of a lexical NP in subject position.

The asymmetry in Case licensing for lexically Case-marked subjects versus objects shows up when we compare the failure of passive morpho-logy to block (lexical) Case licensing (as, for example, in (27)) with the following paradigm.

(39) a. [að [PRO   batna   veikin]]   er venjulegt
         PRO-DAT to-recover-from the-disease-NOM is usual

    b. *[að [Jóni   batna   veikin]]   er mikilvægt
         Jon-DAT to-recover-from the-disease-NOM is important

The bracketed construction in (39) is an infinitival sentential subject. Crucially, the verb in this construction is one that selects a lexical Case subject (in the dative). Given the PLS, we assume that PRO is Case-marked dative[22] so that the lexical property of Case selection is satisfied in (39a). The fact that a lexical subject in the selected Case is not possible in this construction shows that lexical Case selection for subjects is not sufficient to license the presence of a lexical NP in that position. Thus, (39b) is ruled out as a violation of Case licensing.[23] Under this analysis, the lexical Case subjects in the following examples must be licensed configurationally, and not via lexical Case selection.

(40) a. Jóni   batnaði   veikin.
         Jon-DAT recovered-from the-disease-NOM

    b. Ég tel   [Jóni   hafa   batnað   veikin].
         I believe Jon-DAT to-have recovered-from the-disease-NOM

In (40a–b) the actual Case of the subject of *batna* is determined by the verb, but the licensing of the lexical NP is done independently in terms of its structural position. In (40b), for example, the licensing of the lexical NP *Jóni* is done by the matrix verb *tel*, which governs the NP. Thus, Case assignment and Case licensing appear to be distinct processes.

This same asymmetry holds with respect to lexically Case-marked derived subjects where lexical Case selection is to an object position. The paradigm corresponding to (39) is given in (41).

(41) a. [að PRO$_i$ vera hjálpað   e$_i$] er erfitt
         PRO-DAT to-be helped-PPP   is difficult

     b. *[(að) Jóni$_i$ vera hjálpað   e$_i$] er erfitt
         Jon-DAT to-be helped-PPP   is difficult

Given the PLS, we assume once again that PRO is Case-marked dative to satisfy the lexical Case selection property of *hjálpa* (namely, that it selects a dative object). Though this Case selection is sufficient to license the presence of a lexical NP in the object position of the passive predicate, it has no effect when the lexical object is moved to subject position, as illustrated in (41b). Thus, in (42) we have yet another example where Case assignment is determined via lexical Case selection, whereas the licensing of the lexical NP is done configurationally.

(42) Ég tel   [Jóni$_i$ hafa   verið hjálpað   e$_i$].
     I believe Jon-DAT to-have been helped-PPP

In this way, (41)–(42) provide striking confirmation of the subject-object asymmetry for lexical Case selection and that Case licensing is primarily a configurational phenomenon, with the exception of lexical objects in passive constructions, which can be licensed by lexical Case selection.

The separation of Case assignment and the licensing of lexical NPs leads us to a reconsideration of what have been assumed to be Case Filter effects. Our investigation of lexical Case phenomena suggests that the determination of the Case of an NP is not the relevant factor; rather, it is whether a lexical NP occurs in a configuration that licenses the presence of a lexical NP. If this view is correct, then the Case Filter as formulated in section 1 should be replaced by a licensing principle along the lines of (43).

(43) *Case Licensing Principle*
     A lexical NP (that is, one containing phonetic material) must occur
     in a Case-licensed position.

Under this analysis, (39b) and (41b) constitute violations of Case Licensing.[24]

Though it seems that the Case-licensed positions are exactly those where a configurationally Case-marked NP can occur, there is in Icelandic and

German the notable exception of the object position for passive predicates, where a lexically Case-marked NP can occur but the canonical configurational Case (accusative) cannot. One way to deal with this exception is to assume that a lexical NP can occur only in positions that receive a "structural index." Thus, objects of verbs and prepositions receive a structural index under government, and presumably subjects of finite clauses receive such an index via identification with respect to agreement. If, for reasons yet to be determined explicitly, a passive predicate cannot assign such a structural index, then its lexical object must get one from some other position. If, however, lexical Case selection for objects can assign such an index as a marked option (for instance, Icelandic versus Russian), then the Icelandic facts would follow. Note that we would have to assume that assignment of the structural index is to a position and remains on the position even when a lexical NP in that position is moved to another position (as in (41b)). Assuming that structural indices are assigned within a government domain, the asymmetry of licensing with respect to lexically Case-marked subjects and objects would follow since subject position (the position designated as SPEC of IP) is outside the government domain of V.[25]

What we have demonstrated in this paper is that lexical Case phenomena manifest some rather different properties from configurational Case phenomena. With configurational Case phenomena, Case assignment and Case licensing are not distinguished. The analysis of lexical Case, in contrast, requires a distinction between the assignment and licensing of Case —the former being a lexical property of certain heads and the latter a configurational property of constructions. As we have shown with the analysis of Icelandic, it is licensing rather than Case assignment that distinguishes well-formed from ill-formed constructions. Since this analysis will apply equally well to configurational Case phenomena, it is possible to revise Case theory by replacing the Case Filter with a principle of Case Licensing, as we have proposed.

Notes

1. Lasnik and Freidin (1981) give an argument that *wh*-trace must also be subject to the Case Filter. The argument concerns the deletion of *wh*-phrases in infinitival relative clauses where the deleted *wh*-phrase binds a trace in a subject position that is not marked for Case. The relevant paradigm is given in (i), where "∅" indicates the deletion site of the relative pronoun.

(i) a. [$_{NP}$ The man [$_{CP}$ who$_i$ [$_{IP}$ it is believed [$_{CP}$ t$_i$ [$_{IP}$ t$_i$ is lying]]]]] is a friend of mine.

    b. [$_{NP}$ The man [$_{CP}$ $\emptyset$ [$_{IP}$ it is believed [$_{CP}$ t$_i$ [$_{IP}$ t$_i$ is lying]]]]] is a friend of mine.

    c. *[$_{NP}$ The man [$_{CP}$ who$_i$ [$_{IP}$ it is believed [$_{CP}$ t$_i$ [$_{IP}$ t$_i$ to be lying]]]]] is a friend of mine.

    d. *[$_{NP}$ The man [$_{CP}$ $\emptyset$ [$_{IP}$ it is believed [$_{CP}$ t$_i$ [$_{IP}$ t$_i$ to be lying]]]]] is a friend of mine.

In the examples where the *wh*-phrase originates in the subject of a finite clause (ia–b), the relative pronoun may freely delete. In corresponding examples where the *wh*-phrase originates in the subject of an infinitival that is not marked for Case, an overt *wh*-phrase results in a Case Filter violation. The deletion of the *wh*-phrase, which would eliminate the Case Filter violation, does not change the unacceptability of the example. Lasnik and Freidin (1981) conclude that this results because the Case Filter holds for *wh*-trace as well as lexical NP. It seems to us that there may be another explanation for these data. For example, we might reasonably conjecture that deletion operations can only affect elements that are "properly licensed." If being marked for Case is part of proper licensing for lexical NPs, then the example that otherwise leads to the conclusion that *wh*-trace must be subject to the Case Filter can be ruled out on other (perhaps more general) grounds. This eliminates the apparent anomaly of grouping phonetically realized NP with *wh*-trace as being subject to the Case Filter.

2. Discussion of how Case assignment and movement transformations are ordered will be deferred to section 6. For the present discussion we will assume that Case assignment follows movement—that is, all movements.

3. We assume here that the relation *governs* is defined in terms of symmetric m-command, where a category X *m-commands* a category Y if the first maximal phrasal projection dominating X, a lexical category, also dominates Y, where X and Y are in a linear relation in the phrase marker. In particular, it is assumed that the matrix V governs the infinitival complement subject NP in both (3) and (4)—but crucially not in (2), where CP is assumed to be a barrier to government.

4. Note that the explanation of Case absorption as a consequence of passive morphology fails to generalize to the nonpassive raising cases shown in (3). Thus, the mechanism that underlies Burzio's generalization remains obscure (but see note 12).

5. This is essentially a principle of "Case checking"—see Jaeggli 1981, Vergnaud 1985, and Chomsky 1981 for discussion.

6. This distinction between lexical and configurational Case is first discussed in Freidin and Babby 1984 (written in 1981), which recasts and extends both the data and some fundamental ideas in Babby 1980b.

7. (12b) is from Babby 1980a: 13. Note that the subject NP may be marked with the genitive of negation only if the sentence is existential. In Freidin and Babby 1984 both the partitive genitive and the genitive of negation are treated neither as instances of lexical nor as instances of configurational Case, but rather as instances of "semantic Case," which is distinct from lexical Case in that it can alternate with configurational Case. See Freidin and Babby 1984 for a more detailed discussion.

8. Crucially, this is true no matter what analysis of Russian word order is adopted.

9. Here we follow the standard practice of giving German examples in the form of subordinate clauses in order to abstract away from effects of verb movements and topicalization. Note also that in German verbs assign Case to the left rather than to the right as in English.

10. The designation "-PPP" stands for "perfect passive participle." Note that there is no reason to suppose that the NP *dem Spion* in (18b) is a syntactic subject. As Cole et. al. (1980) have demonstrated, the D-Structure object in such sentences fails to exhibit any of the identifiable syntactic properties of S-Structure subjects in German: it fails to behave in coordinate structures as nominative Case subjects do, and there is no corresponding infinitival with a PRO subject in its place—properties in fact exhibited by nominative NPs. This is illustrated in the following paradigms, where the derived nominative subject participates in coordination and control structures in which the corresponding lexically Case-marked NP cannot.

(i) a. daß der Spion   beobachtet wurde
         that [the spy]-NOM observed   was
     b. daß der Spion   Angst hatte und beobachtet wurde
         that [the spy]-NOM fear had   and observed   was
     c. daß der Spion   hofft [PRO beobachtet zu werden]
         that [the spy]-NOM hopes   observed   to be

(ii) a. daß dem Spion   geholfen   wurde
         that [the spy]-DAT helped-PPP was
     b. *daß der Spion   Angst hatte und geholfen   wurde
         that [the spy]-NOM fear had   and helped-PPP was
     c. *daß dem Spion   hofft [PRO geholfen   zu werden]
         that [the spy]-NOM hopes   helped-PPP to be

On the basis of the contrast between (ib–c) and (iib–c) it is assumed that whereas the nominative NP in (ia) occurs in derived subject position, the dative NP in (iia) does not.

11. The same diagnostics mentioned in the preceding note support this conclusion. Thus, for the verb *ekeln* 'to be disgusted' in (i), the accusative NP is analyzed as occurring in VP, and not in the canonical subject position (which contains an empty expletive under some analyses).

(i) a. [$_{IP}$[$_{VP}$ Mich   ekelt]].
             me-ACC is-disgusted
     b. *daß ich Angst habe und ekelt
         that I   fear have and is-disgusted
     c. *daß ich hoffe [PRO nicht zu ekeln]
         that I   hope   not   to be-disgusted

12. Note that in Burzio 1986:178 the correlation referred to elsewhere as "Burzio's generalization" is restricted to accusative Case. Burzio does not discuss the possibility of lexical Case. See Babby 1990 for discussion of certain constructions in Russian where Burzio's generalization fails for configurationally Case-marked NPs as well.

13. The seminal studies in this regard are Andrews 1976 and Cole et al. 1980. Other important ones include Thráinsson 1979 and Zaenen, Maling, and Thráinsson 1985.

14. Here we abstract away from double object constructions in which an indirect object can bind (a subpart of) its direct object. See Sprouse 1989:262–307.

15. Yip, Maling, and Jackendoff (1987) observe that a lexical Case selected by a verb may not show up in the corresponding nominalization. The example cited is the verb *kenna* 'to teach', which selects a dative object, where the corresponding nominal *kennsla* 'teaching' occurs with a (presumably configurational) genitive object. Given that lexical Case selection is a lexical property and that lexical properties often change under nominalization, this fact should not be surprising.

16. There are ungrammatical forms that differ from (27) only in that the object is definite rather than indefinite.

(i) *Í gær   var hjálpað   barninu.
    yesterday was helped-PPP the-child-DAT

(ii) *það var hjálpað   barninu.
    it   was helped-PPP the-child-DAT

This is due to a definiteness effect rather than Case absorption via passive morphology, as (27) illustrates. See Sigurðsson 1989 for a detailed analysis.

17. See Zaenen, Maling, and Thráinsson 1985 and Sprouse 1989 for two different approaches to this problem.

18. See Zaenen, Maling, and Thráinsson 1985 for a different analysis based on rules that associate θ-roles and grammatical functions. Crucially, their analysis depends on one language-particular association rule—in contrast to (30), which is assumed to hold at the level of UG.

19. (34b) would be well formed if *pennanum* is interpreted as topic. If *pennanum* is placed in an unambiguous subject position, the sentence is ill formed, as illustrated in (i).

(i) *Var pennanum talið   [$_{IP}$ t$_i$ hafa   verið skilað   stelpunni   t$_i$]?
    was the-pen   believed   to-have been returned-PPP the-girl-DAT

We are indebted to Hálldor Sigurðsson for this information.

20. Here we ignore the standard assumption of the early 1980s that all nonnominative subjects must be VP-internal at D-Structure, an assumption with purely theory-internal motivation. For us, *underlying subject NPs* are NPs that can be syntactically realized only in subject position.

21. Again, see the relevant literature cited in note 6.

22. Even though dative Case is not morphologically realized in such infinitivals, we assume it is present to account for agreement between the subject and a modifier that occurs in the predicate.

(i) a. Barninu   batnaði   veikin   einu.
    the-child-DAT recovered-from the-disease alone-DAT/NEUTER/SG

b. Barnið   vonast til að [PRO]   batna   veikin
   the-child-NOM hopes [PREP] PRO-DAT to-recover-form the-disease
   einu.
   alone-DAT/NEUTER/SG

c. [að [[PRO]   batna   veikin   einum]]   er
      PRO-DAT to-recover-from the-disease-NOM alone-DAT/MASC/SG is
   venjulegt/erfitt
   usual/difficult

Joan Maling informs us that the ϕ-features of the predicative adjective in these constructions can vary and that they impose an interpretation on noncontrolled PRO. Interestingly, when the infinitival verb does not select a lexical Case for the subject, the predicative adjective shows up with nominative Case.

23. Case assignment is not the relevant mechanism to distinguish between (39a) and (39b). It seems to us highly improbable that if lexical Case is assigned to PRO (as required by the PLS), it would fail to be assigned to the lexical NP.

24. Note that this principle is distinct from the of Proper Assignment discussed in section 1. The latter is needed to rule out examples like *John saw he* that do not violate Case Licensing or the Case Filter.

25. There remains the question of where Case assignment applies with respect to movement operations. Among the several options that are available (for instance, assignment at D-Structure only, or at S-Structure only, or some combination), it is difficult to motivate one proposal over the others. It seems to us that any analysis should be compatible with our proposal regarding Case licensing, and therefore we will not pursue the issue further in this paper.

References

Andrews, A. (1976). "The VP Complement Analysis in Modern Icelandic." In *Proceedings of the Sixth Annual Meeting, NELS*. GLSA, University of Massachusetts, Amherst.

Babby, L. (1980a). *Existential Sentences and Negation in Russian*. Karoma Publishers, Ann Arbor, Mich.

Babby, L. (1980b). "The Syntax of Surface Case Marking." In *Cornell Working Papers in Linguistics* 1. Department of Modern Languages and Linguistics, Cornell University.

Babby, L. (1987). "Case, Prequantifiers, and Discontinuous Agreement in Russian." *Natural Language and Linguistic Theory* 5:91–138.

Babby, L. (1990). "Noncanonical Configurational Case Strategies." In *Cornell Working Papers in Linguistics* 10. Department of Modern Languages and Linguistics, Cornell University.

Burzio, L. (1986). *Italian Syntax*. Reidel, Dordrecht.

Chomsky, N. (1981). *Lectures on Government and Binding*. Foris, Dordrecht.

Chomsky, N. (1986). *Knowledge of Language: Its Nature, Origin, and Use.* Praeger, New York.

Cole, P., W. Harbert, G. Hermon, and S. N. Sridhar (1980). "On the Acquisition of Subjecthood." *Language* 56:719–743.

Freidin, R. and L. Babby (1984). "On the Interaction of Lexical and Structural Properties: Case Structure in Russian." In *Cornell Working Papers in Linguistics* 6. Department of Modern Languages and Linguistics, Cornell University.

Jaeggli, O. (1981). *Topics in Romance Syntax.* Foris, Dordrecht.

Lasnik, H., and R. Freidin (1981). "Core Grammar, Case Theory, and Markedness." In A. Belletti, L. Brandi, and L. Rizzi, eds., *Theory of Markedness in Generative Grammar: Proceedings of the 1979 GLOW Conference.* Scuola Normale Superiore, Pisa.

Sigurðsson, H. (1989). "Verbal Syntax and Case in Icelandic." Doctoral dissertation, University of Lund.

Sprouse, R. A. (1989). "On the Syntax of the Double Object Construction in Selected Germanic Languages." Doctoral dissertation, Princeton University.

Thráinsson, H. (1979). "On Complementation in Icelandic." Doctoral dissertation, Harvard University. Published by Garland Press, New York.

Vergnaud, J.-R. (1985). *Dépendances et niveaux de représentation en syntaxe.* Benjamins, Amsterdam.

Yip, M., J. Maling, and R. Jackendoff (1987). "Case in Tiers." *Language* 63:217–250.

Zaenen, A., J. Maling, and H. Thráinsson (1985). "Case and Grammatical Functions: The Icelandic Passive." *Natural Language and Linguistic Theory* 3:441–483.

Chapter 14

Some Notes on Economy of Derivation and Representation

Noam Chomsky

The past few years have seen the development of an approach to the study of language that constitutes a fairly radical departure from the historical tradition, more so than contemporary generative grammar at its origins. I am referring to the principles-and-parameters approach,[1] which questions the assumption that a particular language is, in essence, a specific rule system. If this approach is correct, then within syntax (excluding phonology)[2] there are no rules for particular languages and no construction-specific principles. A language[3] is not, then, a system of rules, but a set of specifications for parameters in an invariant system of principles of Universal Grammar (UG); and traditional grammatical constructions are perhaps best regarded as taxonomic epiphenomena, collections of structures with properties resulting from the interaction of fixed principles with parameters set one or another way. There remains a derivative sense in which a language L is a "rule system" of a kind: namely, the rules of L are the principles of UG as parameterized for L.

In the course of this recent work, certain unifying concepts have emerged —unifying in the sense that they appear throughout the components of a highly modular system: c-command and government, for example. There also seem to be fairly general principles involving these concepts, with wide-ranging effects. The Empty Category Principle (ECP), belonging to the theory of government, is one such principle, which has been the subject of much fruitful work. Such concepts and principles play a pervasive role in a tightly integrated system; slight modifications in their formulation yield a diverse and often complex array of empirical consequences, which have also been fruitfully explored in a large number of languages. And we may be fairly confident that much remains to be learned about just how they should be expressed.

I think we can also perceive at least the outlines of certain still more general principles, which we might think of as "guidelines," in the sense that they are too vaguely formulated to merit the term "principles of UG." Some of these guidelines have a kind of "least effort" flavor to them, in the sense that they legislate against "superfluous elements" in representations and derivations. Thus, the notion of "Full Interpretation" (FI) requires that representations be minimal in a certain sense. Similarly, the "last resort" condition on movement, which yields a partial explanation for the requirement that A-chains be headed by a Case position and terminate in a θ-position (the "Chain Condition"), has the corresponding effect of eliminating superfluous steps in derivations, thus minimizing their length.[4] What I would like to do here is to search for some areas where we might be able to tease out empirical effects of such guidelines, with a view toward elevating them to actual principles of language, if that is indeed what they are.

1 Preliminary Assumptions

Let us begin with a range of assumptions concerning language design, generally familiar though often controversial, which I will adopt without specific argument.

I will assume the familiar Extended Standard Theory (EST) framework, understood in the sense of the principles-and-parameters approach. We distinguish the lexicon from the computational system of the language, the syntax in a broad sense (including phonology). Assume that the syntax provides three fundamental levels of representation, each constituting an "interface" of the grammatical system with some other system of the mind/brain: D-Structure, Phonetic Form (PF), and Logical Form (LF).

The lexicon is a set of lexical elements, each an articulated system of features. It must specify, for each such element, the phonetic, semantic, and syntactic properties that are idiosyncratic to it, but nothing more; if features of a lexical entry assign it to some category K (say, consonant-initial, verb, or action verb), then the entry should contain no specification of properties of K as such, or generalizations will be missed. The lexical entry of the verb *hit* must specify just enough of its properties to determine its sound, meaning, and syntactic roles through the operation of general principles, parameterized for the language in question. It should not contain redundant information, for example, about the quality of the vowel, properties of action verbs generally, or the fact that together with its complement, it forms a VP.[5]

It has been suggested that parameters of UG relate, not to the computational system, but only to the lexicon. We might take this to mean that each parameter refers to properties of specific elements of the lexicon or to categories of lexical items—canonical government, for example. If this proposal can be maintained in a natural form, there is only one human language, apart from the lexicon, and language acquisition is in essence a matter of determining lexical idiosyncrasies. Properties of the lexicon too are sharply constrained, by UG or other systems of the mind/brain. If substantive elements (verbs, nouns, and so on) are drawn from an invariant universal vocabulary, then only functional elements will be parameterized. The narrower assumption appears plausible; what follows is consistent with it.[6]

The level of D-Structure is directly associated with the lexicon. It is a "pure" representation of θ-structure, expressing θ-relations through the medium of the X-bar-theoretic conditions in accordance with the Projection Principle. It may meet some strong "uniformity condition"[7] and in this sense be invariant across languages. I will assume here a two-level X-bar theory of the conventional sort, perhaps restricted to binary branching in accordance with Kayne's (1984) theory of "unambiguous paths."[8]

The level of PF is the interface with motor-perceptual systems, and the level of LF, the interface with conceptual systems.

Each of these levels is a system of representation of a certain type, its properties specified by principles of UG.[9] For a particular language, the choice of D-Structure, PF, and LF must satisfy the "external" constraints of the interface relation. Furthermore, the three levels must be interrelated by mechanisms permitted by the language faculty. The *structural description* of an expression E in language L includes—perhaps *is*—the set $\{d, p, l\}$, representations at the levels of D-Structure, PF, and LF, respectively, each satisfying the "external" conditions.[10] We may understand the *structure* of L to be the set of structural descriptions, for all expressions E. The language L itself consists of a lexicon, a specific choice of values for parameters of UG, and such rules as there may be, perhaps restricted to phonology. I understand *language* here in the sense of what I have called elsewhere *I-language*, where the terminology is intended to suggest "internalized" and "intensional." Intuitively, a language, so construed, is "a way of speaking and understanding," in a traditional sense; to have such a way of speaking and understanding (that is, to "have a language" or to "know a language") is to have the I-language as a component of the mind/brain. Note that although they are "external" to the computational system of language, the interface constraints are "internal" to the mind/brain. Other interactions—for example, those entering into the study of reference and truth—are a different matter.

In accordance with the general EST framework, I assume that the three levels are related to one another not directly, but only through the intermediary level of S-Structure, which is the sole point of interaction among the three fundamental levels. From this standpoint, S-Structure is a derivative concept. For a specific language L, its properties are determined by those of the fundamental levels, and by the condition that it be related to them by the appropriate principles. The level of S-Structure for L is the system that satisfies these conditions, something like the solution to a certain set of equations. Presumably, the principles of language design require that this "solution" be unique.

Exactly how these principles of interaction among levels should be understood is not entirely clear. I will adopt the general assumption that S-Structure is related to LF by iterated application of the principle Move α (substitution and adjunction), deletion, and insertion—that is, by the principle Affect α in the sense of Lasnik and Saito (1984)—and to PF by this principle and the rules of the phonological component.

The relation of S-Structure to the lexicon has been construed in various ways. I will assume that the relation is mediated by D-Structure, in the manner just outlined, and that D-Structure is related to S-Structure as S-Structure is related to LF and (in part) PF, that is, by iterated application of Affect α. Alternatively, it might be that D-Structure is determined by a chain-formation algorithm applying to S-Structure (or perhaps LF), and in this sense is "projected" from S-Structure as a kind of property of S-Structure; this algorithm will then express the relation of S-Structure to the lexicon.

The choice between these two options has been open since the origins of trace theory, before the principles-and-parameters approach crystallized. It has never been entirely clear that there is a real empirical issue here. There is, at best, a rather subtle difference between the idea that two levels are simply related, and the idea that the relation is a "directional mapping." Similarly, it is a subtle question whether the relation of S-Structure to the lexicon is mediated by a level of D-Structure with independent properties, serving as one of the fundamental "interface" levels. My own rather tentative feeling is that there is an issue, and that there is mounting, if rather subtle and inconclusive, evidence in support of the picture sketched earlier, with three fundamental interface levels and the D- to S-Structure relation interpreted as a directional mapping.[11] I will adopt this interpretation for expository purposes; it is rather generally adopted in practice, with results then sometimes reconstructed in terms of the alternative conception, a suggestive and possibly meaningful fact. Much of what follows is neutral between the several interpretations of this system.

S-Structure may also have to satisfy independent conditions, for example, the binding theory principles, conditions on identification of empty categories, and perhaps X-bar theory.[12]

2 Some Properties of Verbal Inflection

Of the many specific areas that might be investigated in an effort to clarify general guidelines of the kind mentioned earlier, I will concentrate on the topic of X^0-movement, a matter of particular interest because of its implications for the study of word formation, though there are other cases, for example, V-movement in the sense of Koopman (1983) and others. With respect to word formation, there are two major categories where the question of X^0-movement arises: complex predicates (causatives, noun incorporation, and so on), and inflectional morphology. There is an ongoing and illuminating debate about whether X^0-movement applies in these cases, and if so, how. I will not consider the first category, but will limit attention to inflection, assuming that it involves syntactic rules such as V-raising to INFL, and INFL-lowering to V (affix-hopping). I am thus assuming a sharp and principled distinction between inflectional morphology, part of syntax proper, and strictly derivational morphology, part of the lexicon, perhaps subject to such principles as right-headedness in the sense of Edwin Williams and others. I am, then, assuming something like the earliest version of the lexicalist hypothesis.

With respect to X^0-movement, there is one salient descriptive fact—the Head Movement Constraint (HMC)—and one central question about it: Is it reducible, partially or completely, to independently motivated principles of syntactic movement? Assume for now that XP-movement (A- and $\bar{\text{A}}$-movement) is given, with its principles, specifically the ECP. I will assume that the ECP reduces to the property of antecedent government, with the requirement that trace be properly governed relating to other conditions that have to do with "identification" of empty categories.[13] We then ask whether these same principles yield the HMC as a special case. If so, we have a true reduction of the HMC, and therefore reduction of properties of word formation to independently established principles of syntax.[14]

Let us begin with some recent ideas of Jean-Yves Pollock, based on work by Joseph Emonds on verbal inflection in English-type and French-type languages.[15] I will generally follow Pollock's proposals, adapting some of them in a different way and asking how they might bear on "least effort" guidelines and the status of the HMC.

Assume the X-bar-theoretic principle that $S = I''$, so that the basic structure of the clause is (1):[16]

(1)

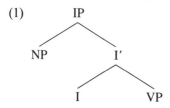

We leave open the question whether the subject NP is base-generated in place or raised from VP, as proposed in several recent studies, and many other questions that are not directly relevant.

Emonds's basic idea is that in French-type languages, V raises to I, whereas in English-type languages, I lowers to V. There is a variety of empirical evidence supporting this conclusion. Assume it to be correct. It will then follow that VP-adverbs, which we take to be generated under VP adjoined to another VP, are preverbal in English and postverbal in French, as in (2):

(2) a. John often kisses Mary.
    b. John completely lost his mind.
    c. Jean embrasse souvent Marie.
    d. Jean perdit complètement la tête.

But the English auxiliaries *have* and *be* behave approximately like ordinary verbs in French, as in (3):

(3) a. John has completely lost his mind.
    b. Books are often (completely) rewritten for children.

Therefore, the distinction is not raising in French versus lowering in English, but some other difference that requires French verbs and English auxiliaries to raise while barring this possibility for other verbs in English.

On other grounds, it has been postulated that the AGR element is "stronger" in French than in English. Assume this to be true. Assume further that weak AGR is unable to "attract" true verbs such as *kiss* or *lose*, though it can attract auxiliaries, whereas strong AGR attracts all verbs.[17]

Why should weak and strong AGR behave in this fashion? One possibility, suggested by Howard Lasnik, is that it is simply a morphological property: only strong AGR can accept a "heavy" element such as a verb, though any AGR can accept a "light" element such as an auxiliary. Another possibility, developed by Pollock, is that the difference reduces to θ-theory: strong AGR allows an adjoined element to head a θ-chain, but weak AGR does not. If the auxiliaries are not θ-markers, then they can raise to AGR without a violation of the θ-Criterion, but raising a true verb to weak AGR will lead to a violation of the θ-Criterion.

Looking at this option more closely, consider the effect of raising Y^0 to adjoin to X^0. This process yields the structure (4), where t is the trace of Y^0:

(4)

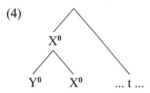

The theory of government must permit Y^0 to govern its trace t in this structure, so as to satisfy the ECP. If the theory of government precludes government of Y^0 from outside of the complex element X^0 formed by adjunction, then successive-cyclic movement of Y^0 will be barred; thus, causative formation, for example, cannot escape the HMC (assuming it to reduce to the ECP) by successive-cyclic movement. I will assume this to be the case, putting a precise formulation aside.

The chain (Y^0, t) will therefore be properly formed in (4) with regard to the ECP. Suppose that Y^0 is a θ-marker. Then t must be able to θ-mark; the θ-marking property of Y^0 must be "transmitted" through the chain. That will be possible if X^0 is strong, but not if it is weak. We will therefore have a θ-Criterion violation if a θ-marker Y^0 is adjoined to weak AGR.

Suppose that instead of raising Y^0 to adjoin to X^0 to yield (4), we lower X^0 to adjoin to Y^0. This process again forms the complex element $[Y^0-X^0]$, but with a structure different from (4)—namely, (5)—t being the trace of X^0:

(5)

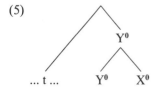

Here the lower Y^0 is the head of the construction, and we may assume that whatever the character of X^0, Y^0 will retain all relevant relations to other elements and will therefore retain the capacity to θ-mark a complement. The normal properties of adjunction, then, have the desired effect, as Pollock observes: lowering of weak AGR to the verb v does not bar θ-marking of the complement, but raising of v to weak AGR does bar θ-marking.

Pollock extends the domain of observation further to negation, proposing the following more articulated structure in a Kayne-style unambiguous path analysis:

(6)

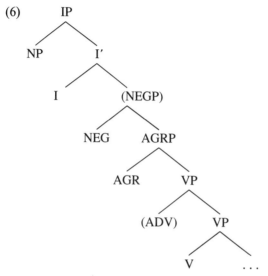

Here I may be [±finite] and NEG is English *not* or French *pas*.[18] This representation, separating I and AGR, eliminates the odd dual-headedness of INFL in earlier treatments. The assumption is that infinitives have (generally vacuous) AGR.

Suppose that V raises to AGR. Then we have the S-Structure order Verb-Adverb-Object, as with English auxiliaries or French verbs generally. If AGR lowers to V, we have the order Adv-V-Obj, as with English nonauxiliary verbs. If V raises to AGR and the complex then raises further to I, we have such forms as (7):

(7) a. John has not seen Bill.

  b. Jean (n') aime pas Marie.
     Jean (*ne*) love NEG Marie
     'Jean does not love Marie.'

If V raises to AGR but not to I, we have (8) in French, where *sembler* 'seem' in (8a) contrasts with *être* 'be' in (8b):

(8) a. ne pas sembler heureux
         ne NEG seem   happy
         'not to seem happy'
     b. n'être pas heureux
         ne be NEG happy
         'not to be happy'

The properties illustrated in (7) and (8) follow on the assumption that [+ finite] is strong and [− finite] is weak. Being strong, [+ finite] allows the verb *aime* to adjoin to it, crossing NEG (*pas*), in (7b). Being weak, [− finite] does not permit the verb *sembler* to adjoin to it, crossing NEG, in (8a), though the auxiliary *être* can raise to weak I just as auxiliaries can raise to weak AGR.

Though the V-raising rule in French is obligatory for tensed clauses, it is optional for infinitives. Thus, alongside (8b) we have the option (9a); and alongside the form V-Adv-NP (obligatory for finite verbs as in (2c)) we have (9b):

(9) a. ne pas être heureux
     b. souvent paraître triste
         often   seem   sad

(9a) results from failure of *être* to raise over NEG to [− finite] I, and (9b) from failure of *paraître* to raise over the adverb to AGR in the infinitive. We return in section 3.2 to the question of why raising should be optional just in the case of the infinitive, and in section 5 to further questions about the nature of AGR. Tentatively, let us assume the analysis just given, putting aside the optionality with infinitives.

At S-Structure the verb must typically be combined with its various affixes, to yield the proper forms at PF; the various affixes in (6) must form a single complex with a verb. Let us suppose that these affixes share some unique feature to guarantee proper association at S-Structure. Thus, any series of rule applications that separates them is barred by an appropriate S-Structure condition, and we need not be concerned if the rule system permits "wild" applications of rules that would leave affixes improperly scattered among the words of the sentence generated. Note that other improper rule applications are barred by the requirement that items lexically identified as affixes be properly "attached" at S-Structure.

Assuming Pollock's parameter, we have strong and weak inflectional affixes. The [+ finite] choice for I (tensed) is strong and the [− finite] choice (infinitive) is weak. AGR is strong in French, weak in English. The basic facts follow, with some idealization of the data.

Pollock observes that earlier stages of English were very much like French, suggesting plausibly that a change in the AGR parameter led to the collection of phenomena that differentiate the languages in their current state. Some of the forms reflect D-Structure directly: for example, (9a–b) in French and their English equivalents. Other forms reflect the consequences of raising of V to AGR or to I, as illustrated. Pollock points out that unitary treatment of the comparative data—with the array of facts involving tense-infinitive, negation and adverbs, verbs and auxiliaries—relies crucially on analysis of Tense and Agreement morphemes "as separate syntactic entities at an abstract level of representation," namely, D-Structure. The analysis, he concludes, provides support for the rigid X-bar-theoretic condition of single-headedness and the consequent distinction between AGR and I, and for the distinction between D- and S-Structure representation.

3   A "Least Effort" Account

3.1   Minimizing Derivations

Let us now see how an analysis of this nature would bear on the guidelines we have been considering. I will put aside the relation of S-Structure to PF and D-Structure to lexicon. Thus, we are considering the relations among D-Structure, S-Structure, and LF. For expository convenience, I will refer to the relation of D- to S-Structure as *overt syntax* (since the consequences of the operations relating these levels are commonly reflected at PF).

The analysis of verbal inflection outlined in section 2 relies crucially on the principle that raising is necessary if possible. This would follow from the assumption that shorter derivations are always chosen over longer ones. The reason is that lowering of an inflectional element INF, as in the case of English true verbs, yields an improper chain $(t, \ldots, \text{INF})$, where INF is adjoined to V at S-Structure to form $[_V \text{V–INF}]$ and t is the trace of INF, which c-commands it. Subsequent LF raising of $[_V \text{V–INF}]$ to the position of t is therefore required to create a proper chain. The result is essentially the same as would have been achieved with the shorter derivation that involves only raising in the overt syntax. Therefore, by a " least effort" condition, only the latter is permissible.

A closer look shows that the "least effort" condition cannot reduce simply to the matter of counting steps in a derivation. Consider English interrogatives. Let us assume that an interrogative construction has the complementizer Q ($[+wh]$) to distinguish it at D-Structure from the corresponding declarative, triggering the appropriate intonational structure at

PF and the proper interpretation at LF. If Q is furthermore an affix, then it must be "completed" in the overt syntax by X^0-raising. The D-Structure representation (10) will yield, by lowering, an S-Structure representation with the verb $[V-AGR-I]^{19}$ and traces in the positions of I and AGR:

(10) Q John I AGR write books

The resulting form is indistinguishable from the declarative at PF and is furthermore illegitimate (at S-Structure) if Q is a real element, as postulated. To permit an output from the legitimate D-Structure representation (10), English makes use of the dummy element *do* to bear the affix, so that lowering does not take place; rather, AGR and I adjoin to *do*. Let us call this process *do*-support, a language-specific process contingent upon the weakness of AGR; for expository purposes, assume it to be a rule of the overt syntax inserting *do* in the Modal position, hence *do*-insertion, attracting the raised affixes and then raising to Q. Given this device, we can form *Did John write books?* from (10).[20]

The same device, however, permits the illegitimate form *John did write books* (*do* unstressed) alongside *John wrote books*, both deriving from the declarative form corresponding to (10) (lacking Q). In fact, this option is not only available but in fact arguably obligatory if shorter derivations are always preferred. The reason is that the illegitimate form requires only the rule of *do*-insertion and raising, whereas the correct form requires overt lowering and subsequent LF raising.

To yield the correct results, the "least effort" condition must be interpreted so that UG principles are applied wherever possible, with language-particular rules used only to "save" a D-Structure representation yielding no output: interrogative forms without modal or non-θ-marking verbs, in this case. UG principles are thus "less costly" than language-specific principles. We may think of them, intuitively, as "wired-in" and distinguished from the acquired elements of language, which bear a greater cost.[21]

Consider now a negative expression with the D-Structure representation (11):

(11) John I NEG AGR write books

The correct derivation involves *do*-insertion and raising of AGR to form the complex verb $[do-I-AGR]$, with the S-Structure representation (12):

(12) John did (does) not write books

But again we face a problem: Why doesn't I lower to AGR, then to V, yielding the complex verb $[V-AGR-I]$ as in the nonnegated form, so that at S-Structure and PF we have *John not wrote (writes) books?* Then LF raising will apply, eliminating the improper chain, exactly as in the case of the nonnegative counterpart. This process involves only the UG principles of overt lowering and LF raising, avoiding the language-particular rule of *do*-insertion. It is therefore not only a permissible derivation, but is actually required by the "least effort" condition, as just revised.

A partial solution to this problem is provided by the HMC. The process of LF raising has to cross NEG, thus violating the HMC. There is therefore only one legitimate derivation: the one involving *do*-insertion, which is therefore required in these cases.

We are thus assuming that, given a well-formed representation at D-Structure, we necessarily apply the least costly derivation that is legitimate to yield an S-Structure and, ultimately, a PF output.

But several further questions immediately arise. Consider the French counterpart to (11) or, equivalently, the English form (13):

(13) John I NEG AGR have written books

Here the correct derivation requires that the verb *have* raise to AGR, then to I, crossing NEG, to yield (14):

(14) John has not written books.

The same will be true of a main verb in French, as in the counterpart to the D-Structure representation (11). If the HMC blocks the unwanted derivation with LF raising over NEG in the case of (11), then why does it not equivalently block the *required* derivation with overt raising over NEG in the case of (14) and the French equivalent to (11)?

Note that a similar question also arises in the case of (11). Thus, the required derivation involves raising of AGR over NEG to I to form the complex verb [*do*–I–AGR] after *do*-insertion. Why, then, does overt raising of AGR over NEG not violate the HMC?[22]

To deal with these questions, we have to consider more carefully the nature of deletion. Clearly, we cannot delete an element if it plays a role at LF: for example, the trace of a verb. But such considerations do not require that the trace of AGR remain at LF, since it plays no role at that level. We might, then, suppose that the trace of AGR is deletable (I will return to this conclusion in a more general setting in section 6.2). We must also determine exactly what we intend the process of deletion to be. There are various possible answers to this question, generally not addressed because they go beyond known empirical consequences. In the present context, however, there are empirical consequences, so a specific decision must be reached. One plausible answer is that deletion of an element leaves a category lacking features, which we can designate [e]. The deletion leaves a position but no features, in particular, no categorial features. Deletion of $[_{AGR} \, t]$, the trace of AGR, leaves $[e]$, and by X-bar-theoretic principles, the dominating category AGRP is now eP, an XP with no features.[23] That is a satisfactory conclusion, since AGRP plays no role at LF.

Making these assumptions, let us return to the problems we faced. Consider first the raising of AGR to I over NEG to form $[do–I–AGR]$ in the correct derivation from the D-Structure representation (11). This process will, in fact, violate the HMC regarded as a condition on derivations, but there will be no ECP violation at LF once the trace of AGR is deleted. Recall that we are taking the ECP to be a condition on chains, along the lines discussed in Chomsky 1986a, thus not applicable to the empty categories PRO, pro, and e, but only to trace. We therefore have no ECP violation, though we do have an HMC violation. But if the HMC is reducible to the ECP, then we can dismiss the HMC as a descriptive artifact, valid only insofar as it does in fact reduce to the ECP. The present case would be one in which the HMC does not reduce to the ECP and is therefore inoperative.

Let us now turn to the more general question. Why does LF raising of $[V–AGR]$ to I over NEG violate the HMC, whereas overt raising of $[V–AGR]$ to I over NEG (as in the case of English auxiliaries and all French verbs) does not violate the HMC? To answer this question, we must again consider more closely the structures formed by adjunction.

Let us return to the D-Structure representations (11) and (13), repeated here in (15):

(15) a. John I NEG AGR write books
      b. John I NEG AGR have written books

Lowering of I to AGR forms the element $[_{AGR} \, AGR–I]$, leaving the trace t_1. Further lowering of the complex element to V forms $[_V \, V \, [_{AGR} \, AGR–I]]$, a verb, leaving the trace t_{AGR}. But this trace deletes, leaving $[e]$, a position lacking features. Applying these processes to (15a), then, we derive the S-Structure representation (16):

(16) John t_1 NEG [e] $[_{VP}[_V \,$ write $[_{AGR} \, AGR–I]]$ books]

We now turn to LF raising. The complex V raises to the position $[e]$, leaving a V-trace; we may assume this to be substitution, not adjunction, on a natural interpretation of recoverability of deletion. We now raise this element to the position t_1, again leaving a V-trace. The latter is of course undeletable, being part of a chain with substantive content at LF. This step violates the HMC; and its residue, (17), violates the ECP at LF:

(17) John [$_V$ write–AGR–I] NEG t$'_V$ [$_{VP}$ t$_V$ books]

Here antecedent government of t$'_V$ is blocked by the intermediate element NEG, under the Minimality Condition. We therefore have a violation of the ECP at LF. In this case the HMC, reducing to the ECP, is a valid descriptive principle, violated by the derivation.

Note that the situation contrasts with overt raising of V to AGR, then to I over NEG, as in the case of (15b) (and all French verbs). Here raising to AGR is permitted, therefore obligatory by the "least effort" condition. Following the derivation step by step, we first raise V to AGR, leaving V-trace and forming [$_{AGR}$ V–AGR]. We then raise this complex element to I over NEG, forming [$_I$ V–AGR–I] and leaving AGR-trace; this step violates the HMC. The AGR-trace now deletes, leaving [e]. We thus derive the form (18):

(18) John [$_I$ have–AGR–I] NEG [e] [$_{VP}$ t$_V$ ...]

This representation induces no ECP violation,[24] though the derivation that formed it violates the HMC. Again, we see that the HMC is descriptively valid only insofar as it reduces to the ECP.

The problems that arise therefore receive straightforward solutions when we consider the nature of adjunction, as standardly defined. Note, however, the crucial assumption that "unnecessary elements" delete at LF; we return to the matter in section 6.2. Also crucial is the assumption that D-Structure relates to S-Structure by a directional mapping, a step-by-step derivational process. In the S-Structure (and LF) representation (18), *have* is "too far" from its trace t_V for the ECP to be satisfied, but the locality requirement has been satisfied in the course of the derivation from D- to S-Structure.[25]

3.2 The Element I

Let us turn to some speculations on the status of IP and the optionality observed earlier in French infinitival constructions. If I is [+finite] (I = T = tense), then it presumably cannot be deleted, since a tensed phrase plays an LF role. Therefore, we have either overt raising to [+finite] or LF raising to the position of its trace.

There is, however, no strong reason to suppose that the same is true of [−finite] (infinitive). If [−finite] and its IP projection play no role at LF, then this element should be deletable, just as AGR (actually, t_{AGR}) is. Suppose that this is the case.[26]

Before considering the consequences, we have to resolve a minor technical question about infinitival inflection: Does [−finite] attach to the base form of the verb or does it not? Little is at stake in the present connection; for concreteness, let us adopt the former alternative.

Keeping now to French, consider verbs that can raise to weak inflection, for example, *être* 'be'. Suppose that we have the form (19), with *être* raised to AGR:

(19) ne I pas être heureux

In this construction, *être* may raise further to I in the normal way, yielding the form (20):

(20) n'être pas heureux

But there is also another option. The form *être* may remain in place, with I lowering to [*être*–AGR], leaving not trace but [*e*]. This is permissible on the assumption we are now considering: that [−finite] is deletable, playing no LF role. The resulting form is (21), identical to (19) but with [*e*] in place of I:

(21) ne pas être heureux

Each of these options involves one rule application. Therefore, the two are equally costly and we have genuine alternatives, in conformity with the "least effort" guideline. As observed earlier, these two cases are both permitted in French.

Consider now a true verb, such as *paraître* 'seem'. We know that it cannot raise to I, so I must lower to AGR, leaving [*e*]. Suppose now that *paraître* is in an adverbial construction, as in the D-Structure representation (22):

(22) souvent paraître triste

If *paraître* raises to AGR in the usual way, we derive the form (23):

(23) paraître souvent triste

Suppose, however, that [AGR–I] lowers to the V-position, leaving [*e*] rather than trace. The resulting form is (22) itself, a legitimate form with no ECP violation. Again we have two options, (22) and (23), each involving a single rule, each legitimate. The reason is that AGR and its projection, exactly like [−finite] I and its projection, play no role at LF and are therefore deletable.

We conclude, then, that although there are no options in the finite forms, their infinitival counterparts allow the options illustrated. Along these lines, we might hope to incorporate Pollock's observations about the range of options for infinitives as distinct from tensed clauses.

We have not settled the precise character of LF raising to the trace of [+finite]. What is required is that the finite (tensed) phrase, functioning at

LF, not be deleted. The requirement is met under LF raising, which might be either adjunction or substitution. If it is adjunction, the resulting form will be (24), which heads TP, where T = [+ finite] (tense):

(24) $[_T[_V V [_{AGR} AGR-T] t_T]]$

We must then take this to be a legitimate form, with T c-commanding its trace t_T. If the LF raising is substitution, we derive (25) in place of (24) in the I-position, now heading VP:

(25) $[_V V [_{AGR} AGR-T]]$

The question of government of t_T does not now arise, but we must ask just how the element (25) in the I-position satisfies the requirement of tense interpretation at LF. The further implications are not clear, and I will leave the question open.

4 Summary: On Economy of Derivation

Summarizing, we have selected one particular option available for sharpening the notion of deletion, previously left undetermined; and we have made a distinction between deletable and nondeletable elements on the basis of their LF role. These moves are natural and seem generally unexceptionable. Apart from this, we have kept largely to familiar assumptions along with Pollock's basic analysis, modified in various ways. Attending to the meaning of the formalism for adjunction and other notions, the basic empirical observations follow.

Some more general conclusions are also suggested. First, the HMC is not a principle, though it is largely accurate as a descriptive generalization. The principle is valid only insofar as it reduces to the ECP, and it can be violated when other processes overcome a potential ECP violation by eliminating an "offending trace." Second, we now have a somewhat more specific interpretation of the "least effort" guidelines. The condition requires that the least costly derivation be used, eliminating the S-Structure and PF consequences of more costly derivations. To a first approximation, cost is determined by length; the condition requires the shortest derivation, so that overt raising is required where it is possible. But "cost" has a more subtle meaning: UG principles are less costly than language-specific rules that are contingent upon parameter choices (see note 20); and *do*-insertion, in particular, functions only as a "last resort," to "save" a valid D-Structure representation that otherwise underlies no legitimate derivation.

Other well-known facts suggest further refinement of the notion of "least costly derivation." Consider, for example, a standard case of long-distance movement, as in (26):

(26) How do you think that John said [that Bill fixed the car t]?

The sentence is well formed by successive-cyclic movement. There is, of
course, a shorter—namely, one-step—derivation, in which case, on the
general principles so far assumed, the sentence should have a status no
different from (27):

(27) How do you wonder why John asked [which car Bill fixed t]?

The shorter derivation does not bar the longer successive-cyclic one in this
case. In fact, the *shorter* derivation is barred; it is not the case that (26) is
structurally ambiguous, with one interpretation given by the legitimate
derivation and another deviant interpretation given by the illegitimate
shorter one. Hence, it must be that the measure of cost prefers short
movement to long movement and thus requires the former where possible.

In such ways as these, we may proceed to refine the "least effort"
conditions on movement, raising them from the status of imprecise guidelines to actual principles of UG.

Notice that this approach tends to eliminate the possibility of optionality
in derivation. Choice points will be allowable only if the resulting derivations are all minimal in cost, as in the case of French infinitival constructions discussed earlier. Any remaining examples of optional rule application would then have to be assigned to some other component of the
language system, perhaps a "stylistic" component of the mapping of
S-Structure to PF. This may well be too strong a conclusion, raising a
problem for the entire approach.

5   The Agreement System: Some Speculations

A number of questions arise about the status of AGR in the system just
outlined. Following Pollock, we have assumed that AGR is dominated by
Tense. But assuming these elements to be dissociated, one might rather
expect AGR to dominate Tense, since it presumably stands in a government relation with the subject in tensed clauses, to yield the standard
subject-verb agreement phenomena. There is morphological evidence, discussed by Adriana Belletti in work to appear, suggesting the same conclusion: in a number of languages where it is possible to obtain relevant
evidence, the agreement element is "outside" the Tense element in the
verbal morphology, as would follow from successive adjunction if AGR
dominates the Tense element. Nevertheless, facts of the kind just illustrated

lead Pollock to postulate a position intermediate between Tense and VP, what he takes to be the AGR-position.

These conflicts might be reconciled by noting that there are actually two kinds of Verb-NP agreement: with subject and with object. Hence, pursuing the basic lines of Pollock's analysis, we should expect to find two AGR elements: the subject-agreement element AGR-S and the object-agreement element AGR-O. On general assumptions, AGR-O should be close to V, and AGR-S close to the subject, therefore more remote from V.[27] The element AGR in Pollock's structure (6), which we have adopted as the basis for discussion, would therefore be AGR-O, providing an intermediate position for raising. It would then be unnecessary to suppose that infinitives necessarily carry (generally vacuous) subject agreement, though we would now be assuming that AGR-O is present even for nontransitives. Pollock's structure (6) would now be more fully articulated as (28), where AGR-S = I, the head of I′ and IP, and F is [±finite]:

(28)

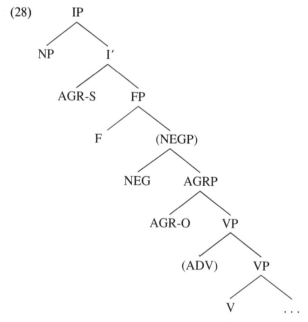

In terms of this proposal, the preceding analysis considered only the structure dominated by FP, which is identical with Pollock's (6) (notations aside).[28]

These conclusions are consistent with Kayne's (1989) analysis of participle agreement in a variety of Romance languages. Kayne assumes an AGR element heading AGRP, with VP as its complement. This element is distinct from the AGR involved in subject agreement; we may take it to be AGR-O. Thus, we have such D-Structure representations as (29), for a French participial construction, putting aside I and AGR-S:

(29) NP V_{aux} [$_{AGRP}$ AGR [$_{VP}$ V-participle NP]]

If the NP object is a *wh*-phrase that undergoes raising, then the participle may or may not agree with it. Kayne assumes that these options correspond to two distinct structures, as in (30), where t, t' are the traces of the *wh*-phrase 'how many tables':

(30) a. combien   de tables [Paul a   [$_{AGRP}$ t' [$_{AGRP}$ AGR [repeint-   t]]]]
        how many (of) tables Paul has   repainted
     b. combien de tables [Paul a [$_{AGRP}$ AGR [repeint- t]]]

The two forms are synonymous, meaning 'How many tables has Paul repainted?' In (30a) the participle surfaces as *repeintes* (plural), in (30b) as *repeint* (lacking agreement).

In the derivation of (30a), the *wh*-phrase raises to the position of the trace t', adjoining to AGRP. In this position, it is in a government relation with AGR (in our terms, AGR-O). The participle thus agrees with its *wh*-phrase object.[29] The underlying assumption is that object agreement is contingent upon a government relation between AGR and an NP, exactly as in the case of subject agreement. In (30b) the *wh*-phrase has not passed through the adjoined position, so there can be no agreement.[30]

Since t', adjoined to AGRP, is in an Ā-position, it follows, Kayne observes, that there will be no participial agreement with the *wh*-phrase in the case of an expletive subject (as is the case), on the assumption of expletive replacement, to which we return in section 6.3. The reason is that expletive replacement would require improper movement of the trace t' of the *wh*-phrase from an Ā- to an A-position.

If an NP remains in the object position, there is no participial agreement, though we again find such agreement in clitic movement, as in (31):

(31) a. Paul a repeint (*repeintes) les tables.
     b. Paul les a repeintes.

The reason is that the object *les tables* in (31a) is not in the appropriate government relation with AGR-O (the relation is barred by the Minimality Condition on government, since the participle intervenes), whereas in (31b) the clitic has raised to a position governed by AGR, perhaps the SPEC of AGRP. Kayne argues further that although the two agreement processes (with *wh*-movement and clitics) are not clearly dissociated in French, comparative evidence shows that they are in fact distinct processes and that the clitic does not adjoin to AGRP.

The question arises why the NP object cannot appear in the postulated position associated with AGR, say, its SPEC position, as in (32):

(32) *Paul a [les tables repeint(es)].

Base generation is excluded if we take θ-marking to be to the right in French; or, as in recent work that assumes raising of the subject from VP to the SPEC of IP position, we might assume that θ-marking must be internal to the projection of the θ-marking head, thus impossible in (33):

(33) ... [$_{\text{AGRP}}$ NP AGR [$_{\text{VP}}$ V]]

Failure of the nonclitic object to raise to the position in (32) follows from the Chain Condition if the participle assigns Case directly to its object, to its right in the base form, as Kayne assumes.[31]

Without reviewing the further consequences that Kayne develops, note that the analysis supports the idea that an AGR position intervenes between tense and the V, and that this element is distinct from the subject-agreement element. Furthermore, we have evidence that object agreement, like subject agreement, is based upon a government relation between AGR (in this case, AGR-O) and the NP.

Koopman (1987) has independently proposed that agreement is always the reflection of a SPEC-head relation.[32] We might revise this proposal to accord with Kayne's: agreement with an NP is always the reflection of a government relation between the head AGR and the NP, either the SPEC-head relation or the relation of the head to an adjoined element, the AGR typically being associated with the verb at S-Structure by the processes we have been discussing. Koopman suggests further that this idea may relate to her earlier proposal that the order parameters of the X-bar system involve two independent factors: directionality of Case marking and θ-marking (Koopman 1983; see also Travis 1984). If Case marking is to the left and θ-marking to the right, then NP will be in prehead and other θ-marked complements in posthead positions.

We might carry the proposals a step further, supposing that structural Case generally is correlated with agreement and reflects a government relation between the NP and the appropriate AGR elements. Thus, subject-verb agreement is associated with nominative Case and is determined by the relation of the specifier to the AGR-S head of AGR-S″ (= IP, in (28)), whereas verb-object agreement is associated with accusative Case and is determined by the relation of the NP to the AGR-O head of AGR-O″, either in specifier position or adjoined to AGR-O. The relations might be uniform at LF, parameterized at S-Structure, with Case checking and Case marking perhaps dissociated.

Note finally that if the proposal just outlined is tenable, with AGR-O distinct from AGR-S, then one of the problems discussed earlier in connection with example (11), repeated as (34), does not arise:

(34) John I NEG AGR write books

The problem was to ensure *do*-insertion and raising of AGR to form the complex verb [$_V$ *do*–AGR–I] with no violation of the HMC, while barring an alternative derivation with overt lowering. If we were to adopt the structure (28) rather than (6), distinguishing AGR-S from AGR-O, then AGR in (34) is actually AGR-O, which would not raise over NEG, but would lower to V (with subsequent LF raising to the position of the trace of AGR-O to form a proper chain). There is, then, no violation of the HMC, straightforwardly. The more general problems discussed earlier remain, however, still motivating the argument presented.

6 Economy of Representation

It has been suggested elsewhere that movement is available only as a "last resort." The preceding discussion suggested that deletion might also be regarded as a "last resort" operation, applicable where necessary, but not otherwise, and that the same is true of whatever is involved in *do*-support: insertion, if that is the proper way to interpret the phenomenon. More generally, then, it may be that the principle Affect α applies only where necessary. This overarching principle, then, expresses a general property of transformational rules—or more properly, of *the* transformational rule, actually a principle of UG. The intuitive meaning is that derivations must be as economical as possible: there is no superfluous rule application. The intuitive content of this idea, however, is spelled out in terms of specific notions of cost that distinguish UG principles from language-particular properties, introduce locality considerations, and so on. We thus have a plausible "least effort" principle, but a principle that is apparently specific to the language faculty in its actual formulation. This is a familiar conclusion elsewhere as well, one that bears on the nature of the language faculty generally.

The analogous principle for representations would stipulate that, just as there can be no superfluous steps in derivations, so there can be no superfluous symbols in representations. This is the intuitive content of the notion of Full Interpretation (FI), which holds that an element can appear in a representation only if it is properly "licensed." Let us proceed now to ask how this intuitive notion might be refined, in an effort to move it too from the status of a guideline toward that of a principle of UG.

It would be natural to expect that FI holds at each of the three fundamental levels that constitute an interface between the computational system of language and other systems: hence, at the levels of D-Structure, PF, and LF. If so, then "licensing" under FI is expressed in terms of conditions relating the syntax, broadly construed, to other systems of the mind/brain.

At D-Structure FI holds by definition, this level simply being a projection of lexical structure in terms of the notions of X-bar theory.[33] At PF it is universally taken for granted, without discussion, that the condition holds in a strong form. That is, a condition on phonetic representation is that each symbol be interpreted in terms of articulatory and perceptual mechanisms in a language-invariant manner; a representation that lacks this property is simply not considered a phonetic representation, but instead is considered a "higher-level" representation, still to be converted to PF. Like D-Structure, PF is understood to be defined by some version of FI. The corresponding notion at LF would be that every element that appears at LF must have a language-invariant interpretation in terms of interactions with the conceptual systems. Let us explore this idea further.

6.1 Operators and Variables

One consequence is that vacuous quantification should be forbidden. That is, language should differ from typical formal systems that permit vacuous quantification freely, with the well-formed expression "$(x) (2 + 2 = 4)$" receiving the same interpretation as "$2 + 2 = 4$." Formal systems are designed this way for ease of description and computation, but the design of human language is different. Thus, we cannot have such expressions as (35a) interpreted as 'John saw Bill', or (35b) interpreted as 'Some person left':

(35) a. Who John saw Bill? Who did John see Bill?

b. Every some person left.

Similarly, if a language permits such structures as (36), the vacuous operator interpretation is excluded:

(36) a. Who did Mary see him?

b. The man that Mary saw him.

These expressions cannot be interpreted to mean 'Mary saw x', 'the man y such that Mary saw x', respectively. If some theory of grammar stipulates specific devices and rules to bar such constructions and interpretations, we conclude that it is the wrong theory: it is generating expressions and structures too accurately and is therefore incorrect. There is nothing paradoxical about this conclusion. The unwanted constructions are excluded on general grounds, in terms of the overarching condition FI; there is no reason to suppose that the mechanisms of language include superfluous devices and rules to achieve, redundantly, the same result in special cases. Similarly, the phonological component contains no rules to express special cases of general properties of universal phonetics or of phonetic representations.

A related question has to do with free variables. What is their status in natural language? Typically, formal systems permit well-formed expressions with free variables, interpreting them as universally quantified or with the free variable treated as an arbitrary name, as in the course of natural deduction and intuitive mathematics generally. One natural language analogue to a free variable would be an empty category bound by an empty operator. There is quite strong evidence that such constructions exist, for example, in complex adjectival constructions such as (37):

(37) a. John is too clever to catch.
   b. John is too clever to expect anyone to catch.
   c. *John is too clever to meet anyone who caught.
   d. Mary expected John to be too clever to catch.

The general properties of these and many other constructions follow from the assumption that the underlying D-Structure representation is as in (38a) (for (37a)) and that empty-operator movement, meeting the usual conditions on $\bar{\text{A}}$-movement, raises the empty category O to the COMP position of the bracketed clause (to the SPEC position of CP), leaving a trace t in the S-Structure representation (38b):

(38) a. John is too clever [$_{CP}$ PRO to catch O]
   b. John is too clever [$_{CP}$ O [PRO to catch t]]

But variables are subject to the property sometimes called "strong binding": a variable must have a range determined by its restricted quantifier (language permitting no unrestricted quantification, as distinct from typical formal systems), or a value fixed by an antecedent that meets certain structural properties: thus *John* but not *Mary* in (37d). The latter condition applies when the operator is an empty category. (37a), for example, cannot mean that John is so clever that he cannot catch everything, or that he cannot catch something (someone) or other, analogous to *John ate*, meaning that John ate something or other. In short, language does not permit free variables: the strong binding property determines the curious semantic properties of these constructions. We might think of this condition as a specific application of the UG condition FI.

In these terms, we would interpret the empty operator binding an empty pronominal, in the sense of Huang's (1984) work on Chinese, as "restricted," in that it is necessarily discourse-related. There are semifree variables such as PRO and *one*, which, however, always appear to have special properties, specifically, human or animate (for instance, *It is easy to roll down a hill* does not refer to a rock). Thus, a true free variable interpretation is disallowed.

6.2 Legitimate LF Elements

A further sharpening of the condition FI is suggested by consideration of what counts as a proper element at the LF level. The question here is analogous to the question of what counts as a phonetic element at the PF level. Each relevant element at the LF level is a chain (39), perhaps a one-membered chain:

(39) $(\alpha_1, \ldots, \alpha_n)$

It seems that the following elements are permitted at LF, each a chain (39):

1. Arguments: each element is in an A-position, α_1 Case-marked and α_n θ-marked, in accordance with the Chain Condition.[34]
2. Adjuncts: each element is in an $\bar{\text{A}}$-position.
3. Lexical elements: each element is in an X^0-position.
4. Predicates, possibly predicate chains if there is predicate raising, VP-movement in overt syntax,[35] and other cases.
5. Operator-variable constructions, each a chain (α_1, α_2), where the operator α_1 is in an $\bar{\text{A}}$-position and the variable α_2 is in an A-position.

These are the only elements that seem to have an interpretation at LF. Suppose, then, that these are the only elements permitted at LF, in accordance with FI. Then the rule Affect α may apply (and must apply) only to yield such an element, given an illegitimate object. We conclude that AGR-trace (and perhaps the trace of [−finite]) must be eliminated, and V-trace may not be eliminated, as required for the proper functioning of the ECP if the argument sketched earlier is correct.[36]

Consider successive-cyclic $\bar{\text{A}}$-movement from an A-position. This will yield a chain that is not a legitimate object; it is a "heterogeneous chain," consisting of an adjunct chain and an $(\bar{\text{A}}, \text{A})$ pair (an operator-variable construction, where the $\bar{\text{A}}$-position is occupied by a trace). This heterogeneous chain can become a legitimate object—namely, a genuine operator-variable construction—only by eliminating intermediate $\bar{\text{A}}$-traces. We conclude, then, that these must be deleted at the point where we reach LF representation.[37] In contrast, intermediate $\bar{\text{A}}$-traces formed by successive-cyclic movement from an $\bar{\text{A}}$-position need not be deleted, since the chain formed is already a legitimate object—namely, an adjunct; since they need not be deleted, they may not be deleted, by the "least effort" principle for derivations already discussed. The same is true for A-chains (arguments) and X^0-chains (lexical elements). On these natural—though of course not logically necessary—assumptions, we derive, in effect, the basic principle for trace deletion stipulated in Lasnik and Saito's theory of the ECP, now a consequence of the general condition FI, with "may delete" strengthened to "must delete." There are further consequences, and interesting questions arise with regard to the specifier of NPs, which shares some properties of A-positions and other properties of $\bar{\text{A}}$-positions, but I will not pursue these matters here.

6.3 FI and Expletives

Consider finally the status of expletive elements, such as English *there* or Italian *ci*, or their various counterparts, null or overt, in other languages. This element receives no interpretation and therefore is not licensed as a legitimate LF object. It must therefore somehow be removed. Elsewhere I have suggested that *there* is eliminated by LF substitution.[38] But *there* has specific features, and we might suppose on these grounds that it is undeletable, by the condition on recoverability of deletion—yet to be precisely formulated. Then we must treat *there* as an LF affix; something must adjoin to it.

The expletive *there* has three salient properties. First, an NP must appear in a certain formal relation to *there* in the construction; let us call this element the *associate* of the expletive and take the expletive to be licensed by its presence. Second, number agreement is not with *there* but rather with the associate. Third, there is an alternate form with the associate actually in the subject position after overt raising. Thus, we have (40), with the associate in italics, but not (41):

(40) a. There is *a man* in the room.
   b. There are *men* in the room.
   c. *A man* is in the room.

(41) a. *There was decided to travel by plane.
   b. *There is unlikely that anyone will agree.

These properties are rather naturally explained on the assumption, deriving from FI, that the expletive is an LF affix, with its associate adjoining to it. Since *there* lacks inherent ϕ-features (including number) and category, these features will "percolate" from its associate on usual assumptions. If agreement is checked at LF, then it will already have to have been established at S-Structure between AGR-S and the associate of *there*, as in (40a–b), yielding the observed overt agreement. This analysis fits readily into the framework already outlined, particularly if agreement and Case are treated in the manner suggested: both assigned by S-Structure since they may appear overtly, both checked at LF since they have LF consequences having to do with visibility (the Case Filter) and the Chain Condition.[39] If we assume further that the SPEC of IP (AGR-S'', if the speculations of section 5 are correct) must be an NP with ϕ-features matching AGR-S, then it will also follow that the associate must be an NP; and it is this NP that raises in overt syntax, as in (40c).

Burzio (1986) argues further that if the expletive is a clitic, it will have to satisfy additional conditions holding generally between a clitic and the position associated with it, specifically, a very restrictive locality condition that, he argues, holds at D-Structure; on this further assumption, he derives an interesting range of phenomena that differentiate English, Italian, French, and Piedmontese expletive constructions. On the general assumptions of the principles-and-parameters approach, we expect to find that expletive constructions of this type have the same basic properties across languages, with differences explicable in terms of the lexical properties of the elements involved.

For such reasons, then, it is plausible to assume that *there* (and its counterparts) is indeed an LF affix, as required by FI.

In (40a) LF adjunction of the associate to the expletive yields the phrase (42) as subject, the complex constituting an NP by percolation:

(42) $[_{NP}$ there$-[_{NP}$ a man]]

Other well-established principles conspire to guarantee that the only element that can adjoin to the expletive is the associate with the appropriate properties.

Given that *there* must have an NP associate, if follows that some other expletive (in English, *it*) is associated with clauses, as in (43), contrasting with (41):

(43) a. It was decided to travel by plane.

     b. It is unlikely that anyone will agree.

It should therefore not be necessary to stipulate distributional conditions on *there* and *it* expletives, or their counterparts in other languages, when their lexical properties are considered.[40]

It also follows that at S-Structure, an expletive E and its associate A must satisfy all LF chain conditions, since there is a chain ($[A-E], \ldots, t_A]$) at LF. Given the Chain Condition holding at LF, it must be that at S-Structure the expletive E is in a Case-marked position and the associate A in a θ-position.[41] Furthermore, if we assume that the binding theory holds at LF, then at S-Structure A and E must be in a relation that satisfies Condition A, since at LF an antecedent-trace relation holds of their S-Structure positions. Similarly, the ECP, a chain condition at LF, will have to hold of the expletive-associate pair at S-Structure. These consequences are largely descriptively accurate, as illustrated in (44):[42]

(44) a. *There* seems that *a man* is in the room. (ECP violation)
    b. *There* seems that John saw *a man*. (Condition A violation)

Similarly, other conditions on movement must be satisfied. Compare the examples in (45):

(45) a. *There* was thought that [pictures of *a man* were on sale].
    b. *We* thought that [pictures of *each other* were on sale].
    c. *A man* was thought that [pictures *t* were on sale].

The italicized elements are properly related in (45b), but not in (45a) or (45c). The problem with (45a) is not the binding theory, as (45b) shows, but rather a condition on movement (the ECP), as we see from (45c).

Such properties of expletives now follow from FI, without further stipulation. Note that it also follows that the binding theory must apply at LF; whether or not it also applies elsewhere (including S-Structure) is a separate question.

Another consequence has to do with Condition C of the binding theory, which requires that an R-expression, such as the associate of an expletive, be unbound. A long-standing question has been why there is no Condition C violation in the case of an expletive and its related associate. But we now assume that the two simply have different indices.[43] There is, therefore, no need to complicate the binding theory to exclude this case, as in a number of proposals over the past years.

Certain problems of scope of the kind discussed particularly by Edwin Williams also are overcome. Consider the sentences in (46):

(46) a. I haven't met many linguistics students.
    b. There aren't many linguistics students here.

(46a) has a scopal ambiguity, but in (46b) *many* unambiguously has narrow scope. The LF representation of (46b) is (47):

(47) [$_{NP}$[there [$_A$ many linguistics students]] are not t_A here]

If *many linguistics students* were literally to replace *there*, it would be expected to have scope over *not*, but in (47) no relation is established between the two, and the scope of *many* can be assumed to be narrow, as in *Pictures of many students aren't here.*[44]

6.4 Further Questions Concerning LF Raising

There is one major exception to the generalization that the expletive *E* and its associate *A* are in a binding theory (Condition A) relation at S-Structure—namely, raising constructions such as (48):

(48) *There* seems [*a man* to be in the room].

Here the expletive-associate pair satisfies all chain conditions, but the expression is ungrammatical.

A natural explanation of these facts is provided by Belletti's (1988) theory of partitive Case assignment. Taking partitive Case to be oblique, therefore θ-related in accord with the uniformity condition on Case assignment (see Chomsky 1986b), partitive Case will not be assigned to the associate in (48) but will be properly assigned at S-Structure to the associate of the expletive after unaccusatives and, we must assume, copula, as in *There arrived a man, There is a man in the room.* Assume as before that Case must be assigned at S-Structure, given that it appears at PF and is relevant at LF. Then (48) is *, since an S-Structure condition is violated. Note that even with these assumptions, it still follows that *there* must be in a Case-marked position, by the Chain Condition, which requires that an LF chain be headed by a Case-marked position.[45]

If this line of argument is correct, there cannot be a process of Case transmission, for that process would allow (48) to satisfy the Case Filter. Rather, Case must be assigned at S-Structure directly by some Case marker or other device.[46] Lasnik (1989) observes that similar conclusions follow from such examples as (49):

(49) a.   I consider [there to be a solution].
       b.   *I consider [there a solution]. (analogous to *I consider John intelligent*)

In (49a) it must be that *be* assigns Case directly to *a solution*; *there* also receives Case (from *consider*), so that the Chain Condition is satisfied after LF raising. There is, it seems, no S-Structure process transmitting Case from the expletive *there* to its associate, the phrase *a solution* in these examples.

Safir (1985) notes the existence of pairs like (50a–b):[47]

(50) a. [$_{wh}$ How many men] did John say that [there were t$_{wh}$ in the room]?

b. *[$_{wh}$ How many men] did John say that [t$_{wh}$ were in the room]?

(50b) is a standard ECP violation; the trace t_{wh} is in a position that is not γ-marked, in Lasnik and Saito's (1984) sense. The question then arises why this is not also true of (50a), if the trace t_{wh}, the associate of the expletive *there*, is raised by LF movement to the position of *there*. Lasnik and Saito's theory provides an explanation, whether we assume LF substitution or, as above, LF adjunction. In either case the trace t_{wh} is γ-marked by the process of *wh*-movement in overt syntax and retains this property when it raises to the position of the expletive, so there is no ECP violation. Similar observations hold with regard to Rizzi's (1982) analysis of *wh*-extraction of subjects in Italian: the subject first extraposes, leaving expletive pro subject, and then undergoes normal *wh*-movement, leaving a trace *t*, γ-marked in overt syntax and then raising at LF to the position of the expletive.

The notion of LF adjunction eliminates much of the motivation for Case transmission theories of expletive-associate relations, and these approaches are still more dubious in the light of the observations just reviewed (see also Pollock 1981 and Kayne 1989). Nevertheless, there is evidence supporting Case transmission.

An indirect though plausible argument for Case transmission is developed by Koopman (1987) in a comparative study of the West African language Bambara and languages of the French-English type. Koopman postulates a parametric difference between languages that have Case chains ([+CC]) and those that do not ([−CC]). Bambara is [−CC] and English-French, [+CC]. Koopman considers three kinds of Case chains:

(51) a. (V, ..., *t*), where V is a Case assigner

b. (O, ..., *t*), where O is an operator and *t* the variable it binds

c. (E, ..., NP), where E is an expletive and NP its associate

Case (51a) results from V-raising. In a [+CC] language, the trace of V will assign the Case "transmitted" from V through the chain. In a [−CC] language, lacking Case chains, the trace will be unable to assign Case, and raising of transitive verbs will therefore be impossible.

Case (51b) is standard operator movement. Typically, the trace must be in a Case-marked position, and, Koopman assumes, the operator must inherit Case from it to satisfy the Case Filter. This will be possible in a

[+CC] language, impossible in a [−CC] language, which will therefore lack overt operator movement.

Case (51c) is the expletive-associate relation. In a [+CC] language, Case can be transmitted from E to NP, as in standard Case transmission theories, and the Case Filter is therefore satisfied. In a [−CC] language, there can be no expletives, for Case transmission will be impossible, Case chains not being permitted.

Koopman observes that in all respects, English-French are of the [+CC] variety, whereas Bambara is of the [−CC] variety. Omitting details, we find in Bambara the following properties. Consider Case chains of type (51a). A verb that does not assign Case raises to I, but a verb that assigns Case remains in place, with a dummy element inserted to bear the affix; the explanation is that the trace could not assign Case if the verb were to raise. In causative formation, an intransitive verb raises to form a complex V-causative construction in the familiar way, but this is impossible for a transitive verb, which allows causative only if the external argument is suppressed, as if prior passivization had taken place. These properties follow on the assumption that the trace of a transitive verb cannot assign Case; since the complex verb assigns its sole Case to the obligatory object, the subject cannot appear.

With regard to property (51b), Bambara has only *wh*-in-situ, as predicted. As for (51c), there are no overt expletives; rather, the associate raises overtly to subject position, again as predicted.

We thus have an indirect argument in favor of Case transmission, absent as a device just when Case chains generally are not permitted.

Can we reinterpret these data so as to resolve the conflict between the argument for Case transmission and the evidence against such a process? Suppose we reinterpret Koopman's parameter in the following way, in accord with the plausible and generally applicable principle that parameters are lexical, that is, stateable in terms of X^0-elements and X^0-categories only. We then consider the property [C], which an X^0-element may or may not have. A [+C] element can enter into Case relations, either assigning or receiving Case; a [−C] element cannot. Suppose further that X^0-elements with lexical content are always [+C], but that languages can differ with respect to whether other X^0-elements are [+C] or [−C]. The parameter is restricted to functional elements, in accordance with the plausible condition discussed earlier. French-English are [+C], meaning that all X^0-elements may enter into Case relations; Bambara is [−C], meaning that only a lexical X^0 enters into such relations.

Turning to the three properties, (51a) follows directly: in Bambara, the trace of V, being [−C], cannot assign Case. As for (51b), the trace of the operator cannot receive Case in Bambara, being [−C], so that we have a typical violation of the Case Filter (or the visibility requirement from which it derives), with a variable heading a (perhaps one-membered) chain that violates the Chain Condition, since it lacks Case. Note that we need not assume that the operator requires Case, an otherwise unmotivated assumption, particularly unnatural for empty operators.

The property that concerns us directly is (51c). Since Bambara is [−C], an expletive cannot receive Case. If the language had expletives, then LF raising (which Koopman assumes) would form a chain headed by an element in a non-Case-marked position, violating the Chain Condition. Consequently, there can be no expletives, and overt raising is required.

There seems, then, to be no strong argument for Case transmission, if this line of argument is viable.[48] We do, however, have evidence for a narrowly specified parametric difference involving Case theory, with a range of interesting consequences. I am not aware of other convincing evidence for Case transmission, so it may be that the property can be eliminated from UG, in favor of LF movement, driven by FI.

7 Some Conclusions on Language Design

Summarizing, we have found evidence to support the basic assumptions on language design sketched in section 1, the more specific assumptions concerning the separate syntactic status of Tense and Agreement elements, and those of subsequent discussion. There is varied evidence suggesting that both derivations and representations are subject to a certain form of "least effort" condition and are required to be minimal in a fairly well defined sense, with no superfluous steps in derivations and no superfluous symbols in representations. Proceeding in the way indicated, we may hope to raise these "least effort" guidelines to general principles of UG. Notice that although these principles have a kind of naturalness and generality lacking in the specific principles of UG such as the ECP, the binding theory, and so on, nevertheless their formulation is, in detail, specific to the language faculty.

As discussed elsewhere (see Chomsky 1988b), these properties of UG, if indeed they are real, are rather surprising in a number of respects. For one thing, they are the kinds of properties that yield computational difficulties, since structural descriptions have to meet "global" conditions. From the point of view of parsing, suppose that we have a process recovering an

S-Structure representation s from the PF representation p. Then to determine the status of s, we have to carry out a number of operations. We have to determine whether s is derived from a properly formed D-Structure representation d licensed by the lexicon, and whether the derivation from d through s to the LF representation l is minimal in the required sense, less costly than any other derivation from d. Furthermore, we have to determine whether l satisfies the conditions of external licensing, FI, and other properties of LF. In general, these computations may be nontrivial. In these respects, language design appears to be problematic from a parsing-theoretic perspective, though elegant regarded in isolation from considerations of use. The basic assumption that the fundamental levels are those that satisfy the external licensing conditions at the "interface" with other systems already illustrates these properties, and the "least effort" conditions, though natural and plausible in terms of empirical consequences, provide further illustration. The discrepancies between natural language design and the structure of formal systems constructed for computational efficiency may also be relevant here, as well as other properties of natural language, such as the existence of empty categories, which might also be expected to yield parsing problems. Note that one cannot easily motivate the conditions on economy of representation in terms of processing considerations, since they hold at LF, and only derivatively at S-Structure. Nor does there appear to be any argument that the particular properties of language design are necessary for language-like systems. These are contingent properties of natural language.

There are "computational tricks" that permit easy determination of the grammatical properties of an S-Structure representation in a large class of cases, broad enough to allow for language to be usable in practice. But language design as such appears to be in many respects "dysfunctional," yielding properties that are not well adapted to the functions language is called upon to perform. There is no real paradox here; there is no reason to suppose, a priori, that the general design of language is conducive to efficient use. Rather, what we seem to discover are some intriguing and unexpected features of language design, not unlike those that have been discovered throughout the inquiry into the nature of language, though unusual among biological systems of the natural world.

Notes

1. This is sometimes called *Government-Binding (GB) Theory*, a misleading term that should be abandoned, in my view; see Chomsky 1988a. Generative grammar

has engendered a good deal of controversy, sometimes for good reason, often not. There has been a fair amount of plain misunderstanding, beginning with the notion of generative grammar itself. I have always understood a generative grammar to be nothing more than an explicit grammar. Some apparently have a different concept in mind. For example, reviewing Chomsky 1986b, McCawley (1988) notes that I interpret the concept here as meaning nothing more than explicit, as I have always done (see, for instance, Chomsky 1965:4), and concludes erroneously that this is a "sharp change" in my usage that gives the enterprise an entirely different cast from that of the 1960s, when the task, as he perceives it, was taken to be "specifying the membership of a set of sentences that is identified with a language" (pp. 355–356; McCawley takes the set of sentences to be what I have called the "structure" of the language, that is, the set of structural descriptions). But the characterization he gives does not imply that "generative" means anything more than "explicit"; there is, furthermore, no change in usage or conception, at least for me, in this regard. The review contains a series of further misunderstandings, and there are others elsewhere, but I will not discuss these matters here.

2. On why phonology alone might be expected to have specific rule structure, see Bromberger and Halle 1989.

3. Or what is sometimes called a *core language*. The core-periphery distinction, in my view, should be regarded as an expository device, reflecting a level of understanding that should be superseded as clarification of the nature of linguistic inquiry advances. See Chomsky 1988a.

4. On these notions, see Chomsky 1986b. General conditions of this sort were investigated in some detail in the earliest work in generative grammar, in the context of the study of evaluation procedures for grammars; see Chomsky 1951.

5. The lexical elements are sometimes called *atomic* from the point of view of the computational operations. Taking the metaphor literally, we would conclude that no feature of a lexical item can be modified or even addressed (say, for checking against another matching element) in a computational operation, and no features can be added to a lexical element. The condition as stated is too strong; just how it holds is a theory-internal question that I will put aside.

6. On restriction to functional elements, see Borer 1983 and Fukui 1988.

7. On this matter, see, among others, Baker 1988.

8. As a matter of notation for X-bar theory, I will use prime instead of bar, X^0 for the lowest-level category, and XP for X'', for each X.

9. I have in mind the notion of "level of representation" discussed in Chomsky 1955–56 and subsequent work.

10. Some have proposed that certain conditions on syntax hold at PF; see, for example, Aoun et al. 1987. It cannot be, strictly speaking, the level of PF at which these conditions apply, since at this level there is no relevant structure, not even words, in general. Rather, this approach assumes an additional level S-P intermediate between S-Structure and PF, the purported conditions holding at S-P.

11. See Burzio 1986 and Chomsky 1987. Some have felt that there is a profound issue of principle distinguishing "two-level" theories that include a relation of D- to

S-Structure from "one-level" approaches, which relate S-Structure to lexical properties in some different way; for some comment, see my response to queries in Longuet-Higgins, Lyons, and Broadbent 1981:63f. and Chomsky 1981. There may be an issue, but as noted, it is at best a rather subtle one.

12. On X-bar-theoretic conditions at S-Structure, see Van Riemsdijk 1989. In lectures in Tokyo in January 1987, I suggested some further reasons why such conditions might hold at S-Structure.

13. I assume here the general framework of Chomsky 1986a, based essentially on Lasnik and Saito 1984, though further modifications are in order that I will not consider here.

14. Note that there also might be a partial reduction, for example, a formulation of the ECP that expresses a generalization holding of X^0-movement and other cases; that would be the import of a proposal by Rizzi (1990). We should also look into the other possible case of movement: X'-movement. For recent evidence supporting this option, see Van Riemsdijk 1989. See also Namiki 1979.

15. See Pollock 1989. I will touch upon only a few of the questions that Pollock addresses. See Emonds 1978 and, for more recent development of his approach, Emonds 1985.

16. Order irrelevant, here and below, for abstract formulations.

17. Pollock's terms for *strong* and *weak* are *transparent* and *opaque*, respectively, for reasons that become clear directly.

18. Pollock treats *ne* in the *ne-pas* construction as the clitic head of NEGP, raising to a higher position. We might think of it as a kind of scope marker.

19. More explicitly, the verb $[_V V [_{AGR} AGR I]]$.

20. The mechanics of how modals and *do* relate to the inflectional affixes remain to be specified. If *do*-support can be shown to be a reflex of parameter fixing (choice of weak AGR, we are assuming), then it is not, strictly speaking, a language-specific rule, though I will continue to use this term for expository purposes. The device of employing dummy elements in this manner is found elsewhere, also plausibly considered to be contingent on parameter fixing; see section 6.4 for one example.

21. Note that there are empirical consequences to these assumptions. They entail that at the steady state attained in language acquisition, the UG principles remain distinct from language-particular properties. Suggestive work by Flynn (1987) on second-language acquisition supports this conclusion.

22. There would in fact be a straightforward solution to this particular problem in terms of an analysis to which we return in section 5, but I will put that aside here, since it will not bear on the other questions just raised.

23. Note that *e* is regarded here as an actual symbol of mental representation, but lacking ϕ-features and categorial features. *e* is not to be confused with the identity element of a syntactic level, regarded as an algebraic construction in the manner of Chomsky 1955–56.

24. Recall that we are assuming, essentially, Lasnik and Saito's (1984) theory of the ECP, as modified in Chomsky 1986a. Under this theory, t_V in (17) is γ-marked

after raising of V to AGR, and subsequent deletion of AGR-trace in this position leaves no ECP violation.

25. On other cases of a similar sort, see Chomsky 1987.

26. Semantic properties of infinitives, then, would be understood as properties of the construction, not its head [−finite].

27. A cursory check suggests that the morphological consequences are as expected, in languages where the hierarchic position of object and subject agreement can be detected.

28. At various points, the reinterpretation would require slight modifications in the exposition and the resulting analysis. I will omit further comment on these matters, which do not seem to raise any serious problem.

29. More precisely, agreement holds between the *wh*-phrase and AGR-O, to which the participle raises so that it agrees with the *wh*-phrase; the same is true of subject-verb agreement.

30. Note that we must assume the two derivations to be "equally costly," each being "minimal" by successive-cyclic movement. This consideration would lead to a further refinement of the notion of "cost."

31. The case of clitic movement depends upon theory-internal assumptions about cliticization, but no new problems appear to arise here. Kayne's argument is slightly different from the above.

32. Koopman is considering the possibility of object raising to SPEC of VP; alternatively, we might suppose that the process in question is raising to SPEC of AGRP.

33. There are further refinements to be considered. For example, should expletives be present at D-Structure or inserted in the course of derivation? What is the status of functional elements? And so on.

34. If we adopt the approach to NP-raising discussed in Chomsky 1986a, then we will have to distinguish the chain (39) formed by movement from the intermediate "derived chain" that takes part in the process of γ-marking of α_n.

35. An alternative possibility, suggested by certain facts about binding and trace interpretation, is that VP-movement is restricted to the PF component (as an optional "stylistic rule") and possibly also to (obligatory) LF movement, along the lines of a reinterpretation of the barriers framework (Chomsky 1986a) discussed in my lectures at Tokyo in January 1987. This conclusion may indeed follow from the considerations discussed above concerning optionality, within the present framework.

36. Note that further precision is necessary to make explicit just when and how this condition applies.

37. They might be present at earlier stages, where licensing conditions do not yet apply, serving, as Norbert Hornstein observes, to permit the application of principles for the interpretation of anaphors in displaced phrases of the sort proposed by Barss (1986).

38. See Chomsky 1986b. For extensive discussion of expletives, which I will largely follow here, see Burzio 1986. See also Travis 1984 on the typology of expletives. The status of *it* (and its counterparts) in extraposition constructions is more convoluted for various reasons, including the question of whether it occupies a θ-position.

39. See Baker 1988 on the role of both Case and agreement in this connection.

40. Such properties had to be stipulated on the assumptions made in Chomsky and Lasnik 1977, but perhaps they are dispensable along the lines just sketched. For these reasons alone, it seems doubtful that what adjoins to the expletive is a small clause of which it is the subject; thus, I assume that what adjoins is *a man*, not the small clause [*a man in the room*], in (40a). There are other reasons for supposing this to be true, Kayne (1989) observes (see his note 6) that the assumption is required for his explanation of the lack of participle-object agreement with object raising in expletive constructions. Consider, furthermore, such expressions as **There seems to be several men sick*, excluded by lack of agreement between *several men* and *seems*. But the phrase [*several men sick*] can be singular, as in [*Several men sick*] *is a sign that the water is polluted* and a range of similar cases discussed by Safir (1987), though many questions remain unsettled. On the possibility of nonagreement between the verb and its associate, see Burzio 1986:132–133. Note that nothing requires that the two kinds of expletives be morphologically distinct.

41. We assume that Case distributes from a category to its immediate constituents, a process that is often morphologically overt, thus from the category of the complex element $[A-E]$ to the adjoined element A, heading the chain $(A, \ldots, t_A)$. Recall that A adjoined to E does head such a chain, by earlier assumptions.

42. Note that these examples could be accounted for by stipulations on the distribution of expletives, as in Chomsky and Lasnik 1977, but we are now exploring the possibility, which seems plausible, that these are dispensable.

43. Or no linking, in Higginbotham's (1983) sense. Note that we cannot assume the expletive to be unindexed—thus, it might have raised, leaving an indexed trace.

44. To account for scopal properties appropriately, more elaborate assumptions are required, taking into account the position of both the head and the terminal position of the associate chain $(A, \ldots, t)$. In a raising construction such as *There appear (not) to have been many linguistics students here*, we have to ensure that the scope of *many* falls within that of *appear* and *not*; no relation is determined by the proposed LF representation, but such a relation would be established in the correct way if the position of the trace is considered, given that the head of the chain has no relation to the other relevant element. Just what is entailed by a wider range of considerations remains to be determined.

45. Similar remarks hold of "quirky Case," assigned at D-Structure under the uniformity condition, but realized in a Case-marked position at S-Structure.

46. See Pollock 1981 for arguments against Case transmission. For additional argument, see Kayne 1989.

47. For discussion of these and the preceding examples, see Shlonsky 1987.

48. Koopman considers other possible Case chains, but the evidence is less convincing.

References

Aoun, J., N. Hornstein, D. Lightfoot, and A. Weinberg (1987). "Two Types of Locality." *Linguistic Inquiry* 18:537–577.

Baker, M. (1988). *Incorporation: A Theory of Grammatical Function Changing.* University of Chicago Press, Chicago.

Barss, A. (1986). "Chains and Anaphoric Dependence." Doctoral dissertation, MIT.

Belletti, A. (1988). "The Case of Unaccusatives." *Linguistic Inquiry* 19:1–34.

Borer, H. (1983). *Parametric Syntax.* Foris, Dordrecht.

Bromberger, S., and M. Halle (1989). "Why Phonology Is Different." *Linguistic Inquiry* 20:51–70.

Burzio, L. (1986). *Italian Syntax.* Reidel, Dordrecht.

Chomsky, N. (1951). "Morphophonemics of Modern Hebrew." Ms., University of Pennsylvania. (Published by Garland, New York, 1979.)

Chomsky, N. (1955–56). *The Logical Structure of Linguistic Theory.* Ms., Harvard University. (Published by Plenum, New York, 1975; University of Chicago Press, Chicago, 1985.)

Chomsky, N. (1965). *Aspects of the Theory of Syntax.* MIT Press, Cambridge, Mass.

Chomsky, N. (1986a). *Barriers.* MIT Press, Cambridge, Mass.

Chomsky, N. (1986b). *Knowledge of Language: Its Nature, Origin, and Use.* Praeger, New York.

Chomsky, N. (1987). "Reply." *Mind and Language* 2:193–197.

Chomsky, N. (1988a). "Generative Grammar, Studies in English Linguistics and Literature." Kyoto University of Foreign Studies, lecture 2.

Chomsky, N. (1988b). "Prospects for the Study of Language and Mind." Ms., MIT.

Chomsky, N., and H. Lasnik (1977). "Filters and Control." *Linguistic Inquiry* 8:425–504.

Emonds, J. (1978). "The Verbal Complex V'-V in French." *Linguistic Inquiry* 9:151–175.

Emonds, J. (1985). *A Unified Theory of Syntactic Categories.* Foris, Dordrecht.

Flynn, S. (1987). *A Parameter-Setting Model of L2 Acquisition: Experimental Studies in Anaphora.* Reidel, Dordrecht.

Fukui, N. (1988). "Deriving the Differences between English and Japanese. A Case Study in Parametric Syntax." *English Linguistics* 5:249–270.

Huang, C.-T. J. (1984). "On the Distribution and Reference of Empty Pronouns." *Linguistic Inquiry* 15:531–574.

Kayne, R. S. (1984). *Connectedness and Binary Branching.* Foris, Dordrecht.

Kayne, R. S. (1989) "Facets of Romance Past Participle Agreement." In P. Benincà, ed., *Dialect Variation and the Theory of Grammar.* Foris, Dordrecht.

Koopman, H. (1983). *The Syntax of Verbs.* Foris, Dordrecht.

Koopman, H. (1987). "On the Absence of Case Chains in Bambara." Ms., UCLA.

Lasnik, H. (1989). "Case and Expletives: Notes toward a Parametric Account." Paper presented at the Second Princeton Workshop on Comparative Grammar, Princeton University, April 1989.

Lasnik, H., and M. Saito (1984). "On the Nature of Proper Government." *Linguistic Inquiry* 15:235–289.

Longuet-Higgins, H. C., J. Lyons, and D. E. Broadbent, eds. (1981). *The Psychological Mechanisms of Language.* Royal Society and British Academy, London.

McCawley, J. (1988). "Review of Chomsky 1986b." *Language* 64:355–366.

Namiki, T. (1979). "Remarks on Prenominal Adjectives and Degree Expressions in English." *Studies in English Linguistics* 7:71–85.

Pollock, J.-Y. (1981). "On Case and Impersonal Constructions." In R. May and J. Koster, eds., *Levels of Syntactic Representation.* Foris, Dordrecht.

Pollock, J.-Y. (1989). "Verb Movement, Universal Grammar, and the Structure of IP." *Linguistic Inquiry* 20:365–424.

Riemsdijk, H. van (1989). "Movement and Regeneration." In P. Benincà, ed., *Dialect Variation and the Theory of Grammar.* Foris, Dordrecht.

Rizzi, L. (1982). *Issues in Italian Syntax.* Foris, Dordrecht.

Rizzi, L. (1990). *Relativized Minimality.* MIT Press, Cambridge, Mass.

Safir, K. (1985). *Syntactic Chains.* Cambridge University Press, Cambridge.

Safir, K. (1987). "'So There'." In M. A. Browning, E. Czaykowski-Higgins, and E. Ritter, eds., *MIT Working Papers in Linguistics* 9. Department of Linguistics and Philosophy, MIT.

Shlonsky, U. (1987). "Null and Displaced Subjects." Doctoral dissertation, MIT.

Travis, L. (1984). "Parameters and Effects of Word Order Variation." Doctoral dissertation, MIT.

Index